Global Vietnam: Across Time, Space and Community

This book series is committed to advancing scholarship on Vietnam and Vietnam-related issues and to nurturing a new generation of Vietnam scholars in arts, humanities, education and social sciences, and interdisciplinary studies. It engages with Vietnam in global contexts and with global Vietnam across time, space and community. It features new writings and understandings that reflect nuances, complexities and dynamic that Vietnam in all of its possible meanings and constructs has inspired, generated and pushed. It recognises the ever expanding circles of Vietnam scholars around the world whose scholarship can be seen as the products of a new era when knowledge production has become increasingly globalized and decentralized. All of these have been reflected and in motion in the well-established over-a-decade-long Engaging With Vietnam conference series, of which this book series is an offspring. For more, visit: https://engagingwithvietnam.org/global-vietnam-book-series/

Thomas Engelbert · Chi P. Pham
Editors

Reading South Vietnam's Writers

The Reception of Western Thought in Journalism and Literature

With contributions from Trương Thuỳ Dung, Duy Lap Nguyen, Wynn Gadkar-Wilcox, Hồ Khánh Vân, Nguyễn Thị Thanh Hương, Nguyễn Minh Thu, Thai Phan Vang Anh, Trịnh Đặng Nguyên Hương, Ngô Thị Quỳnh Nga, Munehiro Nohira

 Springer

Editors
Thomas Engelbert
Universität Hamburg
Hamburg, Germany

Chi P. Pham
Institute of Literature
Vietnam Academy of Social Sciences
Hanoi, Vietnam

ISSN 2731-7552   ISSN 2731-7560 (electronic)
Global Vietnam: Across Time, Space and Community
ISBN 978-981-99-1042-7   ISBN 978-981-99-1043-4 (eBook)
https://doi.org/10.1007/978-981-99-1043-4

This Springer imprint is published by the registered company Springer Nature Singapore Pte Ltd.
The registered company address is: 152 Beach Road, #21-01/04 Gateway East, Singapore 189721,
Singapore

The chapters of this book are selected from the contributions of the conference Literature and Journalism in the Republic of Vietnam (1955–1975) and the Reception of Western Thought *co-organized by Thomas Engelbert and Chi P. Pham. We thank the Ideen - und Risikofonds (University of Hamburg), the Deutsche Forschungsgemeinschaft, and the Hamburger Wissenschaftliche Stiftung for the generous funding they provided to the conference.*

Preface

Brief discussions exist on the influence of some Western thought on the writing and political careers of certain southern Vietnamese intellectuals. Examples can be found in "South Vietnamese Literature" (Văn học Miền Nam) by Thụy Khuê; "Vietnamese Literature of Freedom South" (Văn học Miền Nam Tự Do), by Nguyễn Vy Khanh; *Southern Vietnamese Literature: an Overview* (Văn học Miền Nam: tổng quan), by Võ Phiến; *Women Writers of South Vietnam, 1954–1975* by Công Huyền Tôn Nữ Nha Trang; "The Literature of Vietnam 1954–1973," by Nguyễn Trần Huân; and "Psychoanalysis in South Vietnam's Urban Fiction: Case Study of Thanh Tâm Tuyền" (Phân tâm học trong tiểu thuyết đô thị miền Nam: Trường hợp Thanh Tâm Tuyền), by Đoàn Ánh Dương and Nguyễn Thi Bình.

However, no publication exists that comprehensively analyzes the presence, lively and complex, of a wide range of Western thought in intellectual lives in South Vietnam. This deficiency has many reasons. Ignorance and lack of interest in the subject are two of them. Another issue is still the ideological rule governing the humanities in the contemporary Socialist Republic of Vietnam. In respect to the Republic of Vietnam (South Vietnam), one still finds a reduction of the subject to the idealized legacy of so-called bourgeois individualism and pro-American imperialism. In reunified communist Vietnam, the Republic of Vietnam (South Vietnam) as a political entity and even many of the literary publications and other written materials produced in South Vietnam were indiscriminately seen as embodiments of the intellectual legacy of American imperialism and French colonialism (Nguyen, Lap Duy 2000: 175–213; Tuan Hoang 2013: 24; Nguyen, Tran Huan 1981: 321–345). Generations of Vietnamese studying and doing research were taught to identify the presence of Western literature, particularly non-socialist literature, in South Vietnam as a threat to socialism and national sovereignty (Nguyễn Vy Khanh 2008). Thus, many of these works were collected, especially in the 1975–1976 épuration campaign, and were burned, banned, and eventually caused to disappear from mainstream Vietnamese intellectual life (Thế Uyên 1979; Lữ Phương 1981; Taylor 2015:116–118). In the present-day official histories of Vietnamese literature, several literary authors from South Vietnam still appear as national traitors, hack writers, who promoted an adventurous, luxurious petty bourgeois mentality, and were the supposed enemy of the "class struggle" of the masses (Trần Trọng Đăng Đàn 1991: 28–118; Trần Thục Nga 1987: 89–90; Vũ Hạnh 2008: 80–95).

Since the Reform in 1986, when the Vietnamese government expressed its openness—however cautious and reluctant—the history of Vietnamese literature started incorporating ideologies and styles of artistic expression other than socialist realism, for example, various styles from South Vietnam (Engelbert 2006: 125–129; Đỗ Đức Hiểu et al. 2004). Several researches, in forms of articles and books, dealing with non-communist, socialist ideologies in South Vietnam, appear in official academic, educational forums in Vietnam (Nguyễn Tiến Dũng 1999; Trần Hoài Anh 2009, 2020; Đoàn Ánh Dương and Nguyễn Thị Bình 2013: 20–35; Huỳnh Như Phương 2019, 2020; Vũ Hạnh, Nguyễn Ngọc Phan 2008). These investigations highlight southern intellectuals' active engagement with literature and other sources of intellectual thought not limited to the national politics and boundaries of the time. Nevertheless, the inclusion of South Vietnam's intellectual legacy as an intrinsic part of mainstream Vietnamese intellectual history is still, as already mentioned, reluctant, and cautious.

This book examines how South Vietnam's literary and journalistic authors perceived and were (potentially) influenced by thought generated in the West, including but not limited to phenomenology, hermeneutics, existentialism, romanticism, idealism, essentialism, Marxism, structuralism, and psychoanalytic criticism. The book emphasizes the dynamism and diversity of Western thought in individual literary texts and authors as well as among texts of different authors and different texts by the same author. Historical contexts within which Western thought migrated to Vietnam and also was perceived differently among the various authors are also an interest of the conference. Furthermore, the discussion hopes to shed light on the social and cultural dynamics and the complexities of South Vietnam.

With its openness to such wide and multiple ways of approaching South Vietnam's literature and journalism, the book seeks to show how this writing participated in issues that were, and still very much are, socially, culturally, politically, and philosophically significant to Vietnam and the world. Such an approach to South Vietnam's literature and journalism aims at a new, alternative view of this writing, a view that is pluralistic and inclusive, neither exclusively anti-communist nor "bourgeois individualist" (cá nhân tiểu tư sản), as it has often been interpreted both in and outside of Vietnam. This traditional view has problematically perpetuated the marginal position of South Vietnam's literature within mainstream Vietnamese literature and within the dominant literatures of the host countries where the Vietnamese authors migrated, settled, and continued to write after the Fall of Saigon.

Hamburg, Germany   Thomas Engelbert
                                                                                          Chi P. Pham

Works cited

Công Huyền Tôn Nữ Nha Trang. *Women Writers of South Vietnam, 1954–1975*. Yale University's Vietnam Forum 9, 1987.

Đoàn Ánh Dương and Nguyễn Thi Bình. Phân tâm học trong tiểu thuyết đô thị miền Nam: Trường hợp Thanh Tâm Tuyền. *Nghiên cứu văn học* 2 (2013).

Đỗ Đức Hiểu/Nguyễn Huệ Chi/Phùng Văn Tửu/Trần Hữu Tá. *Từ điển văn học*. Hà Nội: Thế giới, 2004.

Engelbert, Thomas. "Đỗ Đức Hiểu/Nguyễn Huệ Chi/Phùng Văn Tửu/Trần Hữu Tá. Từ điển văn học." Việt Học Niên San. *Annale der Hamburger Vietnamistik*, vol. 2&3 (2006/07): 122–124.

Huỳnh Như Phương. "Văn học Miền Nam Việt Nam 1954–1975: Những khuynh hướng chủ yếu và thành tựu hiện đại hóa." *Hội thảo khoa học quốc tế Việt Nam học lần thứ IV với chủ đề Những vấn đề giảng dạy tiếng Việt và nghiên cứu Việt Nam trong thế giới ngày nay*. Tp Hồ Chí Minh: Đại học Quốc gia Thành phố Hồ Chí Minh, 2019: 710–723.

Lữ Phương. *Cuộc xâm lăng về văn hóa và tư tưởng của đế quốc Mỹ tại miền Nam Việt Nam*. Hà Nội: Văn hóa, 1981.

Nguyen, Duy Lap. *The Unimagined Community: Imperialism and Culture in South Vietnam*. Manchester: Manchester University Press, 2020.

Nguyễn Tiến Dũng. *Chủ nghĩa hiện sinh: lịch sử và sự hiện diện ở Việt Nam*. Hà Nội: Nxb Chính trị Quốc gia, 1999.

Nguyễn Trần Huân. "The Literature of Vietnam 1954–1973." In *Essays on Literature and Society in Southeast Asia: Political and Sociological Perspectives,* Ed. Tham Seong Chee. Singapore: Singapore University Press, 1981: 321–345.

Nguyễn Vy Khanh. "Văn học Miền Nam tự do, 1954–1975." *Nam Kỳ Lục Tỉnh*, 11.2008. https://sites.google.com/site/tuyentapnguyenvykhanh/tuyen-tap/van-hoc-mien-nam-tu-do-1954-75-phan-2-mot-thoi-tuong-tiec [Accessed on 4 October 2021].

Thế Nguyên. "Báo chí và xuất bản miền Nam dưới chế độ Mỹ ngụy". Trong *Văn hóa, văn nghệ miền Nam dưới chế độ Mỹ ngụy*. Tập II. Hà Nội: Văn hóa, 1979.

Thụy Khuê. Văn học Miền Nam. http://thuykhue.free.fr.

Trần Hoài Anh. "Lý luận - phê bình văn học miền Nam trước 1975 và lý luận - phê bình văn học thời kỳ đổi mới - nhìn lại và suy ngẫm ...". *Văn hóa Nghệ An*, September 11, 2020 : http://www.vanhoanghean.com.vn/component/k2/30-nhung-goc-nhin-van-hoa/14407-ly-luan-phe-binh-van-hoc-mien-nam-truoc-1975-va-ly-luan-phe-binh-van-hoc-thoi-ky-doi-moi-nhin-lai-va-suy-ngam [Accessed on 7 October 2021].

Trần Thục Nga. *Lịch sử Việt Nam 1945–1975*. Hà Nội: Nxb Giáo dục, 1987.

Trần Trọng Đăng Đàn. *Văn hóa, văn nghệ Nam Việt Nam 1954–1975*. Hà Nội: Nxb Thông tin, 1993.

Tuan Hoang. Ideology in Urban South Vietnam, 1950–1975. (Dissertation). Pepperdine University, 2013.

Võ Phiến. *Văn học Miền Nam: tổng quan*. Westminster, Calif. : Văn Nghệ, 2000

Vũ Hạnh, Nguyễn Ngọc Phan. *Văn học thời kỳ 1945–1975 ở Thành phố Hồ Chí Minh*. TP Hồ Chí Minh: Tổng hợp & Văn hóa Sài Gòn, 2008.

Contents

Editors and Contributors

About the Editors

Thomas Engelbert received his Ph.D. in Vietnamese Studies and a second doctorate (Habilitation) in Southeast Asian history from Humboldt University, Berlin. Since 2002, he has worked as a Professor of Vietnamese Language and Culture in the Department of Southeast Asian Languages and Cultures at the Asia-Africa Institute, University of Hamburg. His research focuses on Vietnamese and Southeast Asian history, especially Viˆệt folklore, literature, and relations between ethnic minority and majority groups.

Chi P. Pham is a tenured researcher at the Institute of Literature, Vietnam Academy of Social Sciences. She received her first Ph.D. degree in Literary Theory in Vietnam and her second Ph.D. degree in Comparative Literature in the United States. She was an Alexander von Humboldt Postdoctoral Fellow at the Institute of Asian and African Studies, University of Hamburg, Germany. She has published articles in Vietnamese and English on post-colonial literature and nation-building. Her most recent monograph is *Literature and Nation-building in Vietnam: The Invisibilization of the Indians*. New York: Routledge, 2021.

Contributors

Thai Phan Vang Anh Hue University, Hue, Vietnam

Trương Thuỳ Dung Vietnam Academy of Social Sciences, Hanoi, Vietnam

Thomas Engelbert Asia-Africa Institute, University of Hamburg, Hamburg, Germany

Wynn Gadkar-Wilcox Department of History and World Perspectives, Western Connecticut State University, Danbury, CT, USA

Nguyễn Thị Thanh Hương Faculty of Early Childhood Education, Hanoi National University of Education, Hà Nội, Vietnam

Trịnh Đặng Nguyên Hương Institute of Literature, Vietnam Academy of Social Sciences, Ha Noi, Vietnam

Ngô Thị Quỳnh Nga Faculty of Literature, School of Pedagogy, Vinh University, Nghe An, Vietnam

Duy Lap Nguyen Department of Modern and Classical Languages, University of Houston, Houston, TX, USA

Munehiro Nohira Tokyo University of Foreign Studies, Tokyo, Japan

Chi P. Pham Institute of Literature, Vietnam Academy of Social Sciences, Hanoi, Vietnam

Nguyễn Minh Thu Faculty of English, Hanoi Open University, Hanoi, Vietnam

Hồ Khánh Vân University of Social Sciences and Humanities, Viet Nam National University Ho Chi Minh City (USSH, VNU- HCM), Ho Chi Minh City, Vietnam

An Unprejudiced Education and the Development of Literature in South Vietnam in 1954–1975

Trương Thuỳ Dung

South Vietnam, a newly reclaimed land but one inseparable from Vietnamese territory and culture, has never been detached in the course of Vietnam's development. South Vietnamese literature is no exception. Despite many separations and reunifications due to the vicissitudes of Vietnamese history, the literary works of Vietnamese writers, both Northerners and Southerners, were germinated based on actual events and circumstances, thus reflecting Vietnamese people's minds and aspirations. Conflicts, separations, and wars occurring in Vietnam consecutively in most of the centuries in the course of its history led, among some inhabitants, to pessimistic ideas about the destiny of their country being to wrestle with external forces and invaders. In 1954, tragic history repeated, Vietnam experienced a temporary partition, becoming divided into two parts with two co-existing states. Amidst the tragedies of the Vietnam War, South Vietnamese writers explored new avenues and continued creating literary works, thus contributing to collections of modern Vietnamese literature and giving birth to a new dynamic period. In the complexity of a country suffering under war, South Vietnamese writers were still able to take advantage of the challenges, developing a literature upon the basis of a cohort of facilitated elements, comprising the presence of international scholars, the transplanting of modern literary thoughts and movements to South Vietnam, and more importantly, the practice of a new education which accepted all differences. Considering the above factors in a cause-effect relation to one another, it is reasonable to claim that the new education in South Vietnam from the late 1950s to the early 1970s paved and broadened the way for new developments in South Vietnamese literature. This statement will be discussed and examined by an array of evidence in this paper.

T. T. Dung (✉)
Vietnam Academy of Social Sciences, Hanoi, Vietnam
e-mail: truongthuydungvsh@gmail.com

© The Author(s), under exclusive license to Springer Nature Singapore Pte Ltd. 2023
T. Engelbert and C. P. Pham (eds.), *Global Vietnam: Across Time,*
Space and Community, Reading South Vietnam's Writers,
https://doi.org/10.1007/978-981-99-1043-4_1

Academic Freedom

Donald Kennedy emphasized in his work: "The phrase 'academic freedom' is heard so often around colleges and universities that it has come to resemble a mantra. Though the term has only been in use since the early twentieth century, it seems as if it has always been with us."[1] The familiarity of people with this term is rooted in the earlier discussions of *liberal education* (or *liberal-free ideal*), which has been argued by distinguished educators since the seventeenth and eighteenth centuries, or even earlier, when it was inspired by initial ideas of *artes liberales* in Greek and Roman thought. The liberal-free ideal or liberal education was constructed based on a coherent cluster of ideas, including an emphasis on freedom, an emphasis on intellect and rationality, a critical skepticism, and tolerance.[2] "Man was born free and by nature free; education must both awaken the motivation to learn and be a project of personal development. The search for the truth shall set you free."[3] That statement manifests an apparent phenomenon, although it required centuries to realize the idea. In addition, it is worth noting that the practice of liberal education is not always the same but is amended to follow pragmatic requirements. Comparing the changing nature of liberal education, a study conducted by the Association of American Colleges & Universities (AACU) provides a specific example to elucidate the above statement.

The Changing Nature of Liberal Education

	Liberal Education in the Twentieth Century	Liberal Education in the Twenty-First Century
What	• Intellectual and personal development • An option for the fortunate • Viewed as non-vocational	• Intellectual and personal development • A necessity for all students • Essential for success in a global economy and for informed citizenship

(continued)

[1] Kennedy, *Academic Duty*, 1.
[2] Fallis, *Mutiversities, Ideas, and Democracy*, 35.
[3] Ibid., 35–36.

(continued)

	Liberal Education in the Twentieth Century	Liberal Education in the Twenty-First Century
How	• Through studies in the arts and sciences ("the Major") and/or through general education in the initial years of college	• Through studies that emphasize the Essential Learning Outcomes across the entire educational continuum—from school through college—at progressively higher levels of achievement (recommended)
Where	• Liberal arts of colleges or colleges of arts and sciences in larger institutions	• All schools, community colleges, colleges, and universities, as well as across all fields of study (recommended)

Source Association of American Colleges & Universities, *What is Liberal Education?* available at https://www.aacu.org/leap/what-is-liberal-education, accessed on 11 March 2019

Recently, this study of liberal education was updated. The Association of American Colleges & Universities points out the critical components of contemporary liberal education as follows:

- Essential Learning Outcomes: a framework that defines the knowledge and skills required for success in work, citizenship, and life and that can be used to guide students' cumulative progress through college.
- High-Impact Practices: specific teaching and learning practices that have been widely tested and shown to be beneficial for all students, including and especially those from demographic groups historically underserved by higher education.
- Signature Work: an inquiry-based exploration of a significant problem that the individual student identifies and defines, that is conducted over the course of at least one semester, and that involves substantial writing and reflection.
- Authentic Assessment: an approach to learning outcomes assessment that uses rubrics to evaluate the work students produce across their diverse learning pathways and whose results inform efforts to promote student success.[4]

The changed elements regarding the nature of liberal education reveal a deeper and broader understanding of this educational approach. The objectives and operating scope of liberal education were detailed in the recent study of AACU, which clarified and emphasized the necessity of liberal education for the success of students and the mission of all educational institutions in practicing this approach. Adding to this point, Robert Scott claimed that liberal education leads to students gaining "the confidence needed to take initiative, solve problems, and formulate ideas. They develop skills in language, learning, and leadership. They also learn about domestic and foreign cultures, history, mathematics, science, and technology."[5] In short, liberal education aims to facilitate the students' abilities, offering equality for an individual regardless of their place of birth and promising students' competence in adapting

---

[4] "Advocacy for Liberal Education," available at https://www.aacu.org/advocacy-liberal-education-0, accessed on 12 November 2020.

[5] Scott, *Thoughts on a "Liberating" Education.*

to the requirements of labor markets. From the above comparisons, it is requisite to emphasize that the Republic of Vietnam (RVN) education is more consistent with the nature of twentieth-century liberal education. Accordingly, it is inadequate if we study that education in the current situation instead of in the twentieth-century context when examining its liberal-education character. As mentioned, the terminology of liberal education is relatively new and incomplete. Considering this fact, it could be fruitful to assess the RVN education—an education dedicated to the path of liberal education.

The education system in South Vietnam was strengthened at all levels, from preschool, primary school, and secondary school to tertiary education, during the governance of the two Republics. In line with the change of education model from the French to the American one or from elite education to mass education during the 1955–1975 period, the number of schools and students grew remarkably in South Vietnam. By allowing the existence of both public and private schools and conducting the localization in education, the RVN government offered better conditions for South Vietnamese people to pursue their educational path. Among all educational levels, RVN higher education impressed people with its accomplishments when it consolidated itself and developed from a sole branch of Indochinese University to the various presence of the state, religious, and community universities.

The emergence of a university in Vietnam in terms of the universal-modern concept was somewhat late compared to other nations, especially in advanced countries. The idea of academic freedom, which came relatively late, was imported to the community of Vietnamese scholars around the 1950s. Despite the myriad challenges, Vietnamese educators had not missed any chances to gain an open education (so-called liberal education) which stood for both the means and the goal of practicing academic freedom in Vietnam.

After 1954, the partition of Vietnam sowed various problems for education development. Schools were built in insufficient numbers, while curricula and teaching methods were far-reaching in order to meet the development agenda of South Vietnam. Besides, technical education was almost non-existent in Vietnam during the colonial regime and had to be established on all levels to confront and cope with the pressures of national reconstructions and development.[6] In addition, the deficiencies of Vietnam's higher education, such as the shortage of teaching staff and professors, the scarcity of teaching and learning media, the imbalance between the number of students, and the capacities of the universities and colleges, remained unchanged and urgently required a solution. Despite this, it could not be denied that the severe war circumstances had also motivated the growth of South Vietnam's higher education in the 1950s and 1960s. As Dr. Nguyễn Hữu Phước claimed in his work, the context of South Vietnamese society in the late 1950s facilitated the implementation of one of the RVN education philosophies. To be specific, this was the philosophy of *Open Mind for Changes*. In other words, it could be said that RVN education found a fertile environment for development after the late 1950s. He emphasized the conditions which boosted education in South Vietnam, including the

---

[6] Vietnam Virtual Archives, "Information on Education in Vietnam."

intensity of the war after 1959, the continuity of French efforts to perpetuate their cultural and educational influence in South Vietnam, the US assistance to South Vietnam with a preliminary focus on educational projects, the efforts of Vietnamese educators to modernize national education to meet the country's requirements, and the involvement of the US Operation Mission through various educational contracts with American universities to assist and cooperate with the RVN universities.[7]

The educational principles were first proposed in 1958 and were re-affirmed in the Second National Education Convention in 1964, providing a vision of the RVN education which emphasized three concrete parts as follows,

1. Education in Vietnam must be a humanistic education, respecting the sacred character of the human being, regarding man as an end in himself, and aiming at the full development of man.
2. Education in Vietnam must be a national education, respecting the national values, assuring the continuity of man with his natural environment (his family, profession, and country), aiming at safeguarding the nation, its prosperity, and the collective promotion of its people.
3. Education in Vietnam must be an open education, respecting the scientific mind as a factor of progress, attempting to develop the social and democratic mind, and welcoming all the authentic cultural values of the world.[8]

Those principles of the RVN education set a foundation for the RVN education to go further on its developmental path. These principles prevailed in educational speeches and were rapidly applied to RVN higher education institutions. For instance, the characteristic of a national education was illustrated in the curricula of almost all faculties. Parallel to the teaching of Roman and French Code was the impartment of Chinese and Vietnamese Law. The Western knowledge of economic theories was delivered, accompanied by social-economic processes in Vietnam. Furthermore, studying tropical medicine rather than solely digesting Western theoretical knowledge was a mandatory task for students in the School of Medicine.

As its statement, RVN education desired not only to instruct but to humanize, to promote the emergence of free people at once conscious of their transcendent vocation, and to be able to fulfill their technical point of view. Following these educational objectives, curricula were created, enriching students with boundless culture and guiding them toward specialization in higher education. To conduct those objectives, the curricula were required to:

1. lighten the course of study to avoid cramming,
2. favor general education but at the same time promote specialization,
3. honor the national culture; the Vietnamese languages and literature are a basic subject taught in lower secondary schools and have an important place in the upper secondary schools. In addition, Oriental philosophy is one of the main subjects taught in the philosophy classes.

---

[7] Tuong Vu and Sean Fear (eds.), *The Republic of Vietnam*, 94.
[8] Vietnam Virtual Archives, "Information on Education in Vietnam."

4. give students a fair knowledge of a basic foreign language as a cultural factor and a key to the external world.
5. reserve a large place for morals and civics.[9]

Under open education, schools and teachers were free to decide their curricula without being imposed upon by any so-called Propaganda Committee, meaning that teachers could choose which matters they found helpful to impart to their students, given the acceptance of their dean.[10] The political view of an individual neither affected their right to learn nor their position in the academic community in South Vietnam. Several South Vietnamese who are in their sixties living either in Vietnam or abroad recall that RVN education provided most extensive opportunities for South Vietnamese residents pursuing the path of knowledge. The students' right to participate in exams was reserved even they were imprisoned, and when these students passed the exams, the degrees were awarded in prison.[11]

Fulfilling the educational principles and adapting to the requirements of reality, higher education experienced rapid growth after the Partition Agreement in 1954. Before 1954, the University in Saigon was only a branch of Indochinese University, and there were no other institutions of higher learning in South Vietnam. Since 1955, not only did the University of Saigon undergo reform and become an independent entity, but many newly established universities emerged, including public and private universities, namely the University of Huế (1957), Đà Lạt University (1958), Vạn Hạnh University (1964), and the University of Cần Thơ (1966). The increasing number of universities prompted the rising number of students. This number surged in the 1954–1967 period, increasing from 3,000 to 34,000 enrolled university students, to over 11 times the previous number.

The practice of open education in South Vietnam, on the one hand, fostered the increase in the number of students, and on the other hand, led to a breakthrough in terms of teaching methods and teacher-student relations. Prof. Nguyễn Văn Trường, who was a former Minister of Education of the Republic of Vietnam, and also was a professor at the University of Huế, the University of Saigon, and the University of Cao Đài, had shown an unconventional perspective in respect to the relationship between students and teachers.

Throughout the thousands of years of traditional education, Vietnamese had always gratefully respected their teachers and followed teachers' words without questioning. This created a phenomenon common to Vietnamese education, in which teachers were monologists and students were passive listeners. This situation gradually changed in the second half of the twentieth century, as evidenced by the opinion of Prof. Nguyễn Văn Trường on the role of teachers in the teaching-learning process. He emphasized that teaching was not a simple delivery of knowledge, was not propaganda, and definitely not a brainwashing process. According to him, *the learner plays the main role and the teacher plays the supporting role*[12] (Người học là chính và

---

[9] Ibid.

[10] Trần Văn Chánh, *Bàn về giáo dục*, 89.

[11] Ibid., 94.

[12] Nguyễn Thanh Liêm (ed.), *Giáo dục ở miền Nam*, 64.

người dạy là phụ). Therefore, teachers could not force students to follow their criteria. Instead, they were to instruct students on ways of exploring the answers. In doing so, the teachers needed *to silence their own ego* (làm im lặng cái tôi của người thầy), to encourage students to raise their voices, to stimulate the confidence of students, and subsequently, to pave the way for the creation of an individual student and the student's success. The best results to be obtained in the teaching-learning process were not the absorption of specific lessons, but how students grasped the knowledge. In other words, the method for obtaining knowledge was the essential thing to be gained rather than the knowledge itself.

Interestingly, Prof. Nguyễn Văn Trường argued that the students would be the teachers in the teaching-learning process, producing feedback to help their teachers conduct teaching tasks effectively.[13] Agreeing with the arguments and perspectives of Prof. Nguyễn Văn Trường, Prof. Lê Thanh Minh Châu clarified that teachers, in order to accomplish their teaching role, were not only conducting the task of indoctrinating but were instructing the students, understanding the students' abilities, and teaching students with affection.[14]

Open Education and the Development of Literature in South Vietnam

A look at the textbooks used in secondary schools and high schools and syllabuses used in RVN universities could illuminate the non-political nature of South Vietnam's education. Books of eminent Vietnamese writers, both living in North and South Vietnam, were introduced to South Vietnamese students, encouraging them to perceive the entire complexity of Vietnamese literature. In philosophical textbooks and lectures, despite South Vietnam being in an ideological war opposing Socialism, Marxism was treated equally to capitalist theories and ideologies. In order to bring this ideology to the mass of South Vietnamese inhabitants, Marxist-related books were translated, written, and published, such as *Hành trình tri thức của Karl Marx* [The Knowledge Path of Karl Marx] by Prof. Nguyễn Văn Trung, and *Tìm hiểu triết học của Karl Marx* [Studying the Philosophy of Karl Marx] by Prof. Nguyễn Văn Toàn.

South Vietnamese students benefited from the deliberate and crucial preparations for students in the lower levels based on flexible and overarching curricula. In the philosophical curriculum for students of grade 12, majoring in ancient and foreign languages, students spent two out of nine hours per week reading one classical book of Western or Eastern philosophy chosen from a list of recommendations by their professors.[15] Several scholars argued that this curriculum was overloaded and inconsistent with the capabilities of high school students. The curriculum content

---

[13] Ibid., 91.

[14] Ibid., 350.

[15] Ibid., 176–177.

was double that French students had to absorb when studying at the same level. Due to this disagreement, in the 1971–1972 school year, the philosophical curriculum for grade 12 was revised, downsizing the load.[16] The philosophical curriculum before 1971 reflected, on the one hand, how over-ambitious South Vietnamese teachers and professors were in regard to the capabilities of their students, but, on the other hand, had the positive result that it nurtured a "golden generation" of the 1960s and 1970s scholars, who would be able to confidently and professionally discuss fashionable topics of philosophy in a variety of channels, publications, and casual meetings.

A similar situation occurred in the textbooks of Letters. These books contained many writers and poets who were living on "the other bank of Bến Hải River," such as Nguyên Hồng, Tô Hoài, Trần Tiêu, Nguyễn Tuân, Xuân Diệu, Huy Cận, and Chế Lan Viên, regardless of their political perspectives. The non-political nature was not only outstanding in the textbook content but also in the literary works. Prof. Nguyễn Văn Trung asserted that RVN literature owned neither party nor national spirit in terms of ideology; it had only Vietnamese spirit. This phenomenon will be debated more in the following.

Open education, applied in South Vietnam in the 1950s, 1960s, and 1970s, paved the way for a lively atmosphere of academic activities in South Vietnam. The freedom of academia cultivated in schools and universities spread widely to the community via diverse avenues, comprising journals, books, and academic forums. Prominent journals, such as *Bách Khoa* [Encyclopedia], *Đại học* [Higher Education], *Sáng Tạo* [Creation], *Văn* [Literature], and also publishing houses mushroomed in South Vietnam in the years 1955–1975, evidenced the significant influence of open education in South Vietnamese society. The prominent authors for these publications mostly came from RVN universities, for example, Nguyễn Văn Trung, Cao Văn Luận, Thái Văn Kiểm, Trần Thái Đỉnh, Nguyễn Trọng Văn, and Trần Văn Toàn.

A noticeable achievement that should be mentioned in a discourse on RVN education is consideration that this education gave to foreign languages. As known, lectures in RVN universities in the 1950s and 1960s were for the most part taught in English and French instead of Vietnamese. This was due to the lack of precise Vietnamese terminologies in specific fields, especially in the field of sciences. As a consequence, South Vietnamese students were required to use foreign languages, such as English and French, properly. The debates on the ability of South Vietnamese students to wield foreign languages as a medium for their study and research were controversial. A series of writings written by Nguyễn Hiến Lê in *Bách Khoa* shed light on this issue. Nonetheless, the ability of South Vietnamese intellectuals to use French, English, or other foreign languages in the 1960s and 1970s is undeniable.

Prof. Nguyễn Văn Trung reminisced that most South Vietnamese students were capable of reading English, French, and even German books and journals.[17] Fluency in foreign languages was a strength of South Vietnamese scholars in the second half of the twentieth century. Nguyên Đình, a former student at the University of Huế remembers that in the 1960s, like others, he attended the preparation courses and

---

[16] Ibid., 188.
[17] Nguyễn Văn Trung, "Nhìn lại những chặng đường."

had to gain enough "certificates" (*chứng chỉ*) before being accepted at the university. Choosing the French literature section opened up to him an enormous world of literature and its fashionable tendencies in the 1960s, such as Existentialism. He recalled that Existentialism and Sartre's works were introduced to students two hours per week by Prof. Cauro.[18] In the freshman year in the section of Philosophy, there seemed to be no limitations in approaching thoughts and ideologies when he and his fellow classmates attended lectures on ancient Roman philosophy, Zen Buddhist philosophy, Orientation philosophy, and the philosophy of Existentialism. It could be assumed that Existentialism was fairly familiar to South Vietnamese students.

The fluency in foreign languages facilitated South Vietnamese students and scholars in exploring works of international writers and discussing literary tendencies. Nguyễn Văn Sâm, a former student at the faculty of Letters, at the University of Saigon, reminisces that the students of the French and English literature sections in the preparatory courses possessed an impressive command of French and English: "The students at the preparatory course in French literature were pompous and elegant, they spoke fluent French and with a French accent resulting from a deliberate education since childhood, (they) regularly would use French to talk with professors, who mostly came from France."[19]

This skill produced a critical means for students to remain connected to current literature trends in the world. In the 1960s and 1970s, renowned scholars translated many books into Vietnamese. In *Văn hoá, văn nghệ… Nam Việt Nam 1954–1975* [Culture, Literature… in South Vietnam 1954–1975], Trần Trọng Đăng Đàn released an initial result of the 1976 survey which confirms that hundreds of foreign books were translated into Vietnamese during the 1954–1975 period, including 57 German, 58 Italian, 71 Japanese, 97 British-English, 273 American-English, 499 French, 358 Chinese, 120 Russian books as well as 156 translated works from other 38 countries.[20] Besides these publications, several essays and articles were also translated and published in academic journals, for instance, "Văn chương và siêu hình học" [Literature and Metaphysics], written by Nguyễn Văn Trung on *Sáng Tạo* no.10, 07/1957; "Nhận định đại cương về triết học Hiện Hữu" [General Assumptions of Existentialism], written by Nguyên Sa in *Sáng Tạo* no.14, 11/1957, "Khái niệm về chủ nghĩa Hiện sinh" [The Conception of Existentialism], written by Quang Minh, on *Sáng Tạo* no. 28–29, 01–02/1959; "Trình bày và phê bình hai quan điểm nổi loạn của Albert Camus" [Detailing and Criticizing Two Revolutionary Views of Albert Camus], written by Thạch Chương, on *Sáng Tạo* 09/1969.

It could be assumed that the RVN's open education germinated academic freedom in South Vietnam, creating a more expansive and sacred space for South Vietnamese intellectuals to voice their opinions, including anti-government arguments.

---

[18] Nguyên Đình, "Hồi ức về trường Đại học."

[19] The original version in Vietnamese: "Dân Dự bị Pháp hào hoa sang trọng, nói chuyện với nhau bằng tiếng Pháp lưu loát, giọng Pháp chuẩn vì họ học ngôn ngữ nầy từ nhỏ, sử dụng tiếng Pháp hằng ngày với dàn giáo sư hầu hết từ Pháp qua."

Nguyễn Văn Sâm, "Một chút Văn khoa."

[20] Trần Trọng Đăng Đàn, *Văn hoá, văn nghệ*, 427.

The spreading of the open education discipline and the linguistic competence of South Vietnamese scholarship, emerging simultaneously in the context of the Vietnam War, ensured conditions for the flowering of South Vietnamese literature in the 1954–1975 period.

Examining the flows and development of South Vietnamese literature in the twentieth century, we have found that the most free and diverse period for the creativity of South Vietnamese writers was in three decades, from the late 1950s to the early 1970s. An array of philosophical schools were imported to South Vietnam, impacting both the literary creation and criticism of South Vietnamese writers. The philosophies of Personalism, Existentialism, Structuralism, Marxism, and Phenomenology became an invisible part of South Vietnamese literature. The allure of these philosophies is rooted in their novel character as well as the thirst of South Vietnamese writers for a leading theory to use as the spinal framework of their works. Being accepted by South Vietnamese intellectuals, otherwise, those above-mentioned philosophical schools were having different levels of influence during the war.

Compared to other philosophical schools, Personalism was introduced earlier to South Vietnamese, accompanying and engaging with the political propaganda of the Ngô Family. To understand the spread of Personalism in South Vietnam in the late 1950s and the 1960s and the attitude of South Vietnamese scholars toward this philosophical school, it is necessary to recall the situation of South Vietnam after 1954, particularly after the Geneva Agreement. Following the Geneva Agreement decision of temporarily dividing Vietnam into two parts, approximately a million Vietnamese people living in North Vietnam moved to South Vietnam, well-known as the 1954 Southern Exodus. In this migration flow, a considerable portion was intellectual. Their motivations for moving South were varied; a number of these claimed their purpose to be seeking freedom in a new land. If leaving the North was considered an escape from Communism, the choice of Personalism was to furnish a means of seeking and practicing freedom as these people wished.

Nguyễn Trọng Văn, an outstanding scholar in South Vietnam during the Vietnam War, did a psychological analysis of the above matter to clarify the genuine motivation of South Vietnamese writers for choosing Personalism. On the surface, choosing Personalism, in the mind of these people, demonstrated the right to freedom which they would have been unable to obtain if living in North Vietnam (under the Communist-controlled government). However, this does not express the complete truth. Nguyễn Trọng Văn frankly pointed out that the reason was only a justification of the writers who moved to the South and felt self-deprecation toward Northern communists.[21] To persuade themselves, they claimed rightness on their side (South Vietnam). Nguyễn Trọng Văn quoted a paragraph in *Căn nhà vùng nước mặn* [A House in a Mangrove Area] written by Mai Thảo as an example for justification as mentioned earlier:

> … Are people enjoying the party atmosphere on another bank? Xuân Diệu, Lưu Trọng Lư, and Nguyễn Tuân used their works to disguise the fact (…) So, it does not matter whether to go or stay. Going does not mean an exile, a loss of root, what you, the Hanoi people,

---

[21] Nguyễn Trọng Văn, "Hoàn cảnh những người."

and I devoted to contributing to the life surrounding us in Saigon, is a genuine Hanoi - a quintessential part, the most precious part of Hanoi. We brought our homeland with us, we took Hanoi on our journey. In our current life emerged a new conception of homeland in which we are fighting to protect Hanoi and always Hanoi people.[22]

They considered freedom and democracy were the South Vietnamese privileges that could not have been possible for people living under the communist-controlled authority in North Vietnam. They praised love, free creation, new genres, and adventure. These topics were a muse, appearing popularly in their works. Nguyễn Trọng Văn stated that these people were in an illusion, and they did not know that they were sleepwalking people.[23]

It appeared later in South Vietnam, however, Existentialism soon became a leading theory in the literary works of South Vietnamese scholarship. Since the second half of the twentieth century, Existentialism had been taught in South Vietnam's schools, imparted through several subjects, such as Metaphysics and Ethics, at the University of Saigon, the Vạn Hạnh University, the University of Huế, and the Đà Lạt University.[24] After the 1963 coup, the intellectuals in South Vietnam were wakened up from the illusion of freedom and democracy. The belief in their rightness had faded. Disappointed with the reality, the writers sought a muse for creating works on their inner lives. Differing from trending topics in the previous years, after 1963, the foremost and most common sense found in the works of South Vietnamese writers was the emotion of stalemate, loneliness, degradation, and nihilism.

In the latter years, Existentialism was introduced beyond the schools. As elucidated in the Nguyễn Thị Việt Nga's study, while in advance of 1961, Existentialism was only introduced through short writings in several newspapers, after 1961, this theory was brought to readers through arduous studies, for instance: *Heidegger trước sự phá sản của tư tưởng Tây phương* [Heiddeger Confronting the Collapse of Western Philosophies], *Đâu là căn nguyên tư tưởng hay con đường triết lý từ Kant đến Heidegger* [What is the Essence or the Philosophical Path from Kant to Heidegger], *Những vấn đề triết học hiện đại* [Issues of the Modern Philosophy] written by Lê Tôn Nghiêm; *Hiện tượng luận về hiện sinh* [Phenomenology of Existentialism] and *Triết học tổng quát* [Introduction of Philosophy] written by Lê Thành Trị; *Nguyên tử, hiện sinh và hư vô* [Nuclear, Existentialism, and Nihilism] written by Nghiêm Xuân Hồng; and *Tư tưởng hiện đại* [Modern Thoughts].[25] The circulation of Existentialist philosophy paved the way for the creations based on this theory by South Vietnamese

---

[22] The original version in Vietnamese: "... Bờ bên đó vui như một đêm liên hoan? Bọn Xuân Diệu, Lưu Trọng Lư, Nguyễn Tuân chỉ viết láo (…) Cho nên đi hay ở không thành vấn đề. Đi không phải là tị nạn, là mất gốc, những cái mà tôi, mà anh, những người Hà-nội hiến dâng, góp phần vào cho sự sống ở Sài-gòn, ở khắp nơi hôm nay mới chính là Hà-nội, cái phần tinh hoa, cái phần quý giá nhất của Hà-nội. Chúng ta đi mang theo quê hương, chúng ta đi mang theo Hà-nội là thế. Mà cũng chính là trong lối sống hiện giờ có từ một ý niệm mới về quê hương mà chúng ta đang chiến đấu, đang bảo vệ cho Hà-nội, để vẫn là người Hà-nội."

   Ibid., 61.

[23] Ibid., 65.

[24] Nguyễn Tiến Dũng, *Chủ nghĩa hiện sinh.*

[25] Nguyễn Thị Việt Nga, "Văn học miền Nam."

writers. Concerning this aspect, Huỳnh Như Phương concluded in his study that Existentialism led to significant changes in South Vietnamese literature, especially in the artistic view of the loneliness of human beings in an irrational world.[26]

Not only philosophical books on Existentialism were translated into Vietnamese and introduced to Vietnamese readers, but literary studies on Existentialist theory were also ever more popular in South Vietnam in the 1960s and 1970s. For example, *Tuyển tập các nhà văn Pháp hiện đại* [The Collection of Modern French Writers] written by Hoàng Ngọc Biên (Trình Bầy Publishing House, 1969); *Mổ xẻ nhà văn hiện sinh Jean Paul Sartre* [Anatomizing an Existentialist Writer—Jean Paul Sartre] written by Nguyễn Quang Lục (Hoa Muôn Phương Publishing House, 1970); *Cuộc phiêu lưu tư tưởng của văn học Âu Châu thế kỷ XX* [The Adventure of Thoughts in European Literature in the Twentieth Century], written by R.M. Albérè, translated by Vũ Đình Lưu (Phủ Quốc vụ khanh đặc trách văn hoá [The RVN Secretariat of State of Culture], 1971); writings on Samuel Backett and J.P. Sartre of Huỳnh Phan An in *Đi tìm tác phẩm văn chương* [Seeking Literary Works] published by Đồng Tháp Publishing House in 1972; and *Văn học thế giới hiện đại* [Contemporary International Literatures] written by Bửu Ý (An Tiêm Publishing House, 1973).[27] The above works contributed to the nourishment and inspiration of South Vietnamese writers in creating works relating to and based on Existentialist philosophy.

Existentialist theory was absorbed into both South Vietnamese authors' literary creations and their criticism. In terms of creations, some poets representing the Existentialist poem were Bùi Giáng, Nguyên Sa, Đinh Hùng, Thanh Tâm Tuyền, Mai Thảo, Du Tử Lê, Nhã Ca, Cung Trầm Tưởng, and Nguyễn Đức Sơn. Existentialism's application seems to be more thoughtful in regard to literary criticism. From classical to contemporary works and even folklore, a range of literature was refracted and anatomized through a new prism of Existentialism. Some eminent writings could be depicted, such as "Thời gian hiện sinh trong Đoạn trường tân thanh" [Existential Time in The Tale of Kiều] and "Chinh phụ ngâm và tâm thức lãng mạn của kẻ lưu đày" [Lament of the Soldier's Wife and the Romantic Mind of the Exile] penned by Lê Tuyên, published on *Đại học* in the years 1960 and 1961, respectively; "Tính chất bi đát trong thi ca Tản Đà" [Tragedies in Tản Đà' Poems] written by Nguyễn Thiên Thụ on *Thời Tập*; "Nguyễn Du trên những nẻo đường tự do" [Nguyễn Du on Freedom Paths] authored by Nguyên Sa, published on *Sáng Tạo*; *Vũ trụ thơ* [The Universe of Poem] written by Đặng Tiến, examining the fate of Kiều through the prism of Existentialism.[28]

Other philosophical theories that were transferred to South Vietnam in the 1950s, 1960s, and 1970s and had considerable influence on South Vietnamese writers were Phenomenology and Structuralism. Although these two theories had gained only a humble influence compared to what Existentialism had obtained, it was still true that these theories, too, were adopted by South Vietnamese scholars, becoming theoretical foundations for their works and contributing to diversify South Vietnamese literary

---

[26] Huỳnh Như Phương, "Chủ nghĩa hiện sinh."
[27] Nguyễn Thị Việt Nga, "Văn học miền Nam."
[28] Ibid.

creations. The imprints of Phenomenology on RVN writers could not be extracted solely but evolved through the penetration of Existentialism. A close relation of Existentialism and Phenomenology was highlighted in the Nguyễn Tiến Dũng's study. He assumed: "The position of Phenomenology founded by Husserl not only provided a philosophical regulation for Existentialism but also directly influenced the fields of Literature and Art, thus creating 'Philosophical Literature' in Modernism."[29]

The case of Structuralism (*Cấu trúc luận* or *Cơ cấu luận* in Vietnamese) was similar to Phenomenology in its influencing scope. As analyzed by Nguyễn Văn Trung,

> In Vietnam, it can be seen that Structuralism began to be introduced. Is Structuralism becoming a trend like Existentialism? It unquestionably could not be like that because Structuralism is a scientific conception, especially a method that is hard to understand for most people, except a for few experts and specialists. Consequently, a vast number of people, even those who are well-educated but not specialized in the fields of anthropology, linguistics, and psychoanalysis, are unable to grasp it.[30]

Despite that, Structuralism was instilled in the RVN scholarly community, providing a new method of studying literary works, which considered a literary work as linguistic architecture rather than a psychosocial reflection. According to Nguyễn Văn Trung, the application of Structuralism to criticize literary works offered a solution for fixing the flaws in this field. For instance, in the conventional concept, the criticism of a literary work was connected to historical contexts and the author's biography. While many works were anonymous, how could we trace them back to when the authors lived and find related information? This challenge was solved when using Structuralism, which focused on literary works and considered them as linguistic structures rather than as being context-based.[31]

Besides the above theories, Marxism, too, was introduced and applied in South Vietnam, showing the academic freedom of RVN scholarship. The hostility of the RVN government toward communists was not a reason to ignore Marxism. Being treated equally to other theories, Marxism was imparted to South Vietnamese students and studied by RVN researchers. Less impactful, but having a position in the South Vietnamese academic community, Marxism offered an example of the open mind of the South Vietnamese, an achievement of open education and of the diversification of South Vietnamese literature in the 1954–1975 period.

---

[29] The original version in Vietnamese: "Địa vị của hiện tượng học do Husserl đặt nền móng không chỉ đưa lại cho chủ nghĩa hiện sinh một quy chế triết học mà còn ảnh hưởng trực tiếp tới văn học, nghệ thuật, tạo thành 'Văn học triết học' trong chủ nghĩa hiện đại."
Nguyễn Tiến Dũng, *Chủ nghĩa hiện sinh*, 31.

[30] The original version in Vietnamese: "Ở Việt Nam cũng bắt đầu thấy có những bài giới thiệu, bàn về cơ cấu. Liệu cơ cấu có trở thành một 'mốt" như hiện sinh trước đây không? Chắc là không vì cơ cấu là một khái niệm khoa học và cơ cấu luận trước hết là một phương pháp khoa học rất khó hiểu và chỉ dành cho một số người chuyên môn. Do đó người thường có lẽ chả hiểu gì, ngay cả những người có văn hoá cao nhưng thiếu cái vốn học về nhân chủng, ngữ học, tâm phân học, v.v... cũng khó mà lãnh hội được."
Nguyễn Văn Trung, "Tìm hiểu cơ cấu," 35.

[31] Nguyễn Văn Trung, "Tìm hiểu cơ cấu."

Conclusion

The RVN education developed under the dire circumstance of the Vietnam War. Despite many challenges it confronted, this education had several achievements, which have an enduring influence on the current education of Vietnam. One notable accomplishment of the RVN education was that it pursued the discipline of open education. The idea of the "open education" discipline was utterly new to the South Vietnamese people, including RVN educators; however, this did not become a hindrance to keep this discipline from becoming a leading philosophy in the education of both the First and Second Republic of Vietnam. The existence of open education, or as in our viewpoint, an unprejudiced education, created a foundation for adopting external and novel philosophical theories, such as Personalism, Existentialism, Structuralism, Marxism, and Phenomenology, which then became theoretical foundations for South Vietnamese writers in creating and criticizing literary works.

In a chain of causes and effects, it could be assumed that the open education operating in South Vietnam created the way for the diversification of South Vietnamese literature from 1954 to 1975. It is noticeable that the theories mentioned above emerge at different levels of influence in the works of South Vietnamese writers. In any case, South Vietnamese writers endeavored to set the boundary between political and literary approaches when wielding those philosophies. This, on the one hand, demonstrates how impartial South Vietnamese scholars are toward external philosophies, regardless of political conflicts; on the other hand, it is an outstanding example of the consequences of open education.

Bibliography

Advocacy for Liberal Education. Available at https://www.aacu.org/advocacy-liberal-education-0. Accessed on 12 Nov 2020

Association of American Colleges & Universities. What is Liberal Education? Available at https://www.aacu.org/leap/what-is-liberal-education. Accessed on 11 Mar 2019

Fallis G (2007) Mutiversities, ideas, and democracy. University of Toronto Press, Toronto, Buffalo, London

Huỳnh NP, Chủ nghĩa hiện sinh ở miền Nam Việt Nam 1954–1975 (trên bình diện lý thuyết). Available at http://www.vns.edu.vn/index.php/vi/nghien-cuu/van-hoa-viet-nam/1674-chu-nghia-hien-sinh-o-mien-nam-viet-nam-1954-1975-tren-binh-dien-ly-thuyet. Accessed on 12 Apr 2020

Kennedy D (1997) Academic duty. Harvard University Press, Cambridge, MA, London, UK

Nguyễn VT (1969) Tìm hiểu cơ cấu luận như một phương pháp, một triết thuyết và đặt vấn đề tiếp thu. Bách Khoa, số 293(3):35–40

Nguyễn VT (1969) Tìm hiểu cơ cấu luận như một phương pháp, một triết thuyết và đặt vấn đề tiếp thu. Bách Khoa, số 294(4):11–18

Nguyễn TL (ed) (2006) Giáo dục ở miền Nam tự do trước 1975. Le Van Duyet Foundation, C.A

Nguyễn TD (2009) Chủ nghĩa hiện sinh: lịch sử và sự hiện diện ở Việt Nam. Nhà xuất bản Chính trị Quốc gia, Hà Nội

Nguyên Đ, Hồi ức về trường Đại học Văn khoa Huế. Available at https://nguyendinhchuc.wordpress.com/2012/07/04/hoi-uc-ve-truong-dai-hoc-van-khoa-hue/. Posted on 4 July 2012

Nguyễn TV, Hoàn cảnh những người cầm bút miền Nam trước và sau 1963. Available at https://liberalarts.temple.edu/sites/liberalarts/files/HoancanhnhungnguoicambutmienNamtruocvasau1963by.pdf

Nguyễn TVN, Văn học miền Nam 1954–1975: Sự hiện diện của Triết học và Văn học hiện sinh ở đô thị miền Nam 1954–1975. Available at http://vanviet.info/van-hoc-mien-nam/van-hoc-mien-nam-1954-1975-23-su-hien-dien-cua-triet-hoc-v-van-hoc-hien-sinh-o-d-thi-mien-nam-1954-1975/. Accessed on 15 May 2020

Nguyễn VL, Hai mươi năm văn học dịch thuật miền Nam 1955–1975. Available at https://bookhunterclub.com/20-nam-van-hoc-dich-thuat-mien-nam-1955-1975/. Accessed on 25 Jan 2021

Nguyễn VS, Một chút Văn khoa Sài gòn năm 60. Available at http://www.dcvonline.net/2018/04/07/mot-chut-van-khoa-saigon-nam-60/. Posted on 7 Apr 2018

Nguyễn VT, Nhìn lại những chặng đường đã qua. Available at http://vanviet.info/tu-lieu/nhn-lai-nhung-chang-duong-d-qua-1/. Posted on 15 July 2019

Phạm CT (1966) Ý thức mới trong văn nghệ và triết học. An Tiêm xuất bản, Sài Gòn

Scott RA, Thoughts on a 'Liberating' Education. Available at https://www.aacu.org/publications-research/periodicals/thoughts-liberating-education. Accessed on 11 Mar 2020

Trần TĐĐ (2000) Văn hoá, văn nghệ... Nam Việt Nam 1954–1975. Nhà xuất bản Văn hoá Thông tin, Hà Nội

Trần HA (2009) Lý luận – phê bình văn học ở đô thị miền Nam 1954–1975. Nhà xuất bản Hội Nhà văn, Hà Nội

Trần VC (2019) Bàn về giáo dục Việt Nam trước và sau năm 1975. Mega Plus và Nhà xuất bản Hà Nội, Hà Nội

Vietnam Virtual Archives, "Information on Education in Vietnam," File 1780839028, The Vietnam Center and Sam Johnson Archive, Texas Tech University

Vu T, Fear S (eds) (2020) The Republic of Vietnam, 1955–1975: Vietnamese perspective on nation building. Cornell SEAP, Cornell University Press, Ithaca

Trương Thuỳ Dung is a researcher at the Institute of History, Vietnam Academy of Social Sciences, Hanoi, Vietnam. Her research interests focus on but are not limited to the educational and cultural developments of the Republic of Vietnam, the Vietnam wars in the twentieth century, Vietnamese literature and linguistics, and Southeast Asian history. She earned her Ph.D. at the University of Hamburg, Germany, in 2020. She was a postdoctoral fellow at Ash Center, Harvard Kennedy School in 2021–2022.

Vietnamese Personalism: The Communitarian Humanism of the Early South Vietnamese State

Duy Lap Nguyen

Introduction

Shortly after founding the Republic of Vietnam in 1955, its first president, Ngô Đình Diệm, announced that the new South Vietnamese state would adopt a doctrine of Personalism as its official philosophy.[1] In the literature on the Vietnam War, this philosophy, as Philip Catton has noted, has been dismissed "either as a confusing curiosity or a thinly veiled cover for the Ngos' dictatorship."[2] Personalism has been characterized as an "unsystematic *mélange* of 'third force' ideas,"[3] seeking a "third way" or a "middle-ground" between "Marxist collectivism and Western individualistic capitalism."[4] Other critics, who "found personalism vague and confusing," regarded the Republic's official philosophy as an elaborate cover for authoritarian rule.[5] As United States Ambassador, Frederick Nolting, explained in a meeting with Diệm, "most Americans, who have never heard of personalism, think that it means glorifying your person as head of state."[6] The perception of Diệm's Personalist Republic, then, was that it was "theoretically a parliamentary democracy but actually a personal dictatorship."[7]

---

[1] Ngo Dinh Diem, *President Ngo Dinh Diem on Democracy*, 15.

[2] Catton, *Diem's Final Failure*, 25.

[3] Donnell, "National renovation campaigns in Vietnam," 77–80.

[4] Bain, *Vietnam, The Roots of Conflict*, 118.

[5] French, "Politics and National Development in Vietnam—1954–1960."

[6] As quoted in Bửu Lịch, *Les idéologies dans la République du Sud Vietnam 1954–1975*, 39.

[7] Daniels, *Year of the Heroic Guerrilla*, 21.

D. L. Nguyen (✉)
Department of Modern and Classical Languages, University of Houston, Houston, TX, USA
e-mail: duynguyn18@gmail.com

© The Author(s), under exclusive license to Springer Nature Singapore Pte Ltd. 2023   17
T. Engelbert and C. P. Pham (eds.), *Global Vietnam: Across Time, Space and Community*, Reading South Vietnam's Writers,
https://doi.org/10.1007/978-981-99-1043-4_2

For Gabriel Kolko, on the other hand, Personalism was not a theory of parliamentary government, but a "corporatist and authoritarian" worldview created "for the private use of power by Diem and... [his] cronies."[8] Hired "to perform a comprador role for... foreign imperialism,"[9] the Ngos, devoid of any political principles, assembled an "incomprehensible hodgepodge" of reactionary ideas taken from both Europe and Asia. These ideas have been cast as "Confucianism in another guise," a feudal ideology revived for the purpose of perpetuating the rule of "Personalist mandarins."[10] Others have asserted that Personalism was an incoherent political doctrine, derived from the foreign religion of Vietnam's former colonial masters, used, opportunistically, "to fill the regime's ideological vacuum,"[11] and to justify the oppression of its own population: "In the hands of Nhu and Diem, personalism supplied an intellectual foundation for an authoritarian regime that alienated Catholics nearly as badly as South Vietnam's Buddhist majority."[12]

This essay argues that, contrary to conventional accounts, the Personalism adopted as the official philosophy of the First Republic of Vietnam (Đệ Nhất Cộng hòa) was not a reactionary ideology. Rather, it was an anti-colonial and anti-capitalist doctrine, derived from a form of Marxist humanism developed by the French Catholic philosopher, Emmanuel Mounier. In his writings, Mounier embraced the ideal of a decentralized form of communitarian communism, one that he opposed to both the alienation of capital as well as to the oppression of the Soviet state, with its centralized political and economic apparatus. The first part of the essay presents a reading of Mounier's political philosophy. The second examines the influence of Mounier's critique of Stalinism and bourgeois democracy on the philosophy of "Oriental Personalism" (Chủ nghĩa nhân vị phương Đông), developed by Ngô Đình Diệm's younger brother and chief political advisor, Ngô Đình Nhu. I argue that Mounier's Marxist humanism informed the Ngos' opposition to both the ideology of the Vietnamese Communist Party as well as the economic and political liberalism prescribed by their American allies. Contrary to the conventional view, the Personalism of the First Republic, therefore, was not a reactionary Christian philosophy. Rather, it was a form of anti-colonialism derived in part from Western Marxism.

Christianity, Communism, and Capitalism

In a memorandum issued in exile by officers who participated in the failed coup against Ngô Đình Diệm in 1960, Vietnamese Personalism is characterized as an "odious, lying ... doctrine," "hastily and arbitrarily" put together by "highly-paid

---

[8] Kolko, *Anatomy of a War*, 84.

[9] Ibid., 208.

[10] Doyle, *Passing the Torch*, 138.

[11] As quoted in Del Boca and Giovana. *I figli del sole*, 334.

[12] Dobson, "Diem, Ngo Dinh." 170.

priests."[13] The official philosophy of the early Republic, however, had not been adopted opportunistically, in a hurried attempt to manufacture a political cause that could rally support for an illegitimate comprador state. Rather, the doctrine had been developed prior to the Republic's establishment. In the manifesto of the Personalist Labor Revolutionary Party (*Cần Lao Nhân Vị Cách Mạng Đảng*), written in 1954, Diệm's younger brother, Ngô Đình Nhu (who, at the time, was a powerful union organizer) announced the need for a "Personalist Revolution for the complete liberation of Man."[14] Employing the principles of Personalism, Nhu's political party, the *Cần Lao*, would create the conditions for his older brother's ascendance to power.[15]

Although Personalism, moreover, was partly derived from a French Catholic philosophy, the emphasis placed on its non-Vietnamese origins in historical works on the war has served to conceal its radical features.[16] The misperception of Vietnamese Personalism as a conservative Catholic philosophy was one that the leaders of the early Republic had repeatedly tried to correct. "We are a reactionary regime, you have been told," said Nhu sarcastically in an interview with *Le Monde*, "are you aware of the fact that we take our inspiration from the thinkers of the Western Left, particularly the French? I don't want to name names [he laughed] or compromise anybody. … But you must realize that we base ourselves on personalism!"[17]

This doctrine of the Western Left was one that Nhu, "*père du personnalisme viêtnamien*," had encountered in France, as a student at the prestigious École Nationale des Chartes.[18] Nhu's conception of "Oriental Personalism" was inspired in particular by the writings of Emmanuel Mounier, who saw Personalism as an alternative to both Soviet communism and liberal democracy. Contrary to the US ambassador, Elbridge Durbrow, however, this alternative was not a "balance between communist collectivism and old fashioned laissez-faire capitalism."[19] This description fails to acknowledge the radically anti-capitalist character of Mounier's thinking. For Mounier, capitalism was in fact a far greater danger than communism, since "the capitalist evil is incorrigible, the soviet evil is curable."[20] Mounier's personalist

---

[13] As quoted in Burchett, *The Furtive War*, 82.

[14] Tuyên ngôn Cần lao Nhân vị Cách mạng Đảng [Manifesto of the Cần Lao Personalist Revolutionary Party].

[15] Đào Thị Diến, "*Nhà lưu trữ Việt Nam thời kì 1938–1946*," 239.

[16] In Vietnam, Personalism was not merely confined to the Vietnamese Catholic community. During the colonial period, its admirers included people such as Xuân Diệu and Huy Cận, two of the most prominent figures in modern Vietnamese poetry, both of whom would join the Communist Party. While neither accepted Catholicism, their criticisms of Confucianism, and of the traditional family for its suppression of the individual, were informed by Mounier's defense of the "person" in his *Manifeste sur le personalisme*. (Donnell, "Politics in South Vietnam: Doctrines and Authority in Conflict," 172.) This affirmation of the individual (or the *tôi*) would become an integral part of the concept of modernity articulated by the Self-Strength Literary Group (*Tự Lực văn đoàn*), the most influential cultural movement to emerge during the colonial era.

[17] As quoted in Lacouture, *Le Vietnam entre deux paix* [Vietnam Between Two Truces], 37.

[18] Bửu Lịch, *Les idéologies dans la République du Sud Vietnam*, 36.

[19] Dispatch from the Ambassador in Vietnam (Durbrow) to the Department of State, Saigon, 2 March 1959.

[20] Bửu Lịch, *Les idéologies dans la République du Sud Vietnam*, 90.

critique of the Soviet Union, moreover, was not that it failed to incorporate the positive elements of capitalism and liberal democracy. On the contrary, the problem was that it was incapable of completely abolishing the capitalist system and its political superstructure.

As the philosopher Lucien Sève noted, therefore, Mounier's "third way" was more directly aligned with Marxism than Western individualistic capitalism: "What characterizes [Mounier's] third way" is not that it is "situated ... at an equal distance between ... two poles." On the contrary, it is "much closer to Marxism." The "factor that unites currents ... like the existentialism of Sartre and his disciples and the Personalism of Mounier and his followers ... [is] precisely that they define themselves ... with reference to Marxism."[21] As Sève's description suggests, then, Mounier's "Marxist Personalism" was a form of Marxist humanist thought, a category more often associated with the work of thinkers such as Jean-Paul Sartre, György Lukács, and Henri Lefebvre.

In Mounier's writings, Personalism is characterized as Christian humanist doctrine that is opposed to the fetishism of commodities, which Marx defined as the foundation of capitalism: "Marx used to say of capitalism that its reduction of things to commodities degrades them: to be made merely instrumental to profit deprives... things... of the[ir] intrinsic dignity."[22] In capitalism, the commodification of things is accompanied by a "depersonalization" of the human subjects of labor.[23] Work becomes a commodity while the persons employed to perform it are changed into what Marx referred to as "*alienable...* object[s]... subjected to the slavery of egoistic need and to the market."[24] The "error of... capitalism," therefore, as Pope John Paul II described, reiterating Mounier's criticism of capitalism, is that "man is... treated... as an instrument and not in accordance with the true dignity of his work – that is to say... he is not treated as subject and maker... as the true purpose of the whole process of production."[25]

In the capitalist mode of production, labor is no longer understood on the model of the divine act of creation. Unlike commodities, creation is not a possession. It cannot be the property of the creator since God exists in and as the world he created,[26] just as humanity, who is made in his image, is both the subject and object of labor, understood as a process in which humanity transforms itself in the act of transforming the world. Under capitalism, creation, which Mounier identifies with the concept of *praxis*, is reduced to an instrumental activity in which subjects are opposed to objects, transformed into commodities.[27] In that sense, the wage labor relation denies the Christian ideal of humanity as *imago Dei*, the image of God as the subject and object of the act of creation.

---

[21] Sève, "Les troisième voies" [The Third Ways], 44.

[22] Mounier, *Personalism*, 12.

[23] Ibid., 14.

[24] Marx, "On the Jewish Question," 241.

[25] Pope John Paul II, *On Human Work: Encyclical Laborem Exercens*, 15.

[26] Ibid., 16.

[27] Mounier, *Personalism*, 13.

As Mounier argued, moreover, the transformation of persons and things into "stuff to be possessed or dominated" results in a modern-day form of idolatry in which persons, reduced to egoistic individuals, are controlled by the very things that they own.[28] By exercising their self-interest in free competition, these individuals create an economy that imposes itself upon the producer as an autonomous power.[29] The result, according to Mounier, is a dehumanizing inversion of the means and ends of society. Money, as a means of exchange, becomes the aim of production itself, subordinating the worker to its impersonal power. In the process, capital develops the attributes of a subject or sovereign: "It is not money that is at the service of the economy and labor, it is the economy and labor that are at the service of money. The first aspect of this sovereignty is the primacy of capital over labor."[30]

In this inversion, the dehumanization of labor is accompanied by a transformation of things (money and capital) into an impersonal subject, a modern-day idol that dominates individuals. While people, therefore, are reduced to alienable objects, money acquires the "anonymous power" to act as an autonomous agent, imposing its will upon individuals who have been "depersonalized" by the alienation of work.[31] Subjected to what Mounier describes, with reference to the concept of commodity fetishism, as the "mystifications into which man has been inveigled by social constructions derived from his material conditions,"[32] humanity is ruled by a sovereign economy that humanity itself has created: "It is not the economy that is at the service of man, but man who is at the service of the economy."[33]

Like Marx, therefore, Mounier proposed to abolish the domination of persons by the things they possess, as the fetishism that underlies the capitalist mode of production. This condition is directly opposed to the Marxist conception of human action as *praxis*, which, according to Mounier, is "a kind of secularization of the central value that the Christian tradition claims for work."[34] In that regard, the Mounier's Catholic doctrine is completely consistent with the Marxist demand for social revolution against capitalism: "The Marxist movement, with its belief that the mission of mankind is... to elevate... things through the humanization of nature... approaches the Christian doctrine that the destiny of man is to redeem... by labor... the nature that has been corrupted with his fall."[35]

For Mounier, however, the tyranny of production for profit cannot be resisted by appealing to the principles of liberal democracy, which arises from the economic infrastructure of capitalism. The institution of representative government or bourgeois democracy represents only the universal interests of egoistic individuals engaged in production for profit. The parliamentary form of the state established

---

[28] Ibid., *Personalism*, 12.

[29] Ibid.

[30] Mounier, *Œuvres*, vol. 1, 271.

[31] Mounier, *Personalism*, 103.

[32] Ibid., xvii.

[33] Mounier, *Œuvres*, vol. 1, 271.

[34] Ibid., 30.

[35] Mounier, *Personalism*, 13.

by the "bourgeois revolution" of 1789, therefore, is part and parcel of the form of society that Mounier proposed to dissolve. The creation of a "personalist democracy," therefore, would require the abolition of both the capitalist tyranny of production for profit as well as the centralized structures of constitutional government. Following Marx's dictum, therefore, that "changes in the economic foundation lead ... to the transformation of the ... superstructure,"[36] Mounier argued that, "the liberal stage of democracy ... will ... be superseded. ... [o]nly on the foundation of a new social structure."[37] "In the place of capitalist tyranny is established, not an irresponsible parliamentary ... democracy," then, "but an organic democracy in which each is the sanction and source of responsibility."[38]

For Mounier, however, this new infrastructure could not be identified with the official state communism of the Soviet Union. If the concept of the Person was opposed to parliamentary government, it was also incompatible with "the massive Soviet state," and its centralized economic and political structure.[39] While the Person in liberal capitalism is reduced to the egoism of the abstract individual, under the communism of the Soviet Union, the Person was dissolved within the collective. As Ngô Đình Nhu described, reiterating Mounier's argument, a "Person [*Nhân vị*] who is not associated with the community is merely a cover for selfish individualism." Conversely, a "community that is detached from the Person is a collectivism that conceals the enslavement of human beings."[40]

In orthodox Marxism, this oppressive collectivism was justified as a transitional stage needed to create the conditions for a withering away of the state, and the establishment of a society in which Persons are freed from the constraints imposed by the collective. As thinkers like Giorgio Agamben have argued, however, the idea that the centralization of power by a communist government is a necessary prerequisite for completely dissolving the state was the great "weakness" of orthodox Marxism: The "dictatorship of the proletariat as the transitional phase leading to the stateless society ... is the reef on which the revolutions of our century have been shipwrecked."[41] Instead of establishing a stateless society, these revolutions, which imposed the dictatorship of the proletariat as a temporary measure, created what Mounier described as enduring forms of dictatorship and permanent states of emergency:

> When one reproaches Marxism for not taking up the problem of man as... person, the communists reply... that the collective... dictatorship of the proletariat is but a provisional necessity and that Marxism has always had as ultimate goal of its revolution "the enfranchisement of the individual"... and the complete disappearance of the state. These formulas

---

[36] Marx, "A Contribution to the Critique of Political Economy," 426.

[37] Mounier, *Personalism*, 114.

[38] Mounier, *De la propriété capitaliste à la propriété humaine*, 121.

[39] Mounier, "Prague." *Œuvres*, vol. 4, 160.

[40] As quoted in Nguyễn Văn Minh. *Dòng họ Ngô Đình*, 425–426.

[41] Agamben, *Homo Sacer*, 12.

were… [presented by] defenders of a "temporary dictatorship" that has already endured for 20 years.[42]

For Mounier, then, this temporary Marxist dictatorship had become a permanent obstacle to the immediate aim of liberating Persons and things, just as the egoism that prevails under capitalism engenders the sovereign power of money and the depersonalization of labor. But as such, the anti-capitalist form of democracy that Mounier envisioned cannot be conceived as a middle ground between Marxist collectivism and Western individualistic capitalism. Rather, for Mounier, such a democracy could only arise from a rejection of both forms of society. In a Personalist democracy, the "oppression" produced by the "overly centralized apparatus" that characterizes both the communist and parliamentary forms of the state would be superseded in the creation of autonomous "decentralized communities." At the same time, the "tyranny" of the market economy and production for profit, together with the centralized communist system of wage labor and planning, would be replaced by a "decentralized economy," based on the principle of the Person.[43]

This Christian ideal of the Person is one that converges with the concept of autonomy within the anarchist tradition, autonomy as a law (*nomos*) that is given to oneself (*autos*).[44] This law, however, is not one that is imposed by the collective, as in a communist regime. Rather, it is the law of a Personalist community whose aim is to develop the freedom of all of its members. These freedoms, conversely, can only be fully developed by fulfilling the communal obligations imposed upon persons for the sake of their individual freedom.

In Mounier's Personalist program, this "voluntary discipline" or "responsible liberty" is opposed to both capitalism, as the tyranny of production for profit, and the principles of freedom and formal equality in liberal democracy.[45] This liberty or autonomy, then, is not that of "Man in the abstract… the… lord of an unlimited liberty." While the Person, in this new social structure, would be subject to the bonds of the community or the collective, internalizing its discipline, this discipline, as a condition of personal freedom, would constitute a "collective [form] of control, not statist, but decentralized."[46] The person, therefore, becomes the "sanction and source" of an internalized discipline, forming the foundation for a decentralized form of direct communal production, free from the external compulsion of the capitalist and communist state and the bourgeois economy.

---

[42] Mounier, *Le Manifeste au service du personnalisme*, 44.

[43] Mounier, *Révolution personnaliste et communautaire*, 198.

[44] Bookchin, *Social Ecology and Communalism*, 91.

[45] Mounier, *Manifeste*, 232.

[46] Ibid., 218.

Personalism in South Vietnam

In South Vietnam, Mounier's philosophy was adopted as official state doctrine by the early Republican government.[47] Contrary to a common assumption, the doctrine did not appeal to South Vietnamese leaders because of "its origins in the writings of conservative Catholic philosophers… and its rejection of communism as a cure for the ills of modern industrialized society."[48] In the scholarship on the war, the emphasis placed on the Christian character of Vietnamese Personalism served, in fact, to obscure the Marxist critique of capitalism and liberal democracy that early Republican leaders had derived from Mounier's writings.[49]

In a remark echoing Mounier's assertion that "the liberal stage of democracy… will surely soon be superseded,"[50] Ngô Đình Nhu maintained that his "Personalism [had] no relationship to the Christian Personalism taught by the Catholic organizations… [T]he Personalism … I advocate is a militant democracy … [aimed at] modifying the superstructure of the present government."[51] While the statement suggests a rejection of Mounier's Christian "metaphysics of the person," it also appears to affirm his Marxist commitment to an "organic democracy," directly opposed to the parliamentary form of government that constitutes the superstructure of capitalism. As Edward Miller has argued, "Diem and Nhu," "[f]ollowing Mounier… thought of Personalism as a form of communitarianism," as opposed to a Christian ideology, or a "corporatist and authoritarian idealization of the state over private and class interests."[52] This communitarianism, based upon the ideal of a decentralized organic democracy, was one that Nhu had developed during his time as a student at the École des Chartes. Influenced by Mounier's "Marxist Personalism," as well as the work of French syndicalist thinkers, Nhu, writing for the journal *Xã hội*, "advocated the creation of workers' and farmers' cooperatives," as anti-capitalist forms of social organization.[53]

For US officials, therefore, the main problem with Personalism was not its Catholicism, but its "acceptance of the Marxist critique of capitalism," which "cause[d] the Vietnamese (and the French) to perceive the … political systems of the West through a Marxist prism."[54] According to the economist Milton Taylor, for example, Personalism was an incoherent amalgam "of Papal encyclicals and kindergarten economics,"

---

[47] Nguyễn Xuân Hoài, "Chế độ Việt Nam cộng hòa ở miền Nam Việt Nam giai đoạn 1955–1963," 43–47.

[48] Jacobs, *Cold War Mandarin*, 36.

[49] Miller, *Misalliance*, 42–47.

[50] Mounier, *Personalism*, 114.

[51] *Press interviews with President Ngo Dinh Diệm, Political Counselor Ngo Dinh Nhu*, 68.

[52] Kolko, *Anatomy of a War*, 84.

[53] Miller, *Misalliance*, 47.

[54] Donnell, "National renovation campaigns in Vietnam," 469. See also Economic and Social Development. Michigan State University Archives.

Christian theology combined with a dogmatic belief in socialist planning, contrary to a rational understanding of the market economy.[55]

For Mounier, of course, this market economy was based on an egoistic conception of man that he described, in Marxian terms, as the "ideology and the prevailing structure of Western bourgeois society in the eighteenth and nineteenth centuries. Man in the abstract, unattached to any natural community, the sovereign lord of a liberty unlimited and undirected." In Nhu's "Oriental Personalism," Mounier's depiction of bourgeois society would be appropriated as a critique of Western civilization itself: "Occidental countries had for their *structure* ... Capitalism ... for their *ideology* ... Liberalism."[56] In the Occidental ideology of liberalism, "man conceived as an individual, like in free capitalism, is an abstract man."[57] For Nhu, following Mounier, this free individual, separated from direct communal production, engendered the tyranny of production for profit and its "depersonalizing" effect upon individuals: "The capitalists ... have trampled on human dignity ... to build a career of wealth on the blood and bones of laboring [*Cần lao*] people."[58]

This view of capitalism, with its apparently crude combination of "Papal encyclicals and kindergarten economics," which was derived in fact from the Marxian critique of political economy, informed the economic and political policies of the early South Vietnamese state: The "official Personalists in the Vietnamese Government ... remained at heart Marxists ... [i]n their concern over the human damage caused by ... rampant ... *laissez-faire* ... capitalism."[59] Thus, according to Nguyễn Ngọc Thơ, who served as the national economy secretary, the goal of the South Vietnamese state was to establish a "Personalist economic system" based on "economic cooperation practiced under the organizational form of cooperatives." This socialist system would "avoid the liberalism of the Capitalistic system with its cyclical evils of unemployment and economic crises."[60]

Against the depersonalizing inversion in capitalism—whereby money, as a means of exchange, becomes the aim of production itself—Nhu, repeating Mounier's slogan, proclaimed that the "goal of production must be the satisfaction of needs."[61] Affirming the principle of Personalist socialism, Nhu declared that "production must serve the people," in contrast to the inhuman condition in capitalism, where "it is man," in Mounier's words, "who is in the service of the economy."[62]

---

[55] As quoted in Fall, "Review: *Problems of Freedom in South Vietnam*," 436.

[56] As quoted in Ahern, *CIA and the House of Ngo*, 157.

[57] "Personalism—Vietnamese Specialists; Also Others Somewhat Relevant." Vietnam Center and Archive.

[58] *Tuyên ngôn Cần lao Nhân vị Cách mạng Đảng* [Manifesto of the Cần Lao Personalist Revolutionary Party].

[59] Donnell, "National renovation campaigns in Vietnam," 135, 469.

[60] As quoted in Trued, "South Viet-Nam's industrial development center," 259.

[61] *Đảng cương Cần lao Nhân vị Cách mạng Đảng* [Political Program of the Cần Lao Personalist Revolutionary Party].

[62] As quoted in Donnell, "National renovation campaigns in Vietnam," 168.

During the colonial period, this capitalist economy was imposed upon the Vietnamese population by the French imperial government. Drawing on Mounier's account of the "anonymous power" that money acquires in a capitalist economy created by the egoistic pursuit of individual interests, Nhu characterized the impact of colonialism in the following manner:

> Under colonial domination, man is subjected to money and power. Such a regime favors the egoistic type of man ... Against colonialism ... the Vietnamese Personalist and communitarian revolution conceives of human value as independent of money ... and as residing in ... responsibility.[63]

With the introduction of capitalism, money became an anonymous power employed by abstract individuals, detached from their roles as Persons within a community. In Marx's terms, the capitalist economy in the colony favored the "egoistic man... man separated ... from the community."[64] In response, Nhu proposed a communitarian revolution, based on the principle of personal responsibility (which is opposed, implicitly, here to the egoistic individual), as an anti-colonial program to be carried out by the South Vietnamese state.

In Nhu's Oriental Personalism, this personal responsibility, which Mounier identified with the Marxist notion of *praxis*, as a secularization of the Christian concept of work, is translated as *cần lao*, or "willingness to work without coercion." *Cần lao*, then, refers to a communal compulsion that is freely imposed on the self in order to develop its personal freedom. In the Personalist government that Diệm sought to establish, this responsible liberty is opposed to the liberal democracy prescribed by the American government. Repeating Mounier's formula, Diệm affirmed that "democracy is [not] ... the supremacy of numbers. Democracy is essentially a permanent effort to find the right political means for assuring to all citizens the right of free development and of maximum initiative, responsibility, and spiritual life."[65]

Personalism and Vietnamese Communism

The word *cần lao* was incorporated into the name of the Ngos' political party, the Đảng Cần Lao Nhân Vị.[66] Although the latter is usually translated as the "Personalist Labor Party," Nhu wanted to distinguish the expression *cần lao* from "labor" or *lao động*. For Nhu, *lao động*, which was "used in the communist party name (*Đảng Lao Động Việt Nam*) ... implies labor under the pressure of an external authority." In contrast, *cần lao* "derives from a classical expression meaning a willingness to work without coercion, which can be translated as 'diligence.'"[67]

---

[63] Tan Phong, "Ấp Chiến lược: một thực hiện mới của chính phủ để diệt cộng và xây dựng nông thôn," 41–42.

[64] Marx. "On the Jewish Question," 229.

[65] *President Ngo Dinh Diem on Democracy*, 15.

[66] See Wehrle, "No more pressing task than organization in Southeast Asia," 277–295.

[67] Taylor, *A History of the Vietnamese*, 556–557.

On the other hand, the word "labor" or *lao động* is a modern expression whose use in the colonial era coincided with the development of a capitalist economy. The word *lao động*, for example, does not appear in Auctore J. L. Taberd's 1838 *Dictionarium Latino-Anamiticum*. In the dictionary, moreover, *lao*, the root of *lao động*, is defined not as labor, but *fessus* or "tired," exhausted from physical exertion.[68] In Đào Duy Anh's 1932 *Chinese-Vietnamese Dictionary* (*Hán-Việt từ điển*), on the other hand, *lao động* is explicitly identified with proletarian labor, defined as a "person who is hired to work by a capitalist," an *"ouvrier."*[69]

In the ideology of the Vietnamese Communist Party, this modern form of production for profit is conflated with creative activity as such, thereby naturalizing a particular form of external compulsion inherited from the Occidental structure of capitalism. Instead of abolishing capitalism, therefore, the Communist Party, in accordance with its official state socialism, merely sought to collectivize the proletarian labor or *lao động* that constitutes the very foundation of capitalism, as a society in which work is reduce to an *"alienable... object... subjected to the slavery of egoistic need and to the market."*[70] In this collectivized form of commodified labor, which supplanted an earlier system of decentralized communal and household production, the worker sells his labor power as a commodity to the state instead of to a private employer or capitalist. In that sense, "the dictatorship of the proletariat," as a Republican government publication described, is "the proletariat under a dictatorship."[71]

If Nhu, then, "equated the 'evil' of capitalism with that of communism," the equation was based on a Personalist critique of the Soviet Union as a collectivized version of capitalism. In the latter, the Party, in organizing the process of production for profit, usurps the role of the capitalist class in securing the exploitation of labor: "Capitalism on one side and communism on the other side are profitable for only one class."[72] To borrow Marx's critique of the Proudhonist conception of the socialist state, the collectivization of proletarianized labor creates a "papacy of production," one in which the Communist Party emerges as the "despotic ruler of production and trustee of distribution."[73] Thus, instead of founding a new socialist society, the Communist Party, according to the Vietnamese Marxist philosopher, Trần Đức Thảo, established a collective regime of commodity production, one in which the alienation of *lao động* or labor is monopolized by a "red capitalist state:" The "people labor so that they [the communist leaders] ... can be satiated, free and happy."[74]

For Nhu, this implied the need for a liberation of human activity from the domination of *lao động* or labor, imposed under both capitalism and communism (or, more precisely, under the liberal and collectivized forms of capitalist production, which

---

[68] Taberd, J. L. et al., *Dictionarium anamitico-latinum*, 255.

[69] Đào Duy Anh, *Hán-Việt từ điển* [Chinese-Vietnamese Dictionary], 334.

[70] Marx, "On the Jewish Question," 241.

[71] Phuc Thien, *President Ngo-Dinh-Diem's Political Philosophy*, 8.

[72] As quoted in Doyle and Weiss, *A Collision of Cultures*, 19.

[73] Marx, *Grundrisse*, 15.

[74] Trần Đức Thảo, *Những lời trăng trối* [A Few Final Words], 61.

Nhu characterized as systems based upon "competing 'Western' philosophies").[75] This liberation was identified with *cần lao*, as "a willingness to work without coercion." In the political philosophy of Personalism, "labor [*lao động*]," as Nguyễn Đức Cung describes it, "becomes diligence [*cần lao*] when it is no longer the slave of profit, as in capitalism, or a slave to the rule of the party, as in the communist regime."[76]

Thus, for Diệm, the "first task" of the South Vietnamese state "was the creation … of institutions that could protect [the person] from the abstract power of market forces on one side and the impersonal state on the other."[77] Drawing on Mounier's concept of an organic democracy, Nhu referred to these anti-capitalist institutions as a real "infrastructure of democracy": "[O]ur Government aims at one major objective: the establishment of a truly democratic infrastructure."[78]

Personalism and the Strategic Hamlet Campaign

As these statements suggests, the Personalism of the early Republic was not simply an academic philosophy that was never put into practice. Contrary to the caricature of Nhu as an "intellectual and an aristocrat" who "made no attempt to conceal his lack of interest in the needs of the Vietnamese people," Nhu's esoteric doctrine of Personalism was one that emphasized *praxis*[79]: "the Personalism … I advocate is a militant democracy in which freedom is … the fruit of [an] … unceasing conquest of living reality, not in an ideal context, but in a given geopolitical condition."[80] Despite its "diffuseness and its lack of discernible application to day to day problems," Nhu's Vietnamese Personalism, as a CIA memorandum reported, was a doctrine that was "quite aware of the need to descend from the plain of philosophy in order to make the problem attractive to the peasants who are the main target."[81]

Indeed, the attempt to actualize a "truly democratic infrastructure" in the South, by waging a "Personalist and communitarian revolution," was the "major objective" of the first republican government, an objective to which it had "devoted all of its effort."[82] In the scholarship on the war, this fact has been obscured by the failure to

---

[75] Paper—The Political Factor in Pacification, VCA.

[76] Nguyễn Đức Cung, "Từ Ấp Chiến Lược Đến Biến Cố Tết Mậu Thân: Những Hệ Luỵ Lịch Sử Trong Chiến Tranh Việt Nam" [From the Strategic Hamlets to the Tet Offensive: Historical Consequences of the Vietnam War]. https://vnthuquan.net/truyen/truyen.aspx?tid=2qtqv3m32 37nvn0n1ntn4n31n343tq83a3q3m3237nvn&AspxAutoDetectCookieSupport=1. Last accessed 8 August 2021.

[77] Christie, *Ideology and Revolution in Southeast Asia*, 148.

[78] As quoted in Donnell, "National renovation campaigns in Vietnam," 578–579.

[79] Halberstam, *The Making of a Quagmire*, 51.

[80] *Press interviews with President Ngo Dinh Diệm, Political Counselor Ngo Dinh Nhu*, 68.

[81] Carter, "Memorandum for the Secretary of Defense on the Strategic Hamlet Program," VCA.

[82] Huynh Van Lang, "Huynh, Lang Van," Vietnamese in the Diaspora Digital Archive (ViDDA). https://vietdiasporastories.omeka.net/items/show/110. Accessed 20 July 2019.

grasp the significance of the particular program that served as the primary vehicle of this Personalist revolution: the Strategic Hamlet campaign.

In the literature on the war, the latter is often described as a counterinsurgency program, based on the model developed by Sir Robert Thompson in his anti-communist campaign in Malaya. As Maxwell Taylor noted, however, Thompson, "like all the rest of us" contributed "very little" to the design of the Strategic Hamlet campaign, which was "Nhu's own project." While American advisors were "too much oriented toward conventional war," Thompson's experience in counterinsurgency was not applicable to the Vietnamese context: The "Malaysian affair was never on the scale of Viet-Nam ... [I]t ... was really a police operation of going out and catching bandits, and it was operated on that scale."[83]

Unlike the counterinsurgency program developed by Thompson, the Strategic Hamlet campaign "was never just a security measure." Rather, for Nhu, its "architect and prime mover,"[84] it was the "vehicle for a full-scale political and social revolution that would put into practice the long-proclaimed... ideals of the regime's own philosophy of 'personalism.'"[85] For the early Republican leaders, therefore, the Strategic Hamlet campaign was not merely a temporary emergency measure used to contain the communist revolution in the countryside. As Nhu explained in an interview, the war was not a crusade against communism *itself*, but against the Stalinist doctrine espoused by the Vietnamese Communist Party: "I am anti-communist from the doctrinal point of view. I am not anti-communist from a political point of view or from a human point of view. I consider the communists as brothers. I am not in favor of a crusade against communism."[86]

But since Personalism was a doctrine that was also opposed to bourgeois democracy, the Strategic Hamlet campaign would also be used against the institutions of "liberal capitalism," which, as Nhu explained, was "associate[d] historically with colonialism." Thus, for the Ngos, as Phạm Văn Lưu pointed out, the establishment of the Republic in 1955, as a constitutional government, "adopting the institutions of parliamentary democracy from [Western] liberal states," was only a preliminary stage in a broader Personalist revolution. This stage would be followed by a "revolution ... occurring within the superstructure" of the government. In a "step toward democratizing the national apparatus," the Ngos would seek to dismantle the ministries and military bureaucracy inherited from the colonial regime.[87] This revolution in the national superstructure in Sài Gòn was directly connected, however, to a "second revolution, building a genuine democracy in the infrastructure. This was the Strategic Hamlet program ... also known as the rural revolution." While the first revolution

---

[83] Taylor, recorded interview by Larry Hackman, 29 December 1969, 61–62, Robert Kennedy Oral History Program of the John F. Kennedy Library.

[84] Booklet—Vietnam's Strategic Hamlets. VCA. See also "Memorandum from the Director of the Vietnam Task Force (Cottrell) to the Assistant Secretary of State for Far Eastern Affairs (Harriman)," in FRUS: Vietnam 1962. Vol. II, 311.

[85] Paper—The Political Factor in Pacification: A Vietnam Case Study [Draft], 4. VCA.

[86] Ngô Đình Nhu, *"Viet Nam, le cerveau de la famille"* [Vietnam, The Brains of the Family].

[87] Goscha, *Vietnam: A New History*, 299.

would serve to dissolve the centralized power of the parliamentary government, the second, in building a system of semi-autonomous villages, would create the communitarian infrastructure for an organic democracy.[88]

For the Ngos, then, the infrastructure created by the Strategic Hamlet campaign was not only intended as a tool in the struggle against the Stalinism of the Vietnamese Communist Party. The campaign would also serve to create a "real democracy from at base (first of all the level of the village…) *against formal and liberal democracy.*" In the place of a "liberal capitalism… associate[d] historically with colonialism," the program, therefore, would create a Personalist democracy founded on "communitarian labor … and justice based on a social plan … rather than … submission to the capitalist order."[89]

This communitarian program has been characterized as a "clumsy copy of the Party form of organization" employed by the communist insurgency in the South.[90] This program, however, was distinguished from that of the Vietnamese Communist Party by its Personalist rejection of what Agamben described as the primary weakness of orthodox Marxism. For the Communist Party, the creation of a decentralized system of semi-autonomous "sections" or "councils" (*xã bộ*) was regarded as a provisional necessity, a means toward the ends of establishing a collective regime of *lao động* or labor under the central authority of a socialist government. For this reason, according to Kolko, the "absolute necessity of decentralizing the war organization throughout the provinces" was continually in conflict with the "centralizing pretensions and … elitist organizational theory" of the Communist Party.[91] For the Party, the withering of the state, as Nhu reminded officials at an intra-ministry meeting on the Strategic Hamlet campaign, was a task to be accomplished only "after … the proletarian revolution, which means that people in the present must … sacrifice themselves for … the future."[92] For Nhu, on the other hand, the ideal of an organic democracy, which would dissolve the functions of the constitutional state, was the aim of the revolution itself: "That is right. I agree with Marx's final conclusion: the state must wither away – this is a condition for the final triumph of democracy. The sense of my life is to work so that I can become unnecessary."[93]

According to Robert Thompson, however, the emphasis placed on the creation of hamlets "all over the country," without any apparent "strategic direction," was

---

[88] Phạm Văn Lưu, *Chính Quyền Ngô Dình Diệm 1954–1963: Chủ Nghĩa và Hành Động* [The Government of Ngô Dình Diệm 1954–1963: Theory and Practice], 30–31.

[89] Gheddo, *Catholiques et bouddhistes au Vietnam* [Catholics and Buddhist in Vietnam], 154.

[90] Nguyễn Xuân Hoài, "*Đảng Cần lao Nhân vị*" [The Cần Lao Personalist Party]. Luutruvn.com, January 4, 2016. http://luutruvn.com/index.php/2016/04/01/dang-can-lao-nhan-vi/. Last accessed 21 July 2019.

[91] Kolko, *Anatomy of a Peace*, 5.

[92] Meeting Minutes (#36), Uỷ-Ban Liên-Bộ Đặc-Trách về Ấp Chiến-Lược tại Dinh Gia Long [Intra-Ministry Committee for the Strategic Hamlets at Gia Long Palace], VCA. On the Party's views on the dictatorship of the proletariat, see Lê Duẩn, *Hăng hái tiến lên dưới ngọn cờ của Cách mạng Tháng Mười vĩ đại* [Moving Proudly Forward Under the Great Banner of the October Revolution], 54.

[93] Maneli, *War of the Vanquished*, 145–146.

indicative of the fact that the "Vietnamese tended to confuse the means with the end."[94] As Nhu argued, on the other hand, such views were based upon the assumption that the Strategic Hamlet campaign was only a temporary security measure, as opposed to end in itself, or a means without ends: "The Americans and the Vietcong imagine that the strategic hamlets are purely military institutions that will be liquidated as unnecessary once victory is achieved. The Americans and the Vietcong are both wrong."[95] The aim of the Strategic Hamlet campaign was in fact exactly the opposite. The program was not a simply an instrument of the state to be "liquidated as unnecessary" once victory was achieved and the government had accomplished its purpose. The hamlets were not purely military organizations, but rather "basic institutions of direct democracy" which, in a "final triumph of democracy," would allow the state itself to be liquidated and its personnel to be rendered unnecessary: "The sense of my life is to work so that I can become unnecessary." Insofar as the establishment of a decentralized organic form of democracy was the ultimate goal of the revolution itself, the possibility of a socialist future (which the Communist Party proposed to postpone until after the dictatorship of the proletariat was secure) was one that, for Nhu, was *already present* in the political form of the hamlet. Whereas the Party, therefore, believed that "people in the present must ... sacrifice themselves for ... the future," "[f]or us ... people in the present possess the same value as those in the future. Therefore, we propose to savor whatever we attain in our struggle" (*đặt vấn đề tranh đấu tới đâu hưởng tới độ*).[96]

This aspect of the Strategic Hamlet campaign conforms to Mounier's account of the "Personalist and communitarian revolution," as a revolution for which there "are no necessary stages: most Marxist revolutions have shown they know how do without them."[97] Contrary to Frances Fitzgerald, therefore, Nhu (who supposedly "lacked the rigorous analysis of Marxism") had not "misinterpreted" Mounier's work "as a doctrine of the corporate state in which the alienated masses would find unity through ... authoritarian social organizations." Rather, Nhu's Strategic Hamlet campaign was in fact an attempt to realize in practice the communitarian Marxism that Mounier opposed to that of "the massive Soviet state."[98]

Conclusion

Contrary to the conventional view, the official philosophy of the First Republic was not a doctrine seeking a middle ground between socialism and liberal democracy. Rather, it was a political theory, derived in part from a form of French Marxist

---

[94] Thompson, *Defeating Communist Insurgency*, 142.

[95] Maneli, *War of the Vanquished*, 145.

[96] Meeting Minutes (#36), Uỷ-Ban Liên-Bộ Đặc-Trách về Ấp Chiến-Lược tai Định Giá-Lòng [Intra-Ministry Committee for Strategic Hamlets], 14.

[97] Mounier, *Révolution personnaliste et communautaire*, 25.

[98] Mounier. "Prague." *Œuvres*, vol. 4, 160.

humanism, which rejected both ideologies as opposing versions of capitalism. Attempting to implement this philosophy, the Republic initiated a social revolution in the South against Stalinism as well as against liberal democracy. For the Ngos, Personalism, then, was not an anti-communist doctrine, but a communism that was more anti-capitalist than the Marxism espoused by the Communist Party: "I am really combating communism in order to put an end to materialistic capitalism."[99] But if the Republic indeed had adopted this Personalist project as its primary objective, then the early phase of the war in Vietnam could not be understood as a conflict between communism and democracy, or Marxism and nationalism. Rather, it would have to be seen as a contest between two different visions of anti-colonial communism.

Bibliography

Agamben G (1998) Homo Sacer. Stanford University Press, Redwood City, CA

Ahern TL (2000) CIA and the House of Ngo: covert action in South Vietnam, 1954–1963. Center for the Study of Intelligence, Washington, DC

Bain CA (1967) Vietnam, the roots of conflict. Prentice-Hall, lnc, Englewood Cliffs, NJ

Bookchin M (2006) Social ecology and communalism. AK Press, Oakland, CA

Booklet – Vietnam's Strategic Hamlets. VCA. 23970130054, February 1963. Box 01, Folder 30. Rufus Phillips Collection

Burchett WG (1963) The furtive war: the United States in Vietnam and Laos. International Publishers, New York

Bửu L (1983/1984) Les idéologies dans la République du Sud Vietnam 1954–1975 [Ideologies in the Republic of South Vietnam]. Ph.D. dissertation, Université de Paris VII

Carter MS (1962) Memorandum for the Secretary of Defense on the Strategic Hamlet Program, 1–2. VCA. 0410693005, July 13. Box 06, Folder 93. Central Intelligence Agency Collection

Catton P (2017) Diem's final failure. University Press of Kansas, Lawrence

Christie CJ (2001) Ideology and revolution in Southeast Asia 1900–1980: political ideas of the anti-colonial era. Curzon Press, Curzon

Đảng cương Cần lao Nhân vị Cách mạng Đảng [Political Program of the Cần Lao Personalist Revolutionary Party]. Folder 29361, Phông Phủ Tổng Thống Đệ Nhất Cộng hòa [Files of the Office of the President, First Republic], Vietnam National Archives No. 2

Daniels RV (1996) Year of the Heroic Guerrilla: world revolution and counterrevolution in 1968. Harvard University Press, Cambridge

Đào DA (2005) Hán-Việt từ điển [Chinese-Vietnamese Dictionary]. Nhà xuất bản văn hoá thông tin, Hà Nội

Đào TD (2013) Nhà lưu trữ Việt Nam thời kì 1938–1946 [Ngô Đình Nhu: Vietnamese Archivist 1938–1946]. Tạp chí Nghiên cứu và Phát triển [J Res Dev] (6–7):104–105

Del Boca A, Giovana M (1965) I figli del sole, Mezzo Secolo di nazi-fascismo nel mondo [The children of the sun: a half-century of Nazi-Fascism]. Feltrinelli editore, Milano, Marzo

Dispatch from the Ambassador in Vietnam (Durbrow) to the Department of State, Saigon, 2 March 1959

Dobson JC, Jr (2006) Diem, Ngo Dinh. In: Domenico RP, Hanley MY (eds) Encyclopedia of modern Christian politics, vol 1. Greenwood Press, London

Donnell JC (1959) National renovation campaigns in Vietnam. Pac Aff 32(March):73–88.

Donnell JC (1964) Politics in South Vietnam: doctrines and authority in conflict. Ph.D. dissertation, Political Science, University of California at Berkeley

---

[99] Maneli, *War of the Vanquished*, 145–146.

Doyle E, Weiss S (1984) A collision of cultures. Boston Publishing Co, Boston, MA

Doyle E, Lipsman S, Weiss S (1981) Passing the Torch (The Vietnam experience) (Ed: Manning R). Boston Publishing, Boston

Economic and Social Development, 15. Michigan State University Archives & Historical Collections Wesley R. Fishel Papers (UA 17.95). Box 1192, Folder 35

Fall BB (1962) Review: problems of freedom in South Vietnam. Inter J 17(4)(Fall):436

French JT, Politics and National Development in Vietnam - 1954–1960. Pol. Sci. 287A. VCA. No Date. Folder 39, Box 01. John B. O'Donnell Collection

Gheddo P (1970) Catholiques et bouddhistes au Vietnam [Catholics and Buddhist in Vietnam]. Groupe des Editions, Alsatia

Goscha C (2016) Vietnam: a new history. Basic Books, New York

Halberstam D (1988) The making of a Quagmire. Rowman & Littlefield Publishers, Lanham, MD

Huynh VL, "Huynh, Lang Van," Vietnamese in the Diaspora Digital Archive (ViDDA). https://vietdiasporastories.omeka.net/items/show/110. Accessed 20 July 2019

Jacobs S (2006) Cold War Mandarin: Ngo Dinh Diem and the origins of America's War in Vietnam, 1950–1963. Rowman & Littlefield Publishers, Lanham, MD

John Paul II (1981) On human work: encyclical Laborem Exercens. Office for Publishing and Promotion Services, United States Catholic Conference, Washington DC

Kolko G (1985) Anatomy of a War. Pantheon Books, New York

Lacouture J (1965) Le Vietnam entre deux paix [Vietnam between two truces]. Éditions du Seuil, Paris

Lê D (1969) Hăng hái tiến lên dưới ngọn cờ của Cách mạng Tháng Mười vĩ đại [Moving proudly forward under the great banner of the October revolution]. Nhà xuất bản sự thật, Hà Nội

Maneli M (1971) War of the vanquished. Harper & Row, New York

Marx K (1973) Grundrisse: foundations of the critique of political economy. Penguin Books, Harmondsworth

Marx K (1992a) A contribution to the critique of political economy. Early Writings. Penguin Books, London

Marx K (1992b) On the Jewish question. Early Writings. Penguin Books, London

Meeting Minutes (#36), Uỷ-Ban Liên-Bộ Đặc-Trách về Ấp Chiến-Lược tại Dinh Gia Long [Intra-Ministry Committee for the Strategic Hamlets at Gia Long Palace]

Memorandum from the Director of the Vietnam Task Force (Cottrell) to the Assistant Secretary of State for Far Eastern Affairs (Harriman), Washington, 6 April 1962 [Source: Department of State, Vietnam Working Group Files: Lot 67 D 54, Pol. 7. Secret] in FRUS: Vietnam 1962. Vol. II

Miller E (2013) Misalliance: Ngo Dinh Diem, the United States, and the fate of South Vietnam. Harvard University Press, Cambridge, MA

Mounier E (1935) Révolution personnaliste et communautaire [The personalist and communitarian revolution]. F. Aubier, Paris

Mounier E (1936a) Le Manifeste au service du personnalisme [Manifesto in the service of personalism] Esprit (1932–1939) 5(49) (1er Octobre)

Mounier E (1936b) De la propriété capitaliste à la propriété humaine [From capitalist property to human property]. Desclée de Brouwer, Paris

Mounier E (1950a) Personalism. Routledge and Kegan Paul Ltd., London

Mounier E (1950b) Prague. Œuvres, vol. 4. Éditions du Seuil, Paris

Ngo DD (1958) President Ngo Dinh Diem on Democracy (Addresses relative to the Constitution). Press Office, Saigon

Ngô ĐN, Viet Nam, le cerveau de la famille [Vietnam, The brains of the family]

Ngo DD, Ngo DN (1963) Press interviews with President Ngo Dinh Diệm, Political Counselor Ngo Dinh Nhu. Republic of Vietnam, Saigon

Nguyễn ĐC, Từ Ấp Chiến Lược Đến Biến Cố Tết Mậu Thân: Những Hệ Luy Lịch Sử Trong Chiến Tranh Việt Nam [From the strategic hamlets to the tet offensive: historical consequences of the

Vietnam War]. https://vnthuquan.net/truyen/truyen.aspx?tid=2qtqv3m3237nvn0n1ntn4n31n34
3tq83a3q3m3237nvn&AspxAutoDetectCookieSupport=1. Last accessed 8 Aug 2021

Nguyễn VM (2003) Dòng họ Ngô Đình: Ước mơ chưa đạt [The Ngô Đình family: dreams unrealized]. Hoàng Nguyên Xuất Bản, Garden Grove, CA

Nguyễn XH (2011) Chế độ Việt Nam cộng hòa ở miền Nam Việt Nam giai đoạn 1955–1963 [The Regime of the Republic of Vietnam in South Vietnam (1955–1963)]. Dissertation, University of Social Sciences and Humanities, Ho Chi Minh City

Nguyễn XH (2016) Đảng Cần lao Nhân vị [The Cần Lao Personalist Party]. Luutruvn.com, January 4. http://luutruvn.com/index.php/2016/04/01/dang-can-lao-nhan-vi/. Last accessed 21 July 2019

Paper – The Political Factor in Pacification: A Vietnam Case Study [Draft], 5. VCA. 21470122001 No Date. Box 01, Folder 22. Vincent Puritano Collection

Personalism – Vietnamese Specialists; Also Others Somewhat Relevant. VCA. January 1, 1953. Folder 14, Box 03. John Donnell Collection. See also Bernard Fall, "Book Review, Problems of Freedom: South Vietnam Since Independence," Journal of Asian Studies. VCA. February 1, 1963. Folder 11, Box 12. Douglas Pike Collection: Other Manuscripts – American Friends of Vietnam

Phạm VL (2017) Chính Quyền Ngô Dình Diệm 1954–1963: Chủ Nghĩa và Hành Động [The Government of Ngô Dình Diệm 1954–1963: theory and practice]. Centre for Vietnamese Studies Publications, Reservoir, VIC

Sève L (1960) Les troisième voies [The third ways]. La Pensée 92 (July–August)

Taberd JL (1838) Pierre-Joseph Pigneau de Béhaine. Dictionarium anamitico-latinum. Frederic-nagori vulgo Serampore: ex typis J. C. Marshman

Tan Phong (Ngô Đình Nhu) (1962) Ấp Chiến lược: một thực hiện mới của chính phủ để diệt cong và xây dựng nông thôn [Strategic Hamlets: A New Government Initiative for Exterminating the Communists and Rural Reconstruction]. Quê Hương 37:41–42

Taylor MD (1969) Recorded interview by Larry Hackman, 29 December, 61–62, Robert Kennedy Oral History Program of the John F. Kennedy Library

Taylor KW (2014) A history of the Vietnamese. Cambridge University Press, Cambridge

Thien P (1956) President Ngo-Dinh-Diem's political philosophy. Review Horizons, Saigon

Thompson R (1967) Defeating communist insurgency: the lessons of Malaya and Vietnam. Praeger, New York

Trần ĐT (2014) Những lời trăn trối [Some final testaments]. Tổ hợp Xuất bản Miền Đông Hoa Kỳ

Trued MN (1960) South Viet-Nam's industrial development center. Pac Aff 33(September):3

Tuyên ngôn Cần lao Nhân vị Cách mạng Đảng [Manifesto of the Cần Lao Personalist Revolutionary Party], hồ sơ 29361, Phông Phủ Tổng Thống, TTII

Wehrle ES (2001) 'No more pressing task than organization in Southeast Asia': the AFL-CIO approaches the Vietnam War, 1947–1964. Labor History 42(3):277–295

Duy Lap Nguyen is associate professor in the Department of Modern and Classical Languages at the University of Houston and is the author of the Unimagined Community: Imperialism and Culture in South Vietnam (Manchester University Press, 2020) and Walter Benjamin and the Critique of Political Economy: A New Historical Materialism (Bloomsbury, 2022).

Continental Philosophy and Buddhism in the Journal *Tư Tưởng* (Thought), 1967–1975

Wynn Gadkar-Wilcox

Introduction

By the 1920s and 1930s, a new generation of scholars was educated in Franco-Annamite schools. Following the educational reforms championed under Governor-General Albert Sarraut, between 1917 and 1919 educational policy in Annam and Tonkin was wrested from the Nguyễn dynasty and local officials, who had presided over a series of informal schools leading up to the imperial examinations. Instead, the French colonial administration put in place a combination of indigenous schools with a traditional curriculum, Franco-Annamite schools with a combined curriculum in French and *quốc ngữ* (Romanized Vietnamese), and *lycées* that offered a French curriculum.[1] In the latter two cases, an initially small but expanding student body was exposed to a curriculum that included substantial classwork in ethics and philosophy emphasizing readings on Plato, Kant, and utilitarian philosophers such as Bentham and Mill.[2]

At that time, Catholic priests were exposed to the basics of ethics and continental philosophy during their ecclesiastical training. Many of these figures emigrated to the south in 1954 and became central figures in the development of the academic field of philosophy in the Republic of Vietnam. These include Father Bửu Dưỡng, who became Professor of Philosophy at the University of Saigon after 1957, and Father Đỗ Minh Vọng (also known as Father Alexis Cras), Philosophy Professor at the University of Dalat.[3]

---

[1] Tai, *Radicalism*, 30–33.

[2] Duong Nhu Duc, "Education in Vietnam," 86–87.

[3] Nguyễn Văn Lục, "20 năm triết học," 91–93.

W. Gadkar-Wilcox (✉)
Department of History and World Perspectives, Western Connecticut State University, Danbury, CT, USA
e-mail: wilcoxw@wcsu.edu

© The Author(s), under exclusive license to Springer Nature Singapore Pte Ltd. 2023   35
T. Engelbert and C. P. Pham (eds.), *Global Vietnam: Across Time,*
Space and Community, Reading South Vietnam's Writers,
https://doi.org/10.1007/978-981-99-1043-4_3

By the 1940s, students who had been educated in these French or Franco-Annamite schools were increasingly going abroad to continue their education. The desire to study abroad stemmed not only from the fact that French Institutions of Higher Education were being disrupted by the First Indochina War but also from a need to keep these young students out of harm's way. Among philosophers, the most well-known was Trần Đức Thảo (1917–1993), who began to study phenomenology under the direction of Maurice Merleau-Ponty in the mid-1930s, wrote an influential defense of the materialist view of phenomenology, and returned to Hanoi only to be swept up in the Nhân văn-Giai phẩm affair and forced by the Hanoi regime to publish self-criticisms.

His fame influenced other Vietnamese intellectuals, particularly with an interest in philosophy, to follow the same path.[4] These included a number of influential academics, including historians such as Nguyễn Phương, who studied American foreign relations in the United States, and Trương Bửu Lâm, who studied history in Belgium.[5] Buddhist monks and scholars of Buddhism went abroad as well. These included famous figures such as Thích Nhất Hạnh, who studied comparative religion at Princeton Theological Seminary in the early 1960s, and Thích Minh Châu, who spent from the late 1940s to the mid-1960s studying and teaching in Sri Lanka and India, where he was exposed to and influenced by New Age Buddhists from the United Kingdom.

The influences on Buddhist scholars from Vietnam varied considerably. Because he studied the philosophy of Vasubandhu at a Buddhist Studies Institute at the University of Wisconsin in the United States, the Buddhist master and scholar Lê Mạnh Thát was more influenced by the Anglo-American analytic philosophy of Bertrand Russell and Willard Van Orman Quine, which led him to a focus on questions of logical structure and perception. On the other hand, Nguyễn Văn Trung, a philosopher and academic who began his study of philosophy in France and Belgium in the early 1950s, finished a PhD on the Buddhist notion of Becoming under the Belgian existentialist philosopher and theologian Albert Dondeyne in 1962. In each of these cases, these scholars were being put in a position of studying Buddhism in the milieu of American or European university Philosophy or Comparative Religion programs in which continental philosophy was also extensively discussed.

Having studied at foreign universities, these monks, scholars, and philosophers returned to Vietnam in an excellent position to help develop the civil society of the Republic of Vietnam. They returned to take positions in the universities that were being established at the time. The public university of Hue was founded in 1957, and the Catholic University of Dalat in 1958. The Buddhist Vạn Hạnh University was founded in 1964. With them came important and influential publications, including *Tư Tưởng* (Thought), published by Vạn Hạnh University.

---

[4] McHale, "Trần Đức Thảo, 1946–1993," 7–31.

[5] "University of San Francisco Commencement Exercises." Nguyễn Đức Cùng claims that Nguyễn Phương also received an MA in Economics, but I cannot find any corroborating evidence for this claim.

This chapter will examine how these scholars, on returning to Vietnam to participate in the construction of universities and an intellectual culture in the Republic of Vietnam, built a body of scholarship on continental philosophy chiefly by comparing it to Buddhism. As a case study, it will focus on articles on the relationship between continental philosophy and Buddhism in the pages of the journal *Tư Tưởng* (Thought), which was published in Saigon between 1967 and 1975. This journal is a good venue for a study of the connections made between continental philosophy and Buddhism because it was the only journal in the Republic of Vietnam so dedicated to contemporary philosophy. Moreover, because it was published by Vạn Hạnh University, an explicitly Buddhist University, it tended to publish articles specifically on these connections.[6] In this journal, scholars from across the Republic of Vietnam examined the influence of Kant, Nietzsche, Heidegger, Sartre, Marcel, and Jaspers on Buddhist thinkers.

This chapter will suggest that these global influences allowed thinkers in Vietnam to develop a Buddhist philosophy that was relevant to the condition of war in their own country. Using language borrowed from thinkers in contemporary continental philosophy, they described a world awash in ideological constructions that political parties offered in bad faith, and argued that Buddhist teachings, unlike misleading Cold War political perspectives, allowed for the attainment of authenticity and for the possibility of action outside of the dictates of ideology. Their views also laid out an ecumenical vision of what civil society in the Republic of Vietnam could be: a society influenced by a rich variety of ideas from Buddhist thinkers from various traditions as well as influenced by phenomenology and existentialism from Europe, and a society of free inquiry, freed from any ideological straitjacket.

The chapter will focus primarily on four thinkers who contributed regularly to *Tư Tưởng* and wrote on the interconnection between Buddhism and continental philosophy. They are: Thích Minh Châu (1918–2012), Lê Tôn Nghiêm (1926–1993), Ngô Trọng Anh (b. 1926), and Thích Chơn Hạnh (b. 1943). These four figures are significant because all of them regularly wrote about continental philosophy and Buddhism and were among the most active regular participants in *Tư Tưởng*. It will focus primarily on their analyses of the connection between Buddhist principles and the thought of Martin Heidegger and Friedrich Nietzsche. Although *Tư Tưởng's* essays considered many important European thinkers from Kant to Husserl, to Foucault and Derrida, the volumes dedicated to Heidegger and Nietzsche have the most explicit and sustained comparisons with Buddhism. The chapter examines the comparisons to ascertain the extent to which they could be understood to offer commentary on the direction of Vietnamese society. I will begin with a longer reflection on the influence of Thích Minh Châu, because he exercised an outsized influence as the Rector of Vạn Hạnh University and the founding editor of *Tư Tưởng*.

---

[6] There are philosophers from the Republic of Vietnam who made substantial contributions to the study of Buddhism and continental philosophy, including Trần Thái Đinh and Nguyễn Văn Trung, which I have considered in a separate article. Wynn Gadkar-Wilcox, "Existentialism and Intellectual Culture," 377–395.

Thích Minh Châu, East/West Connections, and a Pacifist Way Forward

The founder of the journal *Tư Tưởng* was Thích Minh Châu. Though he was born in the south, in Quảng Nam province, Thích Minh Châu (whose birth name was Đinh Văn Nam) hailed from a family of intellectuals from Nghệ An. His father, Đinh Văn Chấp (1893–1953), was a well-known translator of poems and Buddhist texts.[7] In 1946, Thích Minh Châu received his ordination. By the early 1950s, he had arrived in India, where he would spend many years studying manuscripts in the Pali language, resulting in a doctoral dissertation comparing classical Chinese and Pali versions of the *Madhyama Āgama*.[8] In 1964, he returned to Vietnam where he became the rector of Vạn Hạnh University. In the late 1960s and early 1970s, he grew this institution from a relatively small college to a full-fledged university.

One of Thích Minh Châu's goals as Rector was to combine the best elements of the tradition of Buddhist education in the ancient Buddhist universities of India (such as the Nalanda Mahavihara in what is now Bihar, with which he was very familiar) with the educational structure of the modern universities in Europe and North America. To do so, it was necessary to promote the research and teaching activities of the university to the public, both in Vietnam and abroad. For a non-Vietnamese audience, he created *Van Hanh Newsletter* in 1967, which continued as *Van Hanh Bulletin* from 1969 to 1974 and included scholarly work along with more mundane news about university schedules and student affairs. However, the university's flagship journal was *Tư Tưởng* (Thought), which showcased research in Vietnamese. The contributors were primarily faculty members at Vạn Hạnh University, but other intellectuals with interests in Buddhism or continental philosophy from Vietnam and abroad also contributed. For most of its existence, Thích Minh Châu served as the Chairman of the Editorial Board of this journal. He oversaw the gathering of articles and frequently introduced the special topics of each journal with essays of his own which set the tone for each edition.

As with the other contributors, Thích Minh Châu's contributions very frequently drew parallels between Buddhist texts and leading philosophers from Europe. His analysis of the connection between these served two primary purposes. First, it highlighted his vision for the university as a place in which a humanistic view of Buddhist learning, including meditation and training, was combined with a modern university education; and second, it served to highlight his view of pacifism, in which not only a cease-fire but a long-term change in language and attitude was necessary to achieve any true and lasting peace.

Thích Minh Châu used continental philosophy in the service of these ends. One of his most significant ideas was that the context of the late twentieth century in the Republic of Vietnam provided a perfect venue for validating insights from both Buddhism and contemporary phenomenology. In an address to the Vạn Hạnh students

---

[7] Đinh Văn Chấp, "Dịch thơ đời Lý," 238–244; Thích Đôn Hậu, *Muốn hết khổ*.

[8] "Thích Minh Châu (1918–2012)," 905; "Thích Minh Châu," 601; Bhiksu Thich Minh Chau, *The Chinese Madhyama Āgama*, 1–2; *Nava Nalanda Mahvihara*.

during the celebration of the Gautama Buddha's birthday in 1973, he emphasized that the "Law of Anicca" (that impermanence is suffering) was made even more clear by the "fearful invention" of ever-more destructive technologies of warfare. This was no better proven than in the case of the "younger generation" of Vietnamese people who were "born in the war," grew up in the war and reached adulthood, and then "died because of the war."[9]

He then suggested that several contemporary European philosophers expounding what he called "modern humanism" would lead his students to the same insight. German phenomenologist Martin Heidegger (1889–1976) described a contemporary world of "being beset with suffering." The German-Swiss psychiatrist and philosopher Karl Jaspers (1883–1969) explained that technology, in causing us to feel that we had conquered nature, had also sapped us of our creative energy, forcing us to run after benchmarks of "effectiveness" and meeting the newest numerical goal, to get "newer and newer gadgets" that change every month with the "compelling forces of advertising technology." Referencing Arthur Rimbaud (1854–1891) and Nicolai Berdyaev (1874–1948), Thích Minh Châu claimed that we lose ourselves in this instrumentality, that we do not recognize ourselves as ourselves anymore, and that we are at risk of becoming aimless automatons in a purely material world.[10]

The solution to this problem was education. But an education that only concerned the mind rather than all the five *skandhas* (or aggregates) would be insufficient. Instead, a holistic Buddhist education would pay attention to a student's body, feelings, character, intellect, and wisdom, training the body and the mind and using moral precepts, concentration, and wisdom. In short, Thích Minh Châu proposed that the education that Vạn Hạnh students were receiving was the very one that would lead Vietnam and the broader world out of the morass of a meaningless and instrumental existence. This path was not just the one recommended through Buddhist education but also corresponded with addressing the problem of technology and was being so forcefully articulated by the likes of Heidegger and Jaspers.

Moreover, Thích Minh Châu argued that this view would lead his students out of war and toward a lasting, peaceful, and better society in Vietnam. He argued that the twentieth century had seen the rise (in the world generally, but perhaps especially in Vietnam), of political polarization and division. The root cause of this problem was a "crisis in spiritual values." That crisis was also simultaneously a crisis of language. Once the use of language was decoupled from ethical requirements, then "language became an instrument, a weapon of one ideology against another." Words such as "peace," "liberation," and "nation" became ideological cudgels in a partisan battle for people's hearts and minds. Thích Minh Châu believed that for both communists and anticommunists, the goal of peace was manipulated to serve the perpetuation of war. Moreover, concepts that once would yield common ground across religions or ideologies, such as "nation" or "liberation," were now being used to hold up one ideological position and exclude another.[11]

---

[9] Thích Minh Châu, "Đức Phật và con người," 6–7.

[10] Ibid., 7–8.

[11] Thích Minh Châu, "Tôn giáo," 363–364.

What society needed—in Vietnam, perhaps, more than anywhere else—was a spiritual cleansing. Young people needed the kind of sheltered environment that Vạn Hạnh University provided them, to have a space outside of political posturing to reframe these words in the language and meaning of "loving-kindness," of sincerity, and of honesty, as envisioned in the Buddhist principle of right speech, but achievable through a genuine spiritual experience in any religion. This was the path to real peace, in Vietnam and elsewhere.

In making this point, Thích Minh Châu would make use of a number of texts from continental philosophy. In the context of the peace negotiations between Washington and Hanoi in Paris in the summer of 1968, for example, he made extensive use of continental philosophy to make an argument for a Buddhist view of long-term peace in which peace could be understood not as an armistice between parties with conflicting ideologies but a disposition and mindset that would lead to peace. The main thrust of his argument was that the Paris negotiations were disingenuous since both sides were blaming the other for not being willing to carry out a true cease-fire. Peace here was a matter of political gain. Even if an armistice could be achieved, it could only be temporary, and would not be a true peace.[12]

To make this argument, Thích Minh Châu turned to Immanuel Kant's *Essay on Perpetual Peace*. In his first appendix, "On the Opposition between Morality and Politics with Respect to Peace," Kant made the argument that partisan politics could be involved in negotiations for peace, and that therefore peace could be achieved only by appealing to pre-established a priori moral guidelines. In summarizing Kant, Thích Minh Châu claimed that political actors would find ways to do what they saw fit, and then apologize later, blame the other side for their own actions, and sow division to gain an advantage for their side.[13] Politics, in this sense, was in absolute contradiction with truth-telling and with the other elements of the eight-fold path. Thích Minh Châu implicitly saw politics as inherently Machiavellian. The purpose was to gain an advantage for a particular nation, party, or ideology, a particular ingroup, and any manipulation of truth-telling could be justified if it led to a desirable outcome for that ingroup. This contradicts the requirements of right speech to be speech that is consistent with the teachings of the Dhamma, and that those following right speech must speak what is true, at the appropriate time, only if it is beneficial, and with loving-kindness.[14] Without right speech, there could be no basis of mutual trust under which any lasting peace could be established. Under Thích Minh Châu's pacifism, the first order of business was not to produce a cease-fire but to produce a society in which the ethical order superseded the political one through the living of life according to the ethical rules that could be gleaned from a spiritual life.

Thích Minh Châu's bolstered his view of pacifism with reference to multiple twentieth-century existentialists as well. Using Gabriel Marcel (1889–1973), he suggested that it was necessary to set aside political events to first conduct an inner

---

[12] Thích Minh Châu, "Khả tính," 9.

[13] Ibid., 8. See also Kant, "Appendix: Perpetual Peace," 127–128.

[14] See King, "Right Speech," 350.

search for peace, suggesting that ideology was a mirage of self-delusion and that seeking general and universal truths outside of Cold War frames was a prerequisite for peace. "An ideologue is a spirit that lets itself be caught up in the mirage of pure abstractions," Marcel argued; and Thích Minh Châu interpreted this to mean that if peace negotiations were carried out by ideologues (on either side of the Cold War, for example), then "peace" would be a kind of ruse, a temporary rhetorical means to get to the triumph of that ideological formation. Undertaken in such bad faith, such a peace could not be sustained.[15]

Similarly, citing Karl Jaspers (1883–1969), Thích Minh Châu suggested that deception was a necessary part of contemporary politics, and that therefore peace negotiations, and the establishment of a lasting peace, needed to be removed from the hands of a particular political order and elevated to some apolitical body. The United States and the Democratic Republic of Vietnam were negotiating a cease-fire in bad faith and solely for the purposes of their immediate self-interest, which meant that no true peace could be achieved. Instead, drawing from the humanistic psychologist Erich Fromm (1900–1980), Thích Minh Châu claimed that the actors in the Cold War, and especially the United States, could profitably learn from their own anti-colonial traditions.[16] Reflecting on these would allow them to withdraw from active participation in overseas wars and seek sincere and honest dialogue with communist countries instead.

This true peace is derived from following a religious path. Thích Minh Châu is quick to point out that other religions, including Christianity, can offer a contemplative path to peace as well; this is not the sole property of Buddhism. However, since true peace comes from reforming language to conform with right speech and proper intent, Buddhist principles offer some advantages. For example, the non-dual nature of Buddhist language contrasts with a dialectical structure that Thích Minh Châu sees as characterizing Western thought, in which words and ideas are refined through a clash between thesis and antithesis. Similarly, the concept of no-self (anatman) means that Buddhists presumptively reject simple distinctions between self and other.[17] Because they necessarily reject antagonism, non-duality and no-self are both constructive prerequisites to achieving true peace.[18] He approvingly quotes structural anthropologist Claude Levi-Strauss (1908–2009) in suggesting that what can be learned from modern science and philosophy "in which the West takes such a pride" would, "if laid end to end," only "reconstitute the meditations of the Sage at the foot of his tree," because the Buddha grasped "the only enduring presence, which is that in which the distinction between meaning and the absence of meaning disappears: and it is from that presence that we started in the first place."[19]

In making these arguments very frequently in articles that began issues of *Tư Tưởng*, Thích Minh Châu set the tone for the other contributions. His method of

---

[15] Marcel, *Paix sur la terre*, 44; Thích Minh Châu, "Khả tính," 6.

[16] Fromm, *May Man Prevail*, 250.

[17] For the link between this point and Levi-Strauss, see Ivan Strenski, "Levi-Strauss," 16–18.

[18] Thích Minh Châu, "Khả tính," 11–12.

[19] Levi-Strauss, *Tristes Tropiques*, 394; Thích Minh Châu, "Khả tính," 11–12.

mining European philosophy for insights to bolster arguments made in Buddhist contexts was also carried out by the other contributors to the journal, who were mostly but not exclusively on the faculty at Vạn Hạnh University. One of the most important areas of this contribution was on the connection between Buddhist thought and the philosophy of Martin Heidegger. Thích Minh Châu acknowledged a special debt to the ideas of Martin Heidegger about the relationship between Being and Buddhist philosophy. He particularly appreciated the connection between Heidegger's under-standing of being-in-the-world and Buddhist notions of being fully present.[20] In arguing that pursuing peace meant that partisan political values needed to be set aside in favor of a more contemplative search for peace, he approvingly cited Heidegger as saying that "every valuing, even where it values positively, is a subjectivizing," by which he meant that reducing art or science to a human judgment of value rendered those objects tools of subjective human appreciation rather than things in them-selves.[21] Given his interest in Heidegger, it is not surprising that under his editor-ship, *Tư Tưởng* produced a 236-page special issue on Martin Heidegger and Western thought in which members of the faculty at Vạn Hạnh University made a systematic case for the synthesis between Heidegger's ideas and Buddhist thought. It is this issue to which we turn now.

Ngô Trọng Anh (b. 1926), Mahayana, and Being

The October 1969 issue was a special issue devoted to the topic of "Martin Heidegger and the Failure of Contemporary Western Thought." Amid several articles intro-ducing and translating texts were two articles that specifically compared Heidegge-rian thought with Buddhist principles: Ngô Trọng Anh's "The Position of Heidegger's Non-Being in Mahayana Thought" and Lê Tôn Nghiêm's lengthy "Heidegger in the Face of the Bankruptcy of Western Thought."

Ngô Trọng Anh (b. 1926) is a renaissance man of sorts. Born in Thừa Thiên province in Central Vietnam, he went to France by the early 1950s and received a degree in engineering from the *École Spéciale des Travaux Publics* in 1954. In 1955, he returned home to Vietnam and occupied various positions in the public works departments at Dalat and Banmethuot, supervising the construction and paving of roads and bridges throughout the central highlands.[22] In 1965–1966, he briefly served as the Minister of Public Works in the Cabinets under both Prime Minister Phan Huy Quát and Nguyễn Cao Kỳ, but was removed at the beginning of the 1966 Buddhist crisis, perhaps because of his sympathy for the Buddhist movement and criticism of United States policy.[23] During his time in France in the 1950s and in the United States,

[20] Thích Minh Châu, *Trước sự nô lệ*, 36–7.

[21] Thích Minh Châu, "Làm thế nào," 22; Heidegger, "Letter on Humanism," 265.

[22] "Ngo Trong Anh," in *Lists and Bios of Key GVN Officials*, 70.

[23] "Expression of Anti-US Sentiments by Cabinet Members," 2; Central Intelligence Agency Directorate of Intelligence, "The Situation in South Vietnam," 1.

which he visited in the early 1960s, he developed substantial expertise in Buddhism. As a Vajrayana Buddhist, he was especially interested in the analysis of Tibetan Buddhism by Western practitioners and by Western thinkers more generally.[24] From 1965–1975, he served as the Vice-Rector of Vạn Hạnh University and served on the editorial board of *Tư Tưởng*, where he contributed numerous articles. He has lived in the United States since 1984.

Ngô Trọng Anh begins with the observation that Heidegger himself understood that placing European philosophy in dialogue with Buddhist concepts was imperative. Ngô Trọng Anh observed that mutual cross-cultural understanding was only possible if a common foundation on which a dialogue could be based was realized. Heidegger's discussion of Being was, first and foremost, a means to engage with ancient Greek philosophy. But after the conditions for a dialogue between modern phenomenology and the ancient Greeks was established, equally important, to Heidegger, was to establish a dialogue with the first principles of ancient East Asian philosophy as well.[25] Ngô Trọng Anh points out that Heidegger himself said:

> Every reflection upon that which now is can take its rise and thrive only if, through a dialogue with the Greek thinkers and their language, it strikes root into the ground of our historical existence. That dialogue still awaits its beginning. It is scarcely prepared for at all, yet it itself remains for us the precondition for the inevitable dialogue with the East Asian World.[26]

Heidegger's starting point for this inquiry, Ngô Trọng Anh explains, is to try to locate a fundamental principle that lies beyond the cause-and-effect principles that characterize formal logic. Enlightenment logic inevitably falls into what Anh calls "the ideological deadlock of all current philosophical and scientific paths," in which ideas are locked to a particular place in time and therefore cannot be said to be true in a more general sense. For Asian philosophy, Heidegger locates the fundamental principle of Being in the *đạo* or path. Heidegger's idea of *đạo*, as Ngô Trọng Anh explains it, is a prelinguistic, formless, intuitive universalism that gets obscured by human language and precise concepts of time.[27] In other words, *đạo* is compatible with Heidegger's notion of Being, which suggests a mode of relating to the world outside of Western metaphysics, controlled by the instrumentalizing logic of technological progress.

Buddhist teachings also present Heidegger with the same opportunity to illustrate a notion of being. Although the notion of *đạo* Heidegger articulates seems derived from the classical Daoism of Laozi and Zhuangzi, Ngô Trọng Anh notes that these concepts become integrated into Zen (*Thiền*) and Shingon (*Chân ngôn*) Buddhism, with which Heidegger was familiar through his student Tanabe Hajime and through his reading of and discussion with D. T. Suzuki.[28] The major insights that Heidegger gained the principles of transformation and change in those doctrines, which raise the possibility of seeing objects and human subjects as constantly transforming into

---

[24] "University Notes," 2.

[25] These points are also eloquently made in Bret W. Davis, "East-West Dialogue," 335–345.

[26] Heidegger, "Science and Reflection," 158. Quoted in Ngô Trọng Anh, "Vị trí," 4.

[27] Ngô Trọng Anh, "Vị trí," 5. See also Laozi, "The Daodejing," 159–161.

[28] Ngô Trọng Anh, "Vị trí," 8; Davis, "East–West Dialogue," 337.

one another and therefore as part of one Being rather than as mutually opposed categories.[29]

Finally, Ngô Trọng Anh points to the resonance between Heidegger's thought and Yogācāra Buddhist principles of the Three Natures (ideas that are introduced by Ngô Trọng Anh and Heidegger through the Huayan school). The three natures are the mentally constructed nature (*parikalpita*), which we construct in our minds based on our experience an unreal distinction between ourselves and objects in the world by beginning to attach particular concepts and categories to form; other-dependent nature (*paratantra*), in which we pair objects with their other, or perceived opposite; and the perfectly accomplished nature (*parinispanna*), in which we approach and directly know the world outside of the subject/object distinction and see it as representations only. In this third plain, we can see the world as thusness (*tathata*), the "inconceivable as-it-is-ness of reality."[30] At this point, we can see in the Yogācāra conception of the three natures a critique of the fixity of objects, and of the subject/object distinction, very much in keeping with the Heideggerian view of being-in-the-world (*dasein*), which critiques the givenness of our relation with presumably fixed objects as a kind of illusion.[31]

These insights were particularly poignant for the Vietnam of Ngô Trọng Anh's time because reading Heidegger might invigorate Vietnamese concepts of emptiness and impermanence that had been disrupted by war. Whereas previously, according to Anh, Vietnamese people could experience emptiness or impermanence through a carefree sense of humor and joie de vivre that was an essential part of Vietnamese life (expressed most poignantly, in Ngô Trọng Anh's opinion, through the humorous and irreverent poetry of Tản Đà) and could avoid attaching themselves to places and ancestral homelands through recreating Tết (lunar new year) rituals in new places, the events of the Tết offensive in 1968 had destroyed that feeling and replaced emptiness with something very different: despair. But the engagement of "mutual dialogue" between Buddhists and those interested in Western philosophy could lead to new flashes of insight. Just as Descartes had arrived at "I think, therefore I know" in his winter of exile, so Vietnamese thought might experience a renaissance of new Heideggerian insights, *contra* Descartes, in a time of war.[32]

Lê Tôn Nghiêm (1926–1993), Heidegger, and the Decline of Western Thought

Lê Tôn Nghiêm (1926–1993) also offers a long discussion of Heidegger's notions of being, but unlike Ngô Trọng Anh, he is more interested in Heidegger's critique of enlightenment thought than he is an analysis of Yogācāra as phenomenology.

---

[29] Ngô Trọng Anh, "Vị trí," 6.

[30] Harvey, *Introduction to Buddhism*, 110–111.

[31] Ngô Trọng Anh, "Vị trí," 11–13; see also Garfield, *Engaging Buddhism*, 75.

[32] Ngô Trọng Anh, "Vị trí," 34–37.

There are relatively few biographical sources on Lê Tôn Nghiêm. As a young man, he traveled to Europe, where he studied philosophy at the University of Louvain in Belgium, completing a PhD dissertation on the notion of the absolute in Daoist philosophy in 1958.[33] Upon his return to Vietnam, he took up a position as the chair of Western Philosophy at the University of Saigon's Faculty of Letters, which he retained until 1975. After the fall of Saigon, the teaching of Western philosophy became undesirable, and he made ends meet by teaching students introductory French.[34]

Lê Tôn Nghiêm's article presents a fairly standard analysis of *Being and Time*, beginning with his analysis of Aristotle's dispersion of the idea of Being into a description of attributes, a description of presence, a notion of truth, and a prerequisite for categories. He then questions "why such a simple concept has to be dispersed into so many different meanings" and suggests that Heidegger's answer to that question is the same as the answer to the question of why "Being" is largely forgotten, or rather merely assumed, in most of Western philosophy after Plato. That is because "Being has forgotten something rooted."[35] In other words, faced with the multifarious and implicit meanings of Being, Western philosophers have tended to conflate ideas of being and existence with a transcendent idea related to a higher power. To the extent Being is discussed, these discussions tend to be restricted to those topics in the dominant stream of Western metaphysics, such as individual subjectivity (as exemplified by Descartes' *cogito ergo sum*) and the values that go along with that subjectivity, such as rationality.[36]

A consequence of this tendency to elide various meanings of Being into a larger metaphysical sense of a universal deity is that the tradition of Western philosophy is vulnerable to nihilism, a questioning of whether anything exists or has meaning. Though this nihilism is not exceptional to Western philosophy, Lê Tôn Nghiêm tells us that it is still part of "the basic operation of the history of Western thought," because the abstraction of Being allows us to assume our own separateness from the ultimate questions of existence and thus our own responsibility for our actions.[37]

As an alternative to this dissatisfying and delimited notion of Being, Lê Tôn Nghiêm points us to Heidegger's embrace of hermeneutics, in the sense of practical meaning-making, and his notion of Dasein, or a practical experince of Being in a community, as an awareness of one's "bound physical existence."[38] In his final paragraph, Lê Tôn Nghiêm compares this idea of Dasein with the idea of "karma being brought into the body," thus making explicit a comparison of Heidegger's thought and Buddhism found in the work of many other scholars.[39] In other words, one's physical body is always in a process of transformation that is conditioned by elements outside of it.

---

[33] Le-Ton-Nghiem, "L'absolu dans le taoisme Chinois."

[34] Đặng Thái Minh, "Nhớ thầy Lê Tôn Nghiêm."

[35] Lê Tôn Nghiêm, "Heidegger," 40–41.

[36] Heidegger, *Being and Time*, 22.

[37] Ibid., 42–43.

[38] Ibid., 94–96.

[39] Nishitani, *Religion and Nothingness*, 244.

This means that we cannot construct ourselves as a "pure, a priori self" without understanding our interconnection with all other beings and things. In this sense, Heidegger's ontology is not ahistorical any more than Buddhist conceptions of our provisional existence and dependent origination, conditioned by *samsara* and *karma*, make our existence unconnected to time.[40] Rather, both Heideggerian and Buddhist ideas suggest that we are part of a larger web of connections and relationships, which removes us from the primacy of the subject that Lê Tôn Nghiêm sees as a harmful element of Western thought.

Ngô Trọng Anh (b. 1926), Thích Chơn Hạnh (b. 1943), and Nietzsche

The articles suggesting that Heidegger's critique of Being in Western culture opened an avenue for Buddhism also paved the way for similar arguments about Nietzsche. The September 1, 1970, issue of *Tư Tưởng* was a special issue entitled "Nietzsche and Buddhism." It featured a Vietnamese translation of Nietzsche's poem "Out of High Mountains," which is included as a postscript to *Beyond Good and Evil*, an excerpt from *Also Spoke Zarathustra*, and two essays: Thích Chơn Hạnh's "The Buddha and Nietzsche," and Ngô Trọng Anh's "Nietzsche and Vajrayana Buddhism."

Chơn Hạnh's essay argued that Nietzsche was "the black heart of the Buddha," by which he meant that Nietzsche sought to explain the same phenomenon and arrive at similar insights about impermanence and transcendence, but with what Chơn Hạnh believed to be Nietzsche's darker, more polemical language.[41] Nietzsche used that language to eviscerate what he saw to be the hypocrisy of Christian morality and religion. Classical Buddhist teachings also wanted to get "beyond good and evil," but merely expressed this sentiment differently, without the same kind of polemics.[42]

As Chơn Hạnh points out, it is undeniable that Nietzsche was influenced to some extent by basic Buddhist teachings (largely from the *Dhammapada*) via his reading of the second volume of Schopenhauer's *The World as Will and Representation*, which in turn was directly influenced by Buddhist views about time and transcendence.[43] In a trip with the classicist Erwin Rohde in 1865, during the time Nietzsche was

---

[40] Lê Tôn Nghiêm, "Heidegger," 97.

[41] Very little is known about Chơn Hạnh's biography. Chơn Hạnh appears to have been a *nom de plume* that later became his dharma name; he was born Trần Xuân Kiêm in Quảng Nam province in 1943. In the mid-1960s, he was president of Huế's general student union. beyond the fact that he was a monk who was affiliated with Vạn Hạnh University in the late 1960s and early 1970s through his frequent contributions to *Tư Tưởng,* and that he also co-translated Hermann Hesse's novel Steppenwolf into Vietnamese along with his then-wife Phùng Thăng. See Hesse, *Sói Đồng Hoang.* He may or may not be the same Thích Chơn Hạnh who is currently the abbot of the Tây Tạng Temple in Bình Dương. For this biographical information, see Nguyễn Thanh Châu, "Trần Xuân Kiêm."

[42] Chơn Hạnh, "Đức Phật và Nietzsche," 11.

[43] Wirth, *Nietzsche and Other Buddhas*, 15–16.

studying Schopenhauer intensely, he found a place in the Pleisse valley he called "Nirvana" and carved the words "accomplish your true nature into a rock."[44] In 1875, he described reading an English translation of the *Sutta Nipāta* and observed that the text had assisted him in releasing himself from his attachment to the will to knowledge:

> I am of the opinion that the will to knowledge is the last remaining vestige of the will to life; it is an intermediary region between willing and no longer willing, a piece of purgatory, in so far as we look discontentedly and contemptuously on life, and a piece of Nirvana, in so far as, through it, the soul approaches the state of pure disinterested contemplation. I am training myself to unlearn the eager hurry of the will to knowledge.[45]

Chơn Hạnh turned to *Also Spoke Zarathustra* to delve deeply into Nietzsche's connection with Buddhist teaching. In a way, this was a curious choice. This novel was one of the least explicitly Buddhist works, as opposed to *the Antichrist* in which Nietzsche praises Buddhism as having reached beyond the self-deception of morality, and *Ecce Homo* in which he argues that Buddhist teachings are hygienic rather than moral in character.[46] But Chơn Hạnh argued that there were several obvious parallels between *Also Spoke Zarathustra* and Buddhist teachings. First, *Also Spoke Zarathustra* is structured like a sutra. It uses "thus I have heard" "thus told Zarathustra," "Thus have I spoken" as the opening of a description, a clear reference to the "*Evaṃ me suttaṃ*" standard introduction to Buddhist discourses. And Nietzsche has Zarathustra refer to himself as "the advocate of life, the advocate of suffering, the advocate of the circle."[47]

One might claim that Nietzsche's thought and Buddhist thought are not compatible because Nietzsche's tendency to be angry at the world and to wail in lament is evidence of attachment. Moreover, Nietzsche's Zarathustra agrees that "Life is Only Suffering," but then announces that the only solution to this problem is for one to kill oneself, in contravention of essential Buddhist teachings.[48] But Chơn Hạnh insists that this difference is purely rhetorical. He points out that Nietzsche's cries of anger are no different from the Buddha's crying out in fear upon initially leaving society and entering the forest.[49]

The real convergence between Nietzsche and principles of Buddhism, however, lay in Nietzsche's understanding of the necessity of transcending the self, which also involves transcending being. Chơn Hạnh refers to the work of Karl Jaspers, who argued that to grasp the truth of the Buddha, Westerners must give up their notion of Being in order to detach from self to find that "all forms of thought situated within illusory becoming and selfhood are without validity. Here there is neither being nor non-being."[50] Both Nietzsche, (through Zarathustra), and Gautama Buddha

---

[44] Chơn Hạnh, "Đức Phật và Nietzsche," 11.

[45] *Selected Letters of Friedrich Nietzsche*, 107.

[46] Sprung, "Nietzsche's Trans-European Eye," 81.

[47] Nietzsche, *Thus Spoke Zarathustra*, 188; Chơn Hạnh, "Đức Phật và Nietzsche," 11.

[48] Nietzsche, *Thus Spoke Zarathustra*, 40.

[49] Chơn Hạnh, "Đức Phật và Nietzsche," 12.

[50] Jaspers, *Socrates, Buddha, Confucius, Jesus*, 31; Chơn Hạnh, "Đức Phật và Nietzsche," 13.

recognize that attachment to the self is perilous. Moreover, Chơn Hạnh notes the parallel between the Buddha, who after forty years of preaching said that he never said anything, and Zarathustra's wondering if humans know how to listen to his words at all.[51] For all of Zarathustra's talk about "killing the self," the ultimate aim of self-extinguishment is the same: to understand that "the Buddha is a ghost and Being is like a dream."[52]

In "Nietzsche and Vajrayana Buddhism," Ngô Trọng Anh also focuses on Nietzsche's advocacy of understanding Being, knowledge, and the self as transitory and formless, but does so from the perspective of tantric Buddhism. He does so by suggesting that Nietzsche was a practitioner rather than a scholar, and that his lack of adherence to a formal school and unwillingness to be restricted to an academic position puts him in the same kind of position as Tibetan mystics.

Ngô Trọng Anh emphasizes that Nietzsche's writing, influenced by Schopenhauer, portrays things in the universe as being infinite and formless. Particularly in the middle and late writings, such as *Also Spoke Zarathustra*, and *Beyond Good and Evil* (including "Out of High Mountains") this emphasis on the non-essential character of all things resonates with doctrines of non-discernment in Vajrayana Buddhism.[53]

But his essential argument is that Nietzsche's writing is like the vehicle of the thunderbolt. Nietzsche uses "the death of God" in the same way and for the same function as Vajrayana Buddhism might use Yama the God of Death, and the Dharmapalas or wrathful gods. When a Vajrayana Buddhist symbolizes their detachment from the world by smearing themselves with funerary ashes, they are doing something Nietzschean. Their intent is to use "brutal, horrible, creepy" language and practices to "destroy idols" and pierce through the illusion of common knowledge.[54] In other words, Nietzsche's method is tantric. He seeks to shock us out of our commonplace notions of the world in order to cause us to rethink, even to disidentify, with those values that we had previously taken for granted.

Conclusion

At the heart of the intellectual sphere of a place such as Vạn Hạnh University, one finds a series of contradictions. Following their Rector Thích Minh Châu, many of those who participated in Vạn Hạnh's environment wanted to play a part in forging a new Vietnamese cultural and educational environment based on the Buddhist principles of the Nalanda Mahavihara, and yet their frames of reference, more often than not, came from European philosophy. They were skeptical about the Cold War and about direct foreign intervention in Vietnam (by the Soviet Union, by China, and by the United States), but they themselves were steeped in foreign cultural influence,

---

[51] Chơn Hạnh, "Đức Phật và Nietzsche," 13.

[52] Ibid., 13.

[53] Ngô Trọng Anh, "Nietzsche và mật tông," 29.

[54] Ibid., 31.

since most of them had degrees from Europe and the United States. They wished to distance themselves from the colonial past, but they still valued their cosmopolitan, multidisciplinary education in French texts. They wished to live in a Republic of Vietnam that was modern and cosmopolitan in the European sense, but not one that was based solely on European thought. They wanted the cachet of European ideas without the stigma of lingering French influence.

In finding connections between European philosophers such as Kant, Heidegger, and Nietzsche and ideas in various schools of Buddhism, these thinkers found a way to resolve these contradictions. They could do so by focusing on the ways in which modern continental philosophy challenged enlightenment ideas. These texts argue that the study of contemporary continental philosophy inexorably leads one to conclude that the basic assumptions of enlightenment thought, such as the value of reason, the autonomy of the individual, the ontological imperative of Being (that things "exist" as such), were increasingly called into question by European philosophers themselves. Instead, European philosophers themselves, in rejecting the teleological thrust and technological destructive capability of Western culture, were increasingly turning to Buddhist arguments.

Perhaps the Second Indochina War, as Thích Minh Châu had suggested, was the logical endpoint of the kind of instrumental rationality of Western civilization, in which a battle of "good and evil" became increasingly meaningless and in which increasingly technologically sophisticated weaponry could be brought to bear to produce tremendous destruction in the name of ideology. What Vietnamese were experiencing was, in a sense, a perfect reason to join nineteenth- and twentieth-century European thinkers—whether one were to follow the path of Nietzsche, Heidegger, Sartre, or Foucault, in rejecting the excesses of Western rationality. The Vietnam War, with its proliferation of ideologies offered in bad faith by those actually seeking to extend their own power, offered an opportunity to do so.

Bibliography

Central Intelligency Agency Directorate of Intelligence Weekly Report: the situation in South Vietnam, 24 February–2 March 1966, Central Intelligence Agency Collection, Vietnam Center and Sam Johnson Vietnam Archive, Texas Tech University. Item Number 0410335001. https://www.vietnam.ttu.edu/virtualarchive/items.php?item=0410335001. Accessed on 10 Nov 2022

Chơn Hạnh (1970) Đức Phật và Nietzsche [The Buddha and Nietzsche]. Tư Tưởng 5(1):11–26

Đặng Thái Minh (2020) Nhớ thầy Lê Tôn Nghiêm [Remembering teacher Le Ton Nghiem] Vietnam Global Network. Accessed 30 Sept 2021

Davis BW (2018) East-west dialogue after Heidegger. In: Fried G, Polt R (eds) After Heidegger? Rowman and Littlefield, Lanham, MD, pp 335–345

Đinh Văn Chấp (1927) Dịch thơ đời Lý và Trần (Translating poetry from Ly and tran times), Nam Phong: Văn-học Khoa-học Tập Chí (South Wind Lit Sci J) 115(March 1927):238–244

Duong Nhu Duc (1978) Education in Vietnam under the French domination, 1862–1945. PhD Dissertation, Southern Illinois University

Expression of Anti-U.S. Sentiments by Cabinet Members. Intelligence Information Cable, Democratic Republic of South Vietnam - re: F029200020853. 11 June 1965, Box 0002, Folder 0853,

Sam Johnson Vietnam Archive Collection, Vietnam Center and Sam Johnson Vietnam Archive, Texas Tech University. https://www.vietnam.ttu.edu/virtualarchive/items.php?item=F02920002 0853. Accessed 11 Nov 2022

Fromm E (1964) May man prevail? An inquiry into the facts and fictions of foreign policy. Doubleday, Garden City, NY

Gadkar-Wilcox W (2014) Existentialism and intellectual culture in South Vietnam. J Asian Stud 73(2):377–395

Garfield JL (2015) Engaging Buddhism: why it matters to philosophy. Oxford University Press, New York

Harvey P (1990) An introduction to Buddhism: teachings, history, and practices. Cambridge University Press, New York

Heidegger M (1977) The question concerning technology and other essays (trans: Lovitt W). Garland Publishing, New York

Heidegger M (1996) Being and time (trans: Stambaugh J). SUNY Press, Albany, NY

Heidegger M (1998) Letter on humanism. In: McNeill W (ed) Pathmarks. Cambridge University Press, New York, p 265

Hesse H (1970) Sói Đồng Hoang [Steppenwolf] Chơn Hạnh-Phùng Thăng dịch. NXB Ca Dao, Saigon

Ivanhoe PJ, Van Norden BW (2011) Readings in classical Chinese philosophy, 2nd edn. Hackett, Indianapolis

Jaspers K (1985) Socrates, Buddha, Confucius, Jesus: the paradigmatic individuals (ed: Arendt H). Houghton Mifflin Harcourt, New York

Kant I (1891) Principles of politics: including his essay on perpetual peace: a contribution to political science (trans: Hastie W). T & T Clark, Edinburgh

King SB (2017) Right speech is not always gentle: the Buddha's authorization of sharp criticism, its rationale, its limits, and possible applications. J Buddhist Ethics 24:347–367

Lê Tôn Nghiêm (1958) Essai sur la notion de l'absolu dans le taoisme Chinois. PhD Thesis, University of Louvain

Lê Tôn Nghiêm (1969) Heidegger trước sự phá sản của tư tưởng Tây Phương [Heidegger in the face of the bankruptcy of Western thought]. Tư Tưởng [Thought] 5:39–97

Levi-Strauss C (1961) Tristes Tropiques (trans: Russell J). Criterion Books, New York

List and Bio's, List and Bio's of Key GVN Officials—1965, 23970107001. 01 November 1965, Box 01, Folder 07, Rufus Phillips Collection, Vietnam Center and Sam Johnson Vietnam Archive, Texas Tech University. https://www.vietnam.ttu.edu/virtualarchive/items.php?item= 23970107001. Accessed 30 Sept 2021

Marcel G (1965) Paix sur la terre: 2 discours, 1 tragédie. Aubier, Paris

McHale S (2002) Vietnamese Marxism, dissent, and the politics of postcolonial memory: Trần Đức Thảo, 1946–1993. J Asian Stud 61(1):7–31

Ngô Trọng Anh (1969) Vị trí của vô thể Heidegger trong tư tưởng đại thừa [The position of Heidegger's non-being in Mahayana thought] Tư Tưởng 5:3–37

Ngô Trọng Anh (1970) Nietzsche và mật tông [Nietzsche and Vajrayana Buddhism]. Tư Tưởng 5:27–46

Nguyễn Thanh Châu (2017) Trần Xuân Kiêm. Tre Magazine. https://baotreonline.com/van-hoc/gioi-thieu-tho/tran-xuan-kiem.baotre. Accessed 1 Oct 2021

Nguyễn Văn Lục (2006) 20 năm triết học Tây Phương ở miền Nam Việt Nam 1955–1975 [Twenty years of western philosophy in southern Vietnam, 1955–1975]. Hợp lưu 91–93

Nietzsche F (1921) Selected letters of Friedrich Nietzsche (trans: Ludovici A). Doubleday, New York

Nietzsche F (2005) Thus spoke Zarathustra (trans: Parkes G). Oxford University Press, New York

Nishitani K (1982) Religion and nothingness. University of California Press, Berkeley

Sprung M (1996) Nietzsche's trans-European eye. In: Parkes G (ed) Nietzsche and Asian thought. University of Chicago Press, Chicago, pp 76–90

Strenski I (1980) Levi-Strauss and the Buddhists. Comp Stud Soc Hist 22(1):3–22

Tai Hue-Tam Ho (1992) Radicalism and the origins of the Vietnamese revolution. Harvard University Press, Cambridge, MA

Thích Đôn Hậu (1942) Muốn hết khổ [Wanting to end suffering] (trans: Đinh Văn Chấp). Introduced by Tri Đạ. Impr. Đuốc Tuệ, Hanoi

Thích Minh Châu (1964) The Chinese Madhyama Āgama and the Pāli Majjhima Nikāya: a comparative study. Saigon Institute of Higher Buddhist Studies Publication Department, Saigon

Thích Minh Châu (1967) Tôn giáo phải là con đường giải thoát cho Việt-Nam và Thế Giới [Religion is the path of liberation for Vietnam and the world] Tử Tương 1:363–371

Thích Minh Châu (1969) Khả tính của Phật Giáo đối với vấn đề hòa bình [The potential of Buddhism and the issue of peace] Tư Tưởng 2(2):3–13

Thích Minh Châu (1970) Trước sự nô lệ của con người: Con đường thử thách của văn hóa Việt Nam [On the cusp of human slavery: the challenging path of Vietnamese culture]. Viện đại học Vạn Hạnh, Saigon

Thích Minh Châu (1973) Đức Phật và con người hiện đại [The Buddha and modern humanism]. Tư tưởng 6(6–7):5–16

Thích Minh Châu (2005) Tác giả Việt Nam: Vietnamese Authors. Songvan, Gardena, CA, p 601

Thích Minh Châu (2013) 1918–2012. In: Buswell REJ, Lopez DJ (eds) The Princeton dictionary of Buddhism. Princeton University Press, Princeton, NJ, p 905

University of San Francisco Commencement Exercises: June 1956. https://www.sfgenealogy.org/sf/schools/usf56.htm. Accessed 1 Oct 2021

University Notes. Van Hanh Newsletter (July 1967): 2.

Wirth JM (2019) Nietzsche and other Buddhas: philosophy after comparative philosophy. Indiana University Press, Bloomington, IN

Wynn Gadkar-Wilcox is Professor and Co-Chair of the Department of History and World Perspectives at Western Connecticut State University. He specializes in the intellectual history, literary history, and historiography of Vietnam from the eighteenth to the twentieth centuries, and has secondary interests in cross-cultural relations, world history, religion, and philosophy. He is the author of *Allegories of the Vietnamese Past: Unification and the Production of a Modern Historical Identity* (Yale Southeast Asia Studies, 2011), and *East Asia and the West* (with Xiaobing Li and Yi Sun) (Cognella, 2019), and the editor of *Vietnam and the West: New Approaches* (Cornell SEAP, 2010).

The Reception of Western Feminism in Feminist Literature in Urban South Vietnam 1955–1975

Hồ Khánh Vân

Over the last approximately 15 years, Vietnamese literary critics have put more focus on Southern Vietnamese literature from the early twentieth century to 1975, collecting literary texts and documents, and analyzing and explaining them from various perspectives. This has contributed to a deeper understanding of an important Vietnamese literary genre. Đoàn Lê Giang advocated conducting a number of large-scale research projects on Southern Vietnamese literature, such as "Examining, Assessing and Preserving Southern Vietnamese Literature Written in Quốc ngữ in the Late 19th Century and the Early 20th Century" (core scientific research project funded by Vietnam National University Hồ Chí Minh City, conducted from 2005 to 2007), "Examining, Assessing and Preserving Southern Vietnamese Literature 1930-1945" (core scientific research project funded by Vietnam National University Hồ Chí Minh City, conducted from 2008 to 2010), "Southern Vietnamese Literature Written in Sino-Nôm between the 17th century and the early 20th century" (funded by NAFOSTED—National Foundation for Science and Technology Development, conducted from 2014 to 2016). The research team, including the author of this article, made a great effort to gather documentation, provide a systemized description of Southern Vietnamese writers and literary works from the early twentieth century to 1945, and then to present an analysis and evaluation of their characteristics and values. Subsequently, Nguyễn Thị Thanh Xuân chaired projects on Southern Vietnamese literary theory and criticism between the late nineteenth century and 1975, respectively, "Literary Theory and Criticism in Southern Vietnam before 1954 (collecting, selecting and researching)" (funded by Vietnam National University Hồ Chí Minh

This research is funded by Vietnam National University HoChiMinh City (VNU-HCM) under grant number C2022-18b-14.

H. K. Vân (✉)
University of Social Sciences and Humanities, Viet Nam National University Ho Chi Minh City (USSH, VNU- HCM), Ho Chi Minh City, Vietnam
e-mail: vanhokhanh@hcmussh.edu.vn

City, conducted from 2013 to 2016) and "The Adoption of Western Literary Theories into South Vietnam 1954-1975" (funded by NAFOSTED, conducted from 2013 to 2016). These two projects provide a panorama of literary reception in Southern Vietnam during the course of more than seven decades, contributing to a more complete understanding of Southern Vietnamese literature in the past. Besides, Trần Hoài Anh's *Literary Theories and Criticism in Urban South Vietnam 1954–1975* (published by Hội Nhà văn Publication House, Hà Nội, 2009) also contributes to the portrayal of nearly twenty critics in urban South Vietnam during the two decades prior to the end of the Vietnam war, such as Thanh Lãng, Bằng Giang, Nguyễn Văn Trung, Nguyễn Ngu Í, Cao Huy Khanh, and Nguyễn Đăng Thục.

Literary works by female writers during the twenty years between 1955 and 1975 are mentioned, to some extent, in the above books and research projects. Nevertheless, there has been no monograph that has studied this topic systematically and thoroughly. In 1973, *Vietnamese Female Writers 1900-1970* by Uyên Thao[1] was published by Nhân Chủ Publishing House in Saigon. The book depicts modern Vietnamese female writers in great detail, and yet it only outlines their biographies, literary trajectories and the basic content of their works, rather than approaching the subject from a theoretical perspective. *Literature in South Vietnam: An Introduction* by Võ Phiến (published by Văn nghệ Publishing House, California, 1986) also draws attention to and generally acknowledges the value of literary works composed not only by male, but by female writers in this period, albeit without in-depth analysis. This article aims to present a general overview of urban South Vietnamese female authors, followed by an analysis and explanation of the factors influencing the development of this literary genre, as well as its features and values. In accordance with these research objectives, this article employs historical methodology, poetic analysis and feminist criticism to demonstrate the historical, political, social, cultural, educational and ideological factors that influenced the writing of these female writers over the course of two decades, including the reception of Western feminist ideas. It simultaneously analyzes the manifestations and characteristics of their feminist awareness, reflected in both their thought and their literary texts.

The Rise of a Generation of Female Writers in the South Vietnamese Sociocultural and Literary Context 1955–1975

In the early twentieth century, in a series of writings on the relationship between women and literature posted in the newspaper *Phụ nữ Tân văn* in the late 1920s and

---

[1] Uyên Thao, born in Hà Nội in 1933, called Vũ Quốc Châu, was a writer and critic. He moved to Sài Gòn at the age of twenty. He was known for his books of literary criticism, such as *Thơ Việt hiện đại 1900–1960* (*Vietnamese Modern Poetry 1900–1960*), *Các nhà văn nữ Việt Nam hiện đại 1900–1970* (*Vietnamese Modern Female Writers 1900–1970*).

early 1930s, Phan Khôi (signed Phụ Nữ Tân Văn)[2] and Manh Manh nữ sĩ[3] stated that literary composition was an innate ability of women, and that the image of a woman writing was a vision aspired to by Vietnamese feminist pioneers.[4] Female literature began to flourish in the 1950s, but there was no sign of a true boom. Female writings during this period, according to Phan Khôi, were "inadequate."[5] The period from 1954 to 1975 witnessed a stunning breakthrough in women literature, especially in the latter half of the 1960s and the early 1970s.[6] Since then, a new generation of female writers comprised of distinct voices has emerged. The full maturity and the peak flourishing of female literature during this period was a result not only of literary progress, but also arose from the contemporary sociocultural context. Efforts to enhance women's position in the first half of the twentieth century should be mentioned first. In addition, it is worth noting that the contemporary social, cultural, and ideological conditions also facilitated women in composing literary works, and so contributed to two glorious decades of Southern Vietnamese female intellectuals.

---

[2] Phan Khôi (1887–1959), born in Quảng Nam, is considered one of the most outstanding Southern Vietnamese scholars of the early twentieth century. He was not only a journalist, but also a literary writer and critic. His writings always demonstrate his penetrating and candid views of social and artistic issues, and his brilliant reasoning. It is worth noting that he was one of the pioneers in establishing women's periodicals in Vietnam.

[3] Manh Manh nữ sĩ was the penname of the poet Nguyễn Thị Kiêm (1914–2005). She impressed her readers by her plain, emancipated, brilliant and distinct writing style. Manh Manh nữ sĩ was also a well-known speaker. She gave speeches at a number of symposia and forums held all over Vietnam, in which the value of Thơ Mới (New Poetry) and feminist ideas were discussed.

[4] Phụ Nữ Tân Văn, "Về văn học của," 11; Phụ Nữ Tân Văn, "Văn học với," 11; Phụ Nữ Tân Văn, "Văn học của," 11; Phụ Nữ Tân Văn, "Theo tục ngữ"; Nguyễn Thị Manh Manh, "Nữ lưu và văn," 32-35.

[5] Phụ Nữ Tân Văn, "Văn học của," 12.

[6] A variety of magazine Văn's special issues (a highly qualified literary periodical during this time) on female literature were published, which reveals the lively development of this literary organ in the contemporary context. In the 13th issue of this magazine published on 1 July 1964, a brief history of three generations of Vietnamese female literature was presented: Tương Phố, Song Thu, Mộng Tuyết (pre-war generation), Nguyễn Thị Vinh, Vân Trang, Trúc Liên (midway generation) and Nhã Ca, Hoàng Đông Phương (a penname of Nguyễn Thị Hoàng), Tuyết Hương (younger generation). In the no. 84 of Văn published on June 15, 1967, whose main theme was "Mưa đầu mùa" (Early Rains), short stories and poems by remarkable female writers were published, and the magazine's editors claimed that these women authors were at the beginning of fruitful and blooming careers. Six years later, in 1973, the Văn special issue continued this topic with "Five most famous contemporary female novelists," including Túy Hồng, Trùng Dương, Nhã Ca, Nguyễn Thị Hoàng, Nguyễn Thị Thụy Vũ. Literary works by female authors and critical essays on female literature were also occasionally published in other periodicals at the time, such as Khởi hành, Giữ thơm quê mẹ, Bách khoa, Sáng tạo, Thời tập, Trình bày, Tư tưởng, Hiện đại, Nhân loại, Nhân văn Tạp chí. Uyên Thao, in Vietnamese Modern Female Writers 1900–1970, provides an overview of the formation and development of Vietnamese female literature from the early twentieth century to 1970, in the second part of which he focuses on female writers in urban South Vietnam who all began to become famous in 1966.

First of all, during this period, the public became more conscious of women's rights, and thus popular perceptions of women were profoundly altered.[7] Additionally, the adoption of American feminism had a great influence on the South Vietnamese intellectual culture of the time. Existentialism and the hippie movement, which advocated the appreciation of the individual Self and an engaging lifestyle, aiming for absolute freedom, greatly impacted the contemporary South Vietnamese younger generation, especially the urban Saigonese. These ideas stimulated people's valuing of the individual Self in general, and specifically the individual selves of women, motivating them to aspire for more opportunities to speak up and have their voices heard, to express themselves, even their most hidden thoughts. Writing was hence their own calling, an inwardly inspired activity through which they could express their genuine selves and perspectives on life.

Second, the years 1954–1975 were a special period in South Vietnamese and Vietnamese history, with various political and social upheavals. The war context, the opposing political tendencies, and the adoption of a European-American lifestyle in Vietnam, an Eastern country, had an intense impact on the material and mental life of the population, including women. On 20 May 1958, Madame Trần Lệ Xuân (or Madame Nhu) advocated the formation of the Women's Solidarity Movement, and in June 1958, the South Vietnamese government approved the Family Law, including the ban of polygamy and the facilitation of women attaining economic independence after divorce.[8] Despite the fact that the adoption of the law was, to some extent, a political move, the policies—viewed from the gender perspective— had a certain influence on the development of the awareness of women's position, and hence, increased the demand for women's liberation, especially in urban areas. Vietnamese women during this time could thus participate in a wide range of social activities and had more opportunities in various areas of life, which helped transform their social status and position. In such a context, a variety of novel and complex social and personal problems related to women emerged. Literary works were where the transformations of contemporary society and in women's lives were reflected and depicted. Besides, in works written by female authors, the protagonists were mostly women, and the current situation of women was the main theme of these pieces. Literary works about women, as a result, appeared more and more frequently,

---

[7] In the first half of the twentieth century, there were only 7 female periodicals, including *Nữ giới chung, Phụ nữ Tân văn, Đàn bà mới, Nữ công Tạp chí, Nữ giới, Phụ nữ, Trong khuê phòng*. In this period, the number increased twofold (according to our statistics), including *Nữ lưu, Mạch sống, Bạn gái Sài Gòn, Chị cùng em, Nữ lưu, Phụ nữ đẹp, Phụ nữ đẹp (New series), Phụ nữ mới, Phụ nữ ngày mai, Phụ nữ sống, Phụ nữ tân tiến, Sài Gòn Thứ bảy, Tuần san Phụ nữ (Ngàn khơi)*, and *Phụ nữ Diễn đàn*, bringing women to the center of public debate. In addition, there were also articles and columns on women's issues in multidisciplinary periodicals (scientific-social-historical-philosophical-cultural-literary periodicals) during this time, such as *Bách khoa, Bút hoa, Hành trình, Trình bày, Tư tưởng, Đối diện*, and *Đối thoại*, and literary magazines, such as *Văn, Sáng tạo, Khởi hành, Văn nghệ, Hiện đại, Hiện tượng, Văn nghệ Tập san, Văn nghệ Tạp chí*, and *Giữ thơm quê mẹ*. Henceforth, Western feminist ideas were adopted in Vietnam, and simultaneously, issues of Vietnamese women, too, were discussed.

[8] Demery, Monique Brinson, *Finding the Dragon Lady*, 153.

eventually dominating the current writing, and becoming an integral constituent of this literary period.

Third, the cultural and educational environment aided the growth of female literature throughout this period. Campaigns to improve women's education that had been underway since the early twentieth century had achieved tremendous results. More schools for women and girls were instituted, and the number of educated women increased, particularly in urban areas. According to Ngô Minh Oanh[9] (2011, 13–22), in 1880, the French established a high school in Mỹ Tho, a school for the Hoa people in Cholon, and a primary school for both male and female pupils in Cholon. Collège de Jeunes Filles Indigènes was founded in 1915. In fact, in 1908, Lê Văn Trung, a member of Conseil Colonial de la Cochinchine, and Governor Đỗ Hữu Phương's wife proposed to the modern government that schools for girls be built. However, seven years later, in 1915, Collège de Jeunes Fille Indigènes (now Nguyễn Thị Minh Khai High School), also known as Áo tím Girls' School, was founded and became the first multi-level school for female students in Saigon. In 1918, École Primaire Supérieure des Jeunes Filles Françaises (currently Marie Curie High School) was established. In 1919, Collège de Đồng Khánh was opened and became the first girls' school in the 13 provinces of Annam during this period. In the late 1920s and the early 1930s, the women, who were soon aware of the gender issues and aspired to develop education for females, advocated establishing "institutes," "foundations," "educational centers," and "libraries" for women, creating opportunities for them to improve their academic standing and to participate in social activities, contributing to the birth of a totally new generation of Vietnamese women. The establishment of women's organizations such as Đạm Phương nữ sử's[10] Nữ lưu học hội (Women's Education Association) (having branches in 18 provinces and cities across the country)[11] and Phan Thị Bạch Vân's[12] Nữ lưu thư quán Gò Công (Gò Công Women's Bookshop)[13] were important foundations for female activities during this time. Thanks to these supports, Vietnamese women were able to learn and access knowledge more conveniently. The release of European cinematic works with open-minded attitudes toward love, marriage and sexuality had a significant impact on the urban Saigonese perception of gender as well. In addition, the vigorous development of the press, especially

---

[9] Ngô Minh Oanh, "Importation of the Western education to South Vietnam under the French domination (1861 - 1945)," 18.

[10] Đạm Phương nữ sử (1881–1947) was a royal offspring of the House of Nguyễn, a ruling family of Vietnam. She is considered the pioneer of early feminist struggles in Vietnam. Đạm Phương strongly emphasized the crucial role of education and cultural activities in upgrading Vietnamese women's social status. She left behind valuable feminist writings after over 30 years of working as a writer, journalist, and social activist.

[11] Đoàn Ánh Dương, *Đạm Phương nữ sử*, 5.

[12] Phan Thị Bạch Vân was a penname of Phan Thị Mai (1903–1980), who sometimes signed Hoàng Thị Tuyết Hoa under her writings. She usually depicted independent and self-determined heroines in most of her novels, such as *Giám hồ nữ hiệp*, *Nữ anh tài*, and *Kiếp hoa thảm sử*. She was not only a poet, a novelist, a journalist but also a social activist who energetically participated in female movements and contributed much to the flourishing of feminist movements in Southern Vietnam.

[13] Phan Thị Bạch Vân, *Gương nữ kiệt*, 2-3.

women's periodicals, also fueled the growth of female authorship. The increase in the amount of newspaper pages in which female authors' writings appeared encouraged women to write more regularly and consistently, while also facilitating the public's reception of their works. Nevertheless, this also resulted in negative phenomena emerging in the contemporary cultural and literary life: many literary works (usually narrating dramatic and arousing love affairs) were written superficially and perfunctorily in order to entertain and entice readers. Such pieces were often published in newspapers and journals, particularly in the "gutter-press." It is also worth noting that during this period, literary works by internationally renowned female writers, like Fracois Sagan, Simone de Beauvoir (Western authors), and Chiung Yao (Eastern author), were translated into Vietnamese and avidly received by the general audience. Vietnamese female writers were inspired to write after reading works by authors of the same gender, and this contributed to the formation of a female writing movement in South Vietnam. Literary composition had already become a professional vocation at this point in time, and these female authors were well aware of it. Furthermore, publishing houses, largely private, were formed and flourished throughout this time period. According to Huỳnh Như Phương, "there were about 150 publishing houses in metropolitan South Vietnam in 1969."[14] This fact also made it easier for female writers to publish their writings. Hoàng Đông Phương, Trình Bầy, Cửu Long, An Tiêm, Trương Vĩnh Ký, Mây Hồng, Trăm Hoa, Đời Mới, Kim Anh, Nguyễn Đình Vượng, Tay Ngà, Thương Yêu, Đồng Nai, and many other publishing houses printed and published their works. Literary criticism also supported the flourishing of female literature during this period. Critics soon acknowledged, depicted, and put forward analyses of the robust and unique rise of female literature during these three decades. Monographs and periodicals on women's literature were increasingly popular, providing not only multifaceted appraisals of this literary genre, but also an efficient way to sell and "market" female literary works to a wider audience. Last but not least, the modern consumer society and literary marketplace made it easier for female literature to develop.

Over only a ten-year time span (between 1965 and 1975), the most energetic female writers of the time, such as Nhã Ca, Nguyễn Thị Hoàng, Trùng Dương, Nguyễn Thị Thụy Vũ, Trần Thị Ngh, and Túy Hồng published a remarkable number of short stories and novels, far more than the previous generation, including Thụy An, Mộng Sơn, Linh Bảo, and Nguyễn Thị Vinh.[15] The artistic values and qualities of these works might be disputed, and yet, the quantity of female literary pieces and their influence clearly prove the prominent position of women's literature in Vietnamese literary history. Uyên Thao claims that 1966 can be compared to the year 1928 (in which, the poem *Giọt lệ thu* (Autumn Teardrops) by Tương Phố was published, and gave significant impetus to the early development of Vietnamese female literature). The year 1966 could thus be seen as a turning point in which "women's hesitation

---

[14] Huỳnh Như Phương, "Chiến tranh, xã hội," đoạn 19, http://khoavanhoc-ngonngu.edu.vn/ngh ien-cuu/v%C4%83n-h%E1%BB%8Dc-vi%E1%BB%87t-nam/5393-chin-tranh-xa-hi-tieu-th-va- th-trng-vn-hc-min-nam-1954-1975.html.

[15] Uyên Thao, *Các nhà văn nữ*, trang 28.

in participating in art and thus the prejudice that women cannot occupy an official position in the art world will not be seen anymore."[16]

Female writers who started to appear between the 1930s and the 1950s such as Thụy An, Mộng Sơn, Linh Bảo, Nguyễn Thị Vinh, Bà Tùng Long, and Tuệ Mai continued traditional writing styles, depicting social and family issues, emphasizing mainly the plot and dramatic events (in prose literary works), or carrying on the romantic, elegant, and classical expression of sentiments (in poetry) as was done in Vietnamese medieval poetry and Thơ Mới (New Poetry Movement). On the other hand, Vietnamese female authors of the 1960s, including Nhã Ca, Nguyễn Thị Hoàng, Trùng Dương, Nguyễn Thị Thụy Vũ, Trần Thị NgH., Túy Hồng, Trần Thị Gioan, and Tần Vy were responsible a turning point in the history of Vietnamese women's literature and attracted a great deal of readers. An introduction to a *Văn*'s special issue on female literature published in 1975 contains the statement: "Without any statistics, it can be alleged that in the first four years of the decade of the 1970s, there is a literary genre which has always had a prominent position: today, in Vietnam, 90 out of 100 readers of literature are reading fiction, and at least 60 to 70 of these enjoy and read only novels by female writers [...] these female talents have created a whole new era of Vietnamese women writers."[17] The introduction even claims that during this time, female literature "has overturned the normal situation" and "overtaken" male literature, which has resulted in "the flourishing of *yin* and the decline of *yang*."[18]

Vietnamese female writings in the 1960s modified the way of approaching reality, portraying not only social scenes, but also personal human issues, including psychoanalytical and existentialist aspects. In their poems, short stories, and novels, they primarily paid attention to women's essence and to the feminine experience. Female subjectivity is expressed strongly and richly. Their views of life, their sexual complexes and aspirations, their personal mental states, and their perceptions of society, love, marriage, family, personal freedom, and women's position are presented both broadly and profoundly in their writings. Some of them, especially Nguyễn Thị Thụy Vũ, Nguyễn Thị Hoàng, and Túy Hồng created the image of rebellious women, who were against the traditional views and lifestyle, who supported both physical and mental freedom and release. Perhaps, having been influenced by European-American thought and culture for a long period of time, they wrote about these topics out of an internal need, rather than viewing the issues from the exterior. Women's nature is depicted naturally, directly, sincerely, and variously in *Bóng tối thời con gái* (Maiden Darkness) by Nhã Ca, *Vết thương dậy thì* (Adolescent Wound) by Túy Hồng, *Mèo đêm* (Night Cats) by Nguyễn Thị Thụy Vũ, *Vòng tay học trò* (In the Arms of a Student) by Nguyễn Thị Hoàng, and *Mưa không ướt đất* (Raining not Enough to Wet the Ground) by Trùng Dương. In addition, this generation of female writers also updated modern writing, mainly focusing on literary tone, language, and the art of psychological analysis, rather than giving overly much attention to dramatic plots

---

[16] Ibid., 28.

[17] *Văn*, "Vào tập," 1.

[18] Ibid, 28.

and events. It is also worth noticing that in South Vietnamese female literature of this period, poetry was overtaken in popularity by prose fiction. In the late 1960s and the early 1970s, short stories and novels prevailed. The energy and potential contained in writings by female authors at the time ensured the flourishing of their literature: "Their abilities in writing are increasingly improving. Their potentials in these genres are unlimited. [...] Previously, the year of Nguyễn Thị Hoàng's novels. Then, the year of Túy Hồng's, Thụy Vũ's, Nhã Ca's and Lệ Hằng's. These female novelists take turns becoming the queen of each novel year." Henceforth, women were not only the figures depicted, but they also became subjects of literary life.

Manifestations of Feminist Awareness in Works of Female Writers in South Vietnam During the Period 1955–1975

Female Writers' Self-Awareness

South Vietnamese female writers in this period were very conscious of gender issues, especially women's rights and status, and demonstrated them directly and fiercely in their writings. They discussed the characteristics, roles, values, situations, and positions of the women who write, analyzing the writing dynamics of female writers, comparing the writing mindsets of male and female, requesting objective evaluation and acknowledgment of female literature, and demonstrating their passion for creation. In the article, "Khả năng và phương hướng sáng tạo của người đàn bà" (Creative Ability and Orientation of Women) published in Văn, no. 84, Nguyễn Thị Hoàng analyzed various obstacles hindering women's creative careers. Social prejudice and limited social engagement due to Eastern traditions restricted women's life experience, inhibited their ideological and emotional development, "making it hard for them to completely perceive and reflect" reality, causing "the limited number of women in the literary circle" and "their limited artistic achievements compared to men."[19] Women's self-awareness formed the foundation of their feminist awareness, enabling them to perceive their surroundings as they really were, rather than being trapped in social "myths" (words by Betty Friedan), and motivating them to free themselves from those myths. Nguyễn Thị Hoàng compared the two genders from the theoretical point of view and pointed out three distinctive traits of women's creativity, consisting of "intuition, imagination, and sentimentality."[20] Her discussion was based on her own writing experiences and on observing her peer female writers. This article, brief but succinct, provided a profound contemplation on female writing style, the nature and distinctions of the female creative mind with both specific social references and theoretical support. "Providing a momentary escape to another life

---

[19] Nguyễn Thị Hoàng, "Khả năng và," 5.
[20] Ibid, 5.

that has no restrictions like the real life they are living"[21] was a burning desire on the creative journey of female writers.

Even at the peaks of their literary career, both commercially and artistically, female writers of this generation were well aware of their limited creative space. The short story *Nghề mới* (New Job) by Nguyễn Thị Thụy Vũ, published on *Bách khoa*, was a bitterly ironic self-portrait of a writing woman squeezed from all sides by financial need, parental responsibility, and artistic ethics. She struggled with the conflict between her artistic desire and writing integrity on the one hand and the quickly, easily written feuilletons that flooded the publishing market those days on the other. With a similarly sarcastic tone, in *Văn*, no. 84, Thụy Vũ stated in double-voicing, from the viewpoints of the discriminating society and her own generation of female writers who wished to prove themselves, how the society, especially men, underrated and disrespected female writers. She encouraged her male peers to overcome prejudices and stereotypes to evaluate female literature with objective and respectful eyes. In a more formal and graceful voice, Trùng Dương, in a talk show, discussed how female writers had to balance or even choose between family and career, children, and literature. She would have made a less feminist, but very feminine, choice: "Honestly, if I were pushed into a situation in which I had to make a choice, I would choose to live for my family [...] I write, but deep down I am still a woman, the mother of my children. There is no work greater than the work of making a human to live like a human."[22] From their personal experiences, those female writers expressed women's common conflict between social and familial responsibility, touching on an everlasting social and inner conflict that was hard to exhaustively dealt with. Trùng Dương, Thụy Vũ, and Túy Hồng, through their choices, voiced their awareness of the female essence and the boundaries that women found difficult, even impossible, to overcome.

This self-awareness motivated these women to write. The urge to bring the problems of society into literature came from within themselves, from their own gender-related disappointment, and turned into the main dynamic of their writing. At first, they wrote about their own unstable, conflicting reality that was a constant source of distress. Writing was a means to escape from their physical lives, to freely converse with others about their own fates and the fate of women in general. The character Nguyệt in the story *Lạc đạn* (Unintentional Bullets) by Trần Thị NgH poured out onto paper all her mental depression that had been kept to herself, and turned herself inside out. Nguyệt was a persona of Trần Thị NgH, with her desire for writing to ease the pain of loneliness and to handle her daunting conflict with reality: "Coming home every evening, I am eager to sit at my table and write passionately, crazily about what happened during the day with all of my feelings witnessing or experiencing them. I write as a way to liberate myself, but at the same time, I am afraid of being caught in the escape with undeniable evidences [...] Generally, I write in a miserable tone,

---

[21] Ibid, 6.

[22] Trùng Dương, "Đàn bà viết văn," 52. This article is the report of her talk to young audience in Phan Thiết on 4 August, 1974.

like exposing all my misery to myself at first, and then, deep down, I possibly wish for sympathy from someone."[23]

In conclusion, the generation of female writers in South Vietnam during the 1960s and 1970s expressed their self-awareness in respect to different aspects of their lives. Firstly, in respect to gender, they were conscious of their gender characteristics and the differences between male and female in the creative process, which were determined by many factors such as social context, familial background, and biological and mental characteristics. It should be noticed that these female writers compared, did not measure, the two genders. They did not regard themselves as weaker or lower than their male peers. Second, in respect to career, they acknowledged the responsibility of female writers to the society, history, and to themselves. They were serious about writing, regarding writing as a professional activity and skillful work, staying firm in their creative objectives and artistic integrity, nurturing their inspiration, and acknowledging their strong and weak points in order to develop their own writing strengths. All this proves that the female writers were well aware of themselves as creative subjects, and as such they expressed their strong desire for creating, proving their own talents, attaining the positions they deserved, and making women's writing an essential component of human literature.

Female Characters in the Subjective Role

Not only did these writers recognize their status as the artistic subjects but they also built their female characters—the artistic objects—full of subjective traits. The female writers were the subjects of literary discourses, and the female characters were the subjects of literary texts. In terms of narrative viewpoint, the female characters were always the narrative subjects, speaking from the first-person or the limited third-person point of view. In terms of narrative structure, the protagonists were always female, and the series of incidents were developed from them as the subjects of activity, utterances, and inner thoughts. In terms of content, the works reflected real-life experiences of women. Women were no longer the object of narration or poetry but now took the subjective role. Nguyên Sa analyzed the images of women appearing as "liberated subjects" in Nhã Ca's poems: "Subjectively and freely choosing and affirming their tender or vigorous femininity, breaking free from the coffin of social myths, gaining the posture of liberated subjects, bearing the physical, sexual conditions and fate of humankind or the meaning and purpose of life through different conditions of war and love, those are the images of women in contemporary literature, including the poems of Nhã Ca."[24]

In Nhã Ca's poems, women always appeared in the subjective and active mode, with cosmic vibrations and with a devotion to inspiration. Women were the foundation and source of life. They lived in their subjectivity, making their own choices,

[23] Trần Thị NgH., *Lạc đạn*, 40.
[24] Nguyên Sa, "Đề tựa," 1.

even the choice of male partner, creating life for all creatures and for themselves from their beauty, vitality, and fertility:

"Chúng ta đã tạo ra một thiên đường
Đã tạo nên nhiều vị vua
Bởi chúng ta đẹp đẽ và xinh tươi"
(*Đàn bà là mặt trời—Nhã Ca*)

(We have created heaven
Have created kings
Because we are beautiful and fresh)
(*Women Are the Suns*)

Nhã Ca can be considered the poet of the strongest, most obviously feminist tone and spirit in this period. Other popular poets with a modern writing style such as Tần Vy, Trần Thị Gioan, and Phạm Nhã Uyên also created images of women, but they tended more toward femininity than feminism.

In fiction, which was the more prolific genre at that time, feminist awareness was expressed more boldly, diversely, and flexibly. Living in the modern time immersed in the democratic spirit and the development of individuality and gender awareness, women wrote about their gender naturally. Confident in the knowledge that they formed half of humanity, they actively moved from the periphery to the center of the society. They neither raised their voices in philosophical discourses or using social slogans nor hardened their stance to prove any theory or ideology. They experienced life and contemplated themselves and other people in an innocent, natural manner, nurturing their creative spirit, as in this quote: "Writing in a confident manner and in the vivid language of daily life, not getting stuck in intellectual discourses that they hardly pay attention to anyway, the women who are writing as they are living have created the marvelous surprise that their works, rather than the works of male writers, have completely eliminated the distance between fiction and real life."[25]

Analyzing the subjectivity of the female characters as evidence of feminist awareness, we pay attention firstly to their subjective mindset and their independent opinions about life. The initial liberation was the liberation in thinking. The female characters, free from all social norms and stereotypes, expressed their thoughts and perceptions of life, people, and themselves. The character Trâm in *Vòng tay học trò* (In the Arms of a Student), the novel that evoked enormous controversy right from its first release, always raged against the standard opinions. Trâm regarded Saigon as a place to plunge herself into overnight parties and bizarre relationships with the "daring pride to experience, destroy and enjoy her life regardless of other people's opinions," and Đà Lạt as a place to shelter herself in silence and isolation with the "daring pride to build her own way far from the available ways of the society."[26] Between Trâm and Lưu occurred a silent but ferocious conflict about how a woman should live. Lưu believed that "a woman is happy just when she is really womanly"

---

[25] *Văn*, "Văn chương phái nữ," 3.
[26] Nguyễn Thị Hoàng, *Vòng tay học trò*, 3.

and that "the only way [for a woman to gain happiness] is to make a family of her own, have her own husband and children, and keep them with her forever." On the contrary, Trâm defined living as "writing, enjoying literature, doing extraordinary things, and creating her own way to move ahead all by herself."[27] Trâm refused to subject herself to the limitations of mundane traditional life and reached for an active life in which she lived to make changes or to achieve the remarkable: "Being a mother and a wife, a womanly woman in Lưu's opinion, is just like a water drop in the ocean. Trâm believes that life can be different and better. She can use her ability to exploit the surrounding conditions to make something. To destroy to rebuild. Real happiness and meaningful beauty can be born only from the misery of the seeds buried in the soil."[28]

In a different style, Nguyễn Thị Thụy Vũ focused more on plot and characters' conversations than on direct statements discussing life. Zooming in to the snack-bar life, her stories featured many young women of strong personalities, daring minds, and rebellious attitudes, which were typical examples of feminism and individualism. In an interview, Thụy Vũ also affirmed her intention to let her female characters live as they wished, free from the mental restrictions of the society: "Most of my characters are lonely. They could be waiting for a sexual intercourse, which I do not find immoral or offensive. A lonely person can possibly fall for the allure of sexual intercourse. It's unnatural to make them rationally resist it."[29]

Believing strongly in freedom and individuality, the female characters were proudly active and assertive. Their activeness progressed from an abstract idea to specific and real actions. This community of females, especially the female protagonists, neither resigned themselves to hard situations nor did they allow themselves to be affected by the judgment of society. They actively affected the development of the plots, provoking the incidents in the stories, causing series of circumstances, even difficult circumstances, and they reacted to them. Their unconventional actions were not the result of momentary irrational impulses, but rather indicated their continuous yearning to be themselves, to be appreciated for their own values, and to gain the status they deserved. Even poetry, a genre of feelings and emotion, was full of action and the activeness of the poetic subjects. The final departure in "Tomorrow I will leave / Let go of the earthly world" in *Lời rêu* (Words of the Moss) by Nguyễn Thị Hoàng and the adolescent departure from her homeland in "I Left Home at Nineteen" in *Chuông Thiên Mụ* (The Bell of Thiên Mụ) by Nhã Ca obviously indicated the liberated status of these women. Nhã Ca's poems contained many verbs, and her poetic subjects were usually the subjects of actions:

"Suốt cuộc đời nước mắt và hối tiếc
Tôi thúc giục tôi nào sống đi con
Sống đi con sống đi con
Thân thể ai gào thét

[27] Ibid, 13.
[28] Ibid, 73.
[29] Du Tử Lê, *Nói chuyện với Nguyễn Thị Thụy Vũ*, 24.

Những tháng ngày phung phí
(*Sau cơn going*—Nhã Ca, *Thơ Nhã Ca*, Thương Yêu Publisher, 1972)

(For an entire life full of tears and regrets
I urged myself to live.
Live, my dear self. Live, my dear Self.
Whose body is screaming
In wasted days?)
(*After a Windstorm*)

Nguyên Sa stated that "Nhã Ca's poetry is an affirmation of a liberated subject who chooses womanly activeness over passiveness, tries to have reciprocal relationships and refuses to be submissive, be treated like an inanimate object or be tied down by various myths built up from ancient traditions, customs, inherited moral codes, and dominant male attitudes all woven together into countless layers of restrictions."[30] Prose also expressed similar activeness. With her vividly realistic narration, Thụy Vũ featured the life of various women in snack bars: a girl had sex, got an abortion, and took revenge on males with a cursed bed (*Cái giường* [The Bed]), a jailed prostitute set fire to the Bạc Hà Prison to escape (*Đêm nổi lửa* [Inflaming Night]), another prostitute got bored with the man with whom she had a paid relationship and turned to find fresh sexual joy with another man (*Đêm nay và mãi mãi* [Tonight and Forever]), and a no longer young woman painfully yearned for love and sexual feelings (*Mèo đêm* [Night Cats]). At the end of *Đêm tối bao la* (A Boundless Night) by Thụy Vũ, the protagonist—a girl betrayed by her lover and forced to kill her three-month old unborn baby—plotted to take a revenge full of womanly spirit, a revenge with her own body, reputation, and ways: "Trying to get back to my full healthy and beautiful self to deceive the world, I will continue my job as a hired sewer. My life has yet to expire like an afternoon market. I will collect and save each bit of money for cosmetic surgery. I will have the doctor upsize my breasts and repair my hymen. You will see. I will marry an officer from the Thủ Đức Military Academy. My life will absolutely not go into deadlock. There is no need to hire gangs to beat you up just for revenge. I will be an elegant woman."[31] Having a love affair with her student, which went against the moral standards of the society, the teacher Trâm was active through all the various incidents of the affair. She actively confessed her love, followed the man, broke the mundane calmness of the affair with jealousy, and terminated it (*Vòng tay học trò* [In the Arms of a Student]—Nguyễn Thị Hoàng). Breaking free from the cushioned life provided by her husband, Nhung found her way back to her true love—a disabled man living in a hut in an alley—and lived her true self (*Mùa xanh* [Green Season]—Nguyễn Thị Hoàng). The girls in Trùng Dương's fictions tried tirelessly to find their true essences. They always felt unsettled with themselves and others, always detached and lonely. The characters in Nhã Ca's stories, such as *Đêm nghe tiếng đại bác* (Listening to Mortar at Night), *Dải khăn sô cho Huế* (A Funeral

---

[30] Nguyên Sa, "Đề tựa," 1.
[31] Nguyễn Thị Thụy Vũ, *Đêm tối bao la*, 50.

Headband for Huế), *Đêm dậy thì* (Pubertal Night), and *Bóng tối thời con gái* (Maiden Darkness), seemed more womanly and less rebellious than those in stories by other female writers, but they still kept their subjective ways. They expressed their inner world with various moods, feelings, and streams-of-consciousness in various life situations, from wartime to everyday circumstances.

Staying subjective in their actions and in how they viewed life, the female characters in this literary period always decided their fates. They were free and independent, capable of choosing how to live their lives, as in Nhã Ca's poetic lines: "Hãy để ta, tự ta / Làm đàn bà để được sống và được chết" (Let me myself/ Being a woman to live and to die) (*Làm đàn bà* [Being a Woman]). They might be put in bitter situations or pushed down into dark, muddy ditches, but they never let themselves be defined by those situations or the opinions of other people. They reacted to those situations not just to escape them, but to find and live true to their own selves. Therefore, they asserted their subjectivity not only to the society but also to themselves. They lived true to their nature and gender, freed themselves from mundane ways of living and the silent deception of yearning for changes, just like the character created by Nguyễn Thị Hoàng: "Love is necessary for women, the only thing to predict and affect the life of a woman. However, she does not accept just love and nothing else. She wants to live her life to the fullest, to achieve the greatest capacity of her emotions and abilities, to choose and control her own life."[32] The girl who was on the threshold of adulthood in *Lạc đạn* (Unintentional Bullets) by Trần Thị NgH shared the same yearning. These females refused to be the dolls or the "forever little girls" (Simone de Beauvoir) so common in the society, refused the narrow space and the monotonous pace of living: "One is not miserable because of being thwarted in bad situations; one lives flexibly according to the situations. I feel dispirited. I yearn to feel fatal despair or noisy emotions… I have nothing either to lament or to be satisfied with. The calmness irritates me and ignites in me the burning desire for change."[33]

Awareness of the Feminine Individual Self

Women thinking and acting in a subjective manner seemed beyond the available paths of the society and were thus a phenomenal irregularity. Neither ridiculous nor short-lived, it was an irregularity that made sense, in which women analyzed and determined themselves. Therefore, the deep-rooted reason for, and also the core essence of, these women's thoughts, actions, and lifestyles was their awareness of the feminine individual Self, consisting of both the individual essence distinguishing them from the rest of community and the feminine essence distinguishing them from the other gender. The characters of the female writers mentioned above were constructed to be their natural selves with their own natural words, actions, and inner worlds. They created meanings and values on the individual side rather than on the

---

[32] Nguyễn Thị Hoàng, *Vòng tay học trò*, 83.

[33] Trần Thị NgH.,*Lạc đạn*, 63.

socially ideological side. In other words, the values of these characters were formed by and for themselves, and not for the purpose of illustrating available doctrines. In most of the women's writings, the female characters were portrayed on the basis of their feminine essence, not their social virtue and morality. They even went against and beyond, or even tore down, the traditional rules of virtue and morality to form new ideas, new ways of living. The authors of the book *Thơ văn nữ Nam Bộ thế kỷ XX* (Poetry and Prose of Southern Vietnamese Women in the Twentieth Century) had a similar observation: "Unlike their male peers focusing on social moral standards on the general scale to create the images of moral and social human beings, female writers tend to directly explore the moral potentials of individual human beings such as potentials for self-awareness or self-affirmation."[34]

The feminine individual Self was formed and expressed in various ways. Each character was a unique individual. Works of female writers in this period high-lighted the individual Self. The girls in the stories of Trần Thị NgH seemed to have multiple selves that defined them, which made them multi-personality individuals. The passionate, instinctive Self urged them to act upon emotions and desires, the most noticeable of which was the death instinct. Many of her characters had suicidal urges or actually took action in this regard. In the meantime, their rational selves always contemplated, even reasoned against, those instincts objectively and unemotionally. The two selves co-existed within the characters, creating a double-Self, in which the rational Self coldly observed, analyzed, and exposed the instinctive Self. Their actions were for the eyes of the world, while their contemplations were for themselves. They countered or sometimes even denounced themselves. In *Lạc đạn* (Unintentional Bullets), Nguyệt exaggerated, even tragedized, her situations to other people but, simultaneously, she was truly aware of her "acting." In *Hè tiếp tục* (Continuous Summer), the first-person narrator killed herself and meticulously observing herself in the suicide process, in which she chose each specific action. These two characters committed suicide to discover something about themselves in another state of mind, in which they were not reacting to adversity or to the degrading society in the usual way. The external and internal selves, the individual in relationship to the community, and the individual in relationship to herself were on opposite sides. The "look-alike" or "act-alike" was analyzed and uncovered by the "actual being." The streams-of-consciousness of these suicides expressed both the self-awareness and loneliness of the individuals who neither fit in nor reached out to the community. The characters had multiple voices, tones, points of view, creating various conversations within the individual selves and with other people. Also in the conversational mode, the characters created by Trùng Dương ceaselessly contemplated themselves in order to discover their own desires and to determine the purpose, meaning, and value of life. They always felt detached from and out of tune with the community, confused in their search for their own identities and individualities. The tender but prolonged sorrow in the stories such as *Vừa đi vừa ngước nhìn* (Looking up While Walking), *Mưa không ướt đất* (Raining not Enough to Wet the Ground), *Cơn hồng thủy và bông hoa quỳ* (A Deluge and a Lotus), and *Mặt trời*

---

[34] Nguyễn Kim Anh, Vũ Ngọc, Hà Thanh Vân and Hoàng Tùng, *Thơ văn nữ Nam bộ*, 42.

tháng tư (The April Sun) was not a result of being cramped in specific situations or social contexts. The young women of Trùng Dương were put into a broader physical space and a longer timescale, contemplating the more profound philosophical issue of individuals in human history and within the vastness of the universe. She usually compared her characters to the birds in sandy areas that remembered neither their way home nor the color of the leaves, always "looking toward the ocean, searching in bewilderment and waiting."[35] However, that bewildered waiting did not indicate hopelessness or exhaustion but, on the contrary, revealed an individuality passionate about self-searching and self-understanding: "Suddenly a star fell down from the sky, sketched a light trail in the darkness before dying out in the immense universe […]. I had yet to wish for anything, because I did not know what I wanted or, more exactly, because I wanted everything. I had so many wishes – the wishes of a young person so tirelessly passionate at the doorstep to life."[36] The fictional world created by Thụy Vũ or Nguyễn Thị Hoàng is the world of the determined individuality that clearly understands and confidently expresses herself. The female characters born from Thụy Vũ's pen acknowledge their sexual desire, the voice of their flesh and blood, and react to their situations upon the wish of liberated bodies and minds. Hồ Tùng Nghiệp claimed that "Writing, from the view of the author of *Night Cats* and my examining of *Night Cats*, contains no attitude toward the society, no desire for anything other than self-affirmation."[37] The female characters of Nguyễn Thị Hoàng liberate themselves thoroughly yet protect their individuality fiercely. They evade romantic relationship because they love themselves. They also avoid marriage, afraid that familial traditions would destroy their own selves and change them: "Being completely drawn to and then emotionally controlled by someone, incorporating my life in his, obeying and following him, all will cost me myself and my self-love. I am enough for me, and I am the romantic object of myself."[38] It is no exaggeration to say that these ideas constructed the first completed image of the female individual Self in literature, uncovering their multi-covered inner world, releasing their multi-voiced, multi-toned, multi-colored femininity, affirming that the female was a community of different, independent individuals. The individual awareness of the characters usually contained gender awareness, from which they glorified their feminine essence, distinguishing them from the male. The feminine essence was expressed in the writing style of the female writers. With the self-narrative mindset, the female writers exploited their own life experiences as writing resources. Túy Hồng repeated the statement "Women do not write outside their own selves" and confessed that each of her characters carried her own traits and situations. Nguyễn Thị Hoàng asserted that the characters always "remained in the soul and reflected the life"[39] of the female writers. Contemplation of the Self is not only the writer's urge, but it also indicates women's self-love. In *The Second Gender*, Simone de Beauvoir

---

[35] Trùng Dương, *Mưa không ướt đất*, 61.

[36] Trùng Dương,*Vừa đi vừa ngước nhìn*, 79.

[37] Hồ Tùng Nghiệp, "Phê bình Mèo đen," 3.

[38] Nguyễn Thị Hoàng, *Vòng tay học trò*, 110.

[39] Nguyễn Thị Hoàng, "Khả năng và," 8.

claimed that women always loved themselves because the social conditions motivated them to come back to themselves and care about themselves rather than about
men. The characters of Nguyễn Thị Hoàng evade men to achieve self-love. The
characters of Nguyễn Thị Thụy Vũ disregard social standards to live according to
their own wishes. More manifestation of feminine essence can be found, forming a
vivid and complex picture of feminine spiritual reality. The teenage girls in Nhã Ca's
stories with their one-sided love for much older men are reminiscent of the Electra
complex. The women in Thụy Vũ's stories are obsessed with time and fading beauty,
burning with sexual feelings, and proudly appreciating their own bodies. The older
women in Túy Hồng's stories yearn for love, from silently to passionately in a feminine manner. These examples make clear that the female writers in this period, with
their feminist awareness, portrayed female individuals not only as human beings but
also as genuine women with complete, natural, and vivid feminine essences.

From their awareness of the individual Self, these women made it a crucial criterion to determine their living attitudes, and to no longer restrict themselves within
social standards. Their actions, therefore, were regarded as rebellious against society
and morality. Thụy Vũ called her characters "cyniques."[40] Trùng Dương was viewed
as "swinging a rope back and forth over moral lines."[41] Túy Hồng said that a female
writer carried the fate of "a writing prostitute,"[42] entering the darkest niches of the
society, experiencing all life conditions, and always mentally and emotionally ready
for verbal attacks from other people. These actions were not irrational, irresponsible, and selfish overreactions just for the sake of being anti-society; they were the
manifestation of individual essence. The young lady in the story *Mùa hè tiếp tục*
(A Continuous Summer) by Trần Thị NgH calmly enters a same-sex relationship,
which was so unfamiliar back then, to learn about her own essence and eliminate her
loneliness. The snack-bar girls in Thụy Vũ's stories plunge their lives into depravity,
not forced by situations but by their own burning sexual desire: "She's still burning
for the body of a man who can arouse a flame in her gloomy soul and every fiber
of her flesh. That man is the incarnation of the Garden of Eden and she is blindly
groping for the seductive fruit far out of her reach."[43] The immoral love in *Vòng tay
học trò* (In the Arms of a Student) shocked the public just for a short time, but its
everlasting value lies in a woman's philosophical contemplation of her individual
Self. All these examples were remarkable not for posing great challenges to social
standards but for the women's courage in completely exposing the feminine inner
world that had been tightly concealed by Eastern tradition for so long.

---

[40] Văn, "Số đặc biệt," 25.

[41] Ibid, 29.

[42] Ibid, 37.

[43] Nguyễn Thị Thụy Vũ, *Chiếc giường*, 26.

Conclusions

Awareness of gender and individuality, and the contemporary political, economic and sociocultural conditions, gave birth to a generation of female writers, such as Nhã Ca, Nguyễn Thị Hoàng, Nguyễn Thị Thụy Vũ, Túy Hồng, Trần Thị NgH, and Trùng Dương, who composed realistic and modernist pieces, and portrayed women's internal world deeply, subtly and uniquely. A phenomenal female literary movement hence emerged in South Vietnam during the 1960s and 1970s.

The contemporary society and the cultural interaction between the East and the West, particularly, the American hippie movement and Western existentialism, had a great influence on the Vietnamese feminist thought and female literature of this period. The women presented in the literary works were individuals full of self-awareness and feminine awareness. The world of women (social, mental, and sexual world) was depicted realistically and profoundly. These female writers not only expressed their perceptions of their gender and their social community, but also of women's personal space and essence. The feminist thought was transformed from liberal feminism to existentialist feminism, which was closely associated with existentialism, which was adopted from the West and was popular in Saigon during this time.

In general, in urban South Vietnam from 1955 to 1975, feminism had a significant impact in various ways, both ideologically and practically. Feminist ideas can be found in journals, translations, art criticisms, and literary works of that time. During this period, women gradually became subjects in the contemporary social, cultural, and historical spaces, thereby facilitating the later evolution of not only Vietnamese women but of women in general.

Bibliography

Bằng, G (1999) Sài Côn cố sự 1930–1975 (Old stories of Sài Côn 1930–1975). Văn học, Hà Nội
Đặng VB and Hoành S (2014) Nam nữ bình quyền (Equality between men and women). Hồng Đức, Hồ Chí Minh City
Demery MB (2013) Finding the dragon lady: the mystery of Vietnam's Madame Nhu. Public Affairs, New York
Đoàn ÁD (2018) Đạm Phương Nữ Sử—Vấn đề phụ nữ ở nước ta (Đạm Phương Nữ Sử—Women's issues in our country). Phụ nữ, Hà Nội
Đoàn ÁD (2019) Phan Bội Châu—Vấn đề phụ nữ ở nước ta (Phan Bội Châu—Women's issues in our country). Phụ nữ, Hà Nội
Du TL (1973) Interview with Nguyễn Thị Thụy Vũ. "Nói chuyện với Nguyễn Thị Thụy Vũ" (Chat with Nguyen Thi Thuy Vu). Văn, special issue: 21–28
Eagleton M (2003) A concise companion to feminist theory. Blackwell, USA
Friedan B (1963) The feminine mystique. W. W. Norton, New York
Hồ TN (1966) Phê bình Mèo đen—Tập truyện của Nguyễn Thị Thụy Vũ (Literary criticism of night cats—a story collection by Nguyễn Thị Thụy Vũ). Tạp chí Nghệ thuật, no 42: 4
Humm M (1992) Feminisms: a reader. Harvester Wheatsheaf, England

Huỳnh NP (2015) Chiến tranh, xã hội tiêu thụ và thị trường văn học miền Nam 1954–1975 (Warfare, consumer society and literary marketplace in South Vietnam 1954–1975). Nghiên cứu Văn học, no 4: 27–40

Lại NÂ (2016) Phan Khôi—Vấn đề phụ nữ ở nước ta (Phan Khôi—Women's issues in our country). Phụ nữ, Hà Nội

Morris P (1998) Literature and feminism. Blackwell, Massachusetts

Nguyên S (1972) "Đề tựa" (Preface). Thơ Nhã Ca (Poems of Nhã Ca). Thương Yêu Bookcase, Saigon

Nguyễn GH (2010) Văn học của phái nữ và một vài xu hướng văn chương nữ quyền Pháp thế kỷ XX (Female literature and several trends in French feminist literature in the twentieth century). Paper presented at Hội thảo Văn học Nữ quyền (Conference on Feminist Literature), Hà Nội, Việt Nam, 9 September 2010

Nguyễn KA, Vũ N, Hà TV, and Hoàng T (2002) Thơ văn Nữ Nam bộ thế ki XX (Southern Vietnamese female literature in the twentieth century). Hồ Chí Minh City Publisher, Hồ Chí Minh City

Nguyễn TH (1967a) Khả năng và phương hướng sáng tạo của người đàn bà (Creative ability and orientation of women). Văn, no. 84: 3–9

Nguyễn TH (1967b) Vòng tay học trò (In the arms of a student). Kim Anh, Sài Gòn

Nguyễn TMM (1932) Nữ lưu và văn học (Women and literature). Phụ nữ Tân văn, 131:32–35

Nguyễn TTX (2001) Người phụ nữ Việt Nam trong văn học (Vietnamese women in literature). Đại học Mở Bán công, Hồ Chí Minh City

Nguyễn TTV (2016a) Lao vào lửa (Rushing into the fire). Hội Nhà văn (Assocciate of Writers), Hà Nội

Nguyễn TTV (2016b) Chiếc giường (The bed). In: Lao vào lửa (Rushing into the fire). Hội Nhà văn (Associate of Writers), Hà Nội, pp 17–35

Nguyễn TTV (2017) "Đêm tối bao la" (A boundless night). In: Chiều mênh mông (A vast late afternoon). Hội Nhà văn, Hà Nội, pp 25–51

Phan TBV (1928) Gương nữ kiệt (Outstanding women). Nữ lưu thơ quán Gò Công, Gò Công, pp 2–3.

Phụ NTV (1929a) Về văn học của phụ nữ Việt Nam (On Vietnamese female literature). Phụ nữ Tân văn, no 1:11–12

Phụ NTV (1929b) Văn học với nữ tánh (Literature and feminity). Phụ nữ Tân văn, no 2:11–12

Phụ NTV (1929c) Văn học của phụ nữ nước Tàu về thời kỳ toàn thạnh (The properous era of Chinese female literature). Phụ nữ Tân văn no 3:11–12

Phụ NTV (1929d) Theo tục ngữ phong dao xét về sự sanh hoạt của phụ nữ nước ta (An investigation of our national women based on folk poetry). Phụ nữ Tân văn, from no 5 to no 18.

Showalter E (ed) (1985). Feminist criticism—essays on women, literature theory. Pantheon Books, New York

Shukla BA (2007) Feminism—from Marry Wollstonecraft to Betty Friedan. Sarup & Sons, India

Sở CLD (1929) Nữ lưu văn học sử (A history of female literature). Đông Phương thư xã, Hà Nội

Trần TN (2012) Lạc đạn (Unintentional bullets). Hội Nhà văn, Hà Nội

Trương C (1990) Nhìn lại vấn đề giải phóng phụ nữ trong tiểu thuyết Tự lực văn đoàn (A reappraisal of women liberation in novels by authors of Tự lực văn đoàn). Nghiên cứu Văn học, 5:3–9

Trùng D (1966) Vừa đi vừa ngước nhìn (Looking up while walking). Khai Trí, Sài Gòn

Trùng D (1967) Mưa không ướt đất (Raining not enough to wet the ground). Văn, Sài Gòn

Trùng D (1974) Đàn bà viết văn (The women who write). Bách khoa, no. 416:49–53

Túy H (1971) Những sợi sắc không (The threads of existence and nothingness). Khai Trí, Saigon

Uyên T (1969) Thơ Việt hiện đại 1900–1960 (Vietnamese Modern Poetry 1900–1960). Hồng Lĩnh, Sài Gòn

Uyên T (1973) Các nhà văn nữ Việt Nam 1900–1970 (Vietnamese female writers 1900–1970). Nhân chủ, Saigon

Văn (1973) Số đặc biệt về 5 nhà văn nữ nổi tiếng nhất của văn chương tiểu thuyết hiện nay. Văn, special issue

Văn (1975a) Vào tập (Introduction). Văn, special issue: 1–3

Văn (1975b) Văn chương phái nữ 1975 (Female literature 1975), no 1. Văn, pp 1–95.

Vương TN (1996) Phụ nữ và sáng tác văn chương (Women and literary composition). Nghiên cứu Văn học, 5:63–65

Warhol RR, Herndl DP (2010) Feminism: an anthology of literary theory and criticism. Rutgers University, New Jersey

Hồ Khánh Vân is a tenured lecturer of the University of Social Sciences and Humanities, Viet Nam National University Ho Chi Minh City (USSH, VNU-HCM). She received her Ph.D. in Literary Theory from USSH, VNU- HCM in 2020. Her researches focuses on feminist issues in Vietnamese and Asian female writings (in comparison). In March 2018, she presented her paper entitled *Masculinity in Prose Writings by Contemporary Vietnamese and Japanese Female Writers (In the cases of Hoang Dieu Do and Amy Yamada)* at the annual AAS Conference held in Washington DC, USA. Her most recent feminist critical publications include *The Image of Women in Vietnamese Folktales* (Yeol-sang Journal, Korea: Yeol-sang Society of Classical Studies, 2021), *The Feminist Consciousness and the Initial Development of Southern Women's Literature in the process of National Literature Modernization in the Early Twentieth century* (The Journal of Literary Studies: Selected Articles—1960–2020, Vietnam: Social Sciences Publishing House, 2021).

Rewriting the History of Vietnamese Children's Literature: Portrayals of Children in South Vietnamese Literature

Nguyễn Thị Thanh Hương and Nguyễn Minh Thu

Introduction

The children's literature of South Vietnam is prolific and dynamic. It emerged under the unique historic circumstances of a Vietnam divided into two political entities in accordance with the Geneva Agreement of 1954. According to Olga Dror, the war between the Democratic Republic of Vietnam (DRV) and the Republic of Vietnam (RVN) was an armed conflict between two polities identifying themselves as representing the same national ethnicity: Vietnamese. These two polities ignored the course of national unification and deliberately plunged into civil war, fighting for the ideologies that set them apart. It was a struggle between different points of view in respect to the models of society the Vietnamese people desired to live in and to bequeath to the next generation.[1] During the period 1954–1975, in the territory of the Democratic Republic of Vietnam, north of the 17th parallel, Marxist-Leninist doctrine and socialist culture determined the mindset of the people; on the other hand, in the territory of the Republic of Vietnam in the South, ideology from the West competed for influence and caused multi-dimensional and diverse impacts on people's lives. "The South was a mixture of cultural poles in which values desiring to win the first place to receive a wide acceptance had to go through a long time of debate and persuasion."[2] In South Vietnam, in the early period of 1954–1963, a liberal art culture thrived within an atmosphere of the culture and beliefs of that

---

[1] Dror, *Making Two Vietnams*, 3.

[2] Huỳnh, "Vietnamese literature," 2.f.

N. T. T. Hương
Faculty of Early Childhood Education, Hanoi National University of Education, Hà Nội, Vietnam

N. M. Thu (✉)
Faculty of English, Hanoi Open University, Hanoi, Vietnam
e-mail: thu.mn92@gmail.com

T. Engelbert and C. P. Pham (eds.), *Global Vietnam: Across Time, Space and Community*, Reading South Vietnam's Writers, https://doi.org/10.1007/978-981-99-1043-4_5

73

time, but in the following period 1964–1975, though the arts became more diverse, they also became more erratic because of the violence during wartime and because of those who debased the arts. In terms of poetry, if New Poetry (Thơ Mới) was more liberal but within a delicate and poetic framework, in this war era, there were poets who were scornful, like Nguyễn Bắc Sơn (1944–2015), who wanted to show the fluctuation in people's emotions, their hopelessness and their helplessness in the face of the brutality of politics and war. Poetry of this period also had philosophical tendencies, about human fate and the universe, such as the poetry of Bùi Giáng (1926–1998) or Đức Phổ (1909–1987), which served as a means of escaping a difficult life or politics bereft of solutions.[3] In terms of publications, while the DRV emphasized the unified communist agenda authorized by the authorities, the RVN's development was very diverse, and thus hard to summarize. The writing, especially for the South Vietnamese youth, reflected a wide range of thought and culture.[4] Saigon, the capital of the South, was the center for journalism, literary, and artistic activities and many journalists and artists of Central and Northern origin came to settle there or to collaborate with others there. These twenty-one years of literature contributed to many artistic and ideological groups, often concentrated in magazines such as *Sáng Tạo* (Creativity), *Quan Điểm* (Perspective), *Văn Hóa Ngày Nay* (Today's Culture), *Nhân Loại* (Human), or *Văn Học* (Literature). It has also been the time of many political-struggle groups centered around the newspapers *Thái Độ* (Attitute), *Lập Trường* (Standpoint), or *Hành Trình* (The Journey) with committed writers such as Phan Nhật Nam (1943–), Ngô Thế Vinh (1941), Nguyên Vũ (1942–), or Thế Uyên (1935–) or anti-war writers like Kinh Dương Vương (1941–), Nguy Ngữ, Trần Hữu Lục (1941–2021), Thái Luân, or Thế Vũ. The study of the children's literature of South Vietnam potentially provides readers with a diverse perspective on the many different literary lives in South Vietnam.

The manifold children's literature in South Vietnam is part of the general complexity of South Vietnamese literature. In the article "Vietnamese Literature in South Vietnam 1954–1975: Literary Trends and Modernization" of Huỳnh Như Phương (1955–) from the 4th International Conference on Vietnamese Studies, the author states that there is a coexistence of two literatures which intertwined and also opposed each other in the region below the 17th parallel from 1954 to 1975. The first group is liberation or revolution literature, which gathered resistance writers, mainly working in the countryside, forests, and mountains, but still had authors and works appearing in urban areas. This is the extension of the revolutionary literature originating in the North constructed in the socialist model of composition. "In the North, all the newspapers and books were controlled by the state."[5] Owing to its revolutionary nature, along with the government's orientation, this literature did not have much place for the portrayal of children. In addition, in the period of the 1950s and early 1960s, Võ Phiến (1925–2015) describes the notion of *littérature engagée* [văn

---

[3] Nguyễn, *Văn học miền Nam.*

[4] Dror, *Making Two Vietnams*, 139.

[5] Thái Đinh Quang Anh, *Dương Thu Hương: '30 tháng Tư 75, nền văn minh đã thua chế độ man rợ'*, 2012, quoted in Nguyễn Lập Duy, *The Unimagined Community: Imperialism and Culture in South Vietnam* (Manchester: Manchester University Press, 2020), 182.

chương dấn thân] which emphasized the "religious political, social or psychological, depending on the individual artist and his circumstances."[6] *Littérature engagée*
predominates when writers such as Phan Nhật Nam (1943–), Nguyên Vũ (1942–), or
Thảo Trường (1936–2010) confront politics and wars, open deep political and social
battlefields on pages of magazines like *Đất Nước* (Nation), *Thái Độ* (Attitude), and
Hành Trình (The Journey). Nguyễn Văn Trung (1930–), in his book *Lược Khảo Văn
Học* (Literature Review), asserted that writers in his time (1955–1975) produced
literary works to indicate political and social tensions of the time by using indirect-
ness, because of the government's strict monitoring mode.[7] It was his journal *Hành
trình* (The Journey) that was banned by the American-supported South Vietnamese
government in 1966 because of its discussion of social revolution in Vietnam.[8] War
is the main topic, transcending all differences, in Southern newspapers and literature during those years. In suburban areas, empty-handed farmers who had lost their
land and village due to war appeared widely in the writings of Võ Hồng (1922–
2013), Nguyễn Mộng Giác (1940–2012), or Thảo Trường. In cities, people who had
suffered misfortune also become subjects in the literature. Reading *Thềm hoang* (The
Wild Shelves) and *Ánh sáng công viên* (Light of the Park) by Nhật Tiến, we meet
a blind singer, a prostitute, a widow, and an orphan. Lê Tất Diệu's *Đêm dài một
đời* (Life-long Night) evokes boundless compassion for blind children with a bleak
future. The brief, tragic fates of human beings, public anxieties, and worries and
doubts about contemporary society and politics were the persistent problems which
predominated in writing of that time. The typical literary characters representing
these issues are farmers and women, supplemented by supporting characters who
are children in unfortunate situations. It can be said that there are child characters in
the works of this period's literature, but this kind of character only has a minor role
reflecting adults' lives or condemning the brutality of war inflicted upon these little
lives. The emerging political themes, along with the underappreciated importance
of child characters, resulted in a lack of children in the liberation literature of South
Vietnam.

Children occur much more frequently in the second body of literature, which
Huỳnh Như Phương addresses as the group existing in the territory managed by the
government of the Republic of Vietnam. It existed mainly in the urban areas of South
Vietnam although there were also authors who wrote about rural areas. This literature
was divided into many different trends, movements, and confusing concepts, having
either a positive or negative relationship to revolutionary literature, as well as being
influenced by modern Western literature. All were trying to find a way to affirm their
own creativity. In a situation dense with the materials of creation and disruption,
children's literature was again marginalized. Because of the increasing violence in
the countryside, the rural population became separated from the country's overall

---

[6] Phiến, Võ, *Hai mươi năm Văn Học Miền Nam: Tổng Quan*, 1986, quoted in Nguyễn Lập Duy,
The Unimagined Community: Imperialism and Culture in South Vietnam (Manchester: Manchester
University Press, 2020), 186.

[7] Phạm, *Literature and Nation-building*, 61.

[8] Lương, *Vietnamese existential philosophy*, 8.

cultural activities. Following the discipline of the market, South Vietnamese writers produced works that served a mass community that was largely confined to the urban areas. The peasants, their lives and activities, gradually fell into oblivion in the minds of urban populations.[9] Novelists like Bình Nguyên Lộc (1914–1987), Ngọc Linh (1935–2002), Duyên Anh (1935–1997), or Mai Thảo (1927–1998) published their novels in daily newspapers. Childhood became a special theme of prominent authors. Specifically, Duyên Anh wrote novels about childhood and youth, such as the collection of stories *Hoa Thiên Lý* (Heavenly Flower) and *Vẻ buồn Tỉnh Lỵ* (Sadness of Town). Nhật Tiến (1936–2020), with a teacher's conscience and responsibility, wrote a lot about unfortunate children or the poor and the victims of war.

Regardless of the existence of South Vietnamese children literature, it does not form a part of the mainstream history of Vietnamese children's literature. In other words, present-day Vietnamese research into the history of Vietnamese children's literature has not attached special importance to South Vietnamese children's literature. This mainstream history is largely formulated around children's literature of North Vietnamese authors and those who are considered participants of the Party-led national projects. Vân Thanh, the nationally recognized researcher of children's literature in contemporary Vietnam, does not mention South Vietnamese literature in any of her writing. She worked for Viện Văn Học (Institute of Literature) in North Vietnam in 1961 and was responsible for doing research on children's literature. She was also a member of the editorial board of Kim Đồng, the publisher specializing in publications for children in North Vietnam and in post-1975 Vietnam. The most popular research of Vân Thanh about children's literature in Vietnam is her PhD thesis *Truyện viết cho thiếu nhi từ Cách mạng tháng tám* (Tales Written for children since the August Revolution). Not only does Vân Thanh's research show the main themes of stories written for children, such as history, resistance against imperialist invaders, labor, study and daily life, comics, science stories, or animal stories, but she also points out the weaknesses in literature for children and adolescents in the categories struggle for unification, science stories, and stories about animals. The above works show the face of children's literature from 1945 to 1975 through various kinds of stories composed for children. Noticeably, this classification does not include writing for children in South Vietnam. This book, which explicitly aims to depict the whole picture of Vietnamese children's literature, has three parts: 1. Overview, 2. Genre, and 3. Author—Work, in the outline of Vietnamese children's literature first published in 1999. In other research, *Văn học thiếu nhi Việt Nam* (Vietnamese children's literature), which gives a brief history of the formation and development of Vietnamese children's literature, Vân Thanh divides folklore into periods, namely literature before the August Revolution, literature in the period of resistance against the French, literature after peace restoration in the North (from 1954 to 1975), and literature after national reunification (after 1975). And, in her description, South Vietnamese children's literature does not have a place.

In textbooks on Vietnamese children's literature, South Vietnamese children's literature does not appear. *Văn học thiếu nhi Việt Nam* (Vietnamese Children's

---

[9] Nguyễn, *The Unimagined Community*, 203.

Literature 1998) by Trần Đức Ngôn—Dương Thu Hương, published by Education House and *Văn học trẻ em* (Children's Literature 2003) by Lã Thị Bắc Lý, published by Nhà xuất bản Đại học Sư Phạm Hà Nội (University of Education Publishing House), have formalized the presence of children's literature in universities and colleges. These documents have covered the development of Vietnamese children's literature, focusing on typical authors such as Võ Quảng (1920–2007), Tô Hoài (1920–2014), Phạm Hổ (1926–2007), and Trần Đăng Khoa (1958–). In these two textbooks, the formation and the development of Vietnamese children's literature is divided into stages: before the August Revolution, the period of resistance against the French (1945–1954); the Northern period of building socialism (1955–1964), the period of resistance against the United States (1965–1975), and the period after 1975. Similarly, South Vietnamese literature is not mentioned at all in 2011, the PhD thesis *Thể loại truyện đồng thoại trong văn học Việt Nam hiện đại* (Genre of folk stories in modern Vietnamese literature, 2011) by Lê Nhật Ký, which has contributed to enriching the shallow resources of children's literature in Vietnam. This work focuses on learning about children's stories from the perspective of genres. By considering the typical features of this type of story, the author of the thesis also mentions the character system of synonymous tales with a focus on animal characters. In addition to the above work (which was later printed as a book), Lê Nhật Ký also made a significant contribution in creating a picture of children's literature, with many articles and treatises published and printed in various journals, magazines, and personal blogs. In 2012, Bùi Thanh Truyền edited the *Giáo trình văn học 2* (Textbook of Literature 2), in which the process of the formation and development of children's literature is also divided into 5 stages as in the two textbooks of Trần Đức Ngôn and Lã Thị Bắc Lý earlier. A thematic book named *Thi pháp văn học thiếu nhi* (Poetics of Children's Literature 2007), edited by Bùi Thanh Truyền, in the primary-school teacher-development project, with six parts, namely artistic conception of people, art time, art space, plot, structure, and artistic language in children's literature, has presented quite clearly the key contents of poetry in children's literature. However, South Vietnamese children's literature is not included in the works discussed. Other writings about the history of children's literature such as *Từ mục đồng đến Kim Đồng* (From herds-man to Kim Đồng, 2002) and *Văn học thiếu nhi nửa thế kỉ một con đường* (Children's literature—a half century and one road, 2012) by Văn Hồng (1931–2012) exclusively mention names of some novelists and poets, for example, Tô Hoài (1920–2014), Võ Quảng (1920–2007), Thy Ngọc (1925–2012), Văn Linh (1930–2014), Định Hải (1937–), Phạm Hổ (1926–2007), Xuân Sách (1932–2008), Lê Khắc Hoan (1937–2021), Nguyễn Nhật Ánh (1955–), and Trần Đăng Khoa (1958–), who originated in the North or who gathered in the North before 1954. In these portrayals of Vietnamese children's writers, no South Vietnamese writers are listed. In short, there has been no research on South Vietnamese children's literature. The questions about the existence of South Vietnamese children's literature, its appearance, and its contribution to the perception of social life in Southern Vietnam during the period of 1954–1975 remain unanswered.

This article studies the children's character world in children's literature with the hope of rewriting the history of Vietnamese children's literature with the inclusion of

South Vietnamese children's literature. Thereby, we can partly show the depiction of children in South Vietnamese literature not only as a reflection of South Vietnamese society but also as an expression of the adult world. In a review of literary works focusing on children, we have chosen two prominent authors: Duyên Anh (1935–1997) with over fifty publications and Nhật Tiến (1936–2020) with twenty-two, all of them published before 1975. When writing, Duyên Anh focused on many circumstances from the world in which many people, like he, lived and in which they treated each other with sincerity.[10] Meanwhile, Nhật Tiến started his writing career portraying orphans in orphanages, a quiet world that can be boring and monotonous to people outside. Readers can explore the people, psychology, circumstances, and lifestyles in the world of orphans, boarding school students, and even monks. Some of his typical works are *Những Người Áo Trắng* (Those in white shirts, 1969), *Những Vì Sao Lạc* (Lost stars, 1969), *Tay Ngọc* (Jade hand, 1969), or *Chim Hót Trong Lồng* (Birds singing in cages, 1984).[11] In categorizing the characters of children created by these two authors, this essay argues that the depiction of children in South Vietnamese literature reflects South Vietnamese society, and thus, deserves to be recognized as part of the history of the Vietnamese nation, particularly the history of Vietnamese children's literature.

In examining the child characters of Duyên Anh and Nhật Tiến, we can see that the works written for children by these two authors were mostly based on two tendencies: either the reflection of social reality or the return to the peaceful past. On the one hand, the authors delved deeply into the fate of abandoned children in order to reconstruct these children's lives. In the context of constant violence, youth fell into a state of doubt, helplessness, and lack of direction. The fierceness of the war caused many families to be scattered, turned children with parents into street children and orphans. This cruel fact was expressed by the outcast-child character in the literary texts for young children. On the other hand, there was a type of child character who was dreamy and innocent found in some writings. As a way of protesting reality, writers came back to childhood, to the dreams and subtleties of adolescence. Childhood became a shelter for painful souls burdened with melancholy.

The "Outcast Child" Character

During wartime, there was a new group of children, the offspring of American soldiers and local women. They were referred to as "bụi đời" or the "dust of life."[12] These Amerasians were stigmatized by the Vietnamese; however, they are not included in the literary character of outcast child that we have discussed in the writings for young children. The outcast children are rather the children that have been abandoned by their family and have then become wanderers and those who have experienced

---

[10] Huỳnh, *Duyên Anh.*

[11] Nguyễn, *Văn học miền Nam.*

[12] Chonchirdsin, "The Vietnam War."

an unhappy childhood. Such characters appear mostly in Duyên Anh's narratives. Võ Phiến, in his book, mentioned that Duyên Anh had more than once distinguished between two types of novels: rustic youth and wanderers. We can find the dusty youth and orphan characters who have left the orphanage or who polish people's shoes in *Luật Hè Phố* (Street Law) and *Dấu Chân Sỏi Đá* (Footprints on stones, 1975). We can find wanderers, known as the "du đãng," which Chi, P. Phuong defined as being "those who follow a dissolute lifestyle, having sex, drinking wine, using opium, robbing and killing people,"[13] in *Giấc mơ một loài cỏ* (Dream of a grass, 1969) or *Ánh mắt trông theo* (Following sight, 1969). Regarding the type of novel called "wanderers," Duyên Anh carefully emphasized: "A lonely youth, eager to sacrifice himself to save lives, but in the end that chivalrous spirit turned into a wandering spirit." These works painted a vivid picture of the society at that time, in which children became juvenile delinquents.

The "Wanderer" Character

The image of a "du đãng" type emerges in the mainstream documents of the RVN, which used it to indirectly criticize America's neocolonialism. Contemporary intellectuals were aware that South Vietnam faced a rising neocolonialism as it was dependent on the United States and other foreign countries.[14] The child characters with the status of wanderers in the works of Duyên Anh are partly a reflection of the society at that time, in which the symbol of an Americanized society is equated with the emergence of drugs, violent music, or pornography.

In *Giấc mơ một loài cỏ* (Dream of a grass, 1969), the central child character is "Quý đen," whose parents are unknown. He makes the decision to escape from the orphanage and becomes a wanderer in the streets. Also, Danh, after his parents' deaths, leaves the house because of his harsh aunt and works as a shoeshine boy. In *Ánh mắt trông theo* (Following sight, 1969), Dậu, sharing the same familial pattern as "Quý đen," is brought up in a brothel. Hường, a fourteen-year-old girl, lives by being a beggar and sleeps on the street. Her parents, who are indigenous people from the Central region, pass away, killed by bombs and bullets. Such poor children survive by eating leftovers from restaurants: "...this food had fed the children and helped them grow up. And the humiliation on the sidewalk taught them to be wise, to fight for a living."[15] When growing up and beginning to feel a sense of shame at eating leftovers, each of them starts to earn their livelihood on the street by joining shoe-shining groups, becoming beggars or pickpockets. These child characters in Duyên Anh's novels are victimized by the lack of parental protection and social sympathy that have led them to live the lives of tramps.

---

[13] Pham, *Literature and Nation-building*, 70.

[14] Ibid., 71.

[15] Duyên Anh, *Ánh mắt trông theo*, 37.

In addition to the children who are pulled to the side of the road and turn into street children, there are also characters who choose the sidewalk as a shelter and call themselves "du đãng" or "genuine wanderers." These young people, as Duyên Anh considered them in *Điệu Ru Nước Mắt* (The lullaby of tears, 1963), are "the purest guys in society."[16] He stated that genuine wanderers are more honest than those who raise their voices to demand education for the homeless, and the society of wanderers is far better than the hypocritical society. These children's rebellious souls stem from both their discontent with family, school, and fatherland and their idea that life considers them to be landlopers.[17] In this novel, there are various child characters choosing to be on the street rather than to be under parental wings. Take Trần Đại as an example. In spite of being born into a rich and influential family, he is well-aware of his father's coldness and his mother's bitter death. Đại chooses the wandering path as not only a way to take revenge on life, but also as deliverance from the dark quagmire of falsehood and evil in his family and society. Following the same motif, James Dean Hùng, whose parents have prestigious occupations, however, is not able to pass the middle school exam. Due to his depression about not living up to his parent's expectations, Hùng runs away from home. Another child character suffering from severe conditions is Trần Thị Diễm Châu, known as Châu Kool. Her father dies at a young age, her mother is sick, and her sister commits suicide because her face is deformed by jealousy. The combination of her difficulties and hatred turns her into a wandering queen. These young characters reflect the social injustice and the insufficiency of the orientation provided by family and school. As a result, their way of taking revenge on society and its hostility is to revolt, slash, rape, and extort money as if there were no other choice.

Duyên Anh said that in his first rogue novel, *Điệu Ru Nước Mắt* (The lullaby of tears, 1963), the Southern generals opposed each other: "This general captured the other, today one person may be a heroic general, but tomorrow, he may become a crooked general. From a writer's perspective, that situation was so depressing, and I did not see anything worthy of praise anymore. Therefore, I only praised the tramps, that was all."[18] Compared to the South Vietnamese society at that time, the landlopers society of Trần Đại, James Dean Hùng, and Châu Kool was very much better. Their rebellion can be considered a reaction to the fact that their expectations of life were so from the realities of their lives.

Duyên Anh gives a lot of sympathy to his wandering characters. He is indignant in *Ảo vọng tuổi trẻ* (Youthful illusions, 1964): "what punishment is appropriate for a youth deceiver, for those who corrupt a new generation to find a place for the nation under the sun."[19] The images of street children in his writings are based on the people that he himself has met in real life during his years living under the Tân Thuận bridge with his compatriots riding cyclo.[20] Living with all kinds of people

---

[16] Duyên Anh, *Điệu ru nước mắt*, 274.

[17] Ibid., 81.

[18] *Vết thù*.

[19] Duyên Anh, *Ảo vọng*, 228.

[20] Huỳnh, *Duyên Anh*.

such as porters, cyclo drivers, peddlars, shoe shiners, newspaper hawkers, thieves, and wanderers, he "lived with them, lived like them." Their lives reflect a chaotic, violent society where the true values of life fall into oblivion because of social evils. In that society, children are hopeless and lost. In such a society, writers like Duyên Anh must perform a divine mission which is to help and lift the poor souls and comfort them with his belief in love and sympathy. However, those things are too fragile in the face of the storm of violence, as is evident in the ultimate fates of the young wanderer characters. These child characters must pay the price for their spontaneous, impulsive, extravagant actions, for the aspirations of youth, with their own lives. Trần Đại dies on a barbed-wire fence, Châu Kool is shackled in prison, Danh is arrested by the police, and Lựa is killed in the middle of the road. Their deaths left big questions for the South Vietnamese society at that time, and made adults worry about their responsibility for their children.

The "Unhappy Child" Character

Unhappy child characters appear in the books of Nguyên Hồng (1918–1982), Nam Cao (1917–1951), and Nguyễn Công Hoan (1903–1977) before 1945. From 1955 onward, disadvantaged children with bitter fates reemerge again in the works of Duyên Anh and Nhật Tiến. In these literary works, the main characters are children who lack love and care. Reading Duyên Anh's and Nhật Tiến's literary compositions, the fates of unhappy children aside, it can be seen that both authors try to portray the dreams and aspirations of their youth via these young characters. The characters of unhappy children express an inextricably interwoven connection between unfortunate lives and sincere love and humanity.

Being inspired by the people they meet, Duyên Anh and Nhật Tiến use their actual life as material to write about the dark situations of children of that time. These children live in Hòa Hưng—a neighborhood of hookers—on the outskirts of the city. Walking in that neighborhood, which is a meter lower than the street, is like climbing a ladder. At that time, the French soldiers were still out. The neighborhood was busy. Every night, there were raids and soldiers "playing around." Prostitutes ran away from them and cursed them loudly. There were tragedies and adversities everywhere. "I had compassion for half-breed children who did not have a homeland or a childhood." At the age of ten, they knew how to "guard against the police, whenever they see the police entering the village, they were on alert."[21] It is the writer's love and belief in people that help Duyên Anh and Nhật Tiến write about the fate of wandering, unhappy children with a heart full of love. They portray the child characters with various circumstances, for example, those living on the streets, those that are forced into an orphanage, or those suffering family breakdowns as vivid and lively and as living individuals sparkling with the desire to live and rise up

---

[21] Huỳnh, *Duyên Anh.*

out of their conditions. In spite of being crisscrossed with scars, the unhappy child characters are symbols of a passionate faith in life and people.

A myriad of disadvantaged child characters are found in Duyên Anh's works, such as in *Con sáo của em tôi* (My sister's starling, 1960), *Đại dương trong lòng con ốc nhỏ* (The ocean in the heart of a small snail), *Cái diều* (The Kite), *Dấu chân sỏi đá* (Footprints on stones, 1975), and *Điệu ru nước mắt* (The lullaby of tears, 1963), *Giặc ô kê* (OK enemy). For instance, Tâm, in *Dấu chân sỏi đá* (Footprints on stones, 1975), and his mother are helpless after his father's death. Even though the government promised to give his family compensation for the father's death, there is no money despite their belief.[22] Tâm becomes a street child and has to cling to the sidewalks to earn a living. Tâm's friend—Bốn lơ xe grows up in an orphanage. When climbing the wall to escape from the orphanage, Bốn lơ xe is still unaware of how harsh the reality is outside the wall, where people are ready to trample on weak children like him.

The character of the unhappy child is also created by Nhật Tiến in *Những vì sao lạc* (Lost stars, 1968), *Tay Ngọc* (Jade Hand, 1969), *Chuyện bé Phượng* (Phượng's story, 1964), and *Chim hót trong lồng* (Birds singing in cages, 1966). In *Những vì sao lạc* (Lost stars, 1968), while Khánh's mother dies as a result of the bombs, his father commits suicide out of frustration. Following the loss of his family, Khánh and his sibling suffer a series of unfortunate events, from the sibling's illness to imprisonment. Another disadvantaged character in this story is Vũ, who becomes a street child after his grandmother passes away. Hạnh, living in a boarding school, in *Chim hót trong lồng* (Birds singing in cages, 1966), innocently writes a letter to her mother and asks whether she was a prostitute, if her brothel was big, or what she did and sold in a brothel. Reading *Những người áo trắng* (Those in white shirts, 1969), one encounters Phượng, Quỳnh and Liễu, who are parentless children, are raped, bullied, and must live in an orphanage. They are girls and boys with speech impairments. The definition of unhappiness is evident in these child characters.

The "Innocent Child" Character

After 1963, especially after the United States poured troops into South Vietnam, the life of politics as well as literature underwent many changes. Researcher Cao Huy Khanh commented that "After 1963, Southern literature metamorphosed with a constant, fierce obsession: obsession with war and all that surrounds war."[23] Writers sought or portrayed characters with a defiant attitude, going against moral standards or avoiding reality, returning to the past in nostalgia for childhood. Duyên Anh, Từ Kế Tường (1946–), and Nhật Tiến are typical authors who opt to escape from the reality to live in childhood. As a way of protesting reality, these writers go back to childhood, which contains the dreams and subtleties of adolescence. To bridge

---

[22] Duyên Anh, *Dấu chân sỏi đá*, 9.

[23] Nguyễn, *Văn học miền Nam.*

the gap between the author's soul and the magical world of innocence and memory, Duyên Anh, Nhật Tiến, and Từ Kế Tường create child characters that are innocent, lively, realistic, and emotional.

Duyên Anh may be the author who gives the most in-depth description of innocence in a child character. Chương Còm, Huệ Tai Voi, Ngân Quắn, Dũng Dakao, Khoa, Vũ, Côn, and Thúy, in Duyên Anh's works have different personalities and appearances but all of them share the same common trait, which is their innocence, pureness, and impartiality. In Yết Kiêu—Côn, Dã Tượng—Luyến, Quốc Toàn—Vọng, Lê Lai—Lộc, and Lý Thường Kiệt—Long, every child wants to be like a national hero who sacrifices themselves to save the country. The desire of most children to become "a Quang Trung" is vividly expressed by Duyên Anh in his collection of stories. The only problem is that child characters in Duyên Anh's stories do not become young soldiers or real heroes like characters in the stories of Northern authors. Thus, the children only play war games. In his writing, they are still children, the most innocent and purest of children. What Duyên Anh discovers is the innocence and sincere love of children. That passionate love ignites in the children the flame of national pride and love for the fatherland, which is boldly displayed in *Mơ thành người Quang Trung* (Dream to be a Quang Trung, 1969). That innocent love binds young hearts and innocent souls together under all circumstances. They fight not for money, not for interests, and not for selfish desires like adults. Their reason is much simpler. It is fun. The fighting game is a child's imitation of adults. In other words, the adult world judged from children's perspective is more innocent. After each of those "wars," whether winning or losing, the children are all happy, "They all laugh. They forget about losing the battle, and they jump into the river to bathe and scrub."[24] Duyên Anh grasps the psychological characteristics of children, playful and easily distracted, as vividly expressed through his characters. The portrayals of children in his writings are real and sharp, and include the naughtiest, the most innocent, and the kindest of children.

A special feature in children's thinking is that it is strongly influenced by emotions, reflected in the fact that "children only think about things they like, and their thought is often caught up in their own whims, regardless of the influence of objective reality."[25] In Duyên Anh's stories, readers could easily recognize this psychological feature in his innocent child characters. Typically, Khoa, in *Thằng Vũ* (Vu, 1967), Vũ's younger brother: Vũ is the apple of Khoa's eyes. He praises Vũ all the time about everything from playing soccer and shooting birds to fighting and even riding a bicycle. Children's feelings are artless, innocent, impulsive. and full of subjectivity. Khoa's unconditional love toward Vũ is simple as brotherhood. Another exemplary character is Nghiêm, in *Tuổi mười ba* (Thirteen, 1971), who is ready to give Hải the highest score in the contest between Dực and Hải just because Dực gave him "a little copra."

Taking on the perspective of children, Duyên Anh has built a world of lively, lovely, naughty, and innocent characters. Reading his novels, the sequence of joyful

---

[24] Duyên Anh, *Mơ thành*, 44.

[25] Nguyễn, *Tâm lí học*, 286.

images such as sunny schoolyards or spacious playgrounds full of children playing traditional games shows his desire to go back in time. In the chaotic society of that time, the characters of innocent children could be seen as either the embodiment of the author's past or his moral expectation of leaving the present.

The "Dreamy Child" Character

In the South of Vietnam, before 1975, the United States involvement in modernizing the South led to the disappearance of pure images such as child characters in literary works. Recognizing the actual depravity of culture, some authors like Duyên Anh, Từ Kế Tường, or Nhã Ca made an effort to save children's innocence via their publications. *Tuổi Ngọc* magazine, edited by Duyên Anh, was a place to collect the works of writers with coming-of-age stories, namely *Tuổi mười ba* (Thirteen, 1971), *Phượng vĩ* (Poinciana 1972), *Lứa tuổi thích ô mai* (Those like ô-mai, 1971*), Áo tiểu thư* (Lady's shirt, 1971*),* or *Anh Chi yêu dấu* (Dear Chi, 1974). Duyên Anh was a writer moving from the North to the South after 1954, which was not simply a spatial but a major shift, changing both his spiritual life and his perspectives. This historic relocation left traces in his compositions. All literary compositions written before 1975 were Duyên Anh's life. According to Võ Phiến, in his book *Tổng quan văn học Việt Nam* (Southern Literary Review), the separatists were still haunted, they looked back at their vibrant past or, as Nguyễn Vy Khanh (1951–) insisted, Duyên Anh was someone who lived in the past.[26] As Duyên Anh, himself, said, "I am haunted by the past, memories and the small sky of my homeland."[27] He wrote for people like him and for their dreams to live a normal life in which people treated each other with sincerity. Thus, using innocent and dreamy child characters in his writings could be a remedy for Duyên Anh, to ease his soul in a dystopic society.

When the stories are about children, people pay little attention to the gender discrimination between the characters, but when the stories are about teenagers, readers can clearly see the difference in the characters of teenage girls and boys. Taking a psychological point of view, Nguyễn Ánh Tuyết in *Tâm lý học trẻ em* (Children's Psychology 1998) stated that when children are younger, gender discrimination does not attract much attention. However, in children's playing activities, there have also been certain gender orientations. Boys like to play strong, forceful games, such as playing marbles, arm wrestling, and fighting. Girls like to play games about care and using ingenuity, such as dolls, role-playing, and jumping rope. However, at such a young age, when signs of puberty have not physically become visible, it seems that children do not have many concerns about gender, and at the same time, emotions and feelings to the opposite sex have not emerged. At puberty, the sense of gender becomes more pronounced, creeping into friendship relationships, making girls and boys suddenly become different people. A guy who is arrogant, brave, or

---

[26] Nguyễn, *Văn học miền Nam.*

[27] Huỳnh, *Duyên Anh.*

bad, suddenly, encountering friends of the opposite sex may have some physical reactions such as blushing, awkward gestures, and faltering speech. A little girl, formerly sloppy, often yelling at her friends, now knows how to be tactful, discreet, timid, and not so casual with friends of the opposite sex. The degree of this change depends on the depth of the relationship between the teenage boys and girls. Teenage boys and girls particularly have started to have tender sensations that, at times, can disappear as quickly as they appear. In such times, they often fall into a state of "drunkenness" and can absolutize love, considering the lover as their one and only idol. They have impulsive, innocent actions that, surely, will never be possible when they are adults.

In literary texts, teenage boys are described as naive, romantic, and very amorous. Khoa, in *Tuổi mười ba* (Thirteen, 1971), steals his mother's pickled plum and puts it in his mouth to give his girlfriend as a present. Nhân, in *Áo tiểu thư* (Lady's shirt. 1971*)*, raises his eyes and looks dumbfounded because of one charming smile from a girl on the street. Her smile brightens up Nhân's world, encouraging him to eat three more bowls of rice, memorize the lengthy lesson, and stay up a little later.[28] Also in this story is Thủy—a daydreamer who is thinking the about one day Hòa did not come back to see him.[29]

In the stories about the teenagers written by the authors of *Tuổi Ngọc* weekly magazine, the main character is hardly ever a female. Nevertheless, the reverse is seen in the stories of Duyên Anh, Từ Kế Tường (1946–), Đinh Tiến Luyện (1947–), and Hoàng Ngọc Tuấn (1947–2005). The noticeable feature of teenage girls in their writings is shyness and secretiveness. Most of them are illustrated through the eyes of passionate boys, so every girl is the most beautiful, the loveliest, and the cutest person. In Duyên Anh's story named *Phượng vĩ* (Poinciana 1972), the scent of Phượng's hair has made the sloppiest students try to fix their collars and hair. She becomes the symbol of beauty, described with many exaggerations, for instance: "The abusive language is only used when she is absent. She makes the unruly students turn into bewildered yellow deer. She does not understand that she is the authority of the class. She is the late autumn leaves. She is a lost bird. She is a fairy pushed down to earth."[30] The female characters in the coming-of-age stories of the writers of *Tuổi Ngọc* possess the clumsiness, innocence, and purity of a girl who is in the process of becoming an adult.

Conclusion

It can be said that there are disparities in terms of portraying child characters in the children's literature of the North and South of Vietnam in the period of 1954–1975. While Northern children's literature puts emphasis on three types of

---

[28] Duyên Anh, *Áo tiểu thư,* 205.

[29] Ibid., 206.

[30] Duyên Anh, *Phượng vĩ,* 24.

child characters—young heroes, young workers and exemplary young characters—
South Vietnamese children's literature portrays child characters either under difficult
circumstances or in their dreamy innocence. Social, cultural, and historical factors
are responsible for these differences.

In the North, Revolutionary literature gave priority to promoting the resistance
via diverse symbols, from soldiers to young children. The founding of Kim Đồng
publishing house marked a milestone in the development of Vietnamese children's
literature. The topic of the war of resistance against the United States is reflected
in many literary works, such as *Những đứa con trong gia đình* (Children in family,
1966), *Em bé bên bờ sông Lai Vu* (A child by river Lai Vu, 1960), or *Đội thiếu niên
du kích Đình Bảng* (Đình Bảng—A guerilla unit, 1975). Although war is a sensitive
topic, these publications use child characters to highlight the spirit of resistance in
a sophisticated way. The daily life of Northern socialist children is also a source
of inspiration for Northern authors, presented in *Chú bé sợ Toán* (Young boy fears
of Math, 1971), *Mái trường thân yêu* (Dear school, 1964) or *Những tia nắng đầu
tiên* (The first sunlight, 1971). The wide acceptance by readers and the great number
of literary works for children in the North of Vietnam might give the impression
that Southern children's literature is inferior. Despite being a part of the national
history of literature, Southern children's literature attracts only a modest number of
researchers. Thus, the study of Southern children's literature and its establishment
on the Vietnamese literary map is urgent and worth undertaking.

The South of Vietnam between 1954 and 1975 was in general not influenced by
political goals, therefore, child characters either reflect the author's realistic view
of society or their attempt to sustain national values. Portrayals of child characters
in the South Vietnamese literature can be divided into four types: street children
(wanderer character), unhappy children, innocent children, and dreamy children.
Among authors who use children as subjects in their literary production before 1975,
Duyên Anh and Nhật Tiến are the most successful, with over fifty and over twenty
works, respectively. Readers can thus partly grasp the historical and social context of
the South as well as the psychological, hidden corners of the spiritual life of the young
generation in the South at that time. To describe the fierceness and damages of wars,
two authors use wanderers and unhappy child characters who may be the most vulnerable victims, existing without sentiment or orientation. Moreover, since both Duyên
Anh and Nhật Tiến find their intricate society unbearable, writing about a peaceful
childhood may be an appropriate rescue as well as a good way to protest. Innocent
and dreamy child characters are qualified representatives for what the writers desire.

To conclude, South Vietnamese children's literature is an integral part of Vietnamese children's literature. There is no denying that it is a literary heritage that
needs to be studied comprehensively. Although the number of authors using child
characters in this genre of literature is limited and the target audience of these texts is
mainly children over thirteen years old, a considerable number of works written by
Duyên Anh and Nhật Tiến clearly shows the face of this literature. By surveying the
portrayals of children in this genre, there is no denying that this literature from the
South of Vietnam is a vibrant field with a hidden value that is well worth exploring.

Bibliography

Bùi TT (2007) Thi pháp Văn học thiếu nhi (Poetics in children's literature). Dự án phát triển dạy học, Huế

Bùi TT, Nga Quỳnh Thị Trần, và Tâm Thanh Nguyễn (2012) Giáo trình văn học 2 (Textbook of literature 2). Nhà xuất bản Đại học Huế, Huế

Cao KH (1974) Vấn đề khuynh hướng trong tiểu thuyết miền Nam từ 1954 đến 1973 (Trends in south fiction from 1954 to 1973). Thời Tập, no. 4

Chonchirdsin S (2016) Chiến tranh Việt Nam: Trẻ em thời chiến (The vietnam war: children at war). Asian and African Studies Blog, 24 February 2016. https://blogs.bl.uk/asian-and-african/2016/02/the-vietnam-war-children-at-war.html

Dror O (2018) Làm nên hai Việt Nam: Chiến tranh và Bản sắc Thanh niên 1965–1975 (Making two Vietnams: war and youth identities 1965–1975). Cambridge University Press, Texas

Duyên A (1960) Con sáo của em tôi. Tuổi Ngọc, Sài Gòn

Duyên A (1963) Điệu ru nước mắt. Nhà xuất bản Đời mới, Sài Gòn

Duyên A (1964) Ảo vọng tuổi trẻ. Tuổi Ngọc, Sài Gòn

Duyên A (1967) Thằng Vũ. Tuổi Ngọc, Gia Định

Duyên A (1968) Giấc mơ một loài cỏ. Nhà xuất bản Đời mới, Sài Gòn

Duyên A (1969a) Thằng Côn. Tuổi Ngọc, Gia Định

Duyên A (1969b) Mơ thành người Quang Trung. Vàng Son, Gia Định

Duyên A (1969) Ánh mắt trông theo. Nhà xuất bản Đời Mới, Sài Gòn

Duyên A (1970) Mặt trời nhỏ. Nhà xuất bản Đồng Nai, Biên Hòa

Duyên A (1971a) Áo tiểu thư. Nhà xuất bản Đồng Nai, Biên Hòa

Duyên A (1971b) Giặc Ô kê. Nhà xuất bản Đồng Nai, Biên Hòa

Duyên A (1971c) Lứa tuổi thích ô mai. Nhà xuất bản Đồng Nai, Biên Hòa

Duyên A (1971d) Tuổi mười ba. Nhà xuất bản Đồng Nai, Biên Hòa

Duyên A (1971e) Tuổi Ngọc. Nhà xuất bản Đồng Nai, Biên Hòa

Duyên A (1972) Phượng vĩ. Nhà xuất bản Đồng Nai, Biên Hòa

Duyên A (1975) Dấu chân sỏi đá. Sài Gòn: Nhà xuất bản Việt Nam

Đinh LT (1974) Anh Chi yêu dấu. Nhà xuất bản Thời Đại, Sài Gòn

Đinh TQA (2020) Dương Thu Hương: '30 tháng Tư 75, nền văn minh đã thua chế độ man rợ' (Dương Thu Hương: April 30th '75, Civilization loses to a barbaric regime), Người Việt April 12, 2012. Quoted in Nguyễn Lập Duy, Một cộng đồng có thật: Chủ nghĩa đế quốc và văn hóa miền Nam Việt Nam (The unimagined community: imperialism and culture in South Vietnam). Manchester University Press, Manchester, p 182.

Huỳnh AP (2019) Duyên Anh, anh là ai? (Who is Duyên Anh), Văn học Sài Gòn, 19 October, 2019. https://vanhocsaigon.com/duyen-anh-anh-la-ai/

Huỳnh PN (2019) Văn học miền Nam Việt Nam 1954–1975: những khuynh hướng chủ yếu và thành tựu hiện đại hoá (Vietnamese literature in South Vietnam 1954–1975: literary trends and modernization). In: Những vấn đề giảng dạy tiếng Việt và nghiên cứu Việt Nam trong thế giới ngày nay. Nhà xuất bản Đại học Quốc gia Thành phố Hồ Chí Minh, Sài Gòn, pp 710–23.

Lã LBT (2003) Giáo trình Văn học trẻ em (Children's literature textbook). Nhà xuất bản Đại học Sư phạm Hà Nội, Hà Nội

Lương HT (2009) Thuyết hiện sinh tại Việt Nam: Đánh giá phê bình (Vietnamese existential philosophy: a critical reappraisal). PhD thesis, Temple University Graduate Board, Philadelphia

Nguyễn KV (2014) Văn học miền Nam Tự Do 1954–1975 phần 1—Một thời văn chương (South literature: freedom 1954–1975, chapter 1—a literary period). https://nhavannhattien.wordpress.com/van-hoc-mien-nam-tu-do-1954-1975-nguyen-vy-khanh/

Nguyễn KV (2016) Văn học miền Nam Tự Do 1954–1975 phần 2—Thế giới nhân bản của Nhật Tiến (South literature: freedom 1954–1975, chapter 2—the world of humanity of Nhật Tiến). http://vanviet.info/van-hoc-mien-nam/van-hoc-mien-nam-54-75209-nhat-tien-2/

Nguyễn LD (2020) Một cộng đồng có thật: Chủ nghĩa đế quốc và văn hóa miền Nam Việt Nam (The unimagined community: imperialism and culture in South Vietnam). Manchester University Press, Manchester

Nguyễn TTT (2007) Vài nét về văn xuôi đô thị miền Nam giai đoạn 1954–1975 (Some features of urban novels in the South in the period 1954–1975), Tạp chí *Nghiên cứu Văn học*, no 5

Nguyễn TÁ (1998) Tâm lí học trẻ em (Children's psychology). Nhà xuất bản Giáo dục, Hà Nội

Nhật T (1969) Những người áo trắng (In lần thứ 3). Nhà xuất bản Huyền Trân, Sài Gòn

Nhật T (1968) Tay ngọc (In lần thứ 2). Nhà xuất bản Đông Phương, Sài Gòn

Nhật T (1966) Chim hót trong lồng. Nhà xuất bản Huyền Trân, Sài Gòn

Phạm CP (2021) Văn học và công cuộc xây dựng đất nước ở Việt Nam (Literature and nation-building in Vietnam). Routledge, New York

Từ TK (1974) Đường phượng bay. Nhà xuất bản Thư Trung, Sài Gòn

Văn H (2012) Văn học thiếu nhi nửa thế kỉ một chặng đường (Children's literature—a half century and one road). Nhà xuất bản Kim Đồng, Hà Nội

Văn H (2002) Từ mục đồng đến kim đồng (From herdsman to Kim Đồng). Nhà xuất bản Kim Đồng, Hà Nội

Vân T (1999) Phác thảo văn học thiếu nhi Việt Nam (Review of Vietnam children's literature). Nhà xuất bản Khoa học Xã hội, Hà Nội

Vết thù trên lưng con ngựa hoang (Back wound on the wild horse), Wikipedia. Accessed November 25, 2021. https://vi.wikipedia.org/wiki/V%E1%BA%BFt_th%C3%B9_h%E1%BA%B1n_tr%C3%AAn_l%C6%B0ng_con_ng%E1%BB%B1a_hoang

Võ P (1986) Hai mươi năm Văn Học Miền Nam (Twenty years of literature in South Vietnam, 1945–1975: overview). Quoted in Nguyễn, Lập Duy. Một cộng đồng có thật: Chủ nghĩa đế quốc và văn hóa miền Nam Việt Nam (The unimagined community: imperialism and culture in South Vietnam). Manchester University Press, Manchester, 2020, p 186

Võ P (2021) Văn học miền Nam: Tổng quan (South Vietnam literature: an overview). Người Việt, California. Accessed November 25, 2021. https://sachtruyen.net/xem-sach/van-hoc-mien-nam-tong-quan.006a3

Nguyễn Thị Thanh Hương did her Ph.D. dissertation at Hanoi National University of Education where she works as a tenured lecturer at the Faculty of Early Childhood Education. Her main research is about children's literature in Vietnam and abroad, children literature and early childhood education, early literacy education, and impacts of culture on the learning environment.

Nguyễn Minh Thu is a tenured lecturer at Faculty of English, Hanoi Open University. She has been a Ph.D. candidate in Foreign Literature at Graduate Academy of Social Sciences in 2021. Her research focuses on Foreign Literature, Vietnamese Literature and Cognitive Linguistics. She first published a paper entitled *Hannibal Lecter in The Silence of the Lambs: From Literature to Cinema* (Journal of Social Sciences Manpower, 2021) and made a presentation of *The Art of Building Psychological Criminal Characters on Korean Screen: Comparison between the Film Dark Figures of Crime (Kim Tae-gyun) and The Silence of the Lambs (Jonathan Demme)* at the International Conference "Studies on Vietnamese and Korean Literature and Films in the Context of Globalization" held by the University of Social Sciences and Humanities, Vietnam National University Ho Chi Minh City (VNUHCM-USSH). In 2022, her most recent researches include *Anti-detective and Paul Auster's novels* (Literary Studies, No. 5, 2022) and *The co-occurrence of Confucianism, Buddhism and Taoism in Nguyen Cong Tru's poems: Reading "Bai ca ngat nguong"* (accepted to present at ARI 17th Singapore Graduate Forum on Southeast Asian Studies of National University of Singapore in late July).

The Wave of Existentialist Feminism in South Vietnamese Literature (1955–1975)

Thai Phan Vang Anh

Introduction

Southern literature in the 1955–1975 period was an integral part of modern Vietnamese literature. However, in the long period since the unification of the country (1975), due to specific historical and political conditions, Vietnamese literature critics and researchers have not really paid due attention to this literature group. The earliest research works on South Vietnamese literature were mainly conducted before 1975 by Southern writers and critics in contemporary literary and artistic magazines. Due to an unnecessary time lag, there were not many summative studies on the literary period. The most notable were the articles "Sơ thảo 15 năm văn xuôi miền Nam (1955–1969)" (First Draft of 15 Years of Southern Prose (1955–1969)),"[1] and a series of editorials by Cao Huy Khanh about Southern fiction published in *Thoi Tap* magazine.[2] These were considered the earliest reviews of a literary period, covering Southern fiction before 1975. In addition, although not generally reviewing the whole of Southern literature, Ta Ty, for the work titled *Ten Artistic Faces Today*,[3] partially shed light on the face of South Vietnamese literature through portraits of representative authors. In particular, the presence and role of female writers was recognized in the general picture of Vietnamese literature from the beginning of the twentieth century, including Southern female writers in the 1955–1970 period. Uyen Thao, for example, authored a work titled *Vietnamese Female Writers in 1900–1970 period*.[4]

---

[1] Cao, "15 năm văn xuôi." (First Draft of 15 Years of Southern Prose (1955–1969)."

[2] Nguyễn, *Văn học miền Nam tự do.*

[3] Tạ, *Mười khuôn mặt.*

[4] Uyên Thao, *Các nhà văn Nữ.*

T. P. V. Anh (✉)
Hue University, Hue, Vietnam
e-mail: tpvanh@hueuni.edu.vn

After 1975, continuous research work on South Vietnamese literature was divided into categories for political reasons. Works and articles on South Vietnamese literature at this time either were just concerned with the Southern liberation literature (Pham Van Sy, with *Southern Liberation Literature*)[5]; or viewed Southern literature from a critical perspective (work titled *The Southern Art and Culture under the American—Puppet regime,* compiled by Tra Linh and Tran Huu Ta[6]; there was also, for example, a work of two volumes titled *American New Colonial Literature in the South Vietnam from 1954 to 1975* by Le Dinh Ky and Tran Trong Dang Dan.[7] It was not until the first decades of the twenty-first century that the research works on South Vietnamese literature gradually began to attract more attention, notably Huynh Nhu Phuong's article "South Vietnamese Literature 1954–1975: Major Tendencies and Modernization Achievements," printed in the proceedings of the 4th Vietnam International Scientific Conference with the title *Issues of Vietnamese Language Teaching and Study on Vietnam in Today's World.*[8] However, there were still not really many general studies on Southern literature in the 1955–1975 period, especially female literature, compared to the research situation for South Vietnamese literature in foreign countries.

Up to now, the elaborate and valuable research works on Southern literature in the 1955–1975 period have mainly been conducted by Southern writers who left the country or Vietnamese intellectuals living and studying abroad. Expressing viewpoints from those currently living abroad, Vo Phien and Nguyen Vy Khanh produced massive research works. The work titled *Twenty Years of Southern Literature: An Overview*[9];Vo Phien's three-volume research work on short stories, *Southern Literature, Stories,*[10] provided a comprehensive and diverse view of Southern literature and also clearly portrayed many Southern writers in the 1955–1975 period. With the article "Literature of the Liberal South Vietnam, 1954–1975,"[11] and a two-volume work titled *1954–1975 Southern Literature, Volume 1—Overview and 1954–1975 Southern Literature, volume 2, Author,*[12] Nguyen Vy Khanh also made elaborate and profound assessments of a part of Southern literature. To attract the attention of readers and the world's research community, a number of conferences on Southern literature were organized, such as *Southern Literature Conference 1954–1975* in Westminster, Southern California, on 6–7 December 2014. In particular, many research works and doctoral theses on South Vietnamese literature, published in English, helped the world understand Southern literature better. Among these works, the most notable was *Women Writers of South Vietnam, 1954–1975* by Cong

---

[5] Phạm, *Văn học giải phóng.*

[6] Trà Linh, *Văn nghệ Miền Nam.*

[7] Lê, *Văn học thực dân.*

[8] Huỳnh, "Văn học miền nam."

[9] Võ, *Hai mươi năm văn học.*

[10] Võ, *Văn học miền Nam, truyện.*

[11] Nguyễn, "Văn học miền Nam tự do."

[12] Nguyễn, *Văn học miền Nam – Tác giả.*

Huyen Ton Nu Nha Trang.[13] This was one of the most elaborate research works on Southern female writers with study and evaluations of the appearance and contributions of female writers, associated with specific literary periods for the 20 years from 1954 to 1975 in South Vietnam.

Thus, up to now in Vietnam there have not been many general studies of South Vietnamese literature, especially female literature. Studies on female literature as a separate trend, contributing to a diverse picture in the writing style of Southern literature, have not yet been taken notice of. This article aims to introduce the emergence, positions, and achievements within the phenomenon of Vietnamese female literature, seen from a gender perspective. It could be said that, in the 60s and 70s of the twentieth century in Vietnam, for the very first time, there were professional female writers who contributed a great deal to female literature and earned a place equal to the male writers. Not only that, from absorbing modern Western thoughts, they, the women of the Vietnam, created a wave of existentialist feminism, contributing to bringing Vietnamese literature into the orbit of modernist literature. The spirit of existentialist feminism was clearly expressed through the conceptions and experiences in the writing style of South Vietnamese female writers.

Receipt of Western Thoughts—Existentialism and Feminism

The cultural, political, and social conditions of the Republic of Vietnam period proved to be favorable for the penetration of Western philosophical-aesthetic thoughts into the life and soul of the Orient. War, social crisis, and the lifestyle of the subsequent materialist civilization and the daily confrontation with death gave rise to anxiety, boredom, and skepticism in a group of contemporary writers and artists. The widely-introduced modern philosophical-aesthetic tendencies were suitable for the mood of a generation of Vietnamese writers who were thirsty for new ideas of universal scope. In particular, existentialist philosophy and feminism were warmly received.[14]

Existentialism is a philosophy of human condition. The question of human dignity was posed by philosophers such as E. Husserl and M. Heidegger, who were considered to be the origin of a meditation literature trend that reflected the human condition. Considered the "ancestor" of existentialism, Jean-Paul Sartre, with his question "Who am I?" more or less decided the fate of world literature, as well as creating a starting point in the formation of an existentialist line of fiction, an important change in twentieth-century Western fiction.

After existentialist philosophy, feminism (consisting of branches with different tendencies) was gradually spread throughout the world. In 1929, the essay *A Room of One's Own* by Virginia Woolf soon raised the question of female literature. Virginia Woolf appealed to women in writing by affirming some certain female styles. According to her, Jane Austen wrote like "role-playing in every word," and Emily

---

[13] Cong Huyen Ton Nu, *Women Writers*.

[14] Võ, *Văn học miền nam: tổng quan*, 153.

Bronte, "instead of writing in wisdom, wrote in madness. Instead of writing about her characters, she wrote about herself."[15] In 1949, when Simone de Beauvoir wrote *Le Deuxième Sexe* (The Second Sex), feminist criticism was established as a fundamental theory. Simone De Beauvoir was both influenced by Sartre's existentialist conception and "contributed to pushing existentialism in a more positive direction. Instead of being tired, bored by the 'meaningless' of life, or like many existentialists, likening the human life to that of 'cockroaches, bugs,' Simone De Beauvoir emphasized active existence."[16] Engaging in dialogue with Sartre, de Beauvoir admitted that existentialists asserted human dignity, but the female presence in works was still obscure and faint.

The reception of modern Western philosophical-aesthetic trends, especially existentialist literature, made Southern literature begin to change its direction. A group of Southern writers and artists found in existentialism a philosophical question about the essence of human dignity "Human, who are you?" This was the essence that made existentialist theory quickly spread and become strongly influential in some Southern literature in the 60s of the twentieth century. On equal footing in both composing and receiving, Southern female writers promptly contributed to the current existentialist literature that was the contemporary mainstream. While male writers raised their voices filled with boredom, protest, and tragedy (Duong Nghiem Mau, Mai Thao, Thanh Tam Tuyen), female writers began to speak out to affirm the human dignity of women. On the other hand, in adopting Western feminist theory, the Southern female writers pioneered in expressing the status of a woman in an absurd existence, and asserted female dignity in the variable historical-social context, in people's worry, confusion, and disbelief. They were also directly influenced by Simone de Beauvoir, the founder of existentialist feminism. Each female writer in the South had a voice of her own, but when female writers "spoke out" and "wanted to be listened" to, they created the first wave of feminism in Vietnam.

Controversial Issues of Women's Writing in Vietnam

In Vietnam, it was not until the early twentieth century that, upon reception of modern Western culture and literature, female writers began to appear in the literary forums and to receive attention, although their voices still did not have a widespread effect in the society. Female literature only really became a major genre in the 1960s, especially in the South, associated with the Republic of Vietnam.

The emergence of the wave of existentialist feminism in South Vietnamese literature (1955–1975) was inevitable and also caused controversies. Contemporary critics raised questions around the following issues: Was there really a writing style that had characteristics unique to women? Did these women's voices make up the discourse of the era, the voice of their gender, or they were just the private voices of the women

---

[15] Woolf, *Căn phòng riêng*, 112, 115.

[16] Lê, "Simone De Beauvoir."

who wrote? "The question was why, by what reason, was there the brilliant presence of Vietnamese female writers?" "How did female literature impact on readers? (Mai Thao)."[17]

From the perspective of affirming and explaining the rise of female writers in the 60s and 70s in South Vietnam, Mai Thao has said: "Women doing literature at present meant speaking up for the rights of life, equality and freedom as in men's life"[18]; "The breaking and rupturing of their old ties to reach this new frontier – that was literature."[19] From a skeptical perspective, Huynh Phan Anh posed the question: "Was women's literature currently just a reaction, a rebellion against old limits? Was it something else aside from being a reaction?"[20] Nguyen Nhat Duat has said that female writers were only concerned with worries about happiness, "the women's everlasting worries, and it's only limited to this"; "Bold contents were not freedom but indulgence. (...) The topics they brought up were no different from the topics dealt with by male writers. That was just an inevitable product of society. Because if there were not this Nguyen Thi Hoang, there would be another Nguyen Thi Hoang.[21] In another direction, Vo Phien said that, from 1963, with the emergency of Nguyen Thi Thuy Vu, Trung Duong, Nguyen Thi Hoang, and Minh Duc Hoai Trinh, women became a ... force."[22]

The above-mentioned opinions show that, at the time, the critics in the South did not clearly see the influences of existentialist philosophy and feminist thought in Southern female literature. Even later, despite clearly identifying the characteristics of Southern female literature, some researchers, such as Cong Huyen Ton Nu Nha Trang, still considered the revelation of female identity in literature and a writing style with strong sexual elements to be a limitation: "Women authors did not make the audience forget that they were women and, furthermore, they were much too preoccupied with sex and overly bold in their depiction of it."[23] However, in fact, with the appearance of Nha Ca, Nguyen Thi Hoang, and Nguyen Thi Thuy Vu as best-selling authors (in 1966)[24] and other beloved female writers such as Tuy Hong, Trung Duong, Tran Thi Ngh, and Le Hang, a female line of literature was established parallel to male literature in the 60s and 70s in South Vietnam. This was considered the first female literature wave in the history of Vietnamese literature. The appearance of a large number of female writers in Southern literature was a sign of gender equality in composition—in the publication field, in terms of the public's reception, in terms of gender. As said by Uyen Thao: "...the timid appearance of women had made them less apparent in cultural and artistic activities, this appearance had often created a prejudice that women could not occupy an official seat in cultural

---

[17] Huỳnh, "Về các nhà văn nữ," 12.

[18] Ibid., 2.

[19] Ibid., 2.

[20] Ibid., 7.

[21] Ibid., 3.

[22] Võ, *Văn học miền Nam, tổng quan*, 247.

[23] Cong Huyen Ton Nu, *Women Writers*.

[24] Uyên Thao, *Các nhà văn nữ*, 20.

and artistic activities."[25] Female writers soon established a discourse of their own: the feminist discourse of a generation of women began to include speaking out against masculinist thoughts; it became an existentialist discourse of egos claiming the right to life.

Expressions of Existential Feminist Perception in Female Writers' Compositions Regarding the Writing Concept

Female writers in the South of the Republic "considered writing work as a profession. They made their living completely by this profession, pursued and continued it to the end,"[26] and overcame social prejudices against women's writing. Nguyen Thi Thuy Vu mainly earned money to raise her children by writing *feuilletons* (stories with many episodes) in the daily newspapers after giving up her career as a teacher. Nha Ca did not hesitate to give up her family and changed her last name to pursue her writing career. Literature was a place for female writers to express a particular ego to establish a way of life, a way of writing. Female writers publicly declared the notion of writing, the sense of composition as a professional activity as an expression of themselves.

The essence of existentialism was to affirm human dignity and promote freedom. From the works of female writers, it could be seen that for them writing was an affirmation of existence. Writing, for female writers of the Republic of Vietnam, was "an act of escape"; "escape from the ruined sunset of a family. Escape from a stagnant space in the province. Escape from the dull and lonely haunts of the girl who lived in the ancient house, listened to the sap in her drying up and her heart loosened in rhythm from languishing."[27] Writing was also a way to respect women, assert female dignity, was "the self-confirmation of their female existence."[28] Talking about "the ability and the direction of women's artistic creation," Nguyen Thi Hoang said: "Objectively and impartially, the fact that we identify women as a minority in the world of literature comes from the strict prejudice of Asian society, the concept that women's writing was romantically loose, a germ that spoiled life and the soul, partly because women's lives were limited and restricted by rules of behavior, and therefore not rich in employment."[29] Set in the context of Vietnamese society at that time, still heavily influenced by feudal ritualistic thought, the decision of living and writing as female writers of the Republic of Vietnam was a challenging one. Consciously, female writers fought for gender equality, for their characters and for themselves, through the medium of stories. Female writers "did not create their admittedly restricted world of fiction based on prescriptive values; rather, they drew

---

[25] Ibid., 28.

[26] Huỳnh, "Về các nhà văn nữ," 2.

[27] Nguyễn, *Chút duyên tình đọc*, 172.

[28] Huỳnh, "Về các nhà văn nữ," 9.

[29] Nguyễn, *Phương hướng sáng tạo*, 4, 5.

their subject matter from keen observation of their own immediate experiences, which rendered the world they described more vivid, more real; and more human."[30]

Existential Topics

Female writers experienced and established an existential feminist writing style, bringing South Vietnamese literature into the period of modernist literature. Female writers delved into existential topics such as anxiety, disbelief, loneliness, rebellion, freedom, and death.[31] In favor of "rebellion," Nguyen Thi Hoang made an impression with her debut work: *Vòng tay học trò* (Students' Arms) is the voice of longing, hidden repression, suppression, and the exuberance of a love that transcended barriers between a young teacher and a high school student. With *Vòng tay học trò* (Students' Arms), and then many other works, Nguyen Thi Hoang spoke out and forced the society to listen to the voice of women, the voice of existential obsessions in the context of Southern society in the years of fierce war. *Tôi nhìn tôi trên vách* (I Look at Myself on the Wall—Tuy Hong) expressed concerns about the status of women in marriages with strong masculine ideology. Trung Duong "became a spokesman for existentialist philosophy in the South, expressed through literature and she followed the footsteps of Francoise Sagan in France.[32] In another direction, Nha Ca chose war topics. In her writings, war, youth, and death were existential obsessions. The repeated deaths in the writer's works showed the fate of people in a turbulent time. In *Đêm nghe tiếng đại bác* (Listening to the Night Cannon), Nha Ca mentioned the mood of a young generation who always had had to face the fierce reality of war: "The youth of blood. The youth of bombs and bullets. The youth of the broken."[33] *Đêm nghe tiếng đại bác* (Listening to the Night Cannon), *Đoàn nữ binh mùa thu* (Autumn Women's Troops), *Tình ca trong lửa đỏ* (Love Song in Red Fire) were fictions that affirmed Nha Ca's name in contemporary female prose.

Nguyen Thi Thuy Vu appeared later. However, her short stories and fictions caused much shock in literary forums. She overcame old prejudices in writing about new topics that were not those usually chosen by women. Characters in Thuy Vu's works were from the scum of society (whores, women married to Americans, bar girls) and had women's fates much affected by war. The familiar spaces in Thuy Vu's works were bars in Saigon. The stuffiness and hustle of life crowded into a narrow space showed the lives of girls who were despised and longed for escaping. According to writer Le Van Nghia: "She became the first and only writer to introduce the status of women into Saigon's literature in a time of bombs and bullets."[34]

---

[30] Cong Huyen Ton Nu, *Women Writers*.

[31] Mounier, *Chủ đề triết hiện sinh*.

[32] Du, *Khác biệt về tính dục*.

[33] Nhã Ca, *Đêm nghe tiếng đại bác*, 69.

[34] Lê, *Văn học Sài Gòn*, 450.

With a generation of female writers, for the first time, the Vietnamese woman dared to simultaneously speak out to demand "smashing everything to rebuild," "not wanting and not needing to think about things afterwards. Present. Just for now. Otherwise, the rest of life would become dismal and insipid" *(Vòng tay học trò/Students' Arms)*. Women's happiness at this time lay in themselves, with the desire to "be their own God" so that "life could be more than that, different from that" *(Bóng tối thời con gái/Maiden Darkness—Nhã Ca, Cho trận gió kinh thiên/For the Dreadful Wind)*. They were conscious of their commitment to finding themselves. The female characters in the literature of Nha Ca, Nguyen Thi Thuy Vu, and Nguyen Thi Hoang had the permanent desire to flee. Ms. Hanh, on her own, broke through the *"maiden darkness"* (name of Nha Ca's work) by deciding "Where do I go. I still go. Take clear steps. But fail to answer." Ms. Nguyet had in mind the "search for another city with a desire to change the atmosphere and life full of sadness in the provincial capital. She had to stay away from her native place which was like arms tightly embracing her when she was a child, luckily she had an opportunity to stand up and live a real life" *(Cho trận gió kinh thiên/For the Dreadful Wind*—Nguyen Thi Thuy Vu). Ms. Tram considered "living as a cold move," "I don't know where to go, but I go," so that "Somewhere else, I will change in the constantly changing performances of a big life stage. It can be fresher, but it can be also worse. But I feel contented to occupy a splendid fairytale life in this place. Putting together a beautiful memory of today for the following few months" *(Vòng tay học trò/Students' Arms*—Nguyen Thi Hoang). Dare to live fiercely, to taste the pain and even pay the costs for a meaningful present is a bold existential choice. Was that why female writers wrote a lot about love? "They saw love as freedom, since it was beyond the control of consciousness. Consciousness is morality; therefore, love is beyond the control of morality rather than being immorality."[35] And, "in almost all literary works created by women Vietnamese existential writers, mutual love is the basis and core value in adopting and establishing other values."[36]

A new point in the conceptions and compositions of female writers is the mention of women's sexuality. In the 60s and 70s of the twentieth century, the explosion of sexual literature in the South caused backlashes. The concept that sexual literature was peripheral was still quite common. According to Huynh Phan Anh, "there has never been a historical period in which sexuality has dominated our literature so heavily. It becomes the ideal climate of literature. It becomes a measure to estimate the 'progress' of a writer, a fashion of art."[37] Taking issue with "prejudices" about sexuality and affirming the existentialist feminist spirit became a cross-cutting topic in the prose of female writers in the Republic of Vietnam. For example, in *Tình yêu như băng sơn* (Love like Iceberg), the author borrowed the words of Ms. Thuy, a woman who was betrayed and forsaken, to question about women's motherhood, about the unjust differences between love in and out of marriage: "Why is it called

[35] Nguyễn, *Chủ nghĩa hiện sinh*, 135.
[36] Luong, *Vietnamese Existential Philosophy*, 49.
[37] Huỳnh, *Đi tìm tác phẩm*, 84–85.

pregnancy out of wedlock?" "And why did I have to run away from home? Meanwhile, many women in the city with a smack showed off their husband's belly? [...] Do they have the right to love while we don't have the right to love each other if we don't get married and put on shackles?" (*Tình yêu như băng sơn/Love like Iceberg*— Le Hang). In order for character Hiep Duc to express herself, Nguyen Thi Thuy Vu also brought up the bitterness of women when they made mistakes or committed crimes: "Women commit crimes because they love someone and then kill a life in their uterus, they have to pay a high price [...]. They must swallow tears, cover their face and go elsewhere, so that tomorrow they will have the opportunity to marry" (*Thú hoang/Wild Animals*). And despite being "enthralled" as well as easily moved by physical lust, the women in the prose of female writers of the Republic of Vietnam also brought up questions about the responsibility of men in love relationships (*Đêm tối bao la/Vast Dark Night*—Nguyen Thi Thuy Vu, *Tình yêu như băng sơn/Love like Iceberg*—Le Hang).

Existentialism conceived the body as the root of existence, "I" could not exist without the body. Upholding their existence together with a body, inside a body, the female writers of the Republic of Vietnam brought sexual desires into literature, promoted the right to consecrate and seek pleasure in love. The female characters in their prose were always female egos who dared to publicize their physical desires (*Vòng tay học trò/Students' Arms, Ngày qua bóng tối/Day through the Darkness* by Nguyen Thi Hoang); accepted having to bury love desires (*Mưa trên cây sầu đông/Rain on Neem Tree, Ngày qua bóng tối/Darkness in the Maiden Period* by Nha Ca) or lost themselves because of love and lust (*Tình yêu như băng sơn/Love as Iceberg, Chết cho tình yêu/Death for Love* by Le Hang).

Experimentation and Establishment of a Female Writing Style

Though diverse in styles, in general the Southern female writers did jointly establish a kind of writing style—the existentialist feminist style. A whole generation of writers "no longer stood on a precarious roadside but existed in daily life, were present in all areas that previously had only had the presence of men").[38]

In her studies on "Gender and Narrative," and "Queering Narratology," Susan Lancer said that "sex," "gender," and "sexuality" were elements of narrative prosody."[39] In narrative works, there was always an intimate relationship between sex and the narrator. However, sex markers were often less evident in heterodiegetic narrators than in homodiegetic narrators. In fictions with homodiegetic narrators, based on gender and sexuality characteristics, readers could know the sex of a character, narrator, or author.

---

[38] Huỳnh, "Về các nhà văn nữ," 16.
[39] Lanser, "Queering Narratology," 396.

In the past, autobiographical writing was often done by men, because women did not dare to reveal themselves. However, with the rise of female voices in the course of literary history, there have been ever more female homogenic narrators. And if the "homogenic narrative voice was considered to be associated with the rise of fiction,"[40] the appearance of the "self-proclaimed" narrator in female fiction was one of the important signs to identify the character of female writing style. This could be clearly seen in the boldly autobiographical fictions of South Vietnamese female writers in the 1955–1975 period. With *Những sợi sắc không* (Bodily Form and Void), Tuy Hong delved into herself and brought herself to the writing page. Nguyen Thi Thuy Vu wrote from the author's family and private life stories. *Mưa không ướt đất* (Rain without Wetting Soil) was created from the physical experiences of author Trung Duong. Nguyen Thi Hoang transformed into the character of teacher Tram in *Vòng tay học trò* (Students' Arms). Many writers also tended to tell stories from the first person perspective, such as Le Hang (*Tình yêu như băng sơn/Love like Iceberg, Bản tango cuối cùng/The Last Tango, Chết cho tình yêu/Die for Love, Mắt tím/Purple Eyes,* and *Tóc mây/Cloud Hair*), and Nguyen Thi Hoang (*Vòng tay học trò/Students' Arms, Bây giờ và mãi mãi/Now and Forever, Hồn muối, Ngày qua bóng tối/Day through Darkness, Tiếng chuông gọi người tình trở về/Ringing Bell to Call Lover Back,* and *Vào nơi gió cát/Into the Area of Wind and Sand*). The sense of gender, especially in the homodiegetic narrator type in the fiction of Southern female writers, not only created a female writing style but also contributed to a female literary tendency, an existentialist feminist tendency.

The French feminist Luce Irigaray, said—"Excitement, laughter and especially the female body are a place of a specific feminine experience."[41] Paying attention to the relationship between body experience and the creative activity of women, in the work *"The Blank Page" and the Issues of Female Creativity,* Susan Gubar also said that: "Many women experience their own bodies as the only available medium for their art, with the result that the distance between the woman artist and her art is radically diminished."[42] Female writing in general was largely shaped by the sex experiences of women who wrote, and South Vietnamese female writers were no exception. South Vietnamese female writers experimented with body language to express existential aspirations and demands for women's rights, especially for gender equality and for physical experience. For the first time in modern Vietnamese female prose, the authors let the characters directly express their beguiling desires, describe in detail the vibrations of the skin and flesh: "His lips are smooth, the man's breath is strange and wonderful, as if I were no longer me, as if I were downstream and the hazy river water took my body away." "I put my hand in his hair like I was digging into a forbidden forest full of passion [...] I was leaning in his arms, I am really changing, because from now on I can only live while breathing with him" *(Chết cho tình yêu/Death for Love).*

---

[40] Ibid., 189.

[41] Đỗ, *Bút pháp,* 439.

[42] Gubar, "'The Blank Page,'" 296.

It could be said that the writing with sensation, with body language, became a prominent feature in the female prose of the Republic of Vietnam. In the context of Vietnamese society in the 60s and 70s, that had just escaped from feudal society and was still heavily influenced by Confucian thought, the female writers of the Republic of Vietnam still chose to write with the body and thus bring the voice of their world to the fore.

Conclusion

In the twentieth century, in the West, there was a generation of writers who was aware of the ontological loneliness inherent in human nature; a lost generation. In the 60s and 70s of the twentieth century, there was also a generation of writers in South Vietnam who were lost, because of gender discrimination in the writing profession— the generation of existentialist feminist writers such as Nguyen Thi Hoang, Nha Ca, Tuy Hong, Nguyen Thi Thuy Vu, Le Hang, Trung Duong, and others.

In contemporary times, within the particular social context of the South, writing was an opportunity for women to raise their voices for their gender, discuss masculine concepts, break the bonds of traditional ritual. As said by Mai Thao: "Creating a women's literature now means speaking out for the rights of life, equality, and freedom equal to those of a man's life". Their writing was therefore a response, an attitude. This explained the destructive atmosphere, the traces of extremeness that we saw in the feminine works at that time.[43] That destructive and rebellious element was the inevitable manifestation of existential desires which were not inherently the prerogative of men. The extremeness was inherent in the protests and struggles of the feminists in order to force the society and men to listen, admit, and understand. Mai Thao was very delicate when he presaged: "Maybe later the extremism will calm down, and the women's writing will become less narrow in the sense of one voice, one reaction."[44] It could be said that by looking deeply at gender misfortunes, fighting against meninism, requiring society to focus on gender equality, the prose of women in the Republic of Vietnam became the expressive language of women, the expressive language of the times.

It could also be said that, for the first time in the history of Vietnamese litera- ture, there was a generation of professional female writers who carried the mood of the times, carried the aspirations of gender and put them into writing. It is worth mentioning that their literature was full of daring when "regaining the privilege of Thinking, Feeling and Living as male writers"[45] (Nguyen Nhat Duat), when already "achieving something rather more superior than equivalent in quality to the male writers" (Vien Linh). As said by Vo Phien: "In terms of gender, Southern literature in

---

[43] Huỳnh, "Về các nhà văn nữ," 2.

[44] Ibid., 2.

[45] Ibid., 6.

the 1954–1975 period was increasingly under the sway of women."[46] Overcoming gender barriers to be on a par with men; rebelling to awaken the society about the right to live, the right to take initiative in love and sexuality, the female writers of the Republic of Vietnam gave a new vitality to Vietnamese literature on the basis of existentialist feminist ideology.

Thereby, it could be said that literature helped female writers establish gender status and the position of writer in the overall picture of South Vietnamese literature from 1955 to 1975 in particular and in the movement of Vietnamese literature in general. Through a bold writing concept, a distinctive female writing style, and works mentioning existentialist topics, Southern female writers created the first wave of existentialist feminism in Vietnamese literature. Not only affirming the great contributions of women in the achievements of South Vietnamese literature, that wave of existentialist feminist literature also contributed significantly to "body praise," bringing literature dealing with sexuality from the periphery to the center of modern Vietnamese literature. For the past few years, in Vietnam, Southern literature, and especially female literature, has received special attention (evidenced by the fact that many works of some female writers such as Nguyen Thi Hoang and Nguyen Thi Thuy Vu have been reprinted and re-introduced in the early decades of the twenty-first century). This is a good sign for South Vietnamese literature, including female literature, and indicates the importance of further study of this field, using the newer approaches.

Bibliography

Bartky S (1988) Foucault, femininity, and the modernization of patriarchal power. In: Diamond, I, Quinby L (eds) *Feminism and Foucault: reflections and resistance*. Northeastern University Press, Boston, pp 119–134

Butler J (1990) Gender trouble: Feminism and the subversion of identity. Routledge, New York

Ca N (1968) Đêm nghe tiếng đại bác (Listening to the Night Cannon). Nam Cường, Sài Gòn

Cao HK (1970) Sơ thảo 15 năm văn xuôi miền Nam (1955–1969) (First Draft of 15 years of Southern prose (1955–1969)). Khởi Hành, No. 74

de Beauvoir S (2010) *The second sex* (trans: Borde C, Malovany-Chevallier S). Vintage Books, New York

Đỗ LT (2009) Bút pháp của ham muốn (Penmanship of desire). Tri thức, Hà Nội

Du TL (2010) Sự khác biệt về tính dục trong truyện Nguyễn Thị Thụy Vũ và các nhà văn nữ khác (Sexuality differences from stories of Nguyen Thi Thuy Vu and other female writers), 27 tháng 10, 12:00 SA. https://dutule.com/a2865/su-khac-biet-ve-tinh-duc

Gubar S (1985) 'The Blank Page' and the issues of female creativity. In: Showalter E (ed) *The new feminist criticism*. Pantheon Books, New York.

Hawkesworth ME (2006) Feminist inquiry: from political conviction to methodological innovation. Rutgers University Press, New Brunswick, NJ

Hoang T (2013) Ideology in urban South Vietnam, 1950–1975. PhD diss., Pepperdine University

Huỳnh PA (1972) Đi tìm tác phẩm văn chương (Looking for literary works). Đồng Tháp, Đồng Tháp

---

[46] Võ, *Văn học miền Nam, tổng quan*, 57.

Huỳnh PA et al (1972) Nói Chuyện Về Các Nhà Văn Nữ (Talking about female writers) Văn (206):1–6

Huỳnh NP (2019) Văn học miền nam Việt nam 1954–1975: những khuynh hướng chủ yếu và thành tựu hiện đại hóa (South Vietnamese literature 1954–1975: Main tendencies and achievements of modernization), Những vấn đề giảng dạy tiếng Việt và nghiên cứu Việt Nam trong thế giới ngày nay (Issues of Vietnamese language teaching and studies on Vietnam in today's world). Vietnam National University, Ho Chi Minh City

Lanser S. Gender and narrative. In: The living handbook of narratology. Hamburg University, Hamburg. http://www.lhn.uni-hamburg.de/article/gender-and-narrative

Lanser S (2005) Queering narratology. In: Hoffman MJ, Murphy P (eds) Essentials of the theory of fiction. Duke University Press, Durham and London

Lê ĐK, Trần, TĐĐ Văn học thực dân mới Mỹ ở miền Nam những năm 1954–1975 (The Southern art and culture under the American—Puppet regime). Sự Thật, Hà Nội, tập 1-1988; tập 2-1991

Lê TQ (2015) Simone De Beauvoir – Nữ quyền không chỉ là phong trào mà là một khoa học (Simone De Beauvoir—feminism is not just a movement but a science), 01tháng 10. http://www.triethoc.edu.vn/vi/ban-tin-triet-hoc/danh-nhan-triet-hoc/simone-de-beauvoir-nu-quyen-khong-chi-la-phong-trao-ma-la-mot-khoa-hoc_581.html

Lê, VN (biên soạn) (2020) Văn học Sài Gòn 1954–1975, những chuyện bên lề (Saigon literature, 1954–1975: The side miscellanies). Tổng hợp, TP Hồ Chí Minh

Linh T, Tá TH (1977) Văn nghệ Miền Nam dưới chế độ Mỹ - Ngụy (The Southern art and culture under the American—Puppet regime). Văn Hóa, Hà Nội

Lương HT (2009) Vietnamese existential philosophy: a critical appraisal. PhD diss., Temple University

Mahon J (1997) Simone de Beauvoir's existentialist feminism: a defence. In: Existentialism, feminism and Simone de Beauvoir. Palgrave Macmillan, London, pp 186–187

Moi T (1990) Feminist theory & Simone de Beauvoir. Bucknell lectures in literary theory. Blackwell, Oxford, UK, Cambridge, MA, USA

Mounier E (1970) Những chủ đề triết hiện sinh (Existentialist philosophies: an introduction/introduction aux existentialismes) (trans: Nhân T). Nhị Nùng, Sài Gòn

Nguyễn TH (1967) Khả năng và phương hướng sáng tạo văn nghệ của người đàn bà (Ability and direction of artistic creation of the women) Văn 84: 3–9

Nguyễn TTV (1967) Khi người phụ nữ làm nghệ thuật (When the women practice art) Văn 84:10–14

Nguyễn VT (1967) Ca tụng thân xác (In praise of the body). Nam Sơn, Sài Gòn

Nguyen VT (1968) Ngôn ngữ và thân xác (Language and the body). Trình Bày, Sài Gòn

Nguyen TD (1999) Chủ nghĩa hiện sinh: Lịch sử, Sự hiện diện ở việt nam (Existentialism: its history, presence in Vietnam). Chính trị Quốc gia, Hanoi

Nguyễn VK (2014) Văn học miền Nam tự do 1954–1975 (Literature of the liberal South Vietnam 1954–1975). Nam Kỳ Lục Tỉnh, 5 tháng 12, 2014. https://sites.google.com/site/tuyentapnguyenvykhanh/tuyen-tap/van-hoc-mien-nam-tu-do-1954-75-phan-1-mot-thoi-van-chuong

Nguyễn VK (2019a) Văn học miền Nam 1954–1975 – Tổng quan (Literature in South Vietnam, 1945–1975—overview). Nhan Anh, Canada

Nguyễn VK (2019b) Văn học miền Nam 1954–1975 – Tác giả (Literature in South Vietnam, 1945–1975—author). Nhan Anh, Canada.

Oaklander LN (1996) Existentialist philosophy: an introduction, 2nd edn. Prentice Hall, New Jersey

Phạm VS (1976) Văn học giải phóng miền Nam (Southern Liberation Literature). Đại học và Trung học chuyên nghiệp, Hà Nội

Sartre JP (2007) Existence is a humanism (trans: Macomber C). Yale University Press

Tạ T (1971) Mười khuôn mặt văn nghệ hôm nay (Ten Literary Faces Today). La Boi, Saigon

Taylor P (2001) Fragments of the present: searching for modernity in Vietnam's South. University of Hawaii Press, Honolulu

Trần HA (2009) Nhà văn nữ – nhìn từ tâm lý sáng tạo mang đặc điểm giới trong phê bình văn học miền Nam trước 1975 (Female writers—from a creative psychology with a gender identity in the literary criticism of the South before 1975). Văn học và giới (Literature and gender). Đại học Huế, Huế

Trần NH (2015) Dẫn nhập về tự sự học nữ quyền luận (An introduction to feminist narratology). Literary Stud 7:40–51

Trang CHTNN (1987) Women writers of South Vietnam, 1954–1975. Yale University's Vietnam Forum 9, 1987, Barnes & Noble Press, 2021. https://www.second-sites.com/nhatrang/womenw riters.html

Thao U (1973) Các nhà văn Nữ Việt Nam 1900–1970 (Vietnamese female writers 1900–1970). Nhân Chủ, Sài gòn

Võ P (1986) Hai mươi năm văn học Miền Nam: Tổng quan (Twenty years of literature in South Vietnam, 1945–1975: overview). Văn Nghệ, Westminster, CA

Võ P (1942) Nhìn lại 15 năm văn nghệ miền nam (Looking back on 15 years of South Vietnamese arts and culture), Bách Khoa, 361–2, 1972, 40

Võ P (1999) Văn học miền Nam, truyện (Literature in South Vietnam, story). Văn Nghệ, California

Võ P (2000) Văn học miền Nam, tổng quan (Literature in South Vietnam, overview). Văn Nghệ, California

Woolf V (2016) Căn phòng riêng (A room of one's own) (trans: Thư, TY). Tri thức, Hà Nội

Thai Phan Vang Anh is a tenured lecturer of The University of Education, Hue University, Viet Nam. She received her PhD in Literary Theory from the Institute of Literature, Vietnam Academy of Social Sciences in 2011. Her research focuses on Modern Literary Theories (such as narratology theory, intercultural theory, existentialism, feminism; neo-historicism) and Contemporary Vietnamese Literature, especially Female Literature. In April, 2017 she presented her treatise entitled: Vietnamese Novels in the early 21st Century—*Unfamiliarize the Play. Some of her other works are: Contemporary Vietnamese Fiction Written about The War from the Gender Perspective* (Bahasa Dan Seni Journal, 2016), *Wounded People in Novels about War and Postwar* (Literary Studies, No 12.2017); *Globalization, Multicuturalism and Interculturalism from Perspectives of Vietnamese Prose in the Twentieth—First Century* (Literary Studies, No 3.2017), *Women, Children and Cultural Dialogues in Khaled Hosseini's Novels* (Literary Studies, No 10.2019), *Literature And Issues of Globalization* (*Studying Linda Lê's Novel*) (Literary Studies, No 8. 2020). Her most recent female literary publications include *Existential Obsessions in Nguyen Thi Hoang's novels* (Literary Studies, No 11.2021), *The Sense of "Overcoming" in the Work of Nguyen Thi Thuy Vu* (Journal of Science, No1, 2022).

Existentialist Elements in Nguyễn Đình Toàn's Literary Works

Trịnh Đặng Nguyên Hương

Vietnamese literature in the period 1954–1975 was divided into two entities: North Vietnamese literature and South Vietnamese literature. Each entity pursued its own ideology and writing style that was derived from the historical context of a divided Vietnam under two different political regimes. North Vietnamese literature was unified by Marxist-Leninist-oriented ideology and mobilized and developed under the Communist Party-led organizations. The typical type of author in North Vietnam was the "writer-soldier" (nhà văn-chiến sĩ). During this same time, South Vietnamese literature was characterized by diversity, liberation, and humanity.[1] "Thought currents from the West competed with each other to influence and cause multi-dimensional and diverse impacts on people's lives in South Vietnam."[2] In addition, in universities and textbooks, trends in literary composition and schools of philosophy, aesthetics, sciences, and literary criticism from the rest of the world were introduced quite abundantly and updated.[3] "Post-war philosophical, cultural, and literary movements from the West such as existentialism and phenomenology soon influenced cultural and artistic activities in the South."[4] All these factors have contributed to supporting that South Vietnam develop strongly and vibrantly in the direction of modernization. Nevertheless, since the unification of Vietnam in 1975 and with the victory of the Party-led Vietnamese government, South Vietnamese literature has still remained marginal in the mainstream history of Vietnamese literature. The study of this literature is essential because it will provide a more comprehensive view of the historical and literary context of Vietnamese literature from 1954 to 1975.

---

[1] Hồ, *Giáo dục*, 13.

[2] Huỳnh, "Văn học," 710.

[3] Huỳnh, "Văn học," 721.

[4] Nguyễn, *Tổng quan*, 92.

T. Đ. N. Hương (✉)
Institute of Literature, Vietnam Academy of Social Sciences, Ha Noi, Vietnam
e-mail: trinhdangnguyenhuongvvh@gmail.com

© The Author(s), under exclusive license to Springer Nature Singapore Pte Ltd. 2023
T. Engelbert and C. P. Pham (eds.), *Global Vietnam: Across Time,*
Space and Community, Reading South Vietnam's Writers,
https://doi.org/10.1007/978-981-99-1043-4_7

What made South Vietnamese literature unique was the influence of philosophy. In South Vietnam, philosophical books were translated and widely distributed. The philosophy of different movements and ideas was taught at the high school and university levels. Even philosophical exchanges among the intelligentsia were considered part of a fashionable lifestyle. Philosophy even influenced literature, changing authors' social conceptions and writing styles. More specifically, in the war situation in which people often faced insecurity and anxiety, many moral and social values were reversed, and people lost faith. South Vietnamese writers were attracted to philosophical thought, especially existentialism, to ease their mental crises. The prominent authors of this tendency include: Mai Thảo, Thanh Tâm Tuyền, Vũ Khắc Khoan, Nguyên Sa, and Dương Nghiễm Mậu. Nguyễn Đình Toàn (1936) was among those writers. He had been a Hanoi writer, who immigrated to the South in 1954, and who continued writing and then succeeded as a writer in the South. This article examines existentialist elements in his prose, highlighting its demonstration of Nguyễn Đình Toàn's nostalgia for Hanoi, his love for Saigon, and his desire for harmony and connection between the two political entities of the country. His works mainly portray young Vietnamese who lived in Vietnam and searched for meaning, the very spirit of existentialism—narrated with descriptive language and tasteful use of captivating internal monologues. Like a creek that plays a role in the water cycle, Nguyễn Đình Toàn's contribution was significant in changing the course of Vietnamese literature toward modernization in general.

This paper examines existentialist themes in novels and short stories by Nguyễn Đình Toàn. Under the influence of existentialism, the largest philosophical movement of the twentieth century, the prose of Nguyễn Đình Toàn presents to readers a world that is both absurd and beautiful, with a sense of freedom in thinking and expressing discoveries through writing styles. Specifically, this paper understands existentialist influences in Nguyễn Đình Toàn's in the world of his characters—young people who were always aware of the absurdity of human existence, determined to achieve self-actualization through action, choosing to face the present upfront, without dwelling on the past or being anxious about the future. The characters of Nguyễn Đình Toàn's are present in the now, and responsible for their every action and decision. This paper also emphasizes his nonchalant portrayal of life, his contemplation of people and things from different perspectives. This paper argues that in existentialism Nguyễn Đình Toàn found a relevant fulcrum from which to venture out and observe, perceive, and reflect on the soul journey of a young Vietnamese generation growing up under war circumstances and the political conflicts of Vietnam from 1954 to 1975.

About Nguyễn Đình Toàn

Nguyễn Đình Toàn was born and raised in Hanoi. In 1954, he moved to the South. He published his first work *Chị em Hải* in Saigon in 1961. The writer quickly became a rather special phenomenon in South Vietnam's arts and literary landscape. Đình Toàn not only wrote stories, but also made his name as a poet, songwriter, and radio host on the Saigon radio station, charming audience across all platforms. As for prose, the majority of Nguyễn Đình Toàn's works were written after 1954, including: *Chị em Hải* (1961), *Những kẻ đứng bên lề* (1964), *Con đường* (1965), *Ngày tháng* (1968), *Phía ngoài* (1969), *Giờ ra chơi* (1970), *Đêm hè* (1970), *Đêm lãng quên* (1970), *Không một ai* (1971), *Đám cháy* (1971), *Tro than* (1972), *Áo mơ phai* (1972), and others. Before 1975, Nguyễn Đình Toàn was a frequent contributor of some of the main journals in South Vietnam, including *Văn*, *Tự Do*, and *Văn Học*. In 1972, he won the *Giải thưởng văn chương toàn quốc* (National Prize for Literature) for *Áo mơ phai* (Fating Printing Shirt), a novel about Hanoi.

In an essay recapitulating a decade of South Vietnamese literature between 1960 and 1970, Tạ Tỵ, a literary critic and painter, designated Nguyễn Đình Toàn as being one of the ten influential authors in the field of literature and art in South Vietnam. Tạ Tỵ asserted that Nguyễn Đình Toàn "writes as if he were piercing into the paper with sharp and steady strokes. His writing has enough strength and endurance to withstand the destructive power of time and change."[5] In 2001, while speaking on a radio program of RFI (21 August 2001), the literary critic Thụy Khuê quoted other critics who complemented Nguyễn Đình Toàn, such as Tạ Tỵ's reading of Nguyễn Đình Toàn's nostalgia for Hanoi (Tạ Tỵ—*Mười khuôn mặt văn nghệ hôm nay*) and Mai Thảo's emphasis on his "literature talent" (Mai Thảo: *Chân dung mười lăm nhà văn, nhà thơ Việt Nam*). Thụy Khuê also shared her own findings about unique artistic tendencies in Nguyễn Đình Toàn's poetry and songs.[6] In 2019, Nguyễn Vy Khanh dedicated an article to Nguyễn Đình Toàn in his book (*Tổng quan văn học miền Nam 1954–1975*) (Overview of Southern Vietnamese literature 1954–1975), summarizing his career, appreciating his achievements in poetry, short stories, and novels. The researcher focuses on the musical rhythms in Nguyễn Đình Toàn's poems, and poetic pace in his prose. He particularly highlights elements in Nguyễn Đình Toàn's stories and poems that reflect "the traces of existentialism." They are, as described by Nguyễn Vy Khanh, the possibility and impossibility of relations among human beings as well as the assertion of how one must be honest with oneself and in what one does, especially in having a devoted attitude: I am a person of this circumstance, I have to live for today, right here, and in every emotion and reality.[7]

Obviously, most researchers acknowledge Nguyễn Đình Toàn's significant contribution to South Vietnamese literature and particularly emphasize some presence of existentialism in his works. This presence is very likely, given the context of pervasive existentialism in South Vietnam. In the midst of the civil war and political divisions, Southern authors found comfort in philosophy. Never before had the intellectual and mainstream public had such a strong need to read and discuss philosophy as in the South during this period. If in the North the influence of Marxism in life and literature was relatively stable and consistent, in the South, ideological trends were constantly imported and widely disseminated. "As described by Schafer, the public

---

[5] Tạ, *Mười khuôn*, 340.

[6] Thụy Khuê.

[7] Nguyễn, *Tác giả*, 1213.

read Françoise Sagan in Saigon at the same time as she was being read in Paris. On the sidewalks, especially at cafes, people talked about Malraux, Camus, and Faulkner, Gorki, Husserl, and Heidegger."[8] In an article on South Vietnamese literature, critic Thụy Khuê mentioned the impact of philosophy on the literature and arts; in particular, she noted the opinion of Professor Nguyễn Khắc Hoạch that existentialism, after its inception in France, "made its way across the world to Vietnam – a country with a similar political and social situation: torn by war, ridden with anxiety, indifference, and disorientation. That is the perfect condition in which the seeds of existentialism will thrive. According to Thụy Khuê, in the latter half of the 1950s some Vietnamese scholars returned to Vietnam after completing their studies in France and Belgium. They quickly popularized the theories of existentialism, such as Jean-Paul Sartre and Merleau Ponty's ideas about phenomenological ontology. In addition, there were Albert Camus's absurdism, the humanist movement, and E. Mounier's personalist ideas – all of those made up and enriched an ideology shared and endorsed by figures of authority at the time, who came from the same religious background as the author."[9]

Amid the context of Nguyễn Đình Toàn's time, many other writers of South Vietnam had found in existentialism a harbor in which they could retreat and contemplate life, to then experiment novel approaches in making art while still carrying and portraying the spirit and soul of the Vietnamese people. As described by Nguyễn Vy Khanh, "such tendencies existed in Southern writers and poets who belonged to literary groups such as Sáng tạo (Creation) and literary journals such as Văn (Literature), Văn học (Literary Studies), and Nghệ thuật (Art). They believed that life was absurd; there was an insurmountable chasm always existing between people and the world, between human aspirations and the inability of the outside world to satisfy individuals. Works by Mai Thảo or Bếp Lửa (Kitchen Fire) and Tuổi Nước Độc (Age of Poisonous Water) convey the message that people who are far from theocracy only know the value of the present and reality, taking care of themselves and of the present day. Works by Phùng Khắc Khoan such as Ngộ nhận (Misconception) and Thành Cát Tư Hãn (Genghis Khan) highlight cynical, suspicious thought."[10] Nguyễn Đình Toàn has a unique way of presenting existentialist elements. By not discussing current affairs and political landscapes, not dwelling on romantic love stories and heartbreaking events, Nguyễn Đình Toàn charms readers common people, by entering inward into the lonely inner world of the characters, filled with emotional storms, where the irrational phenomena of life are challenged, and answers to questions about the meaning of existence are found. That was the direction that the author must have chosen for his first published work, the one that he remained committed to throughout his writing career.

---

[8] See Schafer, "Hiện tượng," talawas.

[9] Thụy Khuê.

[10] Nguyễn, Tổng quan, 93.

Youth and the Awareness of Absurdity

Existentialist philosophy revolves around a variety of themes. E. Mounier describes the main philosophical themes of existentialism, including the tragic conception of human life, the uncertainty of life, nothingness, and the lost life.[11] Trần Thái Đình in Chapter 2 of his book *Triết học hiện sinh* (Existentialist Philosophy) highlights that one of the most important topics of existentialism is "Nausea."[12] Existentialists believe that when a person is awakened and is free to find themselves, they will realize how mundane, repetitive, and monotonous life can be. Sartre referred to this as "Nausea." Camus did not call it nausea, but "Absurdity." Being deeply aware of nausea and the absurdity of life is the first step for a human in breaking away from the status quo, to stop being the object of consciousness, and to "embrace one's consciousness itself, to be free and to take responsibilities for one's actions."[13] This awareness is often found in young and educated characters in Nguyễn Đình Toàn's works, who search for life's meaning only to realize that it is mundane, absurd, plain, and confusing.

The main characters in Nguyễn Đình Toàn's works are, for the most part, young urban men and women (who live in Hanoi or Saigon), in the most glorious years of youth. The author especially emphasizes 17-year-old characters such as Lệ, a beautiful, bohemian young girl who tries her best to understand the meaning of life but is powerless, in *Những kẻ đứng bên lề* (Those on the Margins); or the character of a nameless girl with a birthmark, with a father who died early, a mother who commits adultery and leaves to marry a new husband, is spurned by those around her, and was whipped at her paternal house in the novel *Con đường* (The Road); the character of a Hanoi schoolgirl named Lan, seventeen years old, romantic and dreamy before the moment of parting from the city she is attached to, in the novel *Áo mơ phai*; Thục, a seventeen-year-old schoolgirl on the last summer vacation of her student life in *Giờ ra chơi* (Pause Time); Hải, a beautiful, smart, young girl with a strong personality, with many worries in a large family of only girls in the novel *Chị em Hải* (Hải Sisters). Characters 17 years old, the brightest, most vigorous, proudest time of youth according to the Vietnamese traditional belief (as the saying goes: to turn 17 is to break a buffalo's horn)—occur repeatedly and even obsessively in Nguyễn Đình Toàn's works. In terms of professions, frequent characters of Nguyễn Đình Toàn's works are pupils, students, and young working adults. They are: Phương, Dung, Tâm, Duy, Hảo, and Hiền, young, educated, intellectual boys and girls with many different life choices in *Chị em Hải*; or a 16-year-old, smart, schoolboy, full of personality, named Lãm in *Giờ ra chơi*, the character of the girl is in her twenties, pregnant by her lover, looking for ways to leave the baby in her belly in *Con đường* (The Road); Thái—Mr. Phúc Thành's secretary, a young orphan, once grew up in an orphanage, longing to escape from a boring, monotonous life but unable to find a reason to live in *Những kẻ bên lề*. As we follow these characters, pictures of urban life are revealed,

---

[11] Mounier, *Những chủ.*

[12] Trần, *Triết học.*

[13] Trần, *Triết học*, 44.

and the circumstance of the middle class, who have sidelined away the ongoing war. The majority of these characters are intellectuals, good-looking, educated, and unburdened by the pressures of making ends meet. The inner psychological world of these characters is filled with torments and endless thinking about the absurdity and the meaning of existence. Their sorrows do not come to them from the outside, from class struggle, or the economic condition, but from their inner world which is filled with insecurities and clashes. They are, as described, like flowers that start to wither before full bloom, or trees that have yet to grow tall but are now scorched by the sun. These characters are constantly drained by the exertion of questioning the endless absurdity of life.

The awareness of absurdity appears in Nguyễn Đình Toàn's first novel *Chị em Hải*. The novel is about an affluent urban family that has eight daughters. They are all beautiful, each has their unique personalities, hobbies, and ambitions. The eldest sister is Ms. Phuong, talented, a medical school student, engaged to a lawyer. The second sister is Ms. Dung, gentle and soft-mannered, who is afraid of doing too well in school because she believes a woman who excels in academics will have difficulties finding a husband. Hải is the third daughter, smart and sharp, an avid reader, keen observer, good at giving analyses and asking questions. Next is Khanh, who loves to learn foreign languages, and Hanh, the innocent one with a dream to be able to eat a different fruit every day. The youngest sisters are still little and not featured by the writer. The life of Hải's family is going well, they are happy with what is seen by society as both material and spiritual abundance. However, from the viewpoint of Hải, a 17-year-old girl who is about to graduate from high school, life turns out to be full of absurdity. The first absurd thing Hải notices is the fact that her parents have given birth to so many girls, "Hải thought it was just too many, an excess of…7 daughters!"[14] And even though she does not look like or have any characteristics in common with her sisters Phương, Dung, Khánh, or Hạnh, Hải is still a girl. "And being a girl means you are not very different from one another."[15] And that always irritates Hải, making her annoyed and a bit cranky with her siblings. Watching life go by every day, Hải only sees the meaninglessness of existence. People get married, have kids, then have more kids, generation after generation, as it turns out. "Do people really have nothing else to do?"[16] Hải does not want to be like anyone else in the family. She doesn't want to graduate from the university and then marry a rich husband like Phuong, she also does not want to settle like Dung, no way she would ever want to be like Khanh, Hanh, or her parents. Hải feels miserable because: "No one in this family understood what Hải wanted. And even Hải herself did not know what she wanted. Hải could see she was not certain about any of her ideas."[17] And where do Hải's endless train of thoughts and her wondering come from? In this novel, Nguyễn Đình Toàn introduces a friend named Tâm. Hải meets Tâm at a party at a friend's house, the two separate from the crowd

---

[14] Nguyễn, *Chị em Hải*, 13.
[15] Ibid., 13.
[16] Ibid., 40.
[17] Ibid., 17.

and talk about philosophy. Tâm has tuberculosis, likes reading philosophy books, and doesn't like crowds, just like Hai. Tâm invites Hải to the house to play. Tâm lends Hải "books by Sartre and Camus"[18] before he dies of tuberculosis, telling her to disinfect them before reading because he used to hold them. These details show that reading and discussing philosophy, especially existentialism, was very common among the youth in South Vietnam. Philosophy must have opened new doors to knowledge and ideology for them. These young intellectuals make the first steps away from day-to-day life to gain a new perspective, which helps them realize the dullness, repetitiveness, and passivity of their lives. As a result, a desire to break free from their mundane lives emerges among these intellectuals. For example, Phuong's husband figures out that people like Hải exist not only in his Vietnamese society. Indeed, the youth in Europe are going through the same situation with the associated mental responses. Nguyễn Đình Toàn clearly states this condition: "They are like bomb pieces, or fragments of bullets, already exploded but remain the proofs of destruction. More miserably, they were the explosive pieces with feelings, humble humans searching for themselves."[19]

After *Chị em Hải* (Hải and Sisters), Nguyễn Đình Toàn continued to produce more works about the absurdity among young characters, especially young women, who were considered the more vulnerable gender, more easily found in a position to accept and settle in comparison with their male counterparts.

The unnamed girl in the novel *Con đường* is born with a birthmark on her face. Her father dies when she is 7; her mother has an affair and then leaves to remarry. A little girl who lost her father is then abandoned by her mother and is then seen as a disgrace by her paternal family. She is despised, scolded, and abused:

> I was hit by all kinds of people in the house, but I never cried, or at least I did not cry in front of them. After the beating stopped, I would find a discreet place such as between the door and the wall, in the wooden stick trunk down by the kitchen, or in the bathroom to cry.[20]

As narrated, the girl does not do anything wrong but she has to suffer many absurd aspects of life such as a birthmark on her face and family violence-related trauma in her soul. At the age of 17, she seeks her grandfather's permission to go look for her mother, hoping to reconnect with her and heal her wounded soul. However, the meeting with her mother only makes her realize that her mother is no longer hers. The woman who gave birth to her does not dare to express her love to her daughter out of fear that it will make her new husband displeased, and thus threaten the good life she is having. For Nguyễn Đình Toàn, motherhood and the bond between mother and daughter is supposed to be the most sacred of all, an unbreakable connection by blood; and the daughter is even a continuity of the mother's life. And yet, this story shows astonishing absurdity. The mother character chooses her new family over her daughter. In so doing, she loses herself to the expectations of others, and at the same time, loses her daughter. This novel goes to relate that the girl is aware of things that

---

[18] Ibid., 45.

[19] Nguyễn, *Chị em Hải*, 77.

[20] Nguyễn, *Con đường*, 8.

cause "nausea" in her big family. One such thing is that one envies others and their convenient life with electricity and fresh water. This kind of dreary, stagnant behavior will slowly kill human vitality. Words such as "disgust" and "nausea" appear many times in dialogues between the girl and the little grand-aunt at the end of the novel. Here, characters are aware of their aimless lives; they know that they only exist as lower creatures, and they are shameful of losing the sense of their status as human beings in this world—an indication that this novel embraces existentialist ideas.

Moreover, in this novel, the characters are conscious about having been born into a war-torn country, bringing up more questions about their existence. Hảo, a beautiful, well-educated young man, Dung's lover, and her sister Hải, unfortunately become disabled after a bomb attack (*Chị em Hải*). Hảo is tormented because he is obsessed with the image he first saw when he woke up after a bomb explosion in the past, which was his body with a leg missing. He realizes that he "does not have any right over the wholeness or losses of his own body."[21] He cannot continue to live a normal life upon his discharge from the army, because he knows deeply that "being shot by a bullet in your head is not a lucky thing."[22] The young secretary Mr. Phuc Thanh (*Những kẻ đứng bên lề*) loses his mother and a younger sibling at a young age from a bombing by the French colonists. Painter Duy, a talented young man, Hai's first love, is in a difficult situation: his mother and younger siblings remained trapped on the other side of the country after it was divided (*Chị em Hải*). The young man struggles with the realization that humans grow up amid things that they do not understand at all. Sadness exists everywhere they look. The 17-year-old girl in the novel (*Con đường*) contemplates the forests, mountains, houses, trees, and grass on the way to meet her mother; but she realizes that everything bears a somber mood, something that one just feels forced to accept. Where does that melancholy come from? Who brought it here? Was it true that "I was sad on my own, therefore this was the way I saw everything, or maybe sadness had just been absorbed and infused in our country all over?"[23]

Similar to this young lady, other young characters in Nguyễn Đình Toàn's stories often cannot name the cause of their sadness but they do not stop themselves from constantly wondering, thinking, and aching. They simply cannot be content with and indulge in material abundance or feel fulfilled by romances. The author constructs his young characters as individuals who think critically about life and human experience, who keep seeking something that they cannot explain. That forms the absurdity in Nguyễn Đình Toàn's novels. This absurdity in turn reflects the overall mood and mentality of the urban youth in South Vietnam in this war-torn period.

Nguyễn Đình Toàn's young characters who are ideological, educated, and well-read are all in an appropriate position to recognize the absurdity in multiple aspects of their lives and others' lives. The more aspiration and ambition they have, the more helpless they will find themselves when being faced with life's absurdity. Lan, a dreamy high school student, like a flower in full bloom at 17 (*Áo mơ phai*) suddenly

---

[21] Nguyễn, *Chị em Hải*, 117.

[22] Nguyễn, *Không một*, 188.

[23] Nguyễn, *Con đường*, 18.

realizes that she has lost Hanoi after the Geneva Agreement was signed. Hanoi is still there with its narrow streets and lanes of trees, pristine lakes, and red-bricked roofs covered in fog…But Hanoi as a whole does not belong to her anymore. Lan's family, like many others, is forced to leave, not knowing when they will come back. A wave of educated families moves to the South and there they know that Hanoi will never be the same again. Loss, nostalgia, regret, and the frail layer of vulnerability are all felt by the characters in the novel *Áo mơ phai*. That nostalgia for Hanoi and its external appearance embodies the same nostalgia for the country, a country that is still there but it is not what it used to be. It is no longer theirs.

This very absurdity is incomprehensible for the young soul at 17, like Lan and many others. To them, suffering does not come from the pressure of making ends meet, of romantic struggles, or suppression and injustice. Instead, the misery occurs when they detach themselves from mundane life and contemplate it through the eye of an outsider, as well as of someone who was living in it. In that position, they see the absurdity that they cannot find an answer or a solution for. "The novel suggests that South Vietnamese urban youth was exposed to Western philosophy, culture, and literature and later referred to and reflected on the war-torn reality of their own country, undergoing mental struggles in the post-World War II period common to both South Vietnamese intellectuals and post-WWI young European intellectuals."[24] The characters of young educated men and women, aware of life's absurdity and nausea, do not accept living by social norms or by the expectations of any groups or individuals in their time; they are always wondering and contemplating about their being and the meaning of existence. This indicates the influences of existentialism in Nguyễn Đình Toàn's works. These characters show that Western education, philosophy, and literature, while broadening South Vietnamese intellectuals' viewpoints and liberating their mental worlds, also pushed them into the tragedy of being knowledgeable: their "knowing too much means suffering much."[25] They can no longer believe in what other people lay out. Instead, they have to search for themselves and make the effort to understand what they set out to know. Images of characters who face absurdity and search for a way to rationalize it at all costs indicate Nguyễn Đình Toàn's desire to understand life and his longing for youth's physical and mental freedom.

Choosing Existence

When faced with absurdity, Nguyễn Đình Toàn's characters make different choices. Some choose the existentialist way of life—they live in the present moment, nourish their individual material life, do not care about the future, do not dwell in the past, and are indifferent to history and current affairs. Phúc Thành, the merchant character, openly admits: "I used to paint, once I went to prison for joining the revolution, I was writing poems for my daughter. But all of that was like an excessive gas of vigorous

---

[24] Võ, *Văn học*.

[25] Nguyễn, *Những kẻ*, 12.

youth, which would soon vanish into thin air."[26] Later as a middle-aged man, he scales down his activities and focuses on doing trades, making money, and enjoying an abundant life. This character represents the choices of many intellectuals of South Vietnam—feeling helpless, they choose to be the "sidelined," self-marginalized from the mainstream politics of their country This character also represents the mental and social situation of South Vietnamese intellectuals who were not aware of their roles in reality or their journey, resulting in their choice to indulge themselves in utopian imaginings, wild dreams, and nostalgia for the lost glorious past, and thus not taking any material or practical actions to impact the reality of their war-torn country. In Nguyễn Đình Toàn's novels, there are many young characters who cannot achieve true freedom. Living recklessly, staying in their comfort zone behind cigarette smoke, alcohol, or sexual relationships is the way these characters react to the socially and politically tragic reality of their country. Such characters are the acquaintances of the girl with the birthmark in the play *Con đường*. The main character of this novel, the girl with a birthmark on her face, goes to Đà Lạt to get a job. Here, she lives with a friend who works in the same office, who is much older than she, and has two husbands. Her grandmother is an alcoholic, smoker, likes to watch movies, play cards, and does not hide her need to satisfy the body. During the ride to the plateau, the girl also meets a middle-aged playwright, who is rich, successful, liberal, and amorous. A love triangle takes place between the girl, the roommate, and the writer. In that love, the girl's housemate and the playwright both consider love as a pleasure to satisfy the flesh. They consider sex as a need to be satisfied without worrying about the concept of love or duty and responsibility. Neither of them cares about the meaning of life, they live to enjoy the pleasures of life. The character Tuyết (*Chị em Hải*) is a village girl. Tuyết lives a libertine life, turning night into day and burning up her life in discos with alcohol. The character Lãm (*Giờ ra chơi*), a sixteen-year-old young man who has not left school yet, the younger brother of a classmate of Thục, while on vacation with his sister and her friend casually smokes cigarettes as he tries to conquer her girlfriend, who is one year older. The character of the father (*Tro tàn*) is that of a heavy opium addict, all day doing nothing but lying at the opium lamp table, debilitated both physically and mentally by the smoke. They all lose their selves and become slaves to their instincts and sexual desires, which leads to the loss of their true freedom and future. Some other characters even fall into depression, desperation, and commit suicide. The character Hiền in *Chị em Hải* is an example. She is madly in a love, seeing her lover as her only purpose. In the suicide note left to her friend, Hien wrote: "I know it's not right to live as I've lived, but I don't know how to live right. I pray that you who stay will find the right way to live (…). Don't be bored with life, it's very hard."[27] "How to live a right life?" Perhaps this is the question that Nguyen Dinh Toan's characters often wonder about.

The second traits in Nguyễn Đình Toàn's characters is their way of directly and reflectively facing uneasy truths of life and their turbulent inner selves, resulting in courageous decisions and the determination to find solutions and carry them out.

---

[26] Ibid., 10.

[27] Nguyễn, *Chị em Hải*, 158.

Specifically, they take action, willing to bear responsibility for their actions while confidently standing in life as unique individuals, free from social judgment and expectations. This group of characters shares similar behaviors including "being thoughtful," "making one's own decision," and "being unique," which all embody key points of existentialism.

Hải, the female character in *Chị em Hải*, does not want to resemble anybody in her family. She wants to separate herself from the crowd and try to make sense of all things on her own, in the way of rationalizing her understanding and pursuing the meaning of life. In her reflections, Hải proactively seeks answers by reading books, and she commits herself to actions, actively experiencing disturbing lives to find her true self. Hải visits Tam, a male friend who is passionate about philosophy but is struggling with sickness and living in poverty. Hải feels pity while listening to Tam say that he is dying soon because of tuberculosis since he has never been in love and never been loved by anyone. He regrets that his life is fading during his youth and he has never tasted love and happiness. Listening to Tâm, Hải comes closer to Tam and asks him to kiss her. As narrated, Hải can kiss Tâm passionately although it is also her first kiss. Hải cannot explain the reason for her action, saying to her herself "Hải, you're not in love with Tâm. Why did you kiss Tam so passionately?" "Why did you give Tâm the first kiss of your life?"[28] Although the narrative explicitly emphasizes the unconscious action of the character, it suggests that there is a subjective willingness in this action. That is, the character is encouraged to take the action that is considered abnormal according to the social and cultural norms and is willing to face any consequence of it. The event demonstrates that human beings will take action reflectively in reacting to very special circumstances that life presents to them.

This beyond-convention way of making decisions in special contexts is more explicit in the narrative about Hải's relationship with Duy, a male painter who is madly in love with her, and whom she starts feeling love for. Hải comes over to Duy's house and sees him painting a portrait of her. Incredibly moved to see Hải and being unable to contain his emotions, Duy embraces her and kisses her passionately. As narrated, Hải could have stopped Duy's advances but she intentionally lets go of her feelings. She calculatedly thinks that later she can see it as an accident; and if it is an accident, there will be no point in regretting it. Although she does not regret having sex with Duy on that day, she decides never to see Duy again. She decisively puts an end to a love that has just blossomed between them. Hải does not explain her decision, nor does she give Duy any chance to meet and talk with her. Readers can only understand the reason for this suddenness through examining the narrative about Hải's reaction to Dung, her sibling, who is in a love relationship with another man. She keeps questioning Dung as to whether Dung is in love with that man. Dung does not want to answer, while Hải keeps pushing her. Feeling frustrated, Dung slaps Hải, announcing that she, Hải, does not lose her virginity to other men. The slap makes Hải burst into tears, crying. She says to herself: "that is the cry I should have cried that day at Duy's house [when she lost her virginity to him]."[29] Dung is dismayed at the

---

[28] Nguyễn, *Chị em Hải*, 48.
[29] Ibid., 153.

unstable attitudes and the tears of Hải. Hải is also aware of the unusual contradiction and absurdity in her thought and emotions. On one hand, she desires love, hoping to discover herself in love; thus she does not hesitate to make love with her boyfriend. On the other hand, being aware of the family's dignity, and the shame of having sex before marriage makes Hải feel disgusted with herself. As she knows her sister Dung is still a virgin, she decides to break up with Duy as a way of saving herself from the sin of her sexual relationship with him. She moves on, without looking back to the love in which she once indulged. This shows how decisively and actively the character conducts her action. She is the owner of her actions. When facing a hardship, this character considers it carefully, evaluates its consequences, and makes decisions to resolve it, not being influenced by outside forces such as her parents, her siblings, and her lovers. This autonomous life decision is quite rare among other women of her time. In other words, Hai shows unconventional characteristics of a Vietnamese woman, who is traditionally presented in the image of a soft-mannered beauty and prone to making sacrifices for others. The character Hải also goes beyond motifs in romanticism where female characters are usually willing to die for love.[30] The female character Hải of Nguyễn Đình Toàn's work has a proactive attitude to her life and constantly strives to break free from everyday life's absurdity. The narrative of Hải presents a renewal in the portrayal of female characters in South Vietnamese literature.

Realizing "Hell is the other people,"[31] one of Sartre's sayings that is quoted the most in Vietnamese writing about existentialism, many of Nguyễn Đình Toàn's characters awaken and step out of their illusions about life and love. The novel *Những kẻ đứng bên lề* tells about many individuals who do not participate in the ongoing war between the North and the South. They include the wealthy Phúc Thành, a bourgeois who refuses to commit himself, only cares about making money and enjoying life; his secretary—an intelligent, ambitious young man; and Lệ, Mr. Phúc Thành's niece, whose mother died early and whose father was an alcoholic. She engages in a debauched lifestyle at the disco when she is very young to earn a living. She is always struggling to find a way to understand the meaning of life. Lệ's words are also not the same as those of a typical young girl. For example, Lệ speaks to her boyfriend as if she were posting a question to a philosophy professor: "Between myself and my words, between me and my childhood, there are conflicts. So, did we lose our childhood, or was it taken from us by others? Who took from whom? What are the reasons for those conflicts?"[32] Lệ's continuous questioning reveals the pain of an existentialist self that becomes aware of its turbulent and conflicted inner world. At the age of seventeen, Lệ has lost her youth, her golden years. All that remains of her soul is the "winds and storms of life." "That's just me, who is always making mistakes, and not feeling regretful. I only feel sad. I am a float in the stormy sea,

---

[30] Nguyễn, "Tự Lực."

[31] Trần, *Chủ nghĩa*, 24.

[32] Nguyễn, *Những kẻ*, 20.

wanting to drown but being able to float instead. It is because the float is me, the storm is me, and the sea is me. I have nowhere to sink. I also cannot stop the wind."[33]

Walking into the storm of life, accepting it, take on the resulting challenges and pains to find the true meaning of life is what obviously makes Nguyễn Đình Toàn's characters powerful and unforgettable. More importantly, they demonstrate the existentialist ideas of the time. Most of Nguyễn Đình Toàn's female characters are very determined to take on life head-on, taking matters into their own hands, making decisions for their own lives. Not playing the victim, or not putting the blame on their family or anyone else, these female characters strive to face life. They follow the existentialist motto that "human beings will be what they make of themselves."[34] The female character Hóa in the novel *Tro* rises from the ashes of her life: her mother dies when she is little, her father is a drug addict, she lives with her stepmother and two younger siblings. She goes to school in humiliation and eventually graduates from high school. She then leaves her home to go to Teaching College and works to pay her tuition. However, her mentality is strong and articulate: "What could I have done in that situation?"[35] "I only had one choice: to make all the decisions for my life."[36] She decides to take care of her broken family, assisting her ill father whose health is deteriorating from drug addiction, and raises her two half-siblings who are still in grade school. This attitude in actively dealing with hardships can also be seen in Nguyễn Đình Toàn's construction of the unnamed girl in the novel *Con đường*. Domestic violence is narrated as a force that challenges this seven-year-old girl's destiny and forms in her a longing for the answer to "Who am I?" This girl is aware that she indeed needs the beating, because "only when I get beaten up like that, I knew who I was in this family. These people helped me to find myself and realize the absence of those who had left."[37] The question of identity continues to grow through the years and later urges this young woman to find the answer to this question in action. She figures that, even though her mother has left her, she still needs to see her mother again with the belief that a blood connection between mother and daughter is the most likely thing that can help her understand who she is. Who was she? She needs to get this straight to figure out how she can continue to live her life, and what road she should follow? Struggling to find her roots and herself, she goes to visit her mother twice: the first time when she is 17 years old, and the second time before she takes the job. Whenever she meets with her mother is a chance, it is narrated, for her to "wake up." She figures out that between "I" and "my mother" lies a road. That road is a metaphor for the distance that makes us never be able to see each other. Her own mother is like a stranger, a mother that no longer belongs to her. This young girl must accept this absurd situation in which her lifeboat can leave the harbor—her mother—once and for all "so that I can live my life and she can live hers."[38] The

---

[33] Ibid., 54.

[34] Sartre, *Existentialism Is a Humanism*, 33.

[35] Nguyễn, *Tro than*, tr. 6.

[36] Ibid., 15.

[37] Nguyễn, *Con đường*, 8.

[38] Ibid., 151.

girl then continues to find herself through her relationships with others: her paternal grandfather, her family, her little grand-aunt, the playwright, and her roommate. She has no idea where this journey will lead her, but it is a journey that she decides to take. She is in control of navigating, being ready for the accomplishments as well as the possible failures.

In addition to strong and mature female characters, Nguyễn Đình Toàn also builds characters who are young and innocent women, less experienced and filled with puzzles as they cross the threshold into real life. Examples are Thục (*Giờ ra chơi*) and Lan (*Áo mơ phai*). Though being cocooned by their families, these ladies are consciously willing to step out of their comfort zone to find answers about life. Thục thinks to herself, as she is about to finish the last week of the school year, that she will live this summer as if it were the first summer of her life, because she will "become an adult anyway, I need to get ready for life. Ready for life? Those words, as narrated, keep ringing in her imagination, echoing and making her excited. She also realizes what life is all about, a life in which she is an actor; she is in that life, and that life is there because she is in it. She knows that there will be an encounter between herself and life; she is a part of that life and that life does not belong entirely to someone else."[39] During that summer holiday, Thục wanders with her friend all over Đà Lạt, a city in the central highland of Vietnam. She admires the landscapes and experiences various activities. Although she almost falls into a love affair with another male character, she is in control of her feelings and her decision is not to enter a sexual relationship. At the end of the holiday, she feels like it was just a short recess because she still needs to go back and face real disturbing, changing life "with all the truths, temptations, promises, and threats."[40] The character Thuc, regardless of her existentialist spirit, occurs with the power of strength and her positive attitude in taking on life. She is ready for life, calmly accepts and welcomes everything, be it happiness or sorrows, temptations or downfalls, and promises or threats. Such an attitude suggests a lesson that humans can attain freedom once they embrace existentialism.

The other female character is Lan in the novel *Áo mơ phai*. This character is depicted in another unique way of reflecting existentialist ideas. The novel begins with a chronicle highlight: "Hanoi, 1954. June was not over yet, but Fall had already started to accumulate mist."[41] The two sentences, although short, are truly haunting as they reveal a historic moment in Vietnam's history: 1954, after the signing of the Geneva Agreement on July 21, 1954, the country was divided into two regions North and South, with latitude 17 as the border, and each region following a different political system. It would take Vietnam more than 20 years, until 1975, to unite the country as one. *Áo mơ phai* puts together the feelings, emotions, thoughts, and actions of Lan at this exceptional moment in history. Feeling anxious about having to leave Hanoi, Lan takes a long walk through the streets of her town. She spends every minute she gets to walk, to stroll, to stand in the rain, to wander aimlessly. "Lan

---

[39] Nguyễn, *Giờ ra chơi*, 9, 10.

[40] Ibid., 134.

[41] Nguyễn, *Áo mơ phai*.

wished that she could dissolve, could vanish into Hanoi."[42] She is not dwelling on the heroic past, nor is she capable of worrying about her hometown's future. Through walking aimlessly, she chooses to live every minute with Hanoi, as it is right there and then. How can she immerse herself in Hanoi, to live the life of this city in every breath, in every second when it is still hers? Such actions show her helplessness in the face of reality, but at the same time demonstrate such a deep love a young woman like Lan has for her city, country, and home. Hanoi might not be the same, but the feelings remain and the emotions for this city linger the same in every breath of Lan and other youths. Lan's choices are indeed beautiful reflections of existentialism.

Not only female characters but also male characters in Nguyễn Đình Toàn's novels have a special love for Hanoi. Sơn—a young man from Hanoi, who is working at the Saigon Radio Station in the novel *Đồng cỏ*, holds Hanoi dearly in his heart as he misses it daily while living far away. He "missed many things about Hanoi, every street corner, every roof, every smallest change in the weather. He expressed a sense of regret because he had not taken more photographs of Hanoi before he left."[43] To Sơn, Hanoi is a mesmerizing city, so mesmerizing that it is still tormenting him like "rheumatism." While Sơn misses Hanoi, Phung (a Hanoi girl who comes with her family to Saigon when she is small), anticipates that she will miss Saigon when she works in Japan. This nostalgia is like the "Hanoi-sickness" that her colleague Son is suffering. She contemplates that she will soon miss Saigon just like Son is homesick for Hanoi. She "will miss Viễn Đông sugarcane juice, Mai Huong ice cream, and the snail vermicelli soup by the Casino." She "will miss the streets when the rain pours on this side while the other side remains sunny." And, she "will miss church bells in the afternoon, the afternoons that are both dry and wet…"[44] Missing—or recollecting—about Hanoi and Saigon forms a way by which the youth of South Vietnam cope with the reality of the divided country. Erasing geographical distances through the love for their hometown formed a way for the South Vietnamese intellectuals to escape from the war-torn reality. Nguyễn Đình Toàn's writing indicates the proactivity in the way in which the young Southern Vietnamese attempt to achieve their mental freedom. It is the way of longing for the lost home city.

The world of characters in Nguyễn Đình Toàn's novels is diverse and vibrant. The most dominant characters in that world belong to a group of young urban men and women. In that world, some characters indulge themselves in the existential way of living. They are also characters who self-reflect constantly and strive to create their desired versions of themselves through their actions. These characters walk steadily into the future, accepting the absurdity of reality, and taking responsibility for every action. Interestingly, the majority of these self-reflective characters are female. The way that Nguyễn Đình Toàn portrays these fragile women through their whole life, from an early period to adulthood, when they step into a real life that is full of absurdity, suggests the idea that humans at any age and of any gender are capable of committing themselves to finding a freedom which they truly desire.

---

[42] Nguyễn, *Áo mơ phai*, 309.

[43] Nguyễn, *Đồng cỏ*.

[44] Nguyễn, *Đồng cỏ*.

Writing Style

Nguyễn Đình Toàn explicitly expressed his intention to write in the Nouveau Roman style. As Nguyễn Vy Khanh observes: "Beside the huge existentialist movement and socially engaging movement, the Nouveau Roman that arrived from France made big changes in South Vietnamese intellectual life. Writers such as Huỳnh Phan Anh, Hoàng Ngọc Biên, Nguyễn Đình Toàn, and Nguyễn Xuân Hoàng, embraced a whole new genre of 'anti-roman,' a term first used by Jean-Paul Sartre himself to refer to conversations and monologues, blended with emotional complexity, in the non-chronicological order of this genre. Plots were unnecessary, and there were often no narrators."[45] In Nguyễn Đình Toàn's writings, one rarely finds captivating and thrilling plots. He simply does not focus on building plots and details, but rather captures the hearts of his readers through his writing style. He chooses a poetic voice. His sentences are visually rich and could go on and on like they will never end. His prose sounds like intimate whispering, someone pouring their heart out about a part of their life, a situation that the writer himself has encountered. Even dialogues between characters are sometimes as melodic as a poem. Take this one between Thục and Khôi in the novel *Giờ ra chơi* as one example:

– Do you know of a bridge no one has crossed before?
– Yes, a rainbow?
– Do you know of a field where people plant a kind of tree that never grows?
– Yes, a field of bones and remains.
– Do you know of the night somewhere without darkness?
– Did you mean the night of the blind?

    Khoi giggled and said:

– And that is exactly what I want to write into my song."[46]
– (- Chị có biết một cây cầu nào chưa ai đi qua?
– Có, cầu vồng?
– Chị có biết cánh đồng nào người ta trồng một thứ cây không mọc?
– Có. Cánh đồng xương cốt.
– Chị có biết đêm ở nơi nào không có bóng tối?
– Đêm của những người mù, phải không?
– Khôi cười bảo tôi:
– Vậy thì đó là những gì tôi muốn viết thành những bài hát của tôi")

The poetic quality occurs in the effortless rhyming, the rhythmic pacing, and overall melodic flow in his writing. Visual cues such as a bridge no one has crossed, a field with a kind of tree that never grows, the night without darkness…spark imagination and resonate in readers. It is a subtle way of telling stories about the war seen through their young eyes.

---

[45] Nguyễn, *Tổng quan*, 272.
[46] Nguyễn, *Giờ ra chơi*, 115.

Poetic essence in Nguyễn Đình Toàn's writing sometimes reveals itself as he takes readers through a character's flow of thoughts: "The clocks/in this shop/point at different hours/so do the lives of these people."[47] Phụng (*Đồng cỏ*) is thinking to herself in a poem as though she is looking at a clock shop on the street. Thoughts are condensed into images, and images unlock thoughts, all like the path Nguyễn Đình Toàn must have taken in order to bring poetry into his prose. In other words, the thoughts of characters are presented in the form of a poem. Thus, the poetic essence appears in sensational presentations with witty and uncanny references:

> "Hanoi's a woman because it's cold.
> Saigon's a man because it's hot."
> "Oh, if only that womanly amorous half could integrate with this male rugged half, our country would rejoice in ecstasy!"[48]
> ("Hà Nội đàn bà vì Hà Nội lạnh.
> Sài Gòn đàn ông vì Sài Gòn nóng.
> Ôi, giá cái nửa đàn bà đa tình, quyến rũ đó, kết hợp được với cái nửa đàn ông lực lưỡng này,
> đất nước sẽ sung sướng biết bao?")

Before and after Nguyễn Đình Toàn, no other writers have made such liberated, amorous, and earnest comparisons about the country. The format of these three sentences is special in the way they are broken into 3 lines, which makes them poetic sentences like a poem. It takes a man who loves his country dearly with all his flesh and bones to compare the national division to the separation of a couple in love. Nguyễn Đình Toàn is the only author who has the soul of a poet to harness such wishful thinking: if there were to be a reunion of the amorous woman (Hanoi), and the rugged man (Saigon), the country would "rejoice in ecstasy!"—that is the national reunification. The first two short lines are to identify Hanoi and Saigon; the third line which is longer and more metaphoric, carries waves of emotions that are part aching, part aroused, both passionate and painful. Poetry is an essential characteristic of Nguyễn Đình Toàn's writing style.

A subtle poetic mood occurs throughout Nguyễn Đình Toàn's short stories and novels and is distilled especially beautifully in the novel *Áo mơ phai,* the novel that is filled with nostalgia for Hanoi. For this novel, he writes long sentences that are so visually fascinating that readers do not notice where one sentence ends and the other begins, a feeling that reminds of Hanoi in the fall, with fog building up and leaves falling here and there.

Hanoi is like a bell, and all these voices calling are attempts to make it chime, people tap on their own imagination, tear open their own hearts, to release the heaviness they feel from missing and longing, from their obsession with Hanoi, Hanoi has turned into the face of their first lover when lips touched for the first kiss, that image was engraved deeply in their soul, gentle streets retreating under the midnight mist, the brightness lingering from the moonlight that always looks like the moon they used to see during childhood, and the breeze blowing

---

[47] Nguyễn, *Đồng cỏ.*
[48] Nguyễn, *Đồng cỏ.*

softly on pedestrians' paths, caressing branches on trees, not much different from a lover's breath, they would not know for sure how Hanoi's charming beauty has been absorbed and harmonized into the grace and sensuality of a woman.[49]

This style of writing endless sentences perhaps originate from Nguyễn Đình Toàn's own belief that "it is difficult to distinguish between prose and poetry but it is safe to say that poetry is the climate of literature."[50] He even sometimes thought that "*Áo mơ phai* was a long poem."[51] Before Nguyễn Đình Toàn and until now, no Vietnamese writer has written a novel in this way.

Being influenced by phenomenology, Nguyễn Đình Toàn only describes things and events as they are. He does not insert any emotions, experiences, or biases. Nguyễn Đình Toàn appears to simply present life with a nonchalant attitude. This writing without comments or critiques, without analysis or the inclusion of his feelings makes Nguyễn Đình Toàn's writings difficult to read. While there are very few events and plot twists, Nguyễn Đình Toàn's construction of plot and flow is sometimes messy and random since the narration just follows what the narrator goes to and sees. The endings of his works are often neither closed nor open. These characteristics that add to Nguyễn Đình Toàn's works leave a special emotion in readers as they close the book, leaving them with numerous voids that encourage thinking and contemplating. Even though the stories end, Nguyễn Đình Toàn's characters continue on their private journeys, and readers are welcome to carry on with their flow of thoughts once they have finished reading. *Áo mơ phai* just tells a slice of Lan's life before the Geneva Agreement was signed, *Giờ ra chơi* records a summer trip of the characters Thục, Lãm and Khôi to Da Lat city. *Tro than* is about the days after Hoa graduates from college. *Con đường* tells the story of the road that the main character chooses to take without knowing where it might take her. *Chị em Hải*, *Những kẻ đứng bên lề*, *Không một ai*, *Đồng cỏ*, and other stories by Nguyễn Đình Toàn have open endings, floating somewhere in the middle of the air, as if they had not ended. Nor did the writer make conclusions, nor reveal the characters' future. Such structure helps vividly portray the existentialist condition of every individual in life, and it also shows that being on the path is more important than the destination.

Contemplating reality and people from different points of view and angles is a tool that Nguyễn Đình Toàn uses to reflect reality in his writings. Most characters are described from multiple perspectives, each gives us a different conclusion and perception. In Phuong's eyes, Hải is mentally ill and needs treatment. In Khanh's view, "Hải's mind is distorted by reading too many books,"[52] to Duy (the boyfriend), Hải is "a pitiful angel," while Tan (Phuong's husband) sees Hải as "the kind of people who think more than they live," and when alone with herself, Hải realizes that "inside of her was only disappointment"[53] after erotic moments with her lover. Other characters are also zoomed in on and discovered from many angles and through

---

[49] Nguyễn, *Đồng cỏ*.

[50] Nguyễn, *Tác giả*, 1213.

[51] Ibid., 1213.

[52] Nguyễn, *Chị em Hải*, 42.

[53] Ibid., 110.

different lenses; each of them adds a discovery about the character. Nguyễn Đình Toàn's characters are also often self-reflecting, looking at themselves through their own lens, where they experience an outer-body separation from the self to observe and evaluate themselves as independent, objective, and non-judgmental entities. From the first book, Nguyễn Đình Toàn consistently pursued this style of descriptive writing. In *Áo mơ phai* (*The Blouse in Faded Dreams*), the main character is not a person, but an entity that is Hanoi. It is a Hanoi of the past, of memories, of longing, of aspiration—beautiful, pale, blurry, and also heartbreaking...Hanoi is viewed from Lan's and Quang's points of view, and that of Lan's parents at different points in time, a mix of reality and nostalgia, of what remained and what has been lost, narrated through prose sentences that are a whole page long. All of these give the readers the feeling of reading a novel that never ends while it ultimately adds a whole new mood to literature.

Commenting on Nguyễn Đình Toàn's style, researcher Nguyễn Vy Khanh notes: "The characters and writing style of Nguyễn Đình Toàn's are both unique, a distinguished path shared with no others, and also not conforming to any standards of present-day society."[54] It is through these unique traits that the writer discovers not only the realm of consciousness but also goes deep into the realm of the subconsciousness. He once announced: "A novel, in my opinion, is not a mirror that reflects life, but rather a place to expose what is hidden in real life."[55] Perhaps it is this belief and his style that, as Nguyễn Vy Khanh says, have brought Nguyễn Đình Toàn's writing close to readers of all different social classes over time.

Conclusion

Nguyễn Đình Toàn's literary works present a unique style in South Vietnam (from 1955 to 1975). His writing demonstrates the profound influence of Sartre's existentialist philosophy. Concepts such as "Being precedes essence,"[56] "Hell is the other people,"[57] and "We find ourselves only in the doing"[58] find their embodiments in the world of Nguyễn Đình Toàn's characters, especially the self-reflecting characters, who are always aware of the absurdity of life. These characters commit themselves to finding their ways out of the absurd situation, constructing their selves through actions. In existentialism, Nguyễn Đình Toàn found an ideological pillar to lean on, a means to observe, to discover, and to portray the reality of South Vietnam during a turbulent time of national division. Nguyễn Đình Toàn's profound contribution to Vietnamese literature is that he successfully makes a foreign, distant Western philosophy speak to the state of mind of the Southern Vietnamese youth in the

---

[54] Nguyễn, *Tác giả*, 1222.

[55] Nguyễn, "Nguyễn Đình," 93–96.

[56] Trần, *Chủ nghĩa*, 18.

[57] Ibid., 24.

[58] Ibid., 24.

period of 1954–1975. Nguyễn Đình Toàn's works helped readers, especially young people at that time, realize the absurdity of their day-to-day life, provoking them to seek their own life experience, resulting in their self-committed engagement in their society. They were quite aware that only through those mental and active transformations would they gain freedom for their minds and their souls. Nguyễn Đình Toàn absorbed Sartre's existentialism and manifested his understanding of this philosophy in his stories, that portray social and individual issues that are unique to Vietnamese history, society, and tradition.

Bibliography

Hồ AS, Nguyễn TN, Nguyễn PT (2019) Giáo dục phổ thông miền Nam (1954–1975) (South Vietnam's High School Education 1954–1975). Oanh NM (ed) Nhà xuất bản Tổng hợp Thành phố Hồ Chí Minh, Thành phố Hồ Chí Minh

Huỳnh PN (2019) Văn học miền Nam Việt Nam 1954–1975: những khuynh hướng chủ yếu và thành tựu hiện đại hoá (South Vietnam literature 1954–1975: main trends and achievements of modernization). In: Những vấn đề giảng dạy tiếng Việt và nghiên cứu Việt Nam trong thế giới ngày nay. NXB: Đại học Quốc gia Thành phố Hồ Chí Minh, pp 710–723

Khuê T (2001). Nguyễn Đình Toàn, chương trình phát trên đài RFI (Nguyễn Đình Toàn, a program on RFI radio) Thuykhue, 29 August 2001. http://thuykhue.free.fr/mucluc/nguyendinhtoan-vhnt. html. Accessed 29 Nov 2021

Mounier E (1970) Những chủ đề triết hiện sinh (Themes of existentialism) (trans: Nhân T). Nhà xuất bản Nhị Nùng, Saigon

Nguyễn HX Nguyễn Đình Toàn trên sợi chỉ mành (Nguyễn Đình Toàn—Hanging Thin Thread). Tập san Văn, no. 120, ra ngày 15/12/1968, tr.93-96

Nguyễn KV (2019) Tác giả (Author). In Văn học miền Nam 1954–1975. Nhà xuất bản Nhân Ảnh, San Jose, pp 10–25

Nguyễn KV (2019) Tổng quan (Introduction). In: Văn học miền Nam 1954–1975. Nhà xuất bản Nhân Ảnh, San Jose, pp 2–19

Nguyễn S (2021) Tự Lực văn đoàn với vấn đề phụ nữ ở nước ta [Tự Lực văn đoàn with women's issues in our country]. Văn nghệ quân đội, 25 March 2021. http://vannghequandoi.com.vn/su-kien/tu-luc-van-doan-voi-van-de-phu-nu-o-nuoc-ta_11822.html

Nguyễn TĐ (1961) Chị em Hải. Cơ sở Báo chí và Xuất bản Tự do, Saigon

Nguyễn TĐ (1964) Những kẻ đứng bên lề. Nhà xuất bản Giao điểm, Saigon

Nguyễn TĐ (1965) Con đường. Nhà xuất bản Giao điểm, Saigon

Nguyễn TĐ (1968) Ngày tháng. Nhà xuất bản An Tiêm, Saigon

Nguyễn TĐ (1969) Phía ngoài. Nhà xuất bản Hồng Đức, Saigon

Nguyễn TĐ (1970a) Đêm hè. Nhà xuất bản Hiện đại, Saigon

Nguyễn TĐ (1970b) Đêm lãng quên. Nguyệt san Tân Văn, số 24, tháng 4, 121 trang

Nguyễn, TĐ (1970c) Giờ ra chơi. Saigon: Nhà xuất bản Khai phóng, 1970.

Nguyễn TĐ (1971a) Đám cháy. Nguyệt san Tân Văn, số 37, tháng 5, 112 trang

Nguyễn TĐ (1971b) Không một ai. Nhà xuất bản Khai phóng, Saigon

Nguyễn TĐ (1972a) Tro than. Nhà xuất bản Đồng Nai, Saigon

Nguyễn TĐ (1972b) Áo mơ phai. Nhà xuất bản Nguyễn Đình Vượng, Saigon

Nguyễn TĐ (1972c) Áo mơ phai. Nhà xuất bản Nguyễn Đình Vượng, Saigon. https://vietmesse nger.com/books/?title=ao%20mo%20phai. Accessed 3 Dec 2021

Nguyễn TĐ (1974) Đồng cỏ. Nhật báo Chính luận, Saigon. https://vietmessenger.com/books/?title= ddong%20co. Accessed 4 Dec 2021

Sartre J-P (2016) Thuyết hiện sinh là một thuyết nhân bản (Existentialism is a humanism) (trans: Đinh PH). Nhà xuất bản Tri thức, Hà Nội

Schafer JC (2008) Hiện tượng Trịnh Công Sơn [Trịnh Công Sơn Phenomenon]. Translated by Hoài Phi and Vy Huyền. Talawas. 2 July 2008. http://www.talawas.org/talaDB/showFile.php?res= 12221&rb=0206. Accessed 3 Dec 2021

Tạ T (1972) Mười khuôn mặt văn nghệ hôm nay (Ten Writers Today). Nhà xuất bản Lá Bối, Sài Gòn

Trần ĐT (2001) Chủ nghĩa Hiện sinh và Thuyết Cấu trúc (Existentialism and structuralism). Nhà xuất bản Văn học, Hà Nội

Trần ĐT (2005) Triết học hiện sinh (Existentialist philosophy), 3rd edn. Nhà xuất bản Văn học, Hà Nội

Võ P Văn học miền Nam: Tổng quan (South Vietnam literature: an overview). https://sachtruyen. net/doc-sach/van-hoc-mien-nam-tong-quan.006a3.0009. Accessed 4 Dec 2021

Trịnh Đặng Nguyên Hương is a tenured researcher at the Institute of Literature, Vietnam Academy of Social Sciences. Her expertise is modern Vietnamese literature, with a focus on children's literature. She is particularly interested in the issue of children's education reflected in literature regarding inner freedom, dreams, and will. Her most recent publications (largely in Vietnamese) are *Children's Literature from Nguyên Nhật Ánh's Works* (Journal of Literary Studies, No. 1/2021), *An Overview of Children's Literature in Vietnam at the Dawn of the XXI Century* (Journal of Literary Studies, No. 10/2021), and *Aesthetics of Children's Poetry in Pre-Reform Vietnamese Textbooks* (Military Arts Magazine, No. 973, September 2021).

Vũ Hạnh (1926–2021)—A Typical Left-Leaning Writer

Ngô Thị Quỳnh Nga

Introduction

In the period from 1955 to 1975, especially in the urban areas of South Vietnam, political, social, cultural, religious, aesthetic, philosophical, and literary ideas of the West and the United States poured in, interfered with, and influenced traditional culture, creating a new face of spiritual life.[1] In this context, urban literature in South Vietnam was born, existed and developed with its unique characteristics. Literary composition, theory, and criticism were strongly influenced by Western and American philosophy, culture, and literature.[2] Deep imprints of existentialist and psychoanalytic theories and the footprints of great writers, such as Marcel Proust, Jean-Paul Sartre, Boris Pasternak, and Franz Kafka were obvious in many works.[3] However, the "local" literature also had a group of authors that created a separate way, even in opposition to the majority. These were people deeply influenced by communist ideas. Their compositions aimed at propagating revolutionary ideas and preserving the nation's traditional culture against foreign influences. Typical of these authors was the writer Vũ Hạnh (1926–2021). Focusing on Vũ Hạnh, a typical left-leaning writer, we aim to show the influence of cultural mechanisms and political power on

---

[1] Võ Phiến, *Văn học miền Nam*, 118, 145,150, 151, 289, 296, 307–308.

[2] Trịnh Bá Đĩnh, *Lịch sử lý luận*, 167, 168, 171; Nguyễn Văn Lục, "*20 năm văn học,*" https://nguoitinhhuvo.wordpress.com/2014/12/03/20-nam-van-hoc-dich-thuat-mien-nam-1955-1975-nguyen-van-luc/.

[3] Bửu Ý, "Nhìn lại đời sống," http://tapchisonghuong.com.vn/tap-chi/c371/n25459/Buu-Y-nhin-lai-do-i-so-ng-van-hoc-mien-Nam-giai-doan-tu-1954-1975.html, 30/04/2017; Võ Phiến, *Văn học miền Nam*, 307–308; Nguyễn Văn Lục, "20 năm văn học," https://nguoitinhhuvo.wordpress.com/2014/12/03/20-nam-van-hoc-dich-thuat-mien-nam-1955-1975-nguyen-van-luc/.

N. T. Q. Nga (✉)
Faculty of Literature, School of Pedagogy, Vinh University, Nghe An, Vietnam
e-mail: ngothiquynhnga@gmail.com

Vũ Hạnh's views and how political view is constructed in his short stories. Through Vũ Hạnh's case, we want to demonstrate the diversity, richness and complexity of urban literature in South Vietnam, thereby providing a multi-dimensional picture of Vietnamese literature during the war.

After 1954, South Vietnam had two coexisting literary trends. Revolutionary literature (also known as the liberation literature of South Vietnam) was formed and developed in areas controlled by the People's Army of Vietnam. This literary body gathered together communist writers who composed their works according to the direction and policy of Northern literature under the leadership of the Communist Party of Vietnam. Literature in areas under the management of the government of the Republic of Vietnam, mainly in urban areas (we call it urban literature in South Vietnam for short),[4] was very rich and complex. Writers and artists came from many different backgrounds: some were journalists, some were teachers, some were soldiers of the Vietnamese National Army, some were communists who were assigned secret revolutionary activities in urban areas. This diversity led to complicated literary trends that both opposed and dominated each other.[5] There were works praising nationalism: *Người tù* (Prisoner, 1957), *Mưa đêm cuối năm* (Rain in the Last Night of the Year, 1958) by Võ Phiến (1925–1979), *Giấc ngủ chập chờn* (Restless Sleep, 1967) by Nhật Tiến (1936–2020), *Dấu binh lửa* (The Sign of the Fire Army, 1969), *Mùa hè đỏ lửa* (Red Fiery Summer, 1972) by Phan Nhật Nam (1943); works that were influenced by Western philosophical thought: *Đêm tóc rối* (The Night of Tangled Hair, 1965) by Dương Nghiễm Mậu (1936–2016), *Vòng tay học trò* (The Student's Embrace, 1966) by Nguyễn Thị Hoàng (1939), *Mù khơi* (Blind Sea, 1970) by Thanh Tâm Tuyền (1936–2006); urban literature in South Vietnam also consisted of works that showed the protest of communist writers against the national government.

On assignment by the Communist Party, Vũ Hạnh (1926–2021) and Lê Vĩnh Hòa (1932–1967 participated in the Anti-French Resistance War, stayed in the South after 1954, and engaged in journalism in Saigon[6]; Viễn Phương (1928–2005) participated in the Anti-French Resistance War, stayed in Saigon after 1954 to work in the field of literature and journalism, from 1960 he was active in the free zones of the communist government[7]; Vũ Bằng (1913–1984) went to South Vietnam under the direction of the Party after 1954, continued to write and collaborate with many newspapers and served as a contact person for the Party in Saigon from then until 1975[8]; Nguyễn

---

[4] The term urban literature in South Vietnam is used to refer to a geographical area. The urban area is understood as a place where a contemporary government has its headquarters, the economic, political, and cultural center of a locality or region, in contrast to the rural area. Urban literature is literature that is born in urban areas, influenced by the economic, political, and cultural conditions of this area. During the Vietnam War, the cities in South Vietnam such as Huế, Đà Nẵng, Nha Trang, Đà Lạt, Pleiku, Cần Thơ, and Saigon were the places where the government of the United States—the Republic of Vietnam took power and set up its headquarters. This was the place where crucial cultural and literary activities took place.

[5] Võ Phiến, *Văn học miền Nam*, 70–71.

[6] Trần Hữu Tá, *Nhìn lại*, 1058.

[7] Ibid., 1069.

[8] Ibid., 1053.

Nguyên (real name is Nguyễn Ngọc Lương (1929–2002) was the director of *Tin Văn* newspaper,[9] Lữ Phương (real name is Lữ Văn Phương, born in 1938) was Deputy Minister of Culture and Information in the Provisional Revolutionary Government of the Republic of South Vietnam)[10]; Sơn Nam (1926–2008) participated in the Anti-French Resistance War, stayed in Saigon to work in the field of journalism and literature after 1954[11]; Bình Nguyên Lộc (real name is Tô Văn Tuấn, 1914–1987), was a famous journalist and writer in urban areas in South Vietnam, participated in the revolution in the Southeast region[12]; Trang Thế Hy (real name is Võ Trọng Cảnh, 1924–2015), was a famous journalist and writer in urban areas in South Vietnam, participated in the revolution since the August Revolution of 1945,[13] and remained in the inner city of Saigon while secretly working on revolutionary activities[14] and being a journalist, teaching and writing for living.[15] They expressed their political views in newspapers and magazines, such as *Bách Khoa* (director and editor-in-chief was Huỳnh Văn Lang, 426 issues published from 1957 to 1975)[16]; *Nhân Loại*,[17] *Hành Trình* (chaired by Nguyễn Văn Trung, 1930, a lecturer who taught philosophy)[18] had its first issue published in October 1964, stopped publishing in November 1967 and changed to the *Đất Nước* newspaper. The latter journal was also chaired by Nguyễn Văn Trung[19]; *Tin Văn* (Nguyễn Nguyên, 1929, chairman and editor-in-chief) was issued in the years 1966–1967. Some writers such as Sơn Nam, Bình Nguyên Lộc, and Trang Thế Hy mainly wrote about rural life and customs in the South. The works of writers Lê Vĩnh Hòa, Vũ Hạnh, and Viễn Phương expressed the voice of struggle directly. Among the revolutionary writers, Vũ Hạnh stayed in Saigon the longest (during the wartime)[20] and was the most dedicated to using literature as a political weapon.[21]

Vũ Hạnh's real name is Nguyễn Đức Dũng, born on July 15, 1926, died on August 15, 2021, from Bình Nguyên commune, Thăng Bình district, Quảng Nam province.

---

[9] Ibid., 1066.

[10] Ibid., 1069.

[11] Ibid., 1065.

[12] Nguyễn Đăng Mạnh, *Từ điển tác giả*, 52–53.

[13] Đỗ Đức Hiểu, *Từ điển văn học,* 1767.

[14] Vũ Hạnh, *Tuyển tập Vũ Hạnh*, 13; Trần Hữu Tá, *Nhìn lại*, 1053, 1058, 1065, 1066, 1069; Đỗ Đức Hiểu, *Từ điển văn học,* 1767.

[15] Võ Phiến, *Văn học miền Nam*, 44, 52; Vũ Hạnh, *Tuyển tập Vũ Hạnh*, 26.

[16] Phan Đăng Thanh, *Lịch sử các chế độ báo chí*, 267.

[17] *Nhân Loại* is a political—social newspaper run by revolutionaries, the first issue was published at the end of April 1956 and it ended in 1959, the chairman and editor-in-chief was Anh Đào—who only lent *manchette* but was not involved in the content of the newspaper, Bình Nguyên Lộc (2014–1987), Sơn Nam (1926–2008), Trang Thế Hy (1924–2015), Lê Vĩnh Hòa (1932–1967) were regular authors of the magazine. Ibid., 51.

[18] Thụy Khuê, "Nguyễn Văn Trung," 30/7/2014, http://thuykhue.free.fr/stt/n/NguyenvanTrung01.html.

[19] Phan Đăng Thanh, *Lịch sử*, 258.

[20] Vũ Hạnh, *Tuyển tập Vũ Hạnh, tập* 1, 13.

[21] Ibid., 15.

Vũ Hạnh joined the national liberation movement when he was less than twenty years old. Before and during the Anti-French Resistance War, he joined the Việt Minh Front, actively participated in the art team to propagate the New Life Movement, and encouraged people to participate in the resistance war. During the period from 1956 to 1975, he was a contact person of the Party and worked independently in inner Saigon. Unlike some communist writers who only worked in Southern cities for a short time, then moved to the liberated areas or regrouped in the North, Vũ Hạnh stayed in Saigon during the Vietnam War.[22] In 1966, the National Culture Protection Force was established,[23] Vũ Hạnh was assigned to be General Secretary.[24] As a soldier and later a revolutionary leader, Vũ Hạnh tried very hard to express his voice to protect the national culture and to awaken the spirit of struggle against the United States.[25] As soon as he entered Saigon, he chose the press as a means of propagating revolutionary ideals.[26] His theoretical essays and literary compositions were regularly published in *Bách Khoa* and *Tin Văn* newspapers[27] under the pseudonyms Minh Hữu, Cô Phương Thảo, Nguyễn Phù, and A. Pazz.[28] During this period, Vũ Hạnh was very aware of the role of literature in political struggle and always considered it an effective weapon.[29] Many of his criticisms and researches were written under the direction of his superiors, such as *Người Việt cao quý* (The Noble Vietnamese, 1965),[30] and *Con người Sài Gòn* (Saigonese, 1971).[31] His literary works were also composed with clear propaganda purposes. According to him, the short story *Bút máu* (Blood Pen, 1958) was written in "response to a large number of hack writers at that time,"[32] and the play *Người nữ tì* (The Handmaid, 1959) "referred to the intellectuals who

---

[22] Vũ Hạnh, *Vũ Hạnh tuyển tập, tập 1*, 13.

Lê Vĩnh Hòa (1932-1967, participated in the Anti-French Resistance War, stayed in the South after 1954, worked in the press in Saigon, worked in the communist base area after 1963 (Communist bases (also known as liberated zones) were areas controlled by communists. They were areas that were well-equipped with military weapons and used as the place to build revolutionary forces (including political and armed forces). Communist bases were places that provided material and military strength, symbolized as a source of spiritual and political encouragement in the revolution and resistance war.) Nguyễn Đăng Mạnh, *Từ điển tác giả*, 349. Viễn Phương (real name is Phan Thanh Viễn (1928–2005), participated in the Anti-French Resistance War, after 1954 stayed in Saigon to work in the field of literature and journalism, after 1960 performing arts activities in the liberated area of the revolution. Trần Hữu Tá, *Nhìn lại*, 1069. Giang Nam (real name is Nguyễn Sung, born in 1929, joined the revolution in 1945, after 1954, he worked secretly in many places in Nha Trang, Saigon, Biên Hòa, after 1959 moved into the communist base area. Nguyễn Đăng Mạnh, *Từ điển tác giả*, 214–215.

[23] Nguyễn Đăng Mạnh, Ibid., 25.

[24] Ibid., 26.

[25] Ibid., 15.

[26] Ibid., 13.

[27] Ibid., 14, 25.

[28] Ibid., 51.

[29] Ibid., 15.

[30] Ibid., 20.

[31] Ibid., 33.

[32] Ibid., 15.

claimed to serve an unjust, brutal regime and denied their true origins, because of self-interest, illusion or fear, in order to live and die for the regime."[33]

Carrying out revolutionary activities independently in the heart of Saigon, which was controlled by the United States and the Republic of Vietnam government, and being imprisoned many times, Vũ Hạnh still pursued a purpose: to serve the revolution and to use his writing to defend communist ideas. In the section "Memoirs" printed in *Vũ Hạnh tuyển tập* (The Anthology of Vũ Hạnh), *Volume I*, he recalled his superiors' comments about him: "In terms of cultural struggle in the inner city, [he] actively implemented all the revolutionary policies outlined in the anti-American era, and had only one defect, that was obedience to the Party's requirements."[34]

Vietnamese researchers highly appreciated the propaganda value of Vũ Hạnh's works and considered him an excellent revolutionary writer. Specifically, in the period 1956–1975, Vũ Hạnh was assigned the role of "rather radical nationalist."[35] He enthusiastically participated in literary, artistic, and journalistic activities in inner Saigon. Using several pseudonyms for different political purposes, he composed short stories, novels, plays, and wrote many theoretical, critical, and research articles to protect national culture against the invasion policies of the United States. For example, he took the pseudonym A. Pazzi, using a foreign name to write the essay *Người Việt cao quý* (The Noble Vietnamese, 1965) "to make it less censored and [...] to make praises easier to hear."[36] This pseudonym was taken from the name of Vũ Hạnh's fellow prisoner, Võ Hạnh. He changed Võ to Vũ because "at that time many writers migrated from the North to the South - such as Vũ Hoàng Chương, Vũ Khắc Khoan - so in that trend I wanted to be "in tune" with them."[37] Writing literary criticism, he took the pen name Cô Phương Thảo—his daughter's name—because he thought that "people who were criticized by a female were less angry than if they were attacked by a male."[38] His works were published and circulated in South Vietnam, mainly in *Bách Khoa* and *Tin Văn* journals. *Bách Khoa* journal was founded by Mr. Huỳnh Văn Lang. He was born in 1922 and served as a chairman and an editor. He was also a famous intellectual in South Vietnam and General Director of the Foreign Exchange Agency in the First Republic of Vietnam. *Bách Khoa* journal was published twice a month, on the 1st and 15th. The first issue was published on January 15, 1957, and the last issue, number 426, was published on April 19, 1975. *Bách Khoa* published a collection of articles on religion, philosophy, history, research, literature, economics, and medicine. This journal was collaborated on by many intellectuals, writers, and artists such as: Nguyễn Hiến Lê (1912–1984), Võ Phiến (1925–2015), Bình Nguyên Lộc (1914–1987), Quách Tấn (1910–1992), Đông Hồ (1906–1969), Nguyễn Ngu Í (1921–1979), Võ Hồng (1921–2013), and Vũ Hạnh (1926–2021). Its

---

[33] Ibid., 15.

[34] Ibid., 36.

[35] Vũ Hạnh, *Tuyển tập, tập 1*, 13.

[36] Ibid., 20.

[37] Ibid., 57.

[38] Ibid., 58.

content was divided into two distinct parts: essays and arts.[39] *Tin Văn* journal was originally a semi-monthly journal, then changed to a weekly journal that was chaired and edited by Nguyễn Nguyên, whose real name is Nguyễn Ngọc Lương. Born in 1929, he was a Party member in North Vietnam, then moved to Saigon to spy on the South Vietnamese government.[40] The first issue of *Tin Văn* was published on July 7, 1966, and the last issue was published on August 4, 1967. The journal was an open forum for communists whose viewpoints were against the United States and the Saigon government. The policy of this journal was "protecting the national culture, combating the depraved and 'uprooted' culture."[41] Since Vũ Hạnh's literary works were less popular in South Vietnam, reviews and research works were mainly focused on his essays. Research on Vũ Hạnh was mostly discussion of the writer's views reflected in his criticism. In general, these were scattered articles, which showed some comments about Vũ Hạnh's literary and critical works but did not study his literary and critical style.

After 1975, when the war ended, studies on urban literature in South Vietnam in general and Vũ Hạnh in particular increasingly appeared. In such works as *Nhìn lại một chặng đường văn học*[42] (Looking Back on a Literary Journey) by Trần Hữu Tá (who was born in 1937, a professor and lecturer at Ho Chi Minh City University of Education), *Vũ Hạnh*[43] (Vũ Hạnh) by Nguyễn Ngọc Thiện (who was born in 1947, an editor-in-chief of the Vietnam Forum for Culture and Arts), *Văn học Việt Nam thế kỷ XX*[44] (Vietnamese Literature in the 20th Century) by Phan Cự Đệ (1933–2007, a professor, critic and literary theorist), Vũ Hạnh was considered a typical writer of revolutionary literature in the center of the Southern urban area. These researchers identified several important characteristics in Vũ Hạnh's works, including originality, creativity, sophistication, sharpness, and talent for criticism; a majestic spirit in literary creation; an ambiguous, symbolic writing style, the use of historical Chinese stories, and ghost fairy tales to express revolutionary ideas. Trần Hữu Tá said that the achievements of the body of revolutionary literature (which was called "patriotic and revolutionary literature" by Trần Hữu Tá)[45] in Southern cities were the fighting voice that "denounced and negated a disintegrating society,"[46] and "the fervent appeal and the first step of reaching for the light."[47] Trần Hữu Tá showed these ideas in many works. However, his analyses were mainly the descriptions of denunciation, social negation, and the call to find ethnicity. He did not answer thoroughly why the above-mentioned issues were the basic inspiration reflected in the patriotic and revolutionary literature and how literary works affected people.

[39] Phan Đăng Thanh, *Lịch sử*, 267–268.
[40] Trần Hữu Tá, *Nhìn lại*, 1066; Phan Đăng Thanh, *Lịch sử*, 262.
[41] Phan Đăng Thanh, *Lịch sử*, 262.
[42] Trần Hữu Tá, *Nhìn lại*, 50, 55, 96, 97, 99, 100, 119, 120.
[43] Vũ Hạnh, *Tuyển tập Vũ Hạnh, tập 2*, 798.
[44] Phan Cự Đệ, *Văn học Việt Nam*, 313.
[45] Trần Hữu Tá, *Nhìn lại*, 11.
[46] Ibid., 45.
[47] Ibid., 69.

Trần Hữu Tá also pointed out a basic feature of the story genre: "Patriotic writers thoroughly exploit the ambiguous, symbolic writing style, the use of Chinese folk tales, ghostly fairy tales to express their ideals."[48] When analyzing and supporting his arguments, Trần Hữu Tá often quoted Vũ Hạnh's works.[49] In these works, Vũ Hạnh's literary compositions were only used as evidence but not studied deeply to see the commonalities and uniqueness in these works compared to patriotic and revolutionary literature in Southern cities.

In the doctoral thesis *Truyện ngắn trong khuynh hướng văn học yêu nước ở đô thị miền Nam 1965–1975* (Short stories in the patriotic literary trend in urban literature in South Vietnam from 1965 to 1975), Bùi Thanh Thảo (who was a lecturer at Faculty of Social Sciences and Humanities, Can Tho University, Can Tho City, Vietnam) analyzed the issue of the sense of reality and the sense of struggle in some of Vũ Hạnh's short stories.[50] For example, the author analyzed "a strong voice against the Saigon government"[51] in the short story *Chung giọt mồ hôi* (Same Drops of Sweat, 1972) and the "nostalgia for traditional cultural values"[52] in the story *Tô cháo lòng* (A Bowl of Pork Organ Congee) by Vũ Hạnh. However, Bùi Thanh Thảo's thesis only focused on short stories in the patriotic literary trend in Southern urban areas from 1965 to 1975. Vũ Hạnh did not write many valuable short stories in this period. Therefore, the thesis did not give an overview of Vũ Hạnh's artistic style, his position and his contribution to the patriotic trend.

The book *Lược sử văn học Việt Nam* (A Brief History of Vietnamese Literature) edited by Trần Đình Sử (who was born in 1940, Professor of Literature Faculty, Hanoi National University of Education, Vietnam, specializing in literary theory) devoted a section to Southern literature in the period 1954–1975.[53] The book's authors categorized literature in South Vietnam into five categories: the tendency to uphold nationalism[54]; tendency to express the resistance[55]; tendency to honor national cultural traditions[56]; tendency to recreate the human condition[57]; tendency to attract popular readers.[58] Vũ Hạnh belonged to the "literary tendency to honor national cultural traditions."[59] As a "brief history," the book did not delve into specific phenomena to evaluate the roles and contributions of typical writers in each category. As a result, Vũ Hạnh is only mentioned briefly by name.

---

[48] Ibid., 16–17.

[49] Ibid., 50, 55, 96, 97, 99, 100, 119, 120.

[50] Bùi Thanh Thảo, "Truyện ngắn," 60–125.

[51] Ibid., 73.

[52] Ibid., 83.

[53] Trần Đình Sử, *Lược sử văn học*, 252–276.

[54] Ibid., 254.

[55] Ibid., 257.

[56] Ibid., 261.

[57] Ibid., 265.

[58] Ibid., 268.

[59] Ibid., 263, 264.

Extensive research on literature in South Vietnam by overseas researchers was given the most attention by Võ Phiến in his work *Văn học miền Nam Tổng quan* (An Overview of Literature in South Vietnam). Võ Phiến was born in 1925; he was a writer in South Vietnam, lived and composed in Los Angeles, the United States, from 1975 and died on September 28, 2015, in Santa Ana, California. In this work, Võ Phiến mentioned Vũ Hạnh when discussing the writers in urban areas in South Vietnam. Võ Phiến classified Vũ Hạnh as a writer who "gathered around a political position"[60] along with Lữ Phương (1938) and Nguyễn Nguyên (1929–2002), and who "gathered around a newspaper, usually a journal that existed quite long and had a relatively wide influence."[61] Although not explicitly stated in the book, Võ Phiến considered Vũ Hạnh to be a writer who had political leanings and had a great influence on public opinion. Unfortunately, this book did not provide rich materials as regards Vũ Hạnh's point of view and his writing career.

The systematic research work that was most directly related to Vũ Hạnh was the doctoral thesis *Nhà văn Vũ Hạnh: lí luận, phê bình, nghiên cứu, sáng tác* (The Writer Vũ Hạnh: Theory, Criticism, Research, and Composition) by Nguyễn Xuân Huy (a lecturer at Hùng Vương University, Phú Thọ province, Vietnam). In the thesis, Nguyễn Xuân Huy applied historical and sociological methodology, systematic methods, cultural studies, comparison, analysis, and synthesis to show important characteristics of Vũ Hạnh's theoretical and critical work, his research and compositions. For example, Nguyễn Xuân Huy featured Vũ Hạnh's critical style, including: "Spirit of Honest and Objective Research"; "Ability to Systematize Literary Issues Scientifically"; "Direct, Powerful and Timely Criticism"; "Ability to Write Profoundly and Sensitivity to Literary Issues"; "Rich, Expressive Nuances in Critical Language."[62] Regarding literary creativity, Nguyễn Xuân Huy noticed the following outstanding features: the main topics in Vũ Hạnh's works included "the theme of the mountains," "the theme of the history of the wild," "the theme of the world"[63]; Characters were "epic characters embraced with national cultural traditions" and "worldly characters"[64]; Typical artistic methods were mythization and innovation of artistic language.[65] The methods used in the thesis helped Nguyễn Xuân Huy systematically point out the outstanding features of Vũ Hạnh's style in his essays and literary writing. However, the author did not explain important issues such as: How were these discourses formed? What was the purpose of creating discourse strategies in Vũ Hạnh's compositions? Hence, the thesis did not delve into the tendencies and the typological nature of Vũ Hạnh's writings. Our article is also interested in Vũ Hạnh's choice of topics, how he builds characters and his use of unique artistic techniques. However, we consider these aspects to be ***the writer's***

---

[60] Võ Phiến, *Văn học miền Nam*, 47.

[61] Ibid., 47.

[62] Nguyễn Xuân Huy, "Nhà văn Vũ Hạnh," 81- 87.

[63] Ibid., 118–130.

[64] Ibid., 130–139.

[65] Ibid., 139 -146.

discursive strategy for conveying political messages and his way of propagating his ideas for the struggle of revolutionary forces.

To give an additional perspective on Vũ Hạnh's literary career, and clarify the vibrant and multifaceted picture of urban literature in South Vietnam in the period 1955–1975, we apply discourse theory to figures out of Vũ Hạnh's literary works, analyze the influence that political opinions and ideas had on his way of writing and explaining the advantages and limitations of his way of writing. Specifically, we explore the relationship between political discourse and literary discourse in Vũ Hạnh's compositions, thereby emphasizing the dominance therein of cultural mechanisms, political power, and ways of creating political views. The existence of a left-leaning literary trend in urban literature in South Vietnam at the time of which Vũ Hạnh was a representative shows the diversity and multifaceted political and artistic life in this region.

In terms of methodology, in this article we consider Vũ Hạnh to be a typical writer of the "left-leaning." The term "left-leaning" is used in a political sense in order to distinguish the works of Vũ Hạnh and his fellows from those of the opposite side. The term "left-leaning" is used in contrast to "right-leaning" in terms of ideology. "Left-leaning" is understood as one of the ideologies, such as social liberalism, social democracy, socialism, communism, trade unionism, and anarchism.[66] The official ideology of the Democratic Republic of Vietnam was communism, so writers who supported North Vietnam and followed the Communist Party's aim to unify the country were "left-leaning" writers. We call Vũ Hạnh "a left-leaning writer" to emphasize the political leaning of his artistic consciousness.

Vũ Hạnh wrote many non-fictional and fictional works, including articles, essays, plays, short stories, and long stories. *Tuyển tập Vũ Hạnh* (*Anthology of Vũ Hạnh*), Volume 1 and 2, contains 32 short stories that were composed both before and after 1975,[67] 2 plays,[68] 4 long stories,[69] and 18 essays and criticisms.[70] Within the scope of this article, it is difficult for us to cover all of his writings. So we have chosen only the short stories written in the period 1955–1975, printed in *Vũ Hạnh tuyển tập*, Volume I, published by Ho Chi Minh City General Publishing House in 2015. (This book includes the short stories: *Vượt thác* (Overpassing Waterfall, 1957), *Bút máu* (Blood Pen, 1958), *Chất ngọc* (Quality of Ruby, 1960), *Vàng tháp cổ* (Gold in the Ancient Tower, 1960), *Cây đàn trong núi* (The Violin in the Mountain, 1960), *Giấy nhãn* (Label Paper 1960), *Lòng suối* (Streambed, 1961), *Tết giữa rừng* (Tet in the Middle of the Forest, 1961), *Mùa xuân trên đỉnh non cao* (Spring on the Mountain Peak, 1962), *Lẽ sống* (Reason for Life, 1963), *Người chồng thời đại* (The Husband of the Times, 1966), *Mụ Tư Cò* (Tư Cò, 1966), *Tô cháo lòng* (A Bowl of Pork Organ Congee, 1967), *Câu chuyện mất ngựa* (The Story of Losing a Horse, 1971), *Chung*

---

[66] Quang Đào, *"Nguồn gốc,"* https://baoquocte.vn/nguon-goc-cua-khai-niem-canh-ta-va-canh-huu-109952.html.

[67] Vũ Hạnh, *Vũ Hạnh tuyển tập*, tập 1, 63–506.

[68] Ibid., 507–557.

[69] Vũ Hạnh, *Vũ Hạnh tuyển tập*, tập 2, 13–526.

[70] Ibid., 527–768.

giọt mồ hôi (Same Drops of Sweat, 1972). The short story is a genre in which Vũ Hạnh achieved much. By reading his short stories, we can bring to light the unique nature of Vũ Hạnh's writing—he was dedicated to the goal of propagating and defending the ideals of the Communist Party of Vietnam.

To create a convincing basis for the analysis and arguments in the paper, we rely on documents concerning Vũ Hạnh's life, revolutionary career, creative career, and articles and research on urban literature in South Vietnam, such as *Hồi ký* (Memoirs)[71] by Vũ Hạnh and some documents of writers, journalists, researchers, and critics in Vietnam; material from Võ Phiến's book *Văn học miền Nam tổng quan* (An Overview of Literature in South Vietnam).

Propaganda Strategy in Vũ Hạnh's Short Stories

In the urban area in South Vietnam from 1955 to 1975, literature developed richly, diversely but very complicatedly. There were many literary trends that often inter-fered with each other.[72] At that time, Western and American political, cultural, and philosophical ideas flooded the urban areas in South Vietnam, leaving a deep impres-sion on literature.[73] The colors of existential philosophy and psychoanalysis perme-ated the poetry and prose[74] by Thanh Tâm Tuyền (1936–2006, a famous poet and writer of urban literature in South Vietnam who worked for the government of the Republic of Vietnam); Tô Thùy Yên (real name Đinh Thành Tiên, 1938–2019, who worked for the government of the Republic of Vietnam; a famous poet of urban litera-ture in South Vietnam), Dương Nghiễm Mậu (real name Phi Ích Nghiễm, 1936–2016, a former military reporter for the Republic of Vietnam, a famous writer of urban liter-ature in South Vietnam); Nguyên Sa (real name Trần Bích Lan, 1932–1998, a famous philosophy teacher, journalist, and poet of urban literature in South Vietnam); Nguyên Vũ (real name Vũ Ngự Chiêu, born in 1942, served in the army of the Republic of Vietnam, a famous writer of urban literature in South Vietnam); Nguyễn Thị Thụy Vũ (real name Nguyễn Băng Lĩnh, born in 1937, a famous writer of urban litera-ture in South Vietnam); Nguyễn Thị Hoàng (born in 1939, a famous writer of urban literature in South Vietnam). There were also writers who were classified by some Vietnamese researchers as progressive-patriotic. Most of the works and articles on

---

[71] Vũ Hạnh, *Tuyển tập Vũ Hạnh, tập 1*, 13–60.

[72] Võ Phiến, *Văn học miền Nam*, 70.

[73] Trịnh Bá Đĩnh, *Lịch sử lý luận*, 167, 168, 171; Nguyễn Văn Lục, "20 năm văn học," https://nguoitinhhuvo.wordpress.com/2014/12/03/20-nam-van-hoc-dich-thuat-mien-nam-1955-1975-ngu yen-van-luc/, 3/12/2014.

[74] Bửu Ý, "Nhìn lại đời sống." http://tapchisonghuong.com.vn/tap-chi/c371/n25459/Buu-Y-nhin-lai-do-i-so-ng-van-hoc-mien-Nam-giai-doan-tu-1954-1975.html, 30/04/2017; Võ Phiến, *Văn học miền Nam*, 307–308; Nguyễn Văn Lục, *20 năm văn học*, "Hai mươi năm văn học dịch thuật miền Nam 1955–1975," https://nguoitinhhuvo.wordpress.com/2014/12/03/20-nam-van-hoc-dich-thuat-mien-nam-1955-1975-nguyen-van-luc/, 3/12/2014.

.

urban literature in South Vietnam in the period 1954–1975 in Vietnam shared an important argument: in Southern cities, there was a tendency toward progressive-patriotic/revolutionary patriotic literature, which was composed by communists or those who sympathized with the communist idea.[75] The imprint of Western and American philosophy and literature was still very strong. Composing in the cultural atmosphere of Saigon during the war, regularly interacting with writers who were part of different trends, Vũ Hạnh was aware of new ideologies and their impacts on the writing style of his colleagues. However, he was determined to choose a separate direction and viewpoint in his writing. He did not follow the existentialism, psychoanalysis, and feminism that was "fashionable" at that time but returned to the traditional topics and writing style. He wrote about "the countryside, the mountains and forests,"[76] to create new and attractive themes for readers.[77] In our opinion, political power played a huge role in Vũ Hạnh's choice and form of expression in his short stories. He always had a specific writing strategy for each work in order to maximize propaganda and promotion goals. Writing helped him to carry out his political tasks.

Determined to use literature for politics, from the very beginning Vũ Hạnh thought of "how to write to attract many readers without losing the purpose of the national struggle."[78] And he chose themes and styles that suited the taste of many readers. He wrote about the countryside, mountains, and forests; constructed a space for history and legend, created the feeling of the old days of the nation; wrote about people who had the profiles of epic heroes. His writing strategy, at the same time, achieved many purposes. Firstly, since he conceived that "stories about the countryside as well as the mountains and forests will be liked by urban readers because of their exoticism,"[79] his stories spread widely from the North to the South throughout urban and rural areas.[80] Secondly, composing works with a little of older times, in the context of Saigon's society that was Westernizing and Americanizing, was a way for him to combat the influence of foreign cultures. Thirdly, the metaphorical writing style, which used the past to talk about the present, helped him somewhat avoid repressive retributions by the Saigon government. Although it was well known that his works could provoke

---

[75] Typical for such an idea are: Trần Hữu Tá (born in 1937, professor, lecturer at Ho Chi Minh City University of Education, Vietnam). Trần Hữu Tá, Nhìn lại, 11, 23, 45. Trần Trọng Đăng Đàn (1936–2020, nguyên Tổng biên tập Tạp chí Khoa học Xã hội, Viện Khoa học Xã hội vùng Nam bộ thuộc Viện Hàn lâm Khoa học Xã hội Việt Nam). Trần Trọng Đăng Đàn, Văn học, 8. Bùi Thanh Thảo (lecturer at Faculty of Social Sciences and Humanities, Cần Thơ University, Cần Thơ). Bùi Thanh Thảo, "Truyện ngắn," 26, 60, 126, https://phucvu.thuvientphcm.gov.vn/Viewer/EBook/693919. Nguyễn Thanh Hùng (Lecturer at An Giang University, Vietnam) Nguyễn Thanh Hùng, "Nhìn lại truyện ngắn," 31. Trang Thế Hy (real name is Võ Trọng Cảnh (1924–2015), participating in the revolution since the August Revolution in 1945, famous journalist and writer in Southern urban areas), Bình Nguyên Lộc (real name is Tô Văn Tuấn (1914–1987), participated in the revolution in the Southeast region, a famous journalist and writer in Southern urban areas).

[76] Vũ Hạnh, *Tuyển tập Vũ Hạnh, tập 1*, 15.

[77] Ibid., 16.

[78] Ibid., 15.

[79] Ibid., 15.

[80] Ibid., 15–16.

readers psychologically, it was difficult for the authorities to have enough evidence to arrest him.

Most of Vũ Hạnh's short stories are historical and legendary stories. Surveying 15 short stories composed in the period 1957–1975 included in *Vũ Hạnh tuyển tập* (The Anthology of Vũ Hạnh), Volume 1, we found that there were 9 stories written in the historical style and using legendary elements, including: *Vượt thác* (Overpassing Waterfall, 1957), *Bút máu* (Blood Pen, 1958), *Chất ngọc* (Quality of Ruby, 1960), *Vàng tháp cổ* (Gold in the Ancient Tower, 1960), *Lòng suối* (Streambed, 1961), *Tết giữa rừng* (Tet in the Middle of the Forest, 1961), *Mùa xuân trên đỉnh non cao* (Spring on the Mountain Peak, 1962), *Câu chuyện mất ngựa* (The Story of Losing a Horse, 1971), and *Chung giọt mồ hôi* (Same Drops of Sweat, 1972). The ancient atmosphere made these stories easily touch the hearts of readers, stirring up direct emotions, especially in those who adhered to traditional values. In the context of bombs and bullets, death, turmoil, and chaos, people cannot help but worry, feeling bewildered, longing to escape the situation. Vũ Hạnh's works partly met the readers' need, helping them to relive the old, peaceful and primitive times. These short stories brought readers back to life in the fifteenth and sixteenth centuries through ancient languages; through stories about brave Confucianists, honest, freedom-loving people; and through hidden life lessons. For example, the opening paragraphs of the above-mentioned stories were not different from those of medieval Vietnamese stories: "Lương Sinh - a native of Mân Châu, a son of a wealthy family, had been known for his intelligence since he was a little boy. He was very good at poetry when he was eight, everyone praised him as a child prodigy"[81]; or "In the land of Hào Dương, there was Sầm Hiệu who lived as a plowman, a straightforward, rude and gruff guy."[82] *Lĩnh Nam chích quái* (Selection of Strange Tales in Lĩnh Nam) by Trần Thế Pháp (who lived around the fourteenth century), a prose in Han script that is a collection of legends and fairy tales, consisting of 22 stories, completed at the end of the fourteenth century,[83] and *Truyền kỳ mạn lục* (Collection of Strange Tales) by Nguyễn Dữ,[84] which also had the same opening passages as Vũ Hạnh's *Bút máu* (Blood Pen) and *Chất ngọc* (Quality of Ruby). For example, the tale *Hà Ô Lôi* by Trần Thế Pháp: "During the reign of King Trần Dụ Tông, in the sixth year of Thiệu Phong, there was a man in the Roman village named Đặng Sĩ Doanh. He was a pacification commissioner, to serve the king to go to China"[85] and *Chuyện chức phán sự đền Tản Viên* (The Tale of the Judge of Tản Viên Temple): "Ngô Tử Văn's name was Soạn, from Yên Dũng district, Lạng Giang. He was inherently hot-tempered."[86] Creating a story about the past, Vũ Hạnh implicitly denied the tumultuous contemporary life.

---

[81] Ibid., 63.

[82] Ibid., 74.

[83] Nguyễn Đăng Mạnh, *Từ điển tác giả*, 354; Nguyễn Đăng Na, *Văn xuôi tự sự*, 107.

[84] Nguyễn Dữ is a famous Vietnamese writer who lived and composed around the sixteenth century. *Collection of Strange Tales* is the only collection of stories written by Nguyễn Dữ in 1547, including 20 stories, written in Han script in the genre of legend.

[85] Nguyễn Đăng Na, *Văn xuôi tự sự*, 109.

[86] Nguyễn Dữ, *Truyền kỳ mạn lục*, 105.

The strong fighting voice in these stories was expressed by the writer through artistic symbols in *Bút máu* (Blood Pen*), Chất ngọc* (Quality of Ruby), *Vàng tháp cổ* (Gold in the Ancient Tower), *Mùa xuân trên đỉnh non* cao (Spring on the Mountain Peak), *Vượt thác* (Overpassing Waterfall), *Lòng suối* (Streambed). Constructing these symbols was a way for Vũ Hạnh to use the past to talk about the present. The short story *Blood Pen* (1958) revolved around how to confirm the identity of the Confucian student Lương Sinh. He gave up his uncle's advice to be a soldier to become a writer because he was afraid that "the person who held the blade would not live without harming people."[87] But Lương Sinh was wrong. The pen does not directly cause bloodshed but indirectly creates injustice and death if the writer lacks responsibility. Because of being bribed by bad guys and unable to control his pen, Lương Sinh, without his consciousness, accidentally pushed other people into a situation of misery, injustice, and casualties. The symbol "blood pen" evokes many associations. "Pen" becomes a test of the writer's humanity. "Blood pen" is a lesson of caution for when one is writing something. It was also meant to warn those who ran after profits and positions, who lacked responsibility and conscience. "Ruby" in the story *Quality of Ruby* (1960) is a symbol of the transparent and noble beauty of those who are wholeheartedly for the good of people, bravely fighting to protect justice, not yielding to power and tyranny. The "Ancient Tower" in *Gold in the Ancient Towe*r (1960) is a symbol of the traditional culture that was destroyed by the blind greed of man. At that time, when Western and American cultures were overwhelming South Vietnam, the symbol of gold in the ancient tower easily made readers feel nostalgic for the nation's past and they thus turned away from reality. "Streambed" (*Streambed*, 1961) is a symbol of the human heart. The deep streambed illuminates people's hearts, good and evil are clearly visible. "Spring" (*Spring on the Mountain Peak*, 1962) is a symbol of aspiration and belief in a new and good life. These symbols can move people's hearts, urge them to fight against evil, violence, or the power of foreign cultures, to sacrifice for the common good of the people, to overcome difficulties, and always to keep faith in the present.

The stories *Overpassing Waterfall* (1957), *The Story of Losing a Horse* (1971), *Same Drops of Sweat* (1972) are like fables that contain profound lessons of life. *Overpassing Waterfall* was a wake-up call for those who were weak, lacked courage and feared thorny roads, seeking an easier path. However, they still ended up suffering because there was no easy way to go without perseverance and courage. The king in the story *Same Drops of Sweat* (1972) was the image of those who easily forgot the past, were even willing to shake off the past to reach a higher position. The story was intended to refer to those who were passionate about wealth and power, turning their backs on the country, people, and their benefactors. *The Story of Losing a Horse* (1971) was a lesson of self-esteem. Mr. Thất was not the one who killed the king's horse thief in the past but he felt humiliated because he was falsely accused by his son. So he committed suicide to keep his dignity. The story made readers think of those who did evil things, pushed others into misery but still lived calmly.

---

[87] Vũ Hạnh, *Tuyển tập Vũ Hạnh, tập 1*, 64.

Besides wild historical stories, Vũ Hạnh wrote some stories in a realistic style (6/15 stories).[88] These short stories took place in modern settings. *Cây đàn trong núi* (The Violin in the Mountain, 1960) and *Lẽ sống* (Reason for Life, 1963) praised those who followed the revolution single-mindedly; *Giấy nhân* (Label Paper, 1960), *Người chồng thời đại* (The Husband of the Times, 1966), *Mụ Tư Cò* (Tư Cò, 1966) and *Tô cháo lòng* (A Bowl of Pork Organ Congee, 1967) focused on the alienation of people due to their difficult living circumstances. In these stories, Vũ Hạnh directly exposed the precarious, unsettled, and miserable life of the Saigonese. These stories showed a strong and direct fighting voice.

Choosing expressive methods to propagate the revolutionary struggle become Vũ Hạnh's artistic pursuit throughout his entire career. In fact, his literary propaganda strategy helped him succeed in politics. The short stories *Blood Pen* (1958), *Tet in the Middle of the Forest* (1961), and *The Husband of the Times* (1966) made the authorities in Saigon somewhat afraid of the influences of these stories on people.[89] Vũ Hạnh's initiative and flexibility in fighting-strategies made the Revolutionary forces trust him and they assigned him to be in charge of the inner city press and to write freely. He became General Secretary of the National Culture Protection Force in 1966.[90]

Propaganda Content in Vũ Hạnh's Short Stories

Political consciousness dominated and created consistency in the discourse of Vũ Hạnh's short stories. Whether written in a historical or realistic style, Vũ Hạnh aimed to create a propaganda discourse and promote the revolutionary idea. Unlike other writers who participated in the Anti-French Resistance War and composed in inner Saigon from 1954 to 1975, such as Trang Thế Hy (1924–2015), Bình Nguyên Lộc (1914–1987), and Sơn Nam (1926–2008), the fighting spirit in Vũ Hạnh's short stories was stronger and more direct. Trang Thế Hy (1924–2015), Bình Nguyên Lộc (1914–1987), and Sơn Nam (1926–2008) mainly wrote about customs, the reclamation of Southern people, the beauty of nature, or the people's soul in the South. They hardly mentioned the hot issue of the times—the national conflict. In contrast, Vũ Hạnh's short stories were political discourses. Vũ Hạnh discussed the writer's role in the revolutionary struggle, denounced the aggressive policy of the United States and the Republic of Vietnam government, honored traditional culture and called for spiritual sacrifice by the people. These discourses were all presented and explained by him in the illumination of the communist idea. In *Hồi ký* (Memoirs), Vũ Hạnh wrote: "My superiors allowed me to write freely according to my own will without

---

[88] Vũ Hạnh, *Tuyển tập Vũ Hạnh, tập 1*, 276–365.

[89] Ibid., 15, 16, 16, 57.

[90] Ibid., 26, 58.

consulting and reporting to them, as long as what was written was more or less beneficial to the struggle."[91]

During the war, revolutionary writers and artists were assigned dual tasks by the Communist Party of Vietnam: artists—soldiers. (In a letter to painters on the occasion of the 1951 national painting exhibition, President Hồ Chí Minh directed: "Culture and arts belong to the same front, on which you are fighters"[92]). They both fought on the battlefield and on the ideological front. Their voices represented the voice of the Communist Party and the Revolution, which was considered the truth, capable of guiding people's thoughts. As a revolutionary leader and being active in the field of culture, Vũ Hạnh understood the importance of building an ideal group of writers for the cause of the struggle. *Blood Pen* (1958) was a short story that served as a "declaration" for writers. Through the character Lương Sinh, Vũ Hạnh wanted to remind himself and to warn the "group of hack writers"[93] while at the same time expressing his dream of an ideal writer. A careless, unscrupulous, and irresponsible writer can turn ink into blood:

> Writers use the illusion of literature to harm people, which has caused many crimes so far, but because the crimes are obscure, they can't be clearly seen and the writers don't want themselves to be seen clearly [...] Literary crimes in the past and present, if analyzed, may accumulate into thousands of Thiên Sơn ranges?[94]

Lương Sinh's carelessness and permissiveness caused extreme hardship and death for people. Being treated well by the Governor-General of the Lý family, traveling by palanquin, Lương Sinh did not witness the withered fields, the emaciated and scared faces of the people who tried their best to praise the merits of the mandarin. Because of Lương Sinh's viewpoint in respect to the uselessness of the pen, he casually abetted evil without knowing it. The lesson of Lương Sinh's responsibility was also a lesson for all writers. Through Lương Sinh, Vũ Hạnh proposed an ideal writer who was aware of fighting for human interests.

Composing in inner Saigon, Vũ Hạnh could hardly construct the image of a character that put across the motif of a hero in socialist realist literature in the way that revolutionary writers who worked in the liberated areas could. The figure of the ideal hero was conveyed by him in wild historical stories. For example, the short story *Chất ngọc* (Quality of Ruby, 1960) was a discourse that showed Vũ Hạnh's aspiration for the ideal hero. The character Sầm Hiệu lived by plowing and hoeing. Upon his arrest by the Governor-General to join a defense team to suppress people, he resolutely protested with a justification: "We ate the rice grains given to us by mandarins, but the rice was obtained by the people who worked hard."[95] Sầm Hiệu was ordered to be executed by the mandarin but the Governor's sword that was used to kill his mother and wife did not kill him. It was only when the mandarin used the

---

[91] Ibid., 58.

[92] Hồ Chí Minh, "Thư Hồ Chủ tịch," 1. http://baochi.nlv.gov.vn/baochi/cgi-bin/baochi?a=d&d=WNyf19520105&e=-------vi-20--1--img-txIN------#.

[93] Vũ Hạnh, *Tuyển tập Vũ Hạnh, tập 1*, 15.

[94] Ibid., 71.

[95] Ibid., 77.

sword that killed tax evaders, "the sword was stained with the people's blood," that Sầm Hiệu's head fell to the ground. The story expressed a consistent thought—the thought about the people. Sầm Hiệu originated from the masses, lived and died to protect people. This character was a model hero of the revolutionary era, who came from the masses; who had a kind heart, noble personality, who lived and died for the cause and for the people. Vũ Hạnh clearly revealed the propaganda by creating the existence of a ruby in Sầm Hiệu's tomb, which was "like the blood of hatred from the heart."[96] Vũ Hạnh also did not hesitate to promote: "There are many soldiers today who still carry in their hearts the inherited quality of ruby, which symbolizes the resolute defense of the right and the passionate love for the people."[97]

From 1955 to 1975, Western and American cultures flooded the Southern cities, and threatened to destroy the conceptions of morality and the ideals that had existed for thousands of years in Vietnam.[98] Vũ Hạnh's important task, assigned to him by the Communists, was to fight to protect national culture against the influence of foreign cultures and to hinder the loss of national identity.[99] At the request of his superiors, he joined the Pen Club[100] (Vietnam P.E.N Club), also known as the Vietnamese Pen Group. This organization was a non-political arts organization that gathered together many poets, writers, painters, theater artists, cinematographers, essayists, journalists, and educators. It operated in Saigon from 1957 to 1975 and was led by Mr. Đỗ Đức Thu (1909–1979, a writer), Nguyễn Tường Tam (1906–1963, a writer and politician), and Thanh Lãng (1924–1978, a teacher and researcher of literature and linguistics), all of whom alternated as presidents. The Vietnamese Pen Group officially joined the International Pen Organization on September 2, 1957,[101] (International Pen, an association of writers founded in London, England in 1921 in order to promote intellectual cooperation among writers of the world).[102] Vũ Hạnh also aimed at combating the manifestations of the hybridization, enslavement, and decadence of young people by joining the Youth Protection Council and the Vietnam Youth Association[103]; he served as Secretary-General of the National Culture Protection Force[104] in 1966. He wrote essays and literary criticisms to prove nationality in *Truyện Kiều* (The Tale of Kiều) by Nguyễn Du.[105] He wrote *wuxia* stories in response to the *wuxia* books that propagated individuality, violence, and fictionality

---

[96] Ibid., 78.

[97] Ibid., 79.

[98] Võ Phiến, *Văn học miền Nam*, 118, 139, 151.

[99] Vũ Hạnh, *Tuyển tập Vũ Hạnh, tập 1*, 25.

[100] Ibid, 17.

[101] Nhật Tiến, "Từ nhóm Bút Việt," http://tve-4u.org/threads/tu-nhom-but-viet-den-trung-tam-van-but-viet-nam.36276/, 29/2/2021.

[102] Ibid.,   http://tve-4u.org/threads/tu-nhom-but-viet-den-trung-tam-van-but-viet-nam.36276/, 29/2/2021.

[103] Vũ Hạnh, *Tuyển tập Vũ Hạnh, tập 1*, 18.

[104] Ibid., 25.

[105] Ibid., 18. Nguyễn Du (1766–1820) is a famous Vietnamese poet. *The Tale of Kiều* (Truyện Kiều) is a literary work written in Nom script in the genre of "six-eight" syllables, a classic work of Vietnamese literature.

in the market.[106] His short stories bore propaganda value to protect the beauty of traditional culture. He wrote the short story *Vàng tháp cổ* (God in the Ancient Tower, 1960) to criticize those who were blindly greedy, who were digging and excavating the ancient tower to destroy it. At the end of the story, the goldsmiths were in panic and died tragic deaths due to their trying to climb the rocks to seek gems. This was a warning lesson for those who were greedy, despising the spiritual values of the nation, and at the same time it evoked sadness about the disappearance of traditional culture. This touched the conscience of conscientious readers.

Some of Vũ Hạnh's short stories expressed fierce opposition to the authorities in Saigon. The writer did not directly write about the conflict between the United States—the Republic of Vietnam, and the Revolutionary forces, however, he paid attention to the miserable and sloppy life of people in the heart of glitzy Saigon. A miserable life made people corrupt. They had to sell blood and for a living they did petty things like stealing sandals in temples, pagodas, and churches (*Tư Cò*, 1966). The husband in *The Husband of the Times* (1966) accepted the humiliating work of looking after his children while his wife became a prostitute to support the whole family. Although he did not directly write about the opposing side, through these short stories, Vũ Hạnh created a contrast between the poor life of the people and the lavish life of the upper class, implicitly condemning the government's lack of concern for people. The stories *Overpassing Waterfall* (1957), *The Violin in the Mountain* (1960), *Label Paper* (1960), *Tet in the Middle of the Forest* (1961), *Spring on the Mountain Peak* (1962), *The Story of Losing a Horse* (1971), and *Same Drops of Sweat* (1972) indirectly evoked thoughts about loyalty, honor, perseverance in practicing ideals, and fighting against evil and bad things. The story *Reason for Life* (also known as *The Lizard*, 1963) that was written in the form of a memoir was the only work written about the policy of the United States—Ngô Đình Diệm government. Vũ Hạnh criticized the brutality and cunning of the ruling government through the story of a communist named Hùng who was imprisoned by the contemporary government. He compared Ngô Đình Diệm (1901–1963, President of the First Republic of Vietnam from 1955 to 1963) to a lizard that "liked to deceive itself by retelling the glorious past in order to have a few illusions on his way down."[107]

Vũ Hạnh's short stories had a profound impact on people at that time, making an important contribution toward his achieving his political goals.[108] However, it was the dominance of political power issues in his writing, his writing in order to propagate and promote the struggle entrusted to him by the revolutionary organization, that made many of his short stories less valuable in the long term (In his memoir, Vũ Hạnh admitted: "All compositions at that time were for specific political purposes and were written too hastily with only temporary significance, so I am not interested in re-collecting them after liberation").[109] Interested in propaganda and being in the situation of operating secret revolutionary activities in inner Saigon, Vũ Hạnh's

---

[106] Ibid., 18.

[107] Ibid., 373.

[108] Ibid., 15,16.

[109] Ibid., 58.

somewhat lacked a flexibility of expression in his short stories. Some works just followed what had been set forth, with many passages just meant to clumsily "preach" the Communist ideal. The limitations of Vũ Hạnh's literature were also common to Vietnamese revolutionary literature in general, in which literature was used as a tool to propagate political purposes.

Our article has studied the originality of Vũ Hạnh's sense of political struggle expressed through his short stories. We draw the following conclusions.

Firstly, Vũ Hạnh is a sincere and thoroughly Marxist writer. He is a typical author of the left-leaning trend in urban literature in South Vietnam from 1955 to 1975. The voice of struggle is shown throughout Vũ Hạnh's works, ranging from theory, criticism, to literary composition. Choosing literature as a weapon in the center of Saigon, under the control of the United States—Republic of Vietnam government, Vũ Hạnh exhibited the resilience of a writer-soldier.

Secondly, while composing in a diverse and complex Southern urban literary environment, Vũ Hạnh focused on choosing his own path. For him, literature was a practical aspect of revolutionary ideals. Political pressure dominated the strategy, structure, and discourse of his short stories. In order to both achieve the purpose of propagating communist ideas and to ensure his own safety, Vũ Hạnh implemented a unique writing strategy, which was different from other patriotic writers of his time. His short stories were less influenced by the prevailing Western literary theories. He went his own way, applied historical and legendary styles and symbols. This writing style both helped him avoid the censorship of the authorities and met the needs and tastes of many readers. Propaganda discourses in Vũ Hạnh's short stories were used to express the viewpoint of the ideal writer, the hero model of the revolutionary era and the traditional culture in a time of cultural chaos and in the spirit of revolutionary struggle. The issues he dealt with were urgent issues of concern for the revolutionary forces and the ideas they propagated.

Thirdly, the propaganda discourse in Vũ Hạnh's short stories helped to spread communist ideas widely to all classes in both urban and rural areas from the North to the South. This also helped him fulfill his political goals. However, his purposes also led to some limitations in his short stories and made many of his works pure expressions of the Communist Party's ideology.

Fourthly, the presence of Vũ Hạnh and his like-minded artistic friends such as Lê Vĩnh Hòa (1932–1967), Viễn Phương (1928–2005), and Sơn Nam (1926–2008) created the lively dynamics of literary life in urban areas in South Vietnam. Unlike in the North, literature in urban areas in South Vietnam had many groups and trends that both conflicted with and influenced each other. According to Võ Phiến (1925–2015), Saigon at that time was the home of many groups of artists and writers: "There were groups that gathered around a concept of art such as the Culture of Today group,"[110] "there were other artistic groups that gathered

---

[110] Võ Phiến, *Văn học miền Nam tổng quan*, 70.

around a newspaper,"[111] and "several groups gathered around a figure."[112] They collaborated with a newspaper, but sometimes their political views were opposing, as Võ Phiến (1925–2015) described the relationship between him and Vũ Hạnh: "The rightist and the leftist never shared the same mind."[113] This created inconsistencies in writers' ideas, opinions, and writing styles. Saigon literature was multi-voiced, multi-tonal, rich, and very complex. Thus, with the case study of Vũ Hạnh, we have contributed to an understanding of urban literature in South Vietnam in the period 1955–1975 through identifying its typical characteristics: diversity, flexibility, and complexity.

Acknowledgements This article is funded by Vinh University

Bibliography

Bùi Thanh Thảo (2016) Truyện ngắn trong khuynh hướng văn học yêu nước ở đô thị miền Nam 1965–1975 (Short stories in patriotic literary style in Southern urban areas from 1965 to 1975). Luận án Tiến sĩ Ngữ văn, trường Đại học Khoa học Xã hội và Nhân văn, Đại học Quốc gia thành phố Hồ Chí Minh. https://phucvu.thuvientphcm.gov.vn/Viewer/EBook/693919

Bửu Ý. Nhìn lại đời sống văn học miền Nam giai đoạn từ 1954 - 1975 (Revisiting literature in South Vietnam from 1954–1975). Tạp chí Sông Hương, Accessed 30 Apr 2017, http://tapchisonghuong.com.vn/tap-chi/c371/n25459/Buu-Y-nhin-lai-do-i-so-ng-van-hoc-mien-Nam-giai-doan-tu-1954-1975.html.

Du Tử Lê (2014) Phác họa toàn cảnh sinh hoạt 20 năm văn học nghệ thuật miền Nam 1954–1975 (Outlining 20 years of literature and art in South Vietnam from 1954–1975). Người Việt, CA

Đỗ Đức Hiểu, Nguyễn Huệ Chi, Phùng Văn Tửu (2004) Từ điển văn học bộ mới (Literary dictionary: New Edition) Thế giới, Hà Nội

Hồ Chí Minh (1952) Thư gửi Hồ Chủ tịch gửi các họa sĩ trong dịp khai mạc. Triển lãm hội họa 1951. Cứu quốc. (Letter to painters on the occasion of the 1951 painting exhibition) no.1986. http://baochi.nlv.gov.vn/baochi/cgi-bin/baochi?a=d&d=WNyf19520105&e=-------vi-20--1--img-txIN------#

La Khắc Hòa, Lộc Phương Thủy, Huỳnh Như Phương (2015) Tiếp nhận tư tưởng văn nghệ nước ngoài kinh nghiệm Việt Nam thời hiện đại (Receiving foreign cultural ideas and Vietnamese experiences in modern times) Đại học Quốc gia Hà Nội, Hà Nội

Lê Văn Nghĩa (2020) Văn học Sài gòn 1954–1975 những chuyện bên lề (Saigon literature 1954–1975: Side stories). Tổng hợp, Hồ Chí Minh

Nguyễn Dữ (2017) Truyền kỳ mạn lục. (Collection of strange tales). Hội Nhà văn, Hà Nội

Nguyễn Đăng Mạnh (2012) Từ điển tác giả, tác phẩm văn học Việt Nam (Dùng trong nhà trường). (Dictionary of Vietnamese authors and literary works, textbook). Giáo dục, Hà Nội

Nguyễn Đăng Na (1997) Văn xuôi tự sự Việt Nam thời trung đại, tập 1 truyện ngắn. (Narratives in Medieval Vietnamese prose, Volume 1 Short Stories) Hà Nội: Giáo dục.

Nguyễn Ngọc Thiện (2017) Văn học Việt Nam thế kỉ XX. (Vietnamese literature in the 20th century) Văn học, Hà Nội, 2010.

---

[111] Ibid., 70.

[112] Ibid., 71.

[113] Ibid., 72.

Nguyễn Thanh Hùng. "Nhìn lại truyện ngắn trong dòng văn học yêu nước đô thị miền Nam 1954–1965." (Revisiting Short Stories in the Trend of Patriotic Literature in Urban Literature in South Vietnam 1954–1965) *Lý luận phê bình văn học nghệ thuật*, no. 53 (): 31.

Nguyễn Xuân Huy (2013) Nhà văn Vũ Hạnh: lí luận, phê bình, nghiên cứu, sáng tác (The Writer Vũ Hạnh: Theory, Criticism, Research, Composition.) Luận án Tiến sĩ Ngữ văn, Đại học Sư phạm Hà Nội. http://luanan.nlv.gov.vn/luanan?a=d&d=TTcFqWrNMZPm2013.1.8&srpos=1& e=-------vi-20--1--img-txIN-v%c5%a9+h%e1%ba%a1nh

Nguyễn Văn Lục. Hai mươi năm văn học dịch thuật miền Nam 1955–1975. (Twenty Years of Literature and Translation in South Vietnam 1955–1975). Accessed 3 Dec. 2014, https://ngu oitinhhuvo.wordpress.com/2014/12/03/20-nam-van-hoc-dich-thuat-mien-nam-1955-1975-ngu yen-van-luc/.

Nguyễn Vy Khanh (2016) Văn Học Miền Nam 1954–1975: nhận-định, biên-khảo và thư-tịch; (Literature in South Vietnam 1954–1975: Essay, Review and Bibliography) 2 tập Toronto: Nguyễn Publishings.

Nhật Tiến (2021) Từ nhóm Bút Việt đến Trung tâm Văn bút Việt Nam (From the Vietnamese PEN Group to the Vietnam PEN Center), 29 Feb. http://tve-4u.org/threads/tu-nhom-but-viet-den-trung-tam-van-but-viet-nam.36276/

Phan Đăng Thanh, Trương Thị Hòa. *Lịch sử các chế độ báo chí ở Việt Nam, Tập 2 Sau Cách mạng tháng Tám 1945 đến nay.* (History of Press in Vietnam, Volume 2 After the August Revolution, 1945 to the present.) Tp. Hồ Chí Minh: Tổng hợp, 2019.

Quang Đào (2020) Nguồn gốc của khái niệm 'cánh tả' và 'cánh hữu' (The origin of the terms 'lLeft-wing' and 'Right-wing'). Báo Quốc tế, 2 Feb., 19:45.2020. EST, https://baoquocte.vn/nguon-goc-cua-khai-niem-canh-ta-va-canh-huu-109952.html

Trần Đình Sử (Chủ biên), Nguyễn Xuân Kính, Nguyễn Văn Long, Huỳnh Như Phương, Vũ Thanh, Lã Nhâm Thìn, Trần Văn Toàn (2021) Lược sử văn học Việt Nam, (Brief History of Vietnamese Literature.) Hà Nội: Đại học Sư phạm

Trần Hoài Anh (2009) Lý luận - Phê bình văn học ở đô thị miền Nam 1954–1975. (Literary Theory and Criticism in Southern Urban Vietnam 1954–1975) Hội Nhà văn, Hà Nội

Trần Hữu Tá (2000) Nhìn lại một chặng đường văn học. (Revisiting a Literary Journey) Tp. Hồ Chí Minh: Thành phố Hồ Chí Minh

Trần Trọng Đăng Đàn (2015). Văn học trong cuộc đấu tranh tư tưởng tại miền Nam Việt Nam thời kỳ 1954–1975 (Literature in the ideological conflict in South Vietnam in the period 1954–1975) Tp. Hồ Chí Minh: Khoa học xã hội

Trịnh Bá Đĩnh (Chủ biên) (2016) Lịch sử lý luận phê bình văn học Việt Nam (History of Vietnamese Literary Criticism). Đại học Quốc gia Hà Nội, Hà Nội

Võ Phiến (2014) Văn học miền Nam tổng quan (An Overview of Literature in South Vietnam). Người Việt books, CA

Vũ Hạnh (2015) Tuyển tập Vũ Hạnh, Tập 1 (The Anthology of Vũ Hạnh, Volume 1) Tp. Tổng hợp Thành phố Hồ Chí Minh, Hồ Chí Minh

Vũ Hạnh (2015) Tuyển tập Vũ Hạnh, Tập 2 (The Anthology of Vũ Hạnh, Volume 2) Tp. Tổng hợp Thành phố Hồ Chí Minh, Hồ Chí Minh

Ngô Th Quỳnh Nga is a lecturer at the Department of Literature, School of Pedagogy, Vinh University, Vietnam. She received her PhD degree in Vietnamese literature in 2015 from Vietnam Academy of Social Sciences. Her main research area is modern Vietnamese literature, especially that of the wartime 1945–1975 and post-bellum literature since 1975. Some of her recent works are *Feminism in prose works written by female writers in southern Vietnamese cities (1955–1975)* (International Conference on Language Education, Literature and Culture 2020), *Renovation of Vietnamese war novels since 1975—viewed from the perspective of tone* (Scientific Review, Hanoi National University of Education 2, 2020), *General Vietnamese Literature textbook* (co-author) (Nghệ An: Vinh University, 2022).

Phạm Công Thiện's Ontological Dialogue with Martin Heidegger and Henry Miller

Munehiro Nohira

A Shooting Star Over the Vietnam War

In this article, I will discuss the South Vietnamese poet-thinker Phạm Công Thiện (1941–2011), especially focusing on his role in introducing Martin Heidegger and Henry Miller to South Vietnam, and I will feature Thiện's ontological dialogues and the ideas contained therein.[1]

Phạm Công Thiện (hereafter, Thiện) was very well-known, from the age of 23, with the 1964 publication of the 600-page critical essay, *Ý Thức Mới trong Văn Nghệ và Triết Học* (*New Consciousness in Literature and Philosophy*) (hereafter, *Ý Thức Mới*). In the late 1960s, he published a large variety of works consecutively, including literary criticism, novels, poetry, and translations. In these works, Thiện made a great stir with his radical statements, as exemplified by the poetic phrase, "I masturbate with God and create the human race,"[2] or with inflammatory sentences like "Burn all the books throughout the world. Burn everything."[3] Such outrageous declarations were welcomed and supported with enthusiasm by South Vietnamese youth, and his books became bestsellers. Thiện became an idol for the distressed

---

[1] This article is written based on some arguments of chap. 1, 2, 3 of my doctoral thesis in Japanese 『新しい意識; ベトナムの亡命思想家ファム・コン・ティエン』 (*New Consciousness; Vietnamese Exile Thinker Phạm Công Thiện*) published in 2009, with some new information and new arguments. This is my first presentation on Phạm Công Thiện in English.

[2] Phạm, *Ngày Sanh của Rắn*, 14.

[3] Phạm, *Ý Thức Mới*, 124.

M. Nohira (✉)
Tokyo University of Foreign Studies, Tokyo, Japan
e-mail: nohiramune@tufs.ac.jp

© The Author(s), under exclusive license to Springer Nature Singapore Pte Ltd. 2023
T. Engelbert and C. P. Pham (eds.), *Global Vietnam: Across Time,*
Space and Community, Reading South Vietnam's Writers,
https://doi.org/10.1007/978-981-99-1043-4_9

young war-time generation.[4] However, in 1970 he suddenly disappeared from South Vietnam. Thus, the period of his main activity there was only about half a decade. The poet Thanh Tâm Tuyền discussed Thiện's sudden disappearance with the writer Mai Thảo: "Sooner or later you had to see that Phạm Công Thiện did so once again, that he had gone far away, disappeared. That is Phạm Công Thiện exactly. We are some kind of planets. But he is more than a planet. He is a shooting star."[5] The metaphor of "a shooting star" reminds us of Mallarmé's description of Rimbaud. It is no exaggeration to say that Thiện is a Rimbaud of Vietnam who emerged suddenly in 1960s South Vietnam. Indeed, he was called an "incarnation of Rimbaud" by Henry Miller. Although the period during which Thiện was active in South Vietnam was very short, I think his influence, like that of Rimbaud, on the literary scene and the thought of the time had a similarly tremendous impact.

Although there has been a great deal of discussion about the impression made by Thiện's radical statements and actions,[6] and though the importance of his impact in striking the heart of contemporary youth in his time is obvious, it seems nevertheless that the true significance of his thought has not been examined thoroughly up to now because of the difficulty in truly understanding it. In spite of this, I view Thiện as one of the representative Vietnamese thinkers who engaged at that time with thought on the Vietnam War at the most profound philosophical and fundamental level.

Henry Miller, Martin Heidegger, and D. T. Suzuki were the key persons Thiện studied, and he was greatly affected by them in his late teens.[7] His philosophical struggle with them and the resulting dialogue in his works from the 1960s led to the rediscovery of the possibilities of Eastern thought and the revival of Vietnamese traditional thought, which was completely alien to Western philosophy. In this article, focusing mainly on the influence of the two Westerners Heidegger and Miller on Thiện, my discussion aims to underscore the significance of his thought, born out of the war-torn conditions in Vietnam.

In the following sections, I will first introduce Thiện's unprecedented nomadic life and his friendship with Henry Miller, which has been relatively little-noted except by people particularly interested in either Thiện or Miller. Next, I will discuss his thought as it was formed in the Vietnamese War situation and the reasons for the centrality of references to Heidegger's thought in Thiện's thought. Then, I will discuss the reason why Thiện emphasized Miller rather than Heidegger and on which of Miller's points his emphasis is based.

---

[4] Phạm, "Nói chuyện với tập san Văn," 405; Trần Tuấn Kiệt, *Tác Giả Tác Phẩm*, 26–27. In the letter to Miller on 2 August 1966, he wrote "In Vietnam I am being considered now as the voice of my generation".

[5] Mai, *Chân Dung*, 146–147.

[6] Nguyễn Hưng Quốc, "Mỗi khi một tác giả: Phạm Công Thiện," 81–83; Nguyễn Hưng Quốc, "Đọc lại Phạm Công Thiện"; Inrasara, "Chớp lửa thiêng Phạm Công Thiện & tuổi trẻ tôi"; Nguyễn Mạnh Tiến, " Nhà văn nổi loạn hay thần tượng văn nghệ: trường hợp Phạm Công Thiện.".

[7] Phạm, *Ý Thức Mới*, 129. Also see fn.14.

Phạm Công Thiện's Life

I now will briefly introduce Thiện's personal history. Born in 1941 at Mỹ Tho, a riverside city in the Mekong Delta area, Thiện, at the age of 13, engaged his school's head teacher in disputes on academic problems and ultimately left the school. Afterward, he studied linguistics, literature, philosophy, and many languages autodidactically. At the ages of 13–14, he learned Russian, Italian, Spanish, Germany, and Dutch; at the ages of 18–19, he learned Sanskrit, Pali, Greek, and Tibetan.[8] At age 16, he published an English pronunciation dictionary, *Anh Ngữ Tinh Âm Tự Điển*. His ability with foreign languages enabled him to read foreign books in the original. People around him called him a prodigy. However, he was so sensitive that he often felt alone and melancholic, and he was drawn to Giacomo Leopardi's utterances, such as "Now you will rest forever, my tired heart […] You've laboured enough. Bitterness and boredom, life is nothing more. And mud the world […] And the infinite emptiness of all."[9] At the age of 17, he introduced foreign literature to Vietnam in the magazine *Phổ Thông* (*Popularization*).[10] By 1960, however, his wealthy family had gone bankrupt. Thiện taught English in order to feed his parents, brothers, and sisters. Around that time, he developed a special interest in Buddhism, and, at the age of 20, he entered the Buddhist priesthood. He was given a Buddhist spiritual name, Thích Nguyên Tánh. In the early 1960s, he wrote essays on contemporary Western writers and philosophers in Saigon magazines such as *Mai* (*Tomorrow*) to introduce these writers and thinkers to South Vietnamese readers. In 1964, those essays were compiled and published under the title *Ý Thức Mới trong Văn Nghệ và Triết Học*. In this book, Thiện focuses on the following Western writers, poets, artists, and philosophers: William Saroyan, Jean-Paul Sartre, Henry Miller, Martin Heidegger, Daisetz Teitaro Suzuki, Ivo Andritch, Somerset Maugham, Guillaume Apollinaire, Charles Chaplin, William Faulkner, Aldous Huxley, Nikos Kazantzakis, Clément Rosset, Ernest Hemingway, Franz Kafka, Jean-René Huguenin, Erich Fromm, Frederico Schmidt, André Gide, Thomas Wolfe, and Friedrich Nietzsche. His acute but outrageous insight was already exhibited in this early work. Thiện's thoughts on Heidegger and Miller will be discussed later. As for Sartre, he had been introduced to and had captured the attention of the South Vietnamese public around this time, however, Thiện criticized Sartre on the basis that, in his novel, the ideal (=essence) of existentialism preceded existence although he had previously declared that existence precedes essence.[11] Thiện went so far as to regard Sartre as a monkey in comparison with Louis-Ferdinand Céline.[12] The conclusion of the book is written in the style of a letter to Nietzsche. In order to annihilate the existing values and order which had

---

[8] Phạm, "Lời người dịch." In *Tôi Là Ai ?*, 11.

[9] Phạm, *Đi cho hết Một Đêm Hoang Vu trên Mặt Đất*, 207–208.

[10] In this magazine, he reviewed writers such as the Japanese Emperor Meiji, Goethe, Lope de Vega, Alexandre Petöfi, Boris Pasternak, Mark Twain, John Keats, Schiller, and Juan Ramón Jiménez, and published his translation of Johann Peter Hebel's short story "Kannitverstan."

[11] Phạm, *Ý Thức Mới*, 72–73.

[12] Ibid., 55.

caused the war, Thiện appealed to Nietzsche: "We must destroy everything! Thus you spoke, Nietzsche, didn't you? That is the only power of the creator, super-man."[13] This book become a bestseller, to the extent that it was reprinted four times by 1970.

The Friendship with Henry Miller

As far as I can confirm, Thiện may have been the first Vietnamese to read Miller enthusiastically and to appreciate his true greatness. He mentioned Miller in his many essays and articles, published an essay entitled *Henry Miller* in 1969. After Thiện, Nguyễn Hữu Hiệu introduced Miller in *Con Đường Sáng Tạo* (*The Way of Creation*) in 1970; he also translated *The Time of The Assassins* into Vietnamese in 1971. Miller's *The World of Sex* was translated by Hoài Lãng Tử in South Vietnam in 1969.

Thiện first read Miller's works around 1958, when he was about 17. The first book of Miller's that he read was the Greek travelogue entitled *The Colossus of Maroussi* (1941), which made a deep impression on him, causing him to say: "If I had not met Henry Miller in my youth, I would had been dead a long time ago [...] The most important turning point in my life was the day I read H. Miller."[14] As far as Miller is concerned, people frequently have an impression of him as a "sex writer," but Thiện had insight into Miller's more essential aspects. He regarded Miller as a man who railed against the limitations of modern times as well as the material and mechanical civilization of the West, represented by Miller's birthplace the United States. Moreover, Miller called for reclaiming fundamental human life. Miller's works were a saving grace for Thiện's distressed heart. His first essay on Miller, "Consciousness of Liberation: The Images of the Present Youth in Henry Miller's Works," was first published in the magazine *Mai* in 1962 and then later in *Ý Thức Mới*. In this essay, Thiện displays his sympathy for Miller's acrimonious denunciation of modern civilization. The original text below shows the most typical paragraphs:

> Tôi thấy thương hại loài người, thương hại thế giới hấp hối này. Tôi điên, anh điên, chị điên, cả nhân loại đều điên. Đây là một thế giới điên. [I pity mankind, pity this dying world. I am crazy, you are crazy, you are crazy, all of mankind is crazy. It's a mad world.] *It's a mad world*. (Henry Miller, *The Colossus of Maroussi*, p. 130)
>
> [...]
>
> Văn minh. Tiền. Tiền. Tiền. Tiến bộ. Tiến bộ để đưa con người đến bàn mổ, đến nhà tế bần, đến nhà thương điên, đến chiến hào. [Civilization. Money, money, money. Progress, progress, progress which leads to the operating table, to the poorhouse, to the insane asylum, to the trenches.]
>
> *We are making constant progress, but it is a progress which leads to the operating table, to the poorhouse, to the insane asylum, to the trenches.* (*The Colossus of Maroussi*, p. 81)[15]

---

[13] Ibid., 608.

[14] Phạm, *Henry Miller*, 13.

[15] Phạm, *Ý Thức Mới*, 103.

In the quotation above, Miller's sentences in italics are quoted from Miller's text. The Vietnamese sentences (and corresponding parts of the translations in English in []) underlined by the author correspond to Henry Miller's text immediately below. Throughout this essay, Miller's words are quoted and combined as if they were Thiện's own words, his own feelings, as in this quotation. Thiện incorporated Miller's feelings and thinking into his own, in a severe denunciation of modern civilization.

When Thiện had the opportunity to study in the United States in 1965, he contacted Miller as soon as he arrived and was invited to Miller's home in Pacific Palisades. Upon meeting Miller for the first time, Thiện was so excited that he exclaimed, "Henry Miller, I kill you!" to this writer who was half a century older than he. In fact, this apparently shocking phrase originated from the well-known Zen motto, "When you meet Buddha, kill him." Thiện's use of the expression reflected his strong intention not to sanctify or place absolute trust in a person he admired, but in fact to overcome that admiration. Miller understood the meaning of this expression, so he embraced Thiện upon hearing it, and he called this young rebel an incarnation of Rimbaud.[16] We can also see Thiện's enthusiastic style of praising Miller in some of the letters they exchanged. When Miller wrote to Thiện, "Don't put me on the pedestal,"[17] Thiện answered, "you are not high up on a pedestal, you are me" (underlined in original) and wrote "your assassin: Phạm Công Thiện" in the place of the signature.[18] The quotation from his essay above was to prove the truth of the message "you are me." Moreover, on a letter to Miller, Thiện wrote the sender's name as "Arthur Milarepa Pham."[19] They exchanged letters until 1978. During his wanderings, Thiện sometimes asked Miller for help. In response, Miller sent money or asked his friends to find a job for him.

After leaving California, Thiện studied at universities on the East Coast for several months, but he despised the professors, as he "read Heidegger and Heraclitus in tears and with a bleeding heart, but the professors [of Colombia and Yale University] read through shortsighted vision."[20] When he decided to abandoned studying in the United States and instead go to France, a member of the university staff asked him anxiously: "In the future what do you want to be?" Thiện answered, "I will be a Buddha, otherwise I will commit suicide."[21]

When he arrived in Paris, he had no money, so he asked to stay at the houses of friends and relatives, sometimes sleeping on cold winter streets like out of a passage from Miller: "Better a beggar in Paris than a millionaire in New York."[22]

---

[16] Regarding the first meeting with Miller at his home, see Phạm, *Henry Miller*, 92–94; Phạm, *Hố Thẳm của Tư Tưởng*, 3 ed., 94–95, 98–100.

[17] Miller's letter to Phạm on 24 July 1965. Miller, "Lettres de Henry Miller à Pham Công Thiên," 104.

[18] Phạm'S letter to Miller on 13 August 1965.

[19] Written on the envelope of Thiện's letter to Miller on 13 August 1965.

[20] Phạm, *Hố Thẳm của Tư Tưởng*. 3 ed., 158–159. The expression "in tears and with a bleeding heart" may be taken from Suzuki's *Zen Buddhism*, which deeply impressed him in his youth, and from Miller's books. See Suzuki, *Zen Buddhism*, 6.

[21] Phạm, *Henry Miller*, 95–96.

[22] Phạm, *Ý Thức Mới*, 122.

With financial assistance from Miller, Thiện could leave Paris, wander through other countries, and return to South Vietnam in late 1966.

After Returning to South Vietnam

As soon as he returned to South Vietnam, Thiện assumed the role of dean of the faculty of Literature and Human Sciences of the Buddhist private university, Vạn Hạnh University, and he became chief editor of the university's magazine, *Tư Tưởng* (*Thought*). His many books published in the late 1960s were supported by the distressed young generation of South Vietnam. During this time, a trend occurred that was known as the "phenomenon of Phạm Công Thiện."[23] It involved young Vietnamese imitating Thiện's attitude toward the adults who had caused the collapse of Vietnam and thus rebelling against them. Thiện's strict criticism of Nguyễn Văn Trung, who was the representative of Catholic intellectuals at that time, symbolized the rise of Buddhist power in late 1960s, replacing Catholic power in South Vietnam.[24]

In spite of his success, he suddenly vanished from South Vietnam in 1970 and went to France. At the same time, he stopped most of his writing in Vietnamese. He studied at Paris IV university, and from 1975 he served as an associate professor of Western philosophy at Toulouse University. However, he quit the university in 1983 and went to Los Angeles. From 1987, he resumed writing in Vietnamese and in 1988 published a philosophical autobiographical novel entitled *Đi cho hết Một Đêm Hoang Vu trên Mặt Đất* (*Going Ahead to the End of a Desolate Night on the Earth*). Afterward, Thiện continued writing novels, poems, and essays on literature, Buddhism, and philosophy until 2011, when he passed away in Houston.

The Ontological Dialogue Between Martin Heidegger and Zen Buddhism

The Acceptance of Heidegger in Vietnam

I argue that, except for the poet Bùi Giáng, Thiện was the most representative of the thinkers who introduced Heidegger's thought to Vietnam in earnest. He attempted to

---

[23] Phạm, "Nói chuyện với tập san Văn," 404.

[24] Phạm, *Hố Thẳm của Tư Tưởng*. 1 ed., 131–172. In the appendix of the book, he wrote a chapter "Hố thẳm và đánh giá học vấn phá sản của trí thức Việt Nam" (The abyss and the evaluation of the ruined study of a Vietnamese intellectual), an exhaustive critique of Nguyễn Văn Trung's doctoral thesis on Buddhism. In the third edition of the book, this chapter was deleted.

Regarding the changing cultural, intellectual atmosphere, from Catholicism to Buddhism since the mid-1960s, see Võ, *Văn Học Miền Nam Tổng Quan*, 210–213.

engage in dialogue with this thought and struggled with its ideas. However, Wynn Gadkar-Wilcox refrained from mentioning Thiện when he introduced a discussion of the South Vietnamese Buddhists' acceptance of Heidegger in the article "Existentialism and Intellectual Culture in South Vietnam."[25]

Vietnamese references to Heidegger prior to 1954, as far as I can confirm, are limited to the philosopher Trần Đức Thảo in *Triết Lý Đã Đi Đến Đâu* (*Where Philosophy Has Gone*) in 1950 and in *Phenomenology and Dialectical Materialism,* written in French in 1951. In these books, Thảo, writing from the Marxist viewpoint, criticized Heidegger as a petit-bourgeoisie thinker.[26] But as Thiện pointed out, Thảo was not able to recognize that his Marxism was born of the Western philosophical tradition.[27]

In South Vietnam, as far as I can confirm, Bùi Giáng was the first to introduce Heidegger's thought in *Tư Tưởng Hiện Đại* (*Contemporary Thought*) published in 1960 and *Martin Heidegger và Tư Tưởng Hiện Đại* (*Martin Heidegger and Contemporary Thought*) in 1962. Hoàng Châu Thanh also introduced Heidegger's thoughts on Hölderlin in 1961, in the magazine *Đại Học* (*Higher Learning, University*).

Thiện, too, introduced Heidegger in the early 1960s. Having begun reading the philosopher around 1960, he first wrote an essay on Heidegger in 1961 in the magazine *Mai*. Later, this essay was included in *Ý Thức Mới* under the chapter title "Ý thức siêu thoát" (Consciousness of Transcendence) with the subtitle "Considering Zen Buddhism through an Analogism of Heidegger's Philosophy." After that, he also discussed Heidegger in *Hố Thẳm của Tư Tưởng* (*The Abyss of Thinking*, 1966), and *Im Lặng Hố Thẳm* (*The Silence of the Abyss*, 1967). On December 1969, the magazine *Tư Tưởng* published a special issue on Heidegger under the title "Martin Heidegger and the Failure of Western Contemporary Thought" (No. 5 of a new series). In this issue, Thiện contributed a long essay, "The Perfect Failure of Heidegger and the Way of Vietnamese Thought" that explored Heidegger's *Being and Time*, "Time and Being," and Buddhist thought.

Indeed, it could be argued that in the late 1960s in South Vietnam, many intellectuals were interested in Heidegger. In the special *Tư Tưởng* issue on Heidegger mentioned above, Buddhist intellectuals such as Ngô Trọng Anh, Lê Tôn Nghiêm, and Tuệ Sỹ discussed Heidegger's and Buddhist thought. In 1970, Lê Ton Nghiêm published *Đâu là Căn Nguyên Tư Tưởng hay Con Đường Triết Lý từ Kant đến Heidegger* (*Where is the Root of Thought or The Way of Philosophy from Kant to Heidegger*). As far as translations, Thiện translated two of Heidegger's works: *The Essence of Truth* in 1968 and *What is Philosophy* in 1969. Bùi Giáng translated and annotated *Elucidations of Hölderlin's Poetry* and published it as two separate books with the titles *Lời Cố Quận* (*Words of Homeland*) and *Lễ Hội Tháng Ba* (*Festival in March*) in 1971. In 1973, *Time and Being* was translated into Vietnamese by Trần Công Tiến, who also translated *What is Metaphysics* in 1974.

---

[25] Gadkar-Wilcox, "Existentialism and Intellectual Culture in South Vietnam," 386.

[26] Trần, *Triết-Lý Đã Đi Đến Đâu*, 86–87.

[27] Phạm, "lời giới thiệu của người dịch," XXIV–XXV.

"Being" in Heidegger's Thought and the Possibility of an Ontological Dialogue with Zen Buddhism

The noteworthy aspect of the essay "Consciousness of Transcendence"—in which Thiện focuses on Heidegger in his earliest period—lies in the fact that he points out similarities between Heidegger's thought and Mahayana (especially Zen) Buddhist thought. Thiện became interested in Zen when reading D. T. Suzuki's selected writings, *Zen Buddhism*, around the age of 18 or 19. In the preface, the book's editor, William Barrett, referred to Heidegger's praise for Suzuki: "If I understand this man [Suzuki] correctly, […] this is what I have been trying to say in all my writings."[28] This, I believe, might have had a deep impact on Thiện. He also quoted this remark in his essay "Consciousness of Transcendence."[29] Thiện pointed out the following similarities between Heidegger and Zen Buddhism: the negation of humanism, logic, the standard of moral values (virtue and vice), the Supreme (God, Buddha), the consideration of Being as equal to Nothingness, and criticism of and transcendence over ordinary logic and dualism.

In such comparisons between Zen and Heidegger's thought, there are two aspects I will focus on here. The first is Thiện's daring declaration connecting Heidegger's thought with Zen's *Kiến Tính* (literal meaning: seeing one's own nature. Zen's term refers to Buddhist enlightenment). The second is the translation of Heidegger's key term, Being (*Sein*), into Vietnamese. While he acknowledged the difference that Zen aimed for Enlightenment while Heidegger's thought did not, Thiện claimed that "it seems that in reality Heidegger's thought also aimed towards enlightenment: salvaging humans from forgetting the truth of Being." He stated:

> Kiến Tính [seeing one's own nature] is a supreme experience of Zen. If we can provisionally translate *Sein* [Being] into *Tính* (along with the meaning of *Tính* included in *Phật Tính* [Buddha's nature], *Như Lai Tạng Tính* [Tathāgatagarbha's nature], *Chân Tính* [true nature]), it can be said that Heidegger also gradually goes the way of *Kiến Tính*.[30]

Because Thiện considered that Heidegger's Being would finally attain the same goal as that of *Kiến Tính*, he translated Being into the *Tính* of *Kiến Tính*. For East Asians, *tính* (Chinese character: 性) means an aspect of nature or character of something in general, thus making it appear that *Tính* and Heidegger's *Sein* actually do not have the same meaning. However, for Thiện, who read D.T. Suzuki's works in English, Zen was concerned precisely with the problem of Being. Indeed, Suzuki explained—in English—that *Kiến Tính* (*Kensho* in Japanese) meant "seeing into the nature of one's own *being*"[31] (italics by the author). In short, Thiện's term, *Tính*, means "the nature of one's own *being*." On the one hand, Heidegger's Being means the Being of all beings as a whole. On the other hand, it seems that *Tính's* concept of "one's own being" indicates the being of an independent, separate entity but not of all beings as a whole.

---

[28] Barrett, "Zen for the West," xi.

[29] Phạm, *Ý Thức Mới*, 150.

[30] Ibid., 135.

[31] Suzuki, *Zen Buddhism*, 3.

However, for Zen, "one's own being" does not mean a being of an independent entity. The true sense of "one's own being" is realized only afterward, when the subject "I" jumps into *śūnyatā* (emptiness) = *tathatā* (suchness or "things as they *are*") and dissolves into all beings.[32] The world of *śūnyatā* = *tathatā* is the fundamental, true world for Mahayana Buddhism. Thiện rediscovered such a problem of Being in Zen Buddhism, of which Vietnam also had a religious tradition, and thus pursued an ontological dialogue between Heidegger's thought and Zen thought.

The Etymological Reason for Translating Heidegger's Sein *with* Tính

In Japanese, Chinese, and Korean, 存在 (*tồn tại*) is ordinarily employed for the translation of Heidegger's Being (Japanese scholars of Kyoto school employ 有*hữu*). Thiện's translation, *tính* (性), appears very peculiar in countries where Chinese characters have historically been used. Nevertheless, he claimed that "the translation of Heidegger's Being into *tính thể*[33] was not just any translation. Translating Being into *tính thể* was an important event in the thought of the whole of the East."[34] In addition to the semantic reason based on Zen thought provided above, he explained the etymological reason behind his translation. In *An Introduction to Metaphysics*, Heidegger remarks that *bin/bist* in German and φύσις in ancient Greek originated from **bhū-*[35] (ordinarily translated into "nature", but Heidegger interpreted the archaic meaning as emergent-abiding-Power). "Be" in English is similar in this way. Based on this fact, Thiện explored a word originating from **bhū-* in Sanskrit, an Indo-European language such as German, English, and Greek. Referring to Hajime Nakamura's thesis, Thiện confirmed that *bhāva* and *bhava* originated from **bhū-*, and that *bhāva* corresponds to Being (*Sein*) (*bhava* corresponds to Existence). When Mahayana Buddhist scriptures were translated into Chinese, *bhāva* was translated into 有 (*hữu*), 性 (*tính*), and other words. Nakamura criticized the fact that 有 meant "to have" rather than "to be," and was thus a word that reflected the Chinese anthropocentric view of the world, different from Being in general as in *bhāva's* meaning.[36] So Thiện avoided the word 有 (*hữu*) in translating Heidegger's Being. In short, *tính* is one of

---

[32] Ibid., 261–263.

[33] Thiện also translated Heidegger's Being into *Tính thể* (literal meaning: nature-body) and *Thể tính* (literal meaning: body-nature). Each word has a strategic meaning that expresses Heidegger's thought (see Phạm, *Im Lặng Hố Thẳm*, 243–245), but for convenience, in this article, I deal only with the core word: *Tính*.

[34] Phạm, "lời giới thiệu của người dịch," XVII-XVIII. For the following discussion on the translation of Heidegger's *Sein*, see Ibid., XVIII-XXII.

[35] Heidegger, *Einführung in die Metaphysik*, 76. Hubert Hohl (then assistant director of The German Culture Center in Saigon) mentioned this etymological problem of *Sein* by referring to Heidegger at the conference at Vạn Hạnh University on 14 May 1967 (Hohl, "Heidegger and the Crisis of Metaphysics," 407–414).

[36] Nakamura, *Ways of Thinking of Eastern Peoples*, 233.

the Chinese translated words from the Sanskrit word, *bhāva*, which originated from
*bhū- just as *bin/ bist* in German, "be" in English, and φύσις in Greek. Based on
this, and because性 (*tính*) is Zen's key term for "one's own being," Thiện chose 性
(*tính*) to translate Heidegger's Being. To quote Heidegger: "That dialogue [dialogue
with the Greek thinkers and their language] still awaits its beginning. It is scarcely
prepared for at all, and yet it itself remains for us the precondition of the inevitable
dialogue with the East Asian world."[37] It can be said that Thiện set the common
linguistic foundation in preparation of a dialogue between Heidegger and the East
Asian world.

In South Vietnam in the late 1960s, this translation, *tính*, was employed by
Buddhist intellectuals for Heidegger's Being.[38] We may speculate about Thiện's
influence on intellectuals at that time.

The Vietnam War as an Ontological Problem

After the United States became involved directly in the Vietnam War in 1964, Thiện
referred to Heidegger's thought when he discussed the Vietnam War as an ontological
problem in "The Ontological Background of The Present War in Vietnam (An Open
Letter to Henry Miller)" (hereafter, "An Open Letter") in 1965, as well as *Im Lặng
Hố Thẳm* (*The Silence of the Abyss*), which he wrote in 1967, and other articles.
Based on Heidegger's thought, Thiện claimed that the ultimate cause of the Vietnam
War was that in the representative way of thinking in Western metaphysics Being
had been forgotten. He lamented the fact that the technology which had produced
weapons of mass destruction, including the chemical weapons used in the Vietnam
War, had been formed on the basis of Western metaphysics starting with Plato.
Citing Heidegger's assertion that "all metaphysics, including its counterpart, posi-
tivism, speaks the language of Plato,"[39] he aimed a fundamental criticism at Western
metaphysics: "The science of the twentieth century is the accomplishment of Western
metaphysics, which has been fulfilled in the present cruel war in Vietnam."[40] Western
metaphysics is essentially characterized by a way of thinking in which humankind
as a subject represents the world as an object through language, logic, and reason.
The modern West has represented the world as an object that is positioned opposite
a subject in order to appropriate and rule it. For Thiện, his country of Vietnam, too,
had become an object of pacifist as well as bellicose thought based on Western metaphysics: "Both your pacifist thought, as well as your bellicose thought, has given rise

---

[37] Heidegger, *The question concerning technology, and other essays*, 158. This remark was also
quoted by Ngô Trọng Anh in the special *Tư Tưởng* issue on Heidegger (Ngô, "Vị trí của vô thể
Heidegger trong tư tưởng đại thừa," 4).

[38] In the special *Tư Tưởng* issue on Heidegger (No. 5, 1969), Heidegger's *Sein* is translated as
follows: *Tính* (Ngô Trọng Anh), *Tính thể* (Lê Tôn Nghiêm), *Thể tính* (Tuệ Sỹ), *Hữu thể* (Trần Công
Tiến), showing that three of the four correlated with Thiện's translations.

[39] Phạm, *Im Lặng Hố Thẳm*, 217.

[40] Ibid., 224.

to a war […] Even the very word *ob-jectum,* from the Latin, has cut off Vietnam, Germany, the earth, and the Being of humans in two."[41] Therefore, he also intensely denounced Vietnamese poets who were following the West: "The Western aesthetics has been accomplished in the Vietnam war […] from the prewartime new poetry group in Vietnam to the present free poetry group in both South and North Vietnam, all such fellows are the men who support the West's destruction of Vietnam."[42]

Zen Master Không Lộ's Howl and the Emergence of Being

Thiện called for the awakening of Being, which modern humanity, including of course that of contemporary Vietnam, had so far been unable to grasp through representative thinking. Furthermore, modern Vietnamese thought as well as Western metaphysics had forgotten the concept of Being, though it had long existed in Vietnamese Zen Buddhist thought. We can find it in the "howl" of the ancient Vietnamese Zen master Không Lộ (literal meaning "the way of emptiness"; ?-1119) that Thiện brings up at the very beginning of the apocalyptic preface "Passing through between the High Mountain and the Abyss" of *Im Lặng Hố Thẳm* (hereafter, *Im Lặng*). Translating the original ancient Chinese into modern Vietnamese, Thiện introduced to a modern audience the Vietnamese Zen master's poetic verse: "Zen Master Không Lộ of the Lý Dynasty [1009–1225] of our homeland once climbed up a lofty peak of a mountain alone and howled in a lonely voice that chilled the blue sky filled with white clouds."[43] Subsequently, he remarked, "Down there is a desolate abyss, an abyss of homeland, there the silence of the abyss suddenly resonates *Tính* [Being] and *Việt* [Transcendence; also meaning "Vietnam"]."[44] That is to say, Thiện regarded Không Lộ's howl as an emergence of Being. Moreover, I assert that the purpose of Thiện's quotation of Không Lộ's howl was not to make it an object of academic analysis; rather, it was meant to be Thiện's own howl from within the abyss-like situation of the Vietnam War, where "fire and blood of homeland have married a high mountain and an abyss."[45] More accurately, it meant the howl of Being into which both Thiện and Không Lộ, and indeed all things, are dissolved; it was a call for the emergence of the world of *śūnyatā = tathatā,* in Buddhist terms. Thiện howled Không Lộ's howl by himself to revive Being in Vietnam, to present a Vietnamese thought suitable to the abyss of the Vietnam War.

---

[41] Ibid., 212.

[42] Phạm, *Ý Thức Bùng Vỡ*, 469.

[43] Phạm, *Im Lặng Hố Thẳm*, 11. In the original: 有時直上孤峯頂長嘯一声寒太虛.

[44] Ibid., 11.

[45] Ibid., 11.

Henry Miller and His Awakened Smile

For Thiện, Heidegger still remained in the outer reaches of intelligence and had not yet jumped into the abyss of Nothingness (= Being; according to Heidegger, Being is Nothingness in the sense that it is not any being). Thiện thought that it was none other than Henry Miller who had realized such Nothingness and had been living in it. In the following section, I discuss Thiện's reading of Miller in detail.

In "An Open Letter," Thiện regards Miller as being "among the truly significant outsiders in the world."[46] The "outsiders" here refers to those who "have truly awakened and realized their Nothingness and sensed the Inevitability of their own Death as well as the Death of every creature on earth, and that they have miraculously evolved an entirely new type of Consciousness in an ontologically if not mystically excruciating way."[47] Further, this "new type of Consciousness" means one that "is not the consciousness of any being in particular, but in fact the Consciousness of Pure Nothingness which leads to the total Destruction of both *ens* and non-*ens*, and, finally, to the very destruction of the *Nihil* itself."[48] In short, Thiện regarded Miller as a man who (1) destroyed everything and (2) who then awakened with "the Consciousness of Pure Nothingness."

1. Miller's Total Destruction.

We saw in the argument above how Miller's criticism of modern values is embodied in Thiện's feelings in *Ý Thức Mới*. For Thiện, this can be regarded as Miller's destruction. Here, I quote another passage from *Im Lặng*, in which Thiện introduces the author's destruction.

> All Henry Miller's books denounce American civilization, denounce the ruin of the West, denounce the shallow life of modern people, denounce the crazy delusions of society, organizations, religions, parties, ethics and morals; Henry Miller marks the end of literature, poetry, and art: "A year ago, six months ago, I thought I was an artist. I no longer think about it. I *am*" (Henry Miller, *Tropic of Cancer*, p. 1), "Everything that was literature has fallen from me" (*op. cit.*, p. 1); Henry Miller "spits in the face of Art, kicks in the pants to God, Man, Destiny, Time, Love, Beauty" (*op. cit.*, p. 2).[49]

The sentences above illustrate Miller's rebellion against existing authorities and values. We can see how Miller rejects them and is then released from them, there remains only the idea of "I am," i.e., only his own "being." *Im Lặng* did not quote this, but just before the above sentence beginning "A year ago," there appears the paradoxical expression: "I have no money, no resources, no hopes. I am the happiest man alive."[50]

---

[46] Phạm, "An Open Letter," 83.

[47] Ibid., 84.

[48] Ibid., 84.

[49] Phạm, *Im Lặng Hố Thắm*, 93–94.

[50] Miller, *Tropic of Cancer*, 1.

2. Awakening the "Consciousness of Pure Nothingness".

"Pure Nothingness" here doesn't mean a type of nihilism. It is the so-called Oriental Nothingness. In "Consciousness of Transcendence," pointing out the difference between Heidegger's Nothingness and Zen's, Thiện argues:

> Heidegger's Nothingness still remains in intelligence, in ontology. On the other hand, Zen's Nothingness, i.e. *Śūnyatā* [Emptiness] of the Three-Treatises school, has the same meaning as *Prajñā* [wisdom], deliverance, and Zen's Nothingness annihilates even the supreme Nothingness, Heidegger's Nothingness. Only when Heidegger's Nothingness has been destroyed and has vanished will *Śūnyatā* emerge and total deliverance be realized.[51]

We can consider that the Consciousness of Pure Nothingness is this Nothingness of Zen or *Śūnyatā* of Mahayana Buddhism that annihilates even Heidegger's Nothingness. Additionally, the reason Thiện considered that Miller realized this Nothingness of Zen was that Thiện found Zen's consciousness of awakening in Miller's works. As Thiện indicates in *Im Lặng*—"Henry Miller usually considered himself a master of Zen Buddhism"[52]—Miller was actually the earliest Western writer to study Zen through the works of D.T. Suzuki and Alan Watts, and he sympathized deeply with it.[53] We can find Miller's Zen thought reflected in some parts of *The Smile at the Foot of the Ladder* (1948) (hereafter, *The Smile*), quoted in *Im Lặng*.[54]

Miller is praised in *Im Lặng*, portrayed not only as "a thinker, an artist who has absolutely destroyed everything,"[55] but also as "the only one who has awakened completely, who loves the abyss, spreads his wings, and has flown up from the abyss to the blue sky."[56] The latter expression can be understood as Thiện's identification of Miller with the clown named Auguste, the main character in *The Smile*. Near the end of the story, the scene of Auguste's awakening is described as follows:

> Once again he [Auguste] closed his eyes, to descend into darkness. He remained thus a long time, breathing quietly and peacefully on the bed of his own being. When he finally opened his eyes he beheld a world from which the veil had been removed. It was the world which had always existed in his heart, ever ready to manifest itself, but which only begins to beat the moment one beats in unison with it.[57]

Miller paraphrased this description in the epilogue of the story as follows, and Thiện also quotes it in *Im Lặng*:

---

[51] Phạm, *Ý Thức Mới*, 180–181.

[52] Phạm, *Im Lặng Hố Thẳm*, 101.

[53] For details, see Calonne, "Samadhi All the Time: Henry Miller and Buddhism," 14–15. The title is taken from Miller's letter. *Samādhi* means the deepest stage of meditation. Miller wrote "The vulgar think this [Zen] self-hypnosis. It's not. It's Samadhi all the time" (in the letter to Laurence Durrell on 14 March 1949). Calonne also mentioned Thiện as Miller's friend (Ibid., 9).

[54] In Thiện's letter to Miller on 8 September 1972, he wrote "Your greatest Sastras are The Smile at the foot of the Ladder and the Colossus of Maroussi.".

[55] Phạm, *Im Lặng Hố Thẳm*, 92.

[56] Phạm, *Im Lặng Hố Thẳm*, 95.

[57] Miller, *The Smile at the Foot of the Ladder*, 38–39.

We uncover and discover. All has been given, as the mystics say. We have only to open our eyes and hearts, to become one with that which is.[58]

Although I am not certain to whom "the mystics" specifically refers, it is enough that these quotations from Miller remind us of D.T. Suzuki's description of *satori* (Japanese word of Buddhist enlightenment, awakening), as follows in *An Introduction to Zen Buddhism*:

All the causes, all the conditions of satori are in the mind; they are merely waiting for the maturing. When the mind is ready for some reasons or others, a bird flies, or a bell rings, and you at once return to your original home; that is, you discover your now real self. From the very beginning nothing has been kept from you, all that you wished to see has been there all the time before you, it was only yourself that closed the eyes to the fact.[59]

We must observe that, here, "your now real self" does not mean the independent ego. Instead, it means, in Buddhist terms, the world of *śūnyatā = tathatā*, in which the ego and everything are dissolved. Additionally, if employing Heidegger's term, as argued above, it means Being. In Miller's text, quoted in *Im Lặng*, the opposite state is described as follows: "...we die struggling to get born. We never were, never are. We are always in process of becoming, always separate and detached. Forever outside."[60] This is the description of the state in which the ego separates from everything and loses sight of true Being. Thiện notes this state means "no more flowing in the river of the Destiny of Being."[61] If one wants truly to *be*, one ought to open one's eyes and jump into the river of Destiny to "become one with that which *is*" (italics by the author).[62]

At the end of the story, after opening his eyes, Auguste feels immense joy in the ecstatic state (as in the statement "I am the happiest man alive" at the beginning of *Tropic of Cancer*), and passes away with "a broad, seraphic smile,"[63] even though he has been beaten to death. We can find this smile to be similar to Mahākāśyapa's smile. Mahākāśyapa's is known for the famous Zen phrase "holding a flower, subtly smiling," which symbolizes the Zen Buddhist enlightenment that is without words, and that "came out of the deepest recesses of his nature [...] A direct insight across the abyss of human understanding is indicated"[64] (emphasis by the author), as Suzuki explains in *The Essence of Buddhism*. Similarly, Auguste awoke with a smile after his descent into *darkness*, lying on *the bed of his own being*. We can see that the emphasized words in the preceding sentence correspond to those underlined above. Both smiles emerge from Being, the dark abyss-like place which the light of language and reason (understanding by words) cannot reach. Thus, I think that Thiện saw Mahākāśyapa's smile of enlightenment in Auguste's smile. Moreover, it is due to

---

[58] Ibid., 47; Phạm, *Im Lặng Hố Thẳm*, 98.

[59] Suzuki, *An Introduction to Zen Buddhism*, 91.

[60] Miller, *The Smile at the Foot of the Ladder*, 48; Phạm, *Im Lặng Hố Thẳm*, 98.

[61] Phạm, *Im Lặng Hố Thẳm*, 98.

[62] Miller, *The Smile at the Foot of the Ladder*, 47.; Phạm, *Im Lặng Hố Thẳm*, 98.

[63] Miller, *The Smile at the Foot of the Ladder*, 40.; Phạm, *Im Lặng Hố Thẳm*, 99.

[64] Suzuki, *The Essence of Buddhism*, 26.

this similarity between Zen thought and Miller's that Thiện regarded Miller as a man who had attained Buddhist enlightenment, as we can see from his words in a letter to Miller "I think you have attained satori!"[65] It might be said that Thiện needed a Miller, a living Buddha who could "give a merry laugh, a laugh that destroys *nihil*, a laugh that smashes fatality"[66] in the abyss-like situation of Vietnam.

Conclusion

In this article, I have discussed the significant impact of Phạm Công Thiện's activities on literature and thought in South Vietnam in the 1960s, and have introduced his friendship with Miller and their correspondence. Furthermore, to some extent, I have discussed the significance of Thiện's thought. I have gone into detail on how Thiện's thought was formed by the intercultural, ontological dialogues with Heidegger and Miller, both of whom had influenced him since his late teenage years.

Thiện's dialogues with these Westerners might be summarized as follows:

Heidegger criticized Western metaphysics for forgetting Being and in this way forming the modern world as it is, and he inquired into Being itself. On the basis of Heidegger's thought, Thiện came to the conclusion that the ultimate cause of the Vietnam War lay in the representative thinking in Western metaphysics, which had forgotten Being. He furthermore accused Western modernity, which had been constructed on this foundation and which had invaded his motherland. Based on D.T. Suzuki's essays in English, Thiện recognized how the problem of Zen was a problem of Being, and he discovered the affinity between Zen and Heidegger. Thiện translated Heidegger's Being into *Tính*, which is one of the Chinese words for *bhāva* in Sanskrit and which originated from the same stem as *bin/bist*. Thus, Thiện established this common linguistic foundation, preparing the dialogue between Heidegger and the East Asian world.

Thiện wanted to destroy the representative way of thinking and instead to inquire into an alternative way of being, and he found the possibility of Being in the Vietnamese Buddhist tradition, such as that founded on Không Lộ's howl.

Thiện claimed that the Nothingness of Buddhism would destroy even Heidegger's Nothingness, and he praised Miller as a Western writer who awakened such a consciousness of Nothingness. Just as Heidegger censured the modern world, based on Western metaphysics, Miller also radically criticized modern materialistic civilization and its values. Thiện recognized that Heidegger was still in the outer reaches of intelligence, but he saw that Miller had awoken the Buddhist Consciousness of Nothingness = Being and that he actually lived in it.

Thus, it can be said that in Heidegger and Miller Thiện found the key for his fundamental criticism of Western modernity, which he considered the ultimate cause of the Vietnam War. Moreover, it can be argued that Thiện recognized the affinity

---

[65] Phạm'S letter to Miller on 2 August 1966, from Paris.

[66] Phạm, *Im Lặng Hố Thẳm*, 99.

between Mahayana (Zen) Buddhism and their thoughts, and that, during the time of the war, he attempted to seek the possibility of Being in Vietnamese traditional religion.

In this article, I limited the focus to Heidegger and Miller as two of the great influences on Thiện during the time in which he was living in South Vietnam. However, during this period, Thiện also struggled with other Westerns figures, such as Eckhart, Nietzsche, Rimbaud, L-F. Céline, Faulkner, Saroyan, Kazantzakis, and Rilke. These relationships offer opportunities for future investigations into the sources of Thiện's thought.

Here, I have only discussed the case of Thiện and those around him. However, this view should also allow us to capture a glimpse of the rich situation in which intellectuals in South Vietnam had absorbed Western literature and philosophy and were engaging in dialogue with them. I contend that the activity of intellectuals in South Vietnam during the time of the Vietnam War is noteworthy and deserves further investigation.

Bibliography

Barrett W (1956) Zen for the West. In: Suzuki DT, Barrett W (eds), Doubleday & Company, INC, New York

Calonne DS (2007) Samadhi all the time: Henry Miller and Buddhism. In Stroker 67: 9–19. Stroker Press, Honjo City

Gadkar-Wilcox W (2014) Existentialism and Intellectual Culture in South Vietnam. J Asian Stud 73:377–395. https://doi.org/10.1017/S0021911813002349

Heidegger M (1983) Einführung in die Metaphysik: Gesamtausgabe, vol 40. V. Klostermann, Frankfurt am Main

Heidegger M (1977) The Question concerning technology, and other essays (trans.) Lovitt W, Harper Torchbooks, New York

Hohl H (1967) Heidegger và cuộc khủng hoảng của siêu-hình-học. Translated by Ban chủ biên toà soạn Tư Tưởng Viện Đại-học Vạn-Hạnh. Tư Tưởng, số 1:379–416

Inrasara. "Chớp lửa thiêng Phạm Công Thiện & tuổi trẻ tôi." http://inrasara.com/2011/03/12/ch%E1%BB%9Bp-l%E1%BB%ADa-thieng-ph%E1%BA%A1m-cong-thi%E1%BB%87n-tu%E1%BB%95i-tr%E1%BA%BB-toi/

Mai Thảo (1985) Chân Dung. Văn Khoa, Culver City, CA

Miller H (1958) The smile at the foot of the ladder. New Directions, New York, p c1948

Miller H (1961) Tropic of cancer. Grove Press, New York

Miller H (1958) The colossus of Maroussi. New Directions, New York, p c1941

Miller, H (1983) Lettres de Henry Miller à Pham Công Thiên. In Tribu 1:103–157. Centre d'Édition et d'Action Poétique, Toulouse

Nakamura Hajime (c1964) Ways of thinking of Eastern peoples. revised English translation (ed) Wiener PP.. East-West Center Press, Honolulu

Ngô Trọng Anh (1969) Vị trí của vô thể Heidegger trong tư tưởng đại thừa. In Tư Tưởng, bộ mới số 5:4

Nguyễn Hưng Quốc (1998) Mỗi khi một tác giả: Phạm Công Thiện. In Việt, số 1:81–83

Nguyễn Hưng Quốc. Đọc lại Phạm Công Thiện. In Tiền Vệ. https://www.tienve.org/home/literature/viewLiterature.do?action=viewArtwork&artworkId=8043

Nguyễn Mạnh Tiến (2014) Nhà văn nổi loạn hay thần tượng văn nghệ: trường hợp Phạm Công Thiện. In Tạp Chí Sông Hương, số 308:10–14. http://tapchisonghuong.com.vn/tap-chi/c316/n17377/Nha-van-noi-loan-hay-than-tuong-van-nghe-truong-hop-Pham-Cong-Thien.html

Nguyễn Vỹ ed (1957–1962) Phổ Thông. no.1–6, 13, 16, 75, 80. Saigon

Munehiro N (2009) 『新しい意識; ベトナムの亡命思想家ファム・コン・ティエン』. Iwanami Shoten Publishers, Tokyo

Phạm Công Thiện (1965) The ontological background of the present war in Vietnam (an open letter to Henry Miller)." In Thích Nhất Hạnh, Bùi Giáng, Tam Ích, Hồ Hữu Tường, Phạm Công Thiện. *Dialogue*. Saigon: Lá Bối.

Phạm Công Thiện (1970). Ý Thức Mới trong Văn Nghệ và Triết Học.4th ed. Saigon: An Tiêm (1st ed. Saigon: Lá Bối, 1964).

Phạm Công Thiện (1966). Ngày Sanh của Rắn. An Tiêm, Saigon

Phạm Công Thiện (1966) Hố Thẳm của Tư Tưởng. 1st ed. An Tiêm, Saigon

Phạm Công Thiện (1970) Hố Thẳm của Tư Tưởng. 3rd ed. Phạm Hoàng, Saigon

Phạm Công Thiện (1967) Im Lặng Hố Thẳm. An Tiêm, Saigon

Phạm Công Thiện (1968) lời giới thiệu của người dịch. In Martin Heidegger. Về Thể Tính của Chân Lý. Translated by Phạm Công Thiện. Saigon: Hoàng Đông Phương

Phạm Công Thiện (1969) Henry Miller. Phạm Hoàng, Saigon

Phạm Công Thiện (1970) Nói chuyện với tập san Văn. In Nikos Kazantzakis, Saigon: Phạm Hoàng.

Phạm Công Thiện (1970) Lời người dịch." In Friedrich Nietzsche. Tôi Là Ai ?. Translated by Phạm Công Thiện. Phạm Hoàng, Saigon

Phạm Công Thiện (1971) Ý Thức Bùng Vỡ. Đồng Nai, Saigon

Phạm Công Thiện (1988) Đi cho hết Một Đêm Hoang Vu trên Mặt Đất. Trần Thi, Garden Grove, CA

Phạm Công Thiện. Letters to Henry Miller. In UCLA Library, Department of Special Collections.

Suzuki Daisetz Teitaro (1948) The essence of Buddhism. Hozokan, Kyoto

Suzuki Daisetz Teitaro (2003) An introduction to Zen Buddhism. Art Days, Tokyo

Suzuki Daisetz Teitaro (1956) Zen Buddhism. Edited by William Barrett. New York: Doubleday & Company, INC, .

Trần Đức Thảo (1971) Triết-Lý Đã Đi Đến Đâu. Ban đại diện S.V.P.K. văn-học và K.H.V.N., Saigon

Trần Tuấn Kiệt (1973) Tác Giả Tác Phẩm. Đời sống và tác phẩm các văn nghệ sĩ Việt Nam, Saigon

Tư Tưởng (1969) bộ mới số 5. Viện Đại Học Vạn Hạnh, Saigon

Võ Phiến (1986) Văn Học Miền Nam Tổng Quan. Văn Nghệ, Westminster, CA

Munehiro Nohira is an Associate Professor in Vietnamese language and culture at the Institute of Global Studies, Tokyo University of Foreign Studies, Japan. He received his PhD in Vietnamese Literature from Tokyo University of Foreign Studies in 2007. His research focuses on Vietnamese Literature, Buddhist Philosophy in Vietnamese literature and Comparative Philosophy between the East and the West. His recent papers include *The Acceptance of D.T. Suzuki in Vietnam—D.T. Suzuki and Phạm Công Thiện* (Thought, vol. 48-no. 15, 2020), *Re-examining Nguyễn Du's diplomatic route through his poetry in classical Chinese, Bắc Hành Tạp Lục* (Issues of Teaching Vietnamese and Studying Vietnam in the Today's World. Vol. 1, 2019). He has translated Phạm Công Thiện's two works into Japanese: The Silence of the Abyss (2018, originally published in 1967) and *The New Consciousness in Literature and Philosophy* (2022, originally published in 1964).

The Tragic Hero: Nguyễn Mạnh Côn

Thomas Engelbert

* * *

Like many other terms we use in daily life and in the humanities, for instance in myth, the term "tragedy" has both a wide and a narrow meaning. The term "tragedy" is often used in everyday life for something that is bad, terrible, horrible or difficult to bear. In literature, however, the term tragedy is understood to mean that a person, a tragic hero, is "guilty without guilt." In this understanding, the tragic hero cannot escape from his own destiny and has to live with the consequences of throwing himself into his own misfortune. The contradiction between the expectations of the tragic hero or heroine and reality is also a main driver for a tragedy. The difference between tragedy and comedy is that the incompatibility of the relationship between expectation and reality is punished with suffering and sorrow, whereas in comedy the contradiction is resolved with humour and a wink.

What is a hero? The matter is disputed, and there are different voices throughout history. In the broad, general, public understanding of the word, a hero is a real or fictive person who commits extraordinary deeds using, for instance, his superhuman body, e.g., heroic fights or deeds marked by extraordinary bravery, strength and speed. Usually, this is the hero of the folktale or the medieval epos—half-gods, half-humans, who kill monsters and defeat giants, like Beowulf, Siegfried or Thạch Sanh.

A hero can also be a person of extraordinary capacities and virtues such as courage, sacrifice, or the struggle for justice and lofty ideals. For instance, he could be saving the country from foreign invaders.

Those heroes are, among so many others, Alexander Nevsky (1221–1263), the Prince of Novgorod, Kiev and Vladimir, the famed victor in battle against the Swedes (1240) and in the battle at Lake Peipus against the Livonian-Teutonic Order (1242).

T. Engelbert (✉)
Asia-Africa Institute, University of Hamburg, Hamburg, Germany
e-mail: jengelbert@web.de

© The Author(s), under exclusive license to Springer Nature Singapore Pte Ltd. 2023   163
T. Engelbert and C. P. Pham (eds.), *Global Vietnam: Across Time,*
Space and Community, Reading South Vietnam's Writers,
https://doi.org/10.1007/978-981-99-1043-4_10

He refused submission to the Latin papacy, and was, on the other hand, the faithful servant to and ruthless supporter of the Mongolian Khans against his own Slavic subjects. Jeanne d'Arc (1412–1431) liberated Orléans from the English, but was then betrayed and died on an English pyre. Both were canonized after their death and have been national heroes since the seventeenth century.

Vietnam has many national heroes of this kind: Lý Thường Kiệt (1019–1105), Trần Hưng Đạo (ca. 1228–1300), Lê Lợi (1384/1385–1433), Nguyễn Huệ (1753–1792) and, of course, the greatest of the greatest in the national saga of today's Communist historical propaganda: Hồ Chí Minh (1890–1969). The cult of the nation led, in almost all nation-states of the world, to a cult of national heroes, with monuments, squares and street-names (Washington, Leningrad, Quezon City, Ho Chi Minh City), school-book tales and medals. In the Philippines, a "National Heroes Committees Under the Office of the President" was founded in 1993 to bestow the rank of national hero.

False glorification of heroism in the age of nationalism was also criticized. Bertolt Brecht gave us perhaps the most famous literary citation in his play: *The Life of Galileo*:

Andrea (loud):   Unhappy the country that has no heroes! ...

Galileo: No. Unhappy the country that needs heroes.[1]

In literature studies, the hero is simply the main actor of a literary work, regardless of his capacities or his morality. He can be strong, good-hearted and successful, or weak, unsuccessful and even wicked and evil (the so-called anti-hero, in Russian: негерой, 'un-hero').

What is a tragic hero in literature? Since the age of Greek tragedy, a tragic hero is considered a hero who suffers mishaps for reasons to be found in himself. He bears responsibility for his tragic actions, but originally has no negative intentions. Quite often, almost always, his tragic life ends with death. Hans-Dieter Gelfert distinguished seven kinds of tragic deaths in literature, but he considers only three of these deaths tragic, namely resulting from an error atoned for by death, a miscarriage of justice, or suicide as a result of misjudgement. Four deaths are untragic: death because of age, illness, or accident, heroic death in battle or duty, martyrdom and death in battle or the murder of a tyrant.[2]

Gelfert wrote:

The ruin is unnatural, not accidental, unintentional, self-inflicted and not entirely morally deserved. All of these criteria are commonly felt to be connotations of the term 'failure';

---

[1] *"Andrea laut: Unglücklich das Land, das keine Helden hat! ... Galilei: Nein. Unglücklich das Land, das Helden nötig hat."* Brecht, Das Leben des Galileo Galilei, 129–30.

[2] Gelfert stressed, that he only wants to consider tragedies in the form of literary dramas, from Greek antiquity in the fifth century BC up to Lessing and Hebbel in the nineteenth century. He is not interested in the term "tragedy" in a more general sense. Gelfert, Die Tragödie, 6. However, as he has prominently included Kleist's novella *Michael Kohlhaas* in his research, we can assume that he has treated the topic "tragedy in literature" in general. If he writes (on p. 21) that tragedies as dramatic plays appeared only in certain historical periods (in the Western hemisphere, we should add), he might be right. However, tragedy in literature in general seems to be an eternal phenomenon, transcending the borders of time and space.

because it says that someone fights against defeat and yet fails at the same time. The interplay of coincidence and necessity, of rebellion and succumbing, of guilt and excessive suffering are the defining characteristics of the tragic. And as an additional important factor, there must be a turning point in the tragic process, at which the accidental turns into the inevitable, the noble into the guilty, the rebellion into succumbing. But in order for the interaction of such conflicting impulses to be understood by a spectator, it must be consciously experienced by the hero himself. Since Aristotle we call this becoming aware of the tragic entanglement *anagnorisis* (recognition).[3]

Gelfert distinguished between four types of tragedy. He calls them "four archetypic tragic heroes."[4]

A tragic conflict occurs if the tragically failing hero and his antagonist (e.g., a personal adversary, the state or the law) claim the same moral justification for their action. This is the first or "classical" type of tragic hero in literature, e.g., the "Antigone" of Sophocles. Antigone knowingly breaks one law by following another, contrary law. This makes her guilty. The tragic conflict lies in the moral order of the society.

The second type is the unjustified claim against the prevailing moral codex. Gelfert calls it "guilt tragedy," as in *Macbeth* (Shakespeare). Macbeth knowingly becomes guilty because his passion is greater than his understanding. The tragic conflict stems from the psychology of the hero.

The third type is that of a hero driven to guilt against his will by an overpowering fate. This is the fate tragedy, and one typical case would be *Oedipus Rex* (Sophocles). Oedipus becomes guilty precisely because he wants to avoid guilt. The tragic conflict is caused by the order of the world.

The fourth type occurs when a person, in his striving for the realization of a value, gets into a state of delusion from an inherent antinomy of that value, so that his positive striving is reversed. Gelfert cites the novella *Michael Kohlhaas* (Heinrich von Kleist) as a typical example of this kind, which could be called "dialectical tragedy." Michael Kohlhaas wants to push through an absolute value without compromise. Here, the tragic conflict results from the dialectical structure of the value which is defended.[5]

Why is the reader or viewer interested in tragic heroes or in the depiction of tragic failure? Friedrich Schiller was a historical optimist, an ardent supporter of enlightenment. He described the effect of the tragedy on the listener or reader. He distinguished between the "Fine Arts," which are the arts of taste, beauty and mind and the "moving arts," which are the arts of feelings and the human heart. The latter has the good, the sublime and the emotion as its main subjects. Emotion cannot be separated from the beauty, but beauty can exist without emotion. The desires for the beautiful, the sublime and the emotion strengthen our moral feelings, in the same way as the pleasure in doing good deeds or feeling love.[6]

Nietzsche was a historical pessimist. Neither religion, nor belief in progress consoled him. For him, history was the perpetual repetition of the same. He saw

---

[3] Gelfert, Die Tragödie, 14.

[4] Ibid., 15.

[5] Ibid., 15.

[6] Schiller. Über den Grund des tragischen Vergnügens.

the tragedy as a cure from the disgust with the terrible and with the eternal absurdity of the world. His opinion was that knowledge of the absurd does kill action. The absurd being unveiled by illusion is part of action. Now there is no more consolation, the longing goes beyond a world after death, beyond the gods themselves, existence is denied, together with its glittering reflection in the immortal gods or in an immortal hereafter. In the awareness of the truth once seen, man sees everywhere only that which is terrible or the absurdity of his existence. Now, he understands the symbolism in the fate of Ophelia, and he recognizes the wisdom of the forest god Silenus: it disgusts him. Here, in this greatest danger to the human will, art approaches as a saving sorceress. She alone is able to turn those disgusting thoughts about the horrible and absurd into ideas that one can live with. The sublime of the tragic is taming the horrible, and the comical is the artistic discharge of the disgust with the absurd.[7]

Peter Szondi has an interesting and useful objection: that we must distinguish between the poetics of the tragic, which has existed since Aristotle and is largely based on his teachings, and a philosophy of the tragic which has existed since F.W.J. Schelling. The poetics of the tragic usually examines the origin and effect of the tragedy, whereas the philosophy of the tragic is concerned with the theory, with what the tragic is, its inherent structure, and not its effect on the viewer or listener. In Szondi's view, German idealist philosophy has, like no other, analysed the essence of the tragic. He cited especially Schelling: that the essence of the tragic is a dispute within the subject between freedom and necessity. It is a dialectical phenomenon and does not end with the victory of the one or the defeat of the other. Both appear, victorious and defeated at the same time, in total indifference. The victor is, at the same time, the vanquished, and the vanquished is victor. This dispute exists only then when the will is undermined and freedom is being fought for on its own territory. Freedom falls apart within itself and becomes its own opponent. For Hölderlin, the downfall of the hero is the offering of man to nature. Tragic heroes are victims of their times. Their passing makes something new become possible.[8]

Nguyễn Mạnh Côn is an interesting phenomenon in Vietnamese literature. His life seems to be full of mysterious stories, perhaps real, perhaps invented or attributed. The sketchy information about the adventures and tragedies of his life and death must, of course, be taken with a due degree of caution. Stories are told, legends are spun in the vastness of the Internet by Vietnamese authors living abroad, who, for various, partly understandable reasons, want to remain anonymous or publish under a pseudonym. These true or legendary stories are presented here with this due degree of caution, always referring to the unclear sources of the Internet. The first, and the last, third part, will present this unsatisfactory knowledge about his life and death.

The only comprehensible thing are the literary works he has left behind. One of the four works that could be located in the library of our Institute shall be presented and analysed in the second part of this contribution. The author of this contribution is fully aware that his effort will remain unsatisfactory. It is an attempt to approach

---

[7] Nietzsche, Gesammelte Werke, Die Geburt der Tragödie aus dem Geiste der Musik, 35.

[8] Szondi, Versuch über das Tragische, 13–18.

the life and work of this author, who seems to be somewhat neglected and side-lined in the history of modern Vietnamese literature.[9]

The Life

Nguyễn Mạnh Côn was born on 7 May 1920, in Hải Dương. When he was a child, he studied in Hanoi. According to Vương Trùng Dương's sources ("có tài liệu"), he cooperated with (wrote for?) the Journal *Đông Pháp Thời Báo* (*Le Courrier Indochinois*)[10] in 1939, and with the Japanese in 1945. After the 1945 August Revolution, he allegedly wrote articles for the newspaper *Thống Nhất* of the Việt Minh (VM). In addition to his real name, he also wrote under the pseudonyms Nguyễn Kiên Trung, Kỳ Hoa Tử and Đặng Văn Hầu.[11]

According to Vương Trùng Dương, Nguyễn Mạnh Côn entered the Trần Quốc Tuấn Military Preparatory School. This was not the VM Trần Quốc Tuấn infantry school in Sơn Tây (today's Military Academy of the Infantry) which was founded in 1946. It was a school founded by the Vietnamese Nationalist Party in Chapa on 1 January 1946, where nationalist Vietnamese were trained by Japanese advisors. In a private email, the writer Vương Trùng Dương wrote to the author of this contribution:

> Information can be found in the memoir "My Life" of Mr. Hoàng Tích Thông, Colonel of the Marine Infantry of the Republic of Vietnam. He also belongs to my family, so I helped him with the layout of his memoir. According to this document, the Trần Quốc Tuấn Army School was the martial arts school of the Vietnamese Nationalist Party. The school officially opened on 1 January 1946 at Chapa, Lào Cai province. The Board of Directors and Teaching staff of this Trần Quốc Tuấn Army School consisted of Japanese officers, who had left the army before and after the surrender of the Japanese army to the Allies, with the aim to help train future officers of the National Vietnamese army. The school's total capacity was about 300 students. Most of the students were pupils, students and young people from Hanoi and the Northern provinces. In addition, there were brothers from the Central and Southern regions who were sent there to study. When the National Youth Union brothers withdrew from Việt Trì to Yên Báy and merged with the Trần Quốc Tuấn Army School, the students' total number increased to 500. On 22 May 1946, the Việt Minh's Trần Quốc Tuấn Army School in Sơn Tây opened under the chairmanship of Hồ Chí Minh and Võ Nguyên Giáp. So, there is confusion about these two different military schools.[12]

Later, this basic military training offered by the Japanese was not regarded as a formal basis for afterwards including soldiers in the ranks of the South Vietnamese Army. They had to undergo additional training classes. Vương Trùng Dương explained:

---

[9] In his magisterial two-volume work about South Vietnamese literature (1954–1975), Nguyễn Vy Khanh has mentioned Nguyễn Mạnh Côn in two little paragraphs at the beginning of the first chapter. Nguyễn Vy Khanh. Văn học miền Nam 1954–1975, pp. 20, 30–31.

[10] This journal existed from 1923 until 1928 in Saigon. It seems impossible that Nguyễn Mạnh Côn contributed to it in any way.

[11] Vương Trùng Dương, Nguyễn Mạnh Côn, nhà văn can đảm chọn cái chết trong tù.

[12] Private Mail, Vương Trùng Dương, July 30, 2022.

In the Trần Quốc Tuấn Army School of the Nationalist Party, officers graduated with the rank of Second Lieutenant. ... This rank was not accepted by the National Army, so Mr. Hoàng Tích Thông, for instance, later joined the Fourth Class of the Thủ Đức Infantry school.[13]

After the withdrawal of the Guomindang, Chinese troops who had arrived in Hanoi on 9 September 1945 with the official task of disarming the Japanese troops north of the 16th parallel (the withdrawal was deliberately delayed and lasted from March until September 1945), the Communist VM was able to take over the hegemony in the anti-French struggle and gradually destroyed the rivalling nationalist organizations in the north and centre, beginning with purges in the capital and Northern delta provinces and gradually reaching the mountain provinces along the Vietnam-China border. The non-Communist nationalists were arrested, killed or they fled abroad, mostly to mainland China and, when the Communists took over there as well, to Hong Kong. It could be, that Nguyễn Mạnh Côn was among those who temporarily left Northern Vietnam. Where did the writer Nguyễn Mạnh Côn stay in those years? Vương Trùng Dương guessed:

Hoàng Tích Thông went to China for a few years with many members of the Vietnam Nationalist Party during the Chiang Kai-shek period, so, in my opinion, the writer Nguyễn Mạnh Côn also went to Hong Kong.[14]

In 1951, Côn returned to French-held Hanoi, and taught at a private school. In 1954, he emigrated to the South to work at the Saigon Radio station. After that, he worked as the editor-in-chief and editor of the journal *Chỉ Đạo* (Guideline, 1956–1961), and as the editor of *Văn Hữu* (Literary Friend), and wrote for several other newspapers in Saigon. Nguyễn Triệu Nam wrote about this period and Côn's particular writing style:

Before 30 April 1975, I interacted with Nguyễn Mạnh Côn more often than with any other writer. At one time, he was the editor-in-chief of *Chỉ Đạo*, the mouthpiece of the Free Vietnamese Against Communism, I was a copyreader. When this newspaper was assigned to the Sub-Department of Psychological Warfare, the predecessor of the later Department of Psychological Warfare, he was a collaborator. At that time, I was an assistant to the editor Kỳ Văn Nguyên, who was in charge of editing. Nguyễn Mạnh Côn is a talented writer. Extensive knowledge. Magical pen. Simple, bright style. The literature is full, endless. The style changes flexibly according to each situation. When necessary, he writes like a psychoanalyst. However, it is still popular and easy to understand. In him, there is one outstanding feature. He often uses scientific topics to stir up the story. Therefore, readers, whether they want to or not, must pay attention to the content of the main topic. ... A creative, unique way.[15]

As noted by Đỗ Quý Toàn (Ngô Nhân Dụng) cited by Vương Trùng Dương:

The writer Nguyễn Mạnh Côn has a very special intelligence, although he was born during the war, and he did not receive a formal school education, his intelligent mind is very sharp, he is interested in all matters within the intellectual domain of mankind.[16]

---

[13] Ibid.

[14] Ibid.

[15] Nguyễn Mạnh Côn, Đem tâm tình viết lịch sử; "Trược khi vào sách: Kỷ niệm về Nguyễn Mạnh Côn. Hồi tưởng của Nguyễn Triệu Nam."

[16] Vương Trùng Dương, "Nguyễn Mạnh Côn, nhà văn can đảm chọn cái chết trong tù."

About Nguyễn Mạnh Côn's biography as recorded by his literary friend Viên Linh in 2014, cited by Vương Trùng Dương:

I have a picture of Nguyễn Mạnh Côn's identity card in my hand, behind him he neatly writes his name in the font. I think the photo was taken in 1956, or 57, in a military uniform, the collar of which had a peeled can, perhaps the pauldrons of a second lieutenant, or a lieutenant. He is an assimilation officer. The back of the photo reads: 15 March 1920. Hải Dương, North Vietnam. (It seems to be on the Seventh Day of the Fourth Month, Canh Thân year.) He was born in Đông Hy village, Ninh Giang province. He won the National Literature Prize in 1957. In 1975, he was invited to the National Literature Prize Committee of Judges. In his childhood, he followed his parents—as he wrote, 'mother and father'—traveling all over the North. From the age of 13, he studied at Thăng Long private school, Hanoi. In 1940, he crossed the border and came to Hong Kong. No one knows the reason, but according to an article he wrote that I read, Mr. Côn was active in the Vietnam Nationalist Party ... The resistance war against the French broke out, in December 1945, he withdrew to the Việt Bắc war zone. From here, the book *Bringing the Heart to Write History*, written under the pen name Nguyên Kiên Trung, can be said to be a period of his real-life activity, if not exactly the same, but also very close to reality. In 1952, Nguyễn Mạnh Côn returned to Hanoi, the next year he went to Haiphong, taught in this coastal city until 1955, then moved to the South.[17]

Nguyễn Vy Khanh has portrayed Nguyễn Mạnh Côn as a member of a group of authors, who all had migrated from the North to the South and were involved in the building of the cultural life of the First Republic of Vietnam (1955–1963). They were deeply influenced by European and Western thought. They once had fought, some of them even at the sides of the Communist Việt Minh, against the French colonialists, but had left the VM and the North due to its Communist and totalitarian character. They regarded their literary works as weapons in the struggle against the Communist ideology. After 1960, hot-tempered attacks against Communism receded and made way to new tendencies, for instance, scientific utopian literature with Nguyễn Mạnh Côn. This group of writers, which was not a single literary school, included, beside Nguyễn Mạnh Côn, the authors Mai Thảo, Thanh Tâm Tuyền, Nguyên Sa, Kỳ Văn Nguyên, Doãn Quốc Sĩ, Đỗ Thúc Vịnh and Võ Phiến.[18]

When he worked for the journal *Chỉ Đạo,* Nguyễn Mạnh Côn was employed by the RVN Armed Forces. He was integrated with the rank of second lieutenant. Vương Trùng Dương as cited by an eyewitness, Tạ Ty:

One day, I was very surprised when I saw Nguyễn Mạnh Côn wearing the pauldrons of Second Lieutenant, coming to find me at his workplace at the beginning of Hồng Thập Tự Street, near Thị Nghè Bridge, across from the Zoological Garden. He said that he had been assimilated into the Army with the rank of Second Lieutenant to be in charge of a newspaper advocated by the Ministry of Defense, and he asked me to present the cover template for that magazine. Your direct commander is Captain Quân, my friend. Indeed, I also do not understand how he passed the medical examination of health, especially as his addiction was imprinted on his face. This issue I never mentioned, every time I talk to Nguyễn Mạnh Côn.
…

Since it was a newspaper of the Ministry of National Defense, I wanted to help draw the cover, but Nguyễn Mạnh Côn was also very tactful, telling Captain Quân

---

[17] Ibid.
[18] Nguyễn Vy Khanh. Văn học miền Nam 1954–1975, 20.

to pay me, because the newspaper had its own budget to buy articles from writers, whether they were inside or outside the military.

Thanks to the newspaper, Nguyễn Mạnh Côn had the opportunity to prove his talent. The story of the "Three Paratroopers in Distress," written by him, was well received. He used Einstein's theory of mathematical relativity to explain an equation for the reverse velocity of time. The story is both thrilling and scientific, to enthrall the reader.

Then came the memoir, *Bringing My Heart to Write History*, which was published on a regular basis in the journal and then printed as a book (published by Nguyễn Đình Vương, 1958) like the "Tale of Three Paratroopers in Distress." The memoir exposes the cunning plots of the Party and the Communists to destroy the opposing parties to keep all power in their own hands. The book is a lengthy indictment with historical evidence, so it was hard for the Communists to deny.

In addition, Nguyễn Mạnh Côn also wrote many other book series published by the Cơ Sở Giao Điểm. This company belonged to Trần Phong Giao, not to Nguyễn Đình Vương, as many people mistakenly believe. In addition to writing as a journalist, Nguyễn Mạnh Côn also wrote many commentaries in French for Saigon radio... But Nguyễn Mạnh Côn (as well as Mặc Thu) did not stay in the Army for long. A few years later, they all asked to be discharged from the army to become civilians to make their activities easier."[19]

According to Thế Uyên, cited by Vương Trùng Dương:

> I once jokingly asked him: Is the word Côn in your name a stick, like a school of a stick? He answered: Côn is a kind of whale shark of the ocean, similar to an eagle that flies three thousand miles in the sky. His father named Mạnh Côn with the hope that he would be able to move around in the future. But life's answer is often unexpected: He didn't make a name for himself in martial arts, perhaps a result of his physical weakness, although there was a time when he tried by accepting the position of assimilation lieutenant that led nowhere. He also did not succeed in the school exam! But he succeeded in literature and thinking, and with his creative writing style, entered the 'forbidden zone' of Nguyễn Đình Chiểu, the supernatural world of science fiction, and later entered the world. The whole field of political thinking has visionary vision with the rather thick book *Peace. Think What. Doing what?* It is true that he is a type of fish, struggling freely for a while, in the world of words.[20]

It seems, that in personal life, the author Nguyễn Mạnh Côn was a heavy opium smoker. In Thế Uyên's article about him cited by Vương Trùng Dương, the writer Cá Kình recorded a meeting with Côn:

> He comfortably received me next to the lamp and I also comfortably sat on the mat next to him because he knew that my father was also an opium addict who had just quit after emigrating to the South for a few years. The two of us prepared for our next opium pipe, movements that are so familiar to me from the past. During many nights in the North before 1954, my father had the custom, after dinner, to give the job of preparing dinner to me and my sister. The daughter spread out mats, thin cushions and pillows, I brought a pot of hot tea from the living room, put a lamp in the center of the mat ... Once when I asked Nguyễn Mạnh Côn why he was addicted, he answered frankly that he had heard that opium increases

---

[19] Ibid.

[20] Vương Trùng Dương, "Nguyễn Mạnh Côn, nhà văn can đảm chọn cái chết trong tù."

sexual excitement and prolongs lovemaking. When I asked him if the results were correct, he laughed and said yes … but then he sighed very softly: 'But only in the early stages of smoking, when addicted, everything returns to normal.'[21]

An additional note of Vương Trùng Dương about the author's addiction:

Nguyễn Mạnh Côn had been addicted to the 'brown fairy' Phù Dung since his days in Hanoi, when he entered Saigon where he used to hang out with Vũ Hoàng Chương, Triều Đầu … at the lamp table of Đinh Quát, alley 220, Trương Minh Giảng Street. In the mid-1960s, Hồng Tiêu Nguyễn Đức Huy (1902-1985, the husband of Mrs. Tùng Long), Nguyễn Mạnh Côn and Hoàng Hải Thủy asked for a permission to publish the journal *Bút Sắc* (Pointed Pen). I can't understand why all three of them were 'disciples' of the 'brown fairy.' For political reasons, the request was not granted.[22]

In the literary work which we will discuss below, there is also a scene where the protagonist Trọng is introduced by his friend Hoàng to the world of smoking opium. The writer describes extensively the effects this intoxicant produces on the human body and mind, especially the physical elation and spiritual satisfaction it creates at the beginning. He also describes the sexual endurance produced by the consumption of opium. But it also leads to immediate addiction.

In the early 1970s, he earnestly struggled against his addiction. Nguyễn Triệu Nam remembered:

After the suspension of the journal *Chỉ Đạo*, Nguyễn Mạnh Côn and I rarely saw each other. Time past. It was not until the fiery summer of 72 that I saw him again. He was still writing as always. But he wrote less. The writing profession had really become a side job. To make a living was his right-hand job. He did all the honest things one can do to earn extra money with his wife, including freight forwarding services. For an addict like him, spending a whole day struggling with life was not easy. The good thing was that, every day, he gradually reduced the dose of the drug. At the beginning, it was annoying. Afterwards he got used to it. That's why he could save the whole morning running outside for his business.[23]

Nguyễn Mạnh Côn was not an easy-going personality, especially if he felt treated below his worth. Đặng Hà has told several stories about him, which reveal his extraordinary character. Côn seemed aware of his own importance. Outwardly, he seemed eccentric. But behind it was a vulnerable soul and an absolute sense of justice. There is a moment, when he was forced to wait at the entrance of the Independence Palace (Dinh Độc Lập) in Saigon, the seat of the RVN President. The incident occurred in 1967:

---

[21] Ibid.

[22] Ibid. In a private missive to the author, Vương Trùng Dương added: "In his work *A High Love*, he has written about opium smoking. At that time, in the alley 220 of Trương Minh Giang road, near the Buddhist Institute Vạn Hạnh, there were three dens (vòm): Tư Cao, Sơn Cụt and Đinh Quát. Nguyễn Mạnh Côn went to Đinh Cát, together with the writers Hoàng Hải Thủy, Doãn Bình and Mr. Nguyễn Văn Noãn, the Director of the Information Agency of the Capital Saigon. Noãn had studied film in France. After his return to Vietnam, he directed the film *We Want to Live*." Email, Vương Trùng Dương, 15 August 2022.

[23] Nguyễn Mạnh Côn, Đem tâm tình viết lịch sử; "Trước khi vào sách: Kỷ niệm về Nguyễn Mạnh Côn. Hồi tưởng của Nguyễn Triệu Nam."

The next day he took me (Đặng Hà) to see the writer Nguyễn Mạnh Côn in his house in Nguyễn Cư Trinh alley, near Phú Nhuận intersection. After listening to my presentation of the program, fortunately, he happily accepted my request to support my program right away. At that time, Mr. Côn was writing some ideas for Mr. Nguyễn Cao Kỳ, then the 'Chairman of the Central Executive Committee' or Prime Minister. He promised to take me and Mr. Tu the next morning to meet Mr. Đào Xuân Dung, his close friend, who was at that time deputy director in the President's Office in special charge of National Land affairs. He suggested we should have one more person to add to our power. Mr. Trần Dạ Từ decided to invite Prof. Phan Văn Phùng, General Secretary of CPS, which stands for School Youth Activities Program. This group included Đỗ Ngọc Yến, Lê Đình Điều, Đỗ Quý Toàn, Hà Tường Cát, Trần Đại Lộc, Phạm Phú Minh. After 1975, when they moved to the United States, they all worked for the daily newspaper *Người Việt* (The Vietnamese).

As promised, we waited at the left wing of the Independence Palace on Nguyễn Du Street, waited for about five minutes, but were not yet allowed in. Mr. Côn seemed annoyed. He asked the gatekeeper to call the office so that he could talk directly to Mr. Đào Xuân Dung. Perhaps the gatekeeper who saw him often going in and out of the Presidential Palace also agreed to let him speak directly. He picked up the phone and said loudly, looking very angry, 'What is going on, will you receive us or not? We have been waiting for almost ten minutes, if you're busy, we'll go home, but don't let us wait this long.' After he had finished speaking, he put down the phone and said to us: 'I have never waited more than five minutes before, even when I met Nguyễn Cao Kỳ, after five minutes, and he will not answer (Mr. Côn often used *moi*, and *toi*, to refer to me) *moi* will go then.' A few minutes later, the police at the gate informed us that the Deputy Director invited us into his office to have an audience."[24]

The background of this meeting in the Presidential Palace, as Vương Trùng Dương wrote in a private mail to the author of this contribution, was the creation of an anti-Communist youth movement to win over especially the pupils and students of Saigon, first of all with benevolent and charitable activities, but also with singing. The Communists sensed the threat and killed one of the most active participants of this movement, the student Ngô Vương Toại, in the classroom of the Department of Literature, Cường Để street, on 18 November 1967.[25]

The left-wing anti-RVN youth leader Đoàn Văn Toại, who was arrested for short periods several times by the RVN before 1975, and by the Communists for a long period after 1975 under the pretext that they allegedly confused his name with the other Toại, still believed in his United States exile that Ngô Vương Toại's youth

---

[24] Đặng Hà, "Tưởng nhớ Nguyễn Mạnh Côn," In: Vương Trùng Dương. "Nguyễn Mạnh Côn, nhà văn can đảm chọn cái chết trong tù."

[25] Email, Vương Trùng Dương, 27 July 2022. However, Ngô Vương Toại survived the assassination attempt with a shot in the stomach. In 1979, the two Toại met each other in the US, the country of their exile, and agreed to work together in the fight against human rights violations in their homeland. Doan Van Toai, Der vietnamesische Gulag, 26.

movement was sponsored by the "CIA."[26] That was undoubtedly the rumour spread by the assassins to justify their nefarious act.

To fight against Communist narratives, against an extremely clever, meticulously organized and carefully orchestrated propaganda was one of the goals of Nguyễn Mạnh Côn and his literary and intellectual companions. From today's perspective and looking back into the heated anti-US youth movements' atmosphere of the late 1960s—turmoil and uproar in America, in Western Europe and in South Vietnam against the supposedly "dirty war"—Nguyễn Mạnh Côn's project today seems like Don Quixote's struggle with the windmills. That, too, was part of the tragedy of his life. He had the right ideas at the wrong time.

Where did Nguyễn Mạnh Côn's difficult character come from? First of all, we might think it had something to do with his addiction. However, such an explanation may fall short. Other factors could be thought of as well. We will see later in this contribution, that Côn's novel might have been influenced by Arthur Koestler, the former Communist and later fervently anti-Communist writer. Contemporaries described Arthur Koestler as having a mountain of inferiority complexes.

Koestler himself characterized his "illness of absoluteness (*Absolutitis*)" as a persistent characteristic of his approach to many aspects of life. Others saw him as oscillating between sensitivity and callousness, integrity and shadiness, arrogance and humility. Arthur Koestler was characterized as incorrigibly competitive and relentlessly combative, quick to take offence and slow to forgive. In the case of Koestler, his inferiority complexes probably resulted both from his childhood (an unhappy childhood, full of restrictions, with an overbearing mother) and his experiences of discrimination as a Hungarian Jew in Vienna in the 1920s. The Austro-Hungarian empire had vanished, and the Germans in Austria had difficulties accepting their new role both as a diminished nation and as an immigration country for the new national states which once formed the Empire. Especially, the Jews "from the East" were a particular target of discrimination.[27]

In the case of Nguyễn Mạnh Côn, more research is needed to find out where his indomitable rebellious character came from. His absoluteness led him to a seemingly pointless rebellion against the Communist regime. He paid for his revolt with his life. But his tragic death would make him immortal, perhaps even more so than his literary work.

---

[26] "Die Zeugen müssen verschwinden." In: *Spiegel*, 8 June 1980.
[27] Masters, "Arthur Koestler (1905–1983)."

The Literary Work

Several works are known. Vương Trùng Dươnghas cited 13 of them.[28] In the blurb of one his books printed in 1965, Côn himself cited three other titles in addition.[29]

Undoubtedly, Nguyễn Mạnh Côn was a political writer. Two leitmotifs appear again and again in his literary work. First, is his ideological opposition to Marxism or Communism. Second, he keeps asking himself the question: how could the Communists get the upper hand, even the monopoly, in the anti-colonial struggle and set up a dictatorship under the slogan or pretext of fighting the French?

The author of these lines wants to present one of the four works he has found in the library of his university. He is fully aware that the picture will be accidental, arbitrary, and cannot be regarded as complete or exhausting. As a Vietnamese proverb goes: "Eat a piece, know the whole cauldron (ăn một miếng, biết toàn vạc)."

Nguyễn Mạnh Côn's novel *1945. Lạc đường vào lịch sử* (1945. Losing the way into history) appeared in 1966 in the Publishing House Giao Điểm, Saigon. The pedagogical intention of the author is already made clear in the dedication of the book:

> Any youth has many mistakes, sins, as well as doubts and regrets. Since 1958, when I started writing this story until this year, I have and continue to pursue a dream, to make you, modern young people, firmly believe that our youth is nothing more than your youth. We could have been heroes who had lost their way, unwillingly.

And we just have more suffering. But suffering will come as it has come, to all. This story is proof of our endurance. Now it's your turn. N.M.C. 1965."[30]

With other words: He wants to tell us the story of a big error, of a delusion, a "wrong way into history." His example shall serve as a lesson to those a generation

---

[28] Vương Trùng Dương mentioned the following literary works: "Việt Minh, Ngươi Đi Đâu" (Viet Minh, where are you going? 1957); "Đem Tâm Tình Viết Lịch Sử" (Take the emotion to write history, 1958), which won the National Literary Prize of the Republic of Vietnam (Giải Thưởng Văn Chương toàn quốc), "Kỳ Hoa Tử" (Son of Ky Hoa, 1960); "Truyện Ba Người Lính Nhảy Dù Lâm Nạn" (The story of three parachute soldiers who became victims, 1960); "Lạc Đường Vào Lịch Sử" (The Wrong Way into History, 1965); "Con Yêu Con Ghét" (The loved and hated child, 1966); "Mối Tình Màu Hoa Đào" (The peach-coloured love, 1967); "Giấc Mơ Của Đá" (The dream of the stone, 1968), "Tình Cao Thượng" (A noble-minded love 1968); "Đường Nào Lên Thiên Thai" (Which way to the fairy kingdom, 1969), "Hoa Bình… Nghĩ Gì… Làm Gì" (Peace—what to think, what to do, 1969); "Sống Bằng Sự Nghiệp" (Living by work, 1969) and "Yêu Anh Vượt Chết" (Loving you, overcoming death, 1969). See Vương Trùng Dương, "Nguyễn Mạnh Côn, nhà văn can đảm chọn cái chết trong tù."

[29] These are the following titles "Chống Mác-xít" (Against Marxism, s.d.) and two volumes of memoirs which were announced as in the press in 1965: "Hồi ký đảng tranh 45–46" (Memoirs of the Parties' Struggle, 1945–1946) and "Hồi ký kháng chiến 46–51" (Memoirs of the Resistance War, 1946–1951).

[30] In the original: "Tuổi trẻ nào có nhiều phen sai lầm, tội lỗi, và hoài nghi, hối hận. Từ năm 1958 bắt đầu viết truyện nầy cho đến năm nay, tôi vẫn theo đuổi một ước vọng, là làm thế nào cho các bạn thanh niên hiện đại tin chắc rằng tuổi trẻ của chúng tôi chẳng có gì hơn tuổi trẻ của các bạn. Chúng tôi có thể đã là những anh hùng lạc đường, một cách bất đắc dĩ. Và chúng tôi chỉ có nhiều đau khổ. Nhưng đau khổ sẽ đến như đã đến, với tất cả. Cuốn truyện nầy là bằng chứng sự chịu đựng của chúng tôi. Bây giờ đến lượt các bạn."

younger than he not to commit the same errors. The author probably means: to recognize a mistake is to banish it. No one is forced to remain in mental dependence, a stupid member in a flock of sheep, forever.

The book was printed in 1966. The historical background was the escalating American War in Vietnam. After the fall of the authoritarian Ngô Đình Diệm regime in November 1963, turmoil reigned in South Vietnam, as different cliques in the military as well as political parties and factions fought with each other for power and privileges. The South Vietnamese administration did not collapse, but was severely weakened. In the countryside, the Communist insurgents increased their violence, whereas in the streets of Saigon, Đà Nẵng and Huế, a youth movement made itself heard, demanding freedom and democracy, but creating turmoil. It was secretly influenced by Communist perpetrators, who used the anarchy for their own intentions, to weaken the anti-Communist Republic of Vietnam and deconstruct the regime from within. As in 1945, the danger could be felt that the idealistic and restless youth was being used for the ends of a totalitarian regime, which misused these easily inspired youngsters for their gradual rise to undivided power.[31]

Quite a similar case occurred in Iran in 1978. As the Shahbanu Farah Pahlavi once said in an interview granted in their exile in Paris: "The Iranian youth dreamed to march directly into paradise. What they got was hell."[32]

The first chapter of this short novel of 148 pages describes a morning scene at a dike in the Red River Delta. The author describes the attack of a military unit of the Việt Minh guerilla on a Chinese convoy of four junks with the goal of capturing weapons from the enemy (In this case, the enemy were not the French, but troops of Guomindang China, which had occupied the North of Indochina to the 16th parallel, as stated above, to disarm the Japanese troops. The occupation began in September 1945 and lasted officially until March 1945. From March until September 1945, the Chinese left Northern Indochina).

The authorial narrator presents to us the central heroine of his novel: Tuyết Lan. Because of his parents' pressure, her lover Trọng has married another girl. Instead of resigning or committing suicide out of protest against the feudal customs, like the girls and boys of the novels of the Tự Lực Văn Đoàn literary group one generation before, Tuyết Lan becomes a revolutionary fighter to vent her anger. The operation against the Chinese—very bloody—succeeds. The soldiers are killed, the boats burned.

In the second chapter, the authorial narrator tells us the pre-history of Tuyết Lan's revolutionary awakening.

It was the time after 9 March 1945, when the Japanese occupiers had overthrown the French colonial administration. Her former schoolmate, Quang, who also admired the girl, brought her the news of Trọng's marriage to another girl from a rich family in the countryside. Tuyết Lan had in vain waited for five years that he would come and marry her. Lan invited him to her house in the Hàng Kén street in Hanoi's market quarter. There, Quang introduced her to the revolutionary cause. His reasoning was based on the Great Famine of 1944/45, which had killed two million people in

---

[31] For the general situation, see Engelbert, Vom Chaos zum Inferno.

[32] Shahbanu Farah Pahlavi, 23 July 2019. In: youtube, #judithbenhamouhuet #jbhreports #art.

Northern and Northern Central Vietnam. For this reason, the youth of today had not the right to lament or to withdraw into private life, but had to take up the struggle of the revolution to save the nation. For Quang, talking about the revolution was merely empty talk, the fashion of Hanoi's young people in those tumultuous days. How could he expect, that for Lan it would change her life. In order to forget the unfaithful lover Trọng, Lan plunged into the adventure of revolution.

On 26 April 1945, she pledged the blood oath of allegiance to the party. However, she did not become a member of the Communist movement, but joined the Vietnamese Nationalist Party (Việt Nam Quốc Dân Đảng, VNQDĐ). In the first meeting of the party cell, the problems of this party were already clear: After the uprising of Yên Bái in 1931, the French had destroyed the structure of the VNQDĐ. Only once, the Japanese had disarmed the French, was the party reborn. The members lacked experience and training. More serious was the power struggle within the party organization itself, even at the lowest level of a party cell:

> The conflict, to be honest, had already started ten days before. It was from the day when Quang had, gropingly, again found the connections. His timely business of trading weapons helped him tremendously, because the first rule was that each revolutionary party desperately needed weapons, and secondly, people thought that an illegal weapons' dealer could not but be a great hero. The revolutionary atmosphere of those days was full of a heraldic flavour. And in this way, people accepted Quang's oath very quickly. ... According to a usual tactic of the revolution, Quang also had the task of encouraging, restricting, and monitoring Trọng Sơn. This tactic would not have been without charm, had there been experienced cadres who could control both Quang and Trọng Sơn. But there were no such cadres, and after Quang had interfered clumsily into the work of Trọng Sơn, the latter began to realize that Quang could snatch the secretary's post from him in a short time. This was the reason why he always mentioned Quang's quite recent day of party entry. And now Tuyết Lan had come. Every girl in her circumstances should have known that her existence would cause a serious mess in the organization. Only Tuyết Lan, with her honesty towards the revolution, had never ever thought about that. She was exemplary in her will to sacrifice herself for the revolution.[33]

Nguyễn Mạnh Côn is an avid describer of the modern technical achievements of his times. In the first chapter, he meticulously describes a cancer treatment in the *Institut du Radium à Hanoi* (in Vietnamese: Viện Ra-đi), founded in 1923 as a private corporation, subsidized by the colonial administration, first named *Institut Curie de l'Indochine* according to the model of the *Institut Curie* in Paris. It was renamed in 1926 and housed in an imposing two-story neo-classical building at the corner of *Rue Richaud* (today: 43, Quán Sứ) and *Boulevard Borgnis-Débordes* (Tràng Thi). Since 1954, it has been Vietnam's Central Cancer Hospital (Bệnh Viện Ung Bướu Trung Ương or Bệnh Viện K). As the first doctors of that Institute also served at the *Hopitâl Indigène des Soeurs de Saint Paul* (today's Bệnh Viện Việt-Đức at 40, Tràng Thi), the Institute was built in close proximity to the hospital.

Radiotherapy continues to be one of the central pillars of cancer therapy. In contrast to drug-based chemotherapy that acts throughout the body, radiation treatment is a purely local measure. The tumour-destroying effect thus only occurs within the radiation field. However, in the case of Trọng's mother, the dose was too strong, and

---

[33] Nguyễn Mạnh Côn, *Lạc đường vào lịch sử*, 40–41.

she died of dysentery. On her death-bed, Trọng promised his mother to marry the girl she had chosen for him.

In the second chapter, Côn meticulously describes different printing techniques, especially the difference between lithography and offset-rotative printing, and different papers which were useful for printing counterfeit money. Counterfeit money was widespread in the Vietnam-China border region and was exchanged with real Indochinese money at a certain exchange rate. Organizing this activity became the main task of Lan's cell in the lawless and chaotic months preceding the August Revolution of 1945.

In the fourth chapter, Côn describes the reasons for and natural conditions of a flood disaster in Northern Vietnam. Cold water from the Himalaya had penetrated the Red River Delta. Trọng refreshed himself in the cold water and became severely ill, so that he had to be treated in the provincial hospital with camphor injection—that was all that the old male nurse in the provincial hospital had in his medicine cabinet.

In the fifth, sixth and seventh chapter, there are reminiscences about pre-war Hanoi until the first days of the August Revolution. Hanoi had been a small city up to 1945, inhabited by a hundred thousand people.[34] Ninety percent of them were petty traders, who lived, outwardly at least, happily on a territory of 25 square kilometres, as the author recalled. Nguyễn Mạnh Côn describes extensively the borders of the city, its streets and squares, and the extent of the four tram lines. This is like a Baedeker for Hanoi in the year 1945.

Trọng, when he was a school boy, had taken part in the swimming championship of Tongking organized in Hanoi's West Lake. He knew how to swim and, especially, to crawl, and his idol was Johnny Weissmueller, the actor of "Tarzan." The description of Vietnamese coffee or French and foreign beers, wines and alcohols used at those times, or how Hanoi's noodle-soup (phở) is different from Hong Kong's in the sixth chapter are full of Northern flavour. Undoubtedly, Nguyễn Mạnh Côn, who had lived for more than a decade in Saigon when he published this book, had felt home-sick when he wrote these lines.

With utmost precision and sophistication, the author unfolds before our eyes many interesting small details in the life of the colonial period before the 1945 August Revolution, both in Hanoi and in several provinces of Tonking. On the one side, there was the sunny, carefree and relatively affluent Western-style life of the petty bourgeoisie both in Hanoi and in the provinces. On the other, the young people feverishly embraced ideals of how to liberate their country from colonial rule. They wanted immediate liberation and placed their hopes both in the 1945 August Revolution and in the "Western" allies, like the USA and the USSR. At the same time, the young people witnessed how step by step the Việt Minh were using the revolutionary spirit of the youth to build their Communist dictatorship. If you joined them, you were on the side of the historical winners and could hope to become "somebody important," quite like the history and geography teacher Võ Nguyên Giáp of the

---

[34] In 1930, Hanoi had 133.000 inhabitants: 122.000 Vietnamese, 5.900 Europeans, 4.000 Chinese and 138 Minh Hương (male Chinese-Vietnamese métis from a Chinese father). Gouvernement Général, Annuaire Administratif de l'Indochine, 266.

private *Collège Thăng Long* who was part of the General Insurrection Committee and the Việt Minh government. The other Vietnamese political parties, however, were ruthlessly suppressed right from the beginning. Nguyễn Mạnh Côn wrote:

> The revolution, when it still worked illegally, was admired by many people, but also feared and hated by many. In the true peace-loving spirit of the people, they could accept violence to drive out the French or the Japanese, but nobody wanted to hear about bloody clashes between parties who fought with each other for power. That was the reason why the people were embarrassed after the Việt Minh killed political figures that had not supported the French or Japanese.[35]

On 20 September 1945, the party cell was arrested by the Việt Minh police and charged with the crime of printing counterfeit money. They all were kept in the central police station of Hàng Cỏ. Every afternoon, Tuyết Lan was released from her prison cell to have a walk in the yard, but the purpose of this was for her to hear the screaming of the inmates in the torture chamber. The authorial narrator relates the torture of the inmates in great detail, almost technically, until they hold their breath forever. In this moment, Lan realizes the perfidy of the Communists who wanted not only combat, but to erase political rivals from the scene. The fear of death and physical pain she was feeling from seeing and hearing her comrades being tortured is described by the author with great mastery.

Intentionally or not, these scenes remind us of Arthur Koestler's work *A Spanish Testament,* where the author describes the terror of the Franco army in the police headquarters of Malaga, where the inmates were tortured and where every night the inmates were killed one after the other. Whereas in Koestler's book based on biographical events and narrated in the first person, the Spanish Fascists were the torturers and killers, in Nguyễn Mạnh Côn's book, with its authorial writer and the main protagonist Tuyết Lan, these murderers were Hanoi's Communist secret police.[36]

There is a second similarity. Both Koestler and Tuyết Lan are respected by their jailers for their intelligence and courage. Repeated attempts to convince them to switch sides fail. Both remain steadfast in their political ideals: socialism in the case of Koestler,[37] anti-Communist nationalism in the case of Tuyết Lan.

Through outside intervention of the Hearst newspaper group, British diplomats and members of the parliament, Koestler's life was spared. Later he was freed, seemingly as suddenly and without motivation as he had been incarcerated, and exchanged for a Franquist hostage held by the Republican Spanish government.

Tuyết Lan has the support of her former lover Trọng, who had joined the ranks of the Việt Minh and knows the leading figure of Northern police, Lâm Trọng Ngà, personally from school days together. Lâm Trọng Ngà tries hard to turn Tuyết Lan around to make her a member of the VM espionage organization named Hồng Việt.

---

[35] Nguyễn Mạnh Côn, Nguyễn Mạnh Côn. *Lạc đường vào lịch sử 1945*, 99.

[36] Koestler. Ein spanisches Testament, 67–114.

[37] In April 1938, Arthur Koestler left the German Communist Party. From 1938 to 1940, he wrote his most famous novel "Darkness at Noon." It was a reckoning with Stalin's show trials in Moscow. From that time, Koestler changed from a former Communist to a convinced anti-Communist.

In the process of desperately trying to liberate his former lover, Trọng gradually realizes the true nature of the VM regime, but feels emotionally too weak to break with it. The August Revolution had started with the claim of overall liberation of the oppressed and exploited. In reality, it immediately led to a new kind of enslavement, which was harsher and stronger, more unrelenting and inhumane than the oppressive colonial regime it had overthrown.

Did Nguyễn Mạnh Côn know Koestler's novel *A Spanish Testament*? We cannot know that for sure.

The writer and journalist Vương Trùng Dương, who lives in the United States, remembered, that especially European authors, more than American authors, were translated and widely read in pre-1975 South Vietnam. After Albert Camus, for example, had received the Nobel prize in 1957, many of his literary works were translated into Vietnamese. (Nguyễn Mạnh Côn, for instance, translated Camus' honorary speech in Stockholm.) Solzhenitsyn received the Nobel prize in 1970, and afterwards his works appeared in many translations. A translation of George Orwell's *Animal Farm* was published for the first time in 1952, under the title *Cuộc cách mạng trong trại súc vật* (Revolution in the Animal's Farm), and printed in the official French publishing house *Imprimerie d'Extrême Orient*. However, Vương is not sure if a work written by Koestler had already been translated in the period prior to 1975.[38] Nguyễn Mạnh Côn read French fluently, so he was perhaps not dependent on a Vietnamese translation. It is too early to give a definite answer to that question. Nevertheless, the motif resemblance seems striking.

However, one thing can be said for sure: Most of Nguyễn Mạnh Côn's characters have a distinct connection with historical reality. Who was, for instance, Xương Linh really? Is he a fictional character, or a reference, but to whom? Is this character an allusion to the Romantic writer and VNQDĐ leader Nguyễn Tường Tam alias Nhất Linh (1906–1963)? Vương Trùng Dương dismisses this argument.[39]

Here, Nguyễn Mạnh Côn introduces the character of a 27-year-old major of the Chinese infantry, who appears for the first time in the novel as a participant in a meeting of Võ Nguyễn Giáp with members of the United States military secret service (OSS) in Hanoi. We read:

Tôn Xương Linh was determined not to follow his mother's pear-growing profession. After a few years of attending a school in Liễu Châu province (Liuzhou in Guangxi province, TE), Xương Linh had made acquaintances with a large number of Vietnamese people. He dropped out of school and asked to join the cadre training group, like entering a second Huangpu school of South China. After three years of graduation, he was sent to Chongqing, from Chongqing to Kunming to study armoured vehicles. Two years later, with the rank of chariot lieutenant, but without a tank to use, Xương Linh was suddenly sent to work as an interpreter for an American advisory delegation. Until 1942, there was an order from above to place this Vietnamese-speaking officer under the command of the Chariot Training Department based in India.

---

[38] Email, Vương Trùng Dương, 30 July 2022.
[39] Ibid.

Xương Linh went to India only to find out that the title of Residency Chariot Training Board was just a disguise for a school that trained specialists in intelligence. In the first class, more than one hundred students, including representatives of Malaysia, the Philippines, Thailand, Burma, Indonesia and Vietnam were told that the Empire of Japan, despite its decline, was still holding on to the hope of clinging to the whole of Southeast Asia.

The nations still under its rule would need to have brave and talented children like them. They would be the basis for the liberation work in the future. But their job was not to fight, for they were to be even ahead of the soldiers. Their job was to examine, detect, map or document the enemy's military force. Their activities would later be coordinated to form a secret front line, surrounding all branches of the enemy's activities. They, of course, and even if they were scattered, each had an obligation to be closely related to each other as members of one family. In a party. One agency. The one who controlled the agency was of course the United States. The three letters, OSS, which Americans used to refer to their agency, meant it was a specialized agency, in charge of strategic work. The chariot training board bore the two letters SA, to indicate the Southeast Asian region. Then, at the end, each person was assigned a number to use as a password. Ton Xương Linh studied slowly, sat at the back of the room … from that time on in the OSS group, his commanders as well as his classmates only called Captain Tôn Xương Linh by his symbol SA 141."[40]

In 1945, Nguyễn Tường Tam was already 39, not 27. But age seems not to be the most important hint. One fact seems to be correct: During the Second World War, the OSS established overseas training schools in Southern Italy, Algeria, Egypt, India, Ceylon and China.[41]

Perhaps Xương Linh could be, in reality, an allusion to General Huang Chiang alias Gaston Wang of the Guomindang Secret Service (National Bureau of Investigation and Statistics/Military Commission). Gaston Wang, who appeared prominently in the Chinese-French negotiations in Hanoi in 1945–1946, supported, supervised and guided both the Chinese Overseas and the non-Communist Nationalist parties in Northern Vietnam during the Chinese occupation of Northern Indochina (1945–1946). His original, unfulfillable duty was to help the Vietnamese pro-Chinese Nationalist parties to win the upper hand in the power struggle with the Communist VM. In this capacity, he failed utterly. Secondly, he was in charge of the Overseas Chinese organizations. Especially, he was instrumental in taking the issue of the protection of the Chinese population as a pretext to slow down the withdrawal of the Chinese from and the return of the French to Northern Indochina. In this goal, he failed too, since starting in Spring 1946 at the latest, in the evolving civil war, Chiang Kai-shek needed General Lu Han's divisions badly to fight against Mao Zedong's Red Armies. General Lu Han in Hanoi had to obey and sent his troops to Manchuria.

Gaston Wang spoke Vietnamese perfectly well. His brother Wang Chi Lu owned a transportation company in Haiphong, and worked as a branch manager for a

---

[40] Nguyễn Mạnh Côn, Lạc đường vào lịch sử 1945, 110–11.

[41] Chambers, John Whiteclay II. Office of Strategic Services Training During World War II. In: Studies in Intelligence, Vol. 54, No. 2, June 2010 (www.cia.org).

company which was owned by the prominent Chinese tycoon and politician T.V. Soong. Another brother lived in the commercial centre of Cholon, at *Quai Gaudot* (today: Hải Thượng Lãn Ông). After 1946, Gaston Wang occasionally revealed information to the French, and organized, with the help of his brothers, deliveries to the Việt Minh's so-called Liberated Areas. Gaston Wang was especially close to a US-American with the name of Gordon Brown. During the Second World War, Brown had worked as OSS agent in Southern China. After the war, he was a representative for the United States oil company CALTEX in Bangkok. CALTEX delivered fuel to the VM and the guerrilla movements of Burma and Indonesia. A special tax (two Baht per litre) went to representatives of the Thai Military Junta, who closed their eyes to these activities.[42]

However, Gaston Wang was already a general and active in Hanoi in the late 1930s. He would have been in his fifties after the war. He was a venal secret service man, not a political fighter. Officially, he worked on behalf of his government. Secretly, he worked for anyone who paid him. His sympathies for the liberation struggle of the Vietnamese, however, were surely serious—as were the sympathies of many ethnic Chinese (Hoa) living in the country at that time.

Therefore, Gaston Wang cannot be the 27-year-old lad, the political idealist, unselfish supporter of Vietnam's anti-colonial revolution and fervent lover of Tuyết Lan, as the writer Nguyễn Mạnh Côn has described his protagonist Xương Linh. Maybe the writer has attributed certain traits of this notorious general to his literary character. Linh's age (27) corresponds more with the writers' age, who was 25 in 1945 …

The many allusions make the book a special reading pleasure for the historically trained reader. It feels like a kaleidoscope of the 1945 August Revolution. The guessing game is: Who is who?

For instance, there is the professor with the family name of Đặng. Nobody knows when and how, but he seemingly had studied Marx's *Capital* and therefore, during the late 1930s, considered himself a specialist on Marxism, always discussing socialism calmly and resolutely with his discussion partners, in a sour and poisonous way, especially with his colleague, professor Vũ. Trọng, the disciple, was charged with delivering the French language Communist journal *Rassemblement,* in which professor Đặng had published his own articles, to professor Vũ.[43]

The *Collège Thăng Long* at 20 Ngõ Trạm (*Rue Bourret*) once was the school of Nguyễn Mạnh Tôn (born 1920). This school had existed as a primary school before, but was reorganized in 1935 as a private college. Around 1935–1940, the time when Côn possibly was a schoolboy there, the later General Võ Nguyên Giáp, a disciple of the anti-colonial radical teacher Đặng Thái Mai in Huế (*Collège Quốc học*), and already a clandestine Communist party member in those days, was a teacher of history and geography, and used the school for his political activities.

The left-wing patriotic teacher Đặng Thái Mai, since 1937 a member of the French Socialist Party (like his colleagues Phan Thanh, Hoàng Minh Giám and Vũ Đình Hoè)

---

[42] Engelbert, "Die chinesische Minderheit," 460–62, 482.

[43] Nguyễn Mạnh Côn, 1945, 70.

covered these activities up. Đặng Thái Mai's daughter Bích Hà became, after 1945, the second wife of Võ Nguyên Giáp. Several Thăng Long teachers became leading members of the Việt Nam Dân Chủ Đảng (Vietnamese Democratic Party, founded in 1944) and the Đảng Xã Hội Viêt Nam (Vietnamese Socialist Party, founded in 1946). Both were block parties, and acted as camouflage and front organizations for the Communist Party to win over intellectuals and people of middle-class background. The goal was to create the illusion of a multi-party state. Several leading members of these block parties had originally been Communists, delegated to "strengthen" these parties.[44]

Đặng Thái Mai played a prominent role in the reorganization of this private school, which existed until 1945. The list of teachers and pupils of this school reads like a Who's Who of the political and intellectual elites of Communist Vietnam, although some, like Đương Văn Đôn, later defected to the anti-Communist camp. There were, for instance, Hoàng Minh Giám (DRV Foreign Minister 1947–1954, Minister of Culture, 1954–1976), who served as school rector from 1937, Võ Nguyên Giáp (the founder of the Communist Vietnamese army), Phan Thanh (elected Member of Annam's People's Council, died 1939), Nghiêm Xuân Yêm (DRV Minister of Agriculture, 1947–1951 and 1954–1971), Nguyễn Lân (later a teacher at the Pedagogical College Hanoi), Bùi Kỷ (a traditional scholar, who was active in the movement to combat illiteracy, the father of RVN ambassador Bùi Diễm), Phạm Huy Thông (the rector of Hanoi's Pedagogical College, 1956–1966), Ngô Xuân Diệu (a famous poet), Vũ Đình Hòe (DRV Minister of Education, 1945–1946, Minister of Justice, 1946–1960), Nguyễn Cao Luyện (the Corbusier-trained architect of the Thăng Long school building, who designed the simple but elegant Ba Đình conference hall in 1960), Trịnh Văn Bính (DRV Deputy Finance Minister, trained in France and Britain, who taught English at the Thăng Long school in the 1930s), Nguyễn Dương Đôn (who served as Minister of Education under the first RVN president Ngô Đình Diệm, 1954–1957) and Vũ Đình Liên (a poet and head of the department of French Studies at Hanoi University).

After 1935, they were joined by Phan Mỹ, Khuất Duy Các, Nguyễn Văn Lưu, Vũ Bội Liêu, Phạm Hữu Ninh, Hoàng Như Tiếp, Nguyễn Xiển, Lê Thị Xuyến and Phan Anh. The most prominent graduates were Trần Quang Huy, Ngô Duy Cảo, Nguyễn Thành Lê, Lê Quang Đạo, Hồ Lịch, Nguyễn Thọ Chân, Hồ Trúc, Đặng Xuân Kỳ, Đào Thiện Thi, Phan Kế An, Trọng Loan, Vũ Tú Nam, Đào Duy Kỳ, Lý Chính Thắng,

---

[44] Vũ Đình Hoè and Nghiêm Xuân Yên joined the Democratic Party, Nguyễn Xiển, Nguyễn Cao Luyên and Phan Anh the Socialist Party. Hoàng Minh Giám was chairman of the Socialist Party from 1956 until 1988. Hoàng Minh Chính (the Secretary General of the DP from 1947 to 1967) was a Communist Party member from 1939. In 1967, he was charged with "revisionism" and expelled from both parties. (This method to use Communists in leading functions of block parties existed in many Communist countries, like in the GDR.) In 1988, both parties were dissolved by the General Secretary of the Vietnamese Communist Party, Nguyễn Văn Linh, for fear of a peaceful revolution like in Eastern Europe. Since then, Vietnam is de jure and de facto a one-party state.

Trần Hải Kế, Nguyễn Mai Hiến, Lê Tụy Phương, Nguyễn Hồng Lĩnh, Nguyễn Khoa Diệu Hồng, Trần Lâm, Võ Thuần Nho, Trần Sâm, Minh Tranh and Lê Trung Toản.[45]

Đặng Xuân Kỳ (born 1932, later Professor of Marxism-Leninism, Director of the Institute for Marxism-Leninism and Ho Chi Minh ideology) went to the private Collège Thăng Long. His father, Trương Chính alias Đặng Xuân Khu, from 1941 until 1956 and again several months in 1986, was General Secretary of the Communist Party of Indochina, respectively, the Lao Động party (the party's name 1951–1976) or Vietnamese Communist Party (since 1976), and from 1956 until 1986 member of its Political Bureau, responsible for ideology. In the late 1930s, he was the editor of *Rassemblement*, the journal which Trọng delivered to the teacher with the family name of Vũ (may be Vũ Đình Hoè), who often got into heated discussions about socialism with the teacher with the family name of Đặng. All these radical Vietnamese lived or worked in the perimeter of Ngõ Trạm (Rue Bourret), where not only the school building was situated but also the seats of several left-wing newspapers. These young and middle-aged men all knew each other, wrote for the same journals, worked together in the same organizations.

For the young pupil Nguyễn Mạnh Côn, it should have been an exciting environment, both intellectually and politically. In those years that shaped his mind and character, he was exposed to the lively spirit of the 1930s with all its contradictory tendencies. A first generation had graduated from Indochinese and Metropolitan universities. They had the same qualifications as their French peers, but were not equal to them in Indochina's public service. This injustice fuelled their already existing anti-colonial feelings. The most radical anti-colonial trend was communism, followed by socialism, which appeared to be less violent and was therefore more attractive for intellectuals. No wonder that these political tendencies were very popular among the young French-trained graduates. However, Nguyễn Mạnh Tôn chose a different path.

Is Nguyễn Mạnh Tôn's character Trọng perhaps expressing a slight irony about his teacher Đặng Thái Mai, who in those days wrote popular science books propagating Marxist views on literature? How much of Côn's own life experience can we find reflected in his character Trọng?

---

[45] Giang Quân. Ngày ấy có một trường Thăng Long. In: *Ha Nội Mới Online*, 8 March 2010. In his memoirs, Vũ Đình Hoè remembered this time. Only a few teachers held a diploma from the *École Normale de l'Indochine*, for instance Hoàng Minh Giảm, Nghiêm Toản and Đặng Thái Mai. Most were freelancers. Phan Anh and Vũ Đình Hòe, for instance, studied law and served as teachers at both the *Collège Thăng Long* and the *Collège Gia Long*. Phan Anh also gave tutoring lessons at home. Vũ Văn Hiền studied law in the morning, served as corrector of a newspaper in the afternoon, and in the evening taught at the private *Lycée Hồng Bàng*. Most of these part-time teachers were young professionals or students of the *Université de l'Indochine*, who used a teaching job for earning money. Several teachers of the *Collège Thăng Long* were members of the French Socialist Party (S.F.I.O.): Hoàng Minh Giám, Phan Thanh and Vũ Đình Hòe. They cooperated with the Communists in labour disputes, or with the nationalist leader Nguyễn Tường Tam in social housing projects. Vũ Đình Hiền worked in the Attorney's Office of Trần Văn Chương, the father-in-law of Ngô Đình Nhu. All political factions (Socialists, Communists, non-Communist nationalists and unaffiliated) took part in the movement to spread alphabetization among the lower classes. Vũ Đình Hòe, Hồi Ký Thanh Nghị, I, 20–25; Tườ lập thân, 195.

All in all, Côn's school days produced, probably, happy memories. He dedicated a later book to his former teacher Đặng Thái Mai. The title is: *Mối tình mầu hoà đào. Lý thuyết kể bằng đối thoại* (The love in peach colours. Theory told in dialogues). In the opening credits, he wrote a self-confident, but quite emotional dedication:

> Dedicated to Professor Đặng Thái Mai. In the secondary of the Thăng Long school, the professor once corrected an essay, writing: 'I have corrected one hundred essays – like going on a long journey. When I met an interesting essay, it was like enjoying a cool shadow. My pupil Nguyễn Mạnh Côn, later you can become a Jean-Jacques Rousseau, or better try to be the Jean-Jacques Rousseau of the Twentieth Century.' Now, the teacher and the disciple are living on two different sides of the dividing line. It is the hope of Nguyễn Mạnh Côn that the cultural leader of North Vietnam will get this book in his hands, so that he can study it and raise the question again, if necessary.[46]

In other words: the Thăng Long teachers once had taught about human values derived from the philosophical works of Western literature which they introduced in the class room. The students loved and respected them for that. But do they live by it, can they live by it under the conditions of a Communist dictatorship? The teacher with the family name of Đặng, and the teacher with the family name of Vũ—have they not betrayed what they once taught to their students?

That is strong tobacco. Nguyễn Mạnh Côn often expressed his fearlessness with regard to the Communists. Nguyễn Triệu Nam remembered his words from a private conversation. Nguyễn Mạnh Côn said as follows:

> Communism is a scourge for the nation. One must eliminate the scourge. By many ways. My way is to use a pen. I write because I am conscious of myself, and I need to write. It means I write in the spirit of spontaneity. No imperialists can hire me to write and can say that I do it for their money. Whether the Communists classified me as number one or what number so ever reactionary, that doesn't matter. What I know is, that they are very afraid of anti-Communist works. The works of destructive power are more terrible than atomic bombs. Actually, I'm not afraid of Communism at all. I consider their pranks a joke. ... The South is not a wild garden that the Communists can use to for their stick dance.[47]

Nguyễn Mạnh Côn knew quite a lot about the origins of anti-colonial activities and biographies of important men in the late 1930s as well as during and after the August Revolution of 1945. This knowledge, condensed in literary terms, flowed into his novel *A Wrong Way into History: 1945*.

However, anyone, who dares to write something like that makes himself the mortal enemy of the Communists. Criticizing them is bad. Ripping the mask off their face is worse. Laughing at them—the very worst. When it comes to the question of power, Communists are quite humourless, and they especially cannot laugh at themselves. Irony is dangerous, the destructive nihilist weapon of the class enemy.

Nguyễn Mạnh Côn employed all three stylistic devices: criticism, exposure and irony. Don't mess with them: These guys have long memories (and files). One day, revenge would come. And it came.

---

[46] Nguyễn Mạnh Côn. Mối tình mầu hoà đào. Lý thuyết kể bằng đối thoại, VIII.

[47] Nguyễn Mạnh Côn, *Đem tâm tình viết lịch sử*; "Trước khi vào sách: Kỷ niệm về Nguyễn Mạnh Côn. Hồi tưởng của Nguyễn Triệu Nam." Front page.

The Death of the Writer

Vương Trùng Dương mentioned, that Đặng Hà had known Nguyễn Mạnh Côn since 1967. On 1 April 1976, a Communist campaign started to sweep away all the Southern writers, artists and intellectuals. Nguyễn Mạnh Côn, who was seen as a No. 1 enemy of the new regime, was already arrested on 2 March 1976. Đặng Hà himself was locked up in T 20 prison at No. 4, Phan Đăng Lưu Street, Saigon, in zone C2, room 7.[48]

Nguyễn Mạnh Côn was kept in the same prison, Area B. By early 1978, the inmates were scattered into different labour camps, some also moved to Chí Hòa prison, area AH, for a while. Before he was brought to the labour camp, Đặng Hà returned to the FG area for a while, where he met Nguyễn Mạnh Côn again. During the "reform" trip, which means the forced stay in the labour camp, about one hundred people were moved to Xuyên Mộc camp, Area A, in the province of Baria. There, Nguyễn Mạnh Côn and Đặng Hà joined team No. 14, led by the painter Đặng Giao. Every hangar there held about four or five labour teams, each with more than forty people. In the room with two floors, Đặng Hà and Nguyễn Mạnh Côn slept next to the wall in the lower floor at the entrance to the room.[49]

Vương Trùng Dương quoted extensively from Đặng Hà's post about Nguyễn Mạnh Côn's courageous, but tragic act of resistance in the camp:

> The time is close to April 1979, which is nearly three years, the sentence of re-education that the Communist regime had read out to us before we were going to the camp. In those nights he often confided in me. He said, 'What are we supposed to do when three years are up? Should we be imprisoned for the rest of our lives?' … I did not dare to go into the matter, because of the eyes and ears of the 'antennas' which were in the room, and we were subjects they were always watching. Then what had to happen, happened. As usual, the morning of 2 April 1979, when the gong sounded to warn everyone in the camp to prepare to go to the fields, we lined up to go to work as usual. We were about to leave, when suddenly Nguyễn Mạnh Côn also asked to go out and lined up to go to work. Remember, that, in the camp, going to work is forced, it is very difficult to declare illness to take even one day off, and he was even exempted from hard labor, which was a big privilege. I, Mr. Sơn and Mr. Đặng Giao thought that Mr. Côn wanted to go to work today to show how miserable the work was. Therefore, I strongly advised him to stay at home to rest and stay healthy. It's very hard to go to the scene of work to hoe in the sun. But he definitely wouldn't listen. He resolutely went out to line up. Although it is called queuing, everyone had to sit on the floor. When the camp officer calls a team, that team gets up, the captain reports the total number of people in the team, how many sick people, how many workers, and then it leaves the camp to go to work. Because of the same team, that day, Nguyễn Mạnh Côn lined up behind me, sitting in the last row of the team. While the whole camp had sat in full line, waiting for the camp staff to call each team to go to work, suddenly, Mr. Nguyễn Mạnh Côn stood up in the middle of the camp and said loudly: 'I am Nguyễn Mạnh Côn, a writer under the old regime, sentenced to three years of concentration camp for re-education. Today, 2 April 1979, this inmate has served a full three-year sentence. I demand the Board of Supervisors write a letter to the camp to

---

[48] It was a special prison for political prisoners. Usually, they were detained there under one of three charges: being reactionary, being remnants of the former American puppet regime, or taking part in plots to overthrow the revolutionary authorities. From there, the ordeal mostly led to Chí Hòa prison or to a re-education camp. Tam Giáng Hoàng Đình Báu. Nhà tù Phan Đăng Lưu. In *Việt Báo*, Online, 2 April 2015.

[49] Vương Trùng Dương, "Nguyễn Mạnh Côn, nhà văn can đảm chọn cái chết trong tù."

release me, so that I can return to my family. From today I am no longer a prisoner. I won't eat camp rice anymore.' As soon as he finished speaking, all the thousands of prisoners and the prison police were silent, not a sound. Suddenly, the probation officer (I have forgotten his name for a long time) screeched through his teeth and said: 'Mr. Nguyễn Mạnh Côn go to the tree behind to wait.'[50]

One of the inmates had dared to revolt. The jailers were forced to react, to restore their authority. First, they used a sticks-and-carrots' approach. Đặng Hà reported:

The incident that happened that morning, shook the whole camp, not only the prisoners but also the prison police, from the warden of the camp to the little policemen. At first, they treated him softly, as if giving in to his demands. They asked him not to go on a hunger strike, to eat normally, they provided him with meat and fish to eat every day while waiting for them to send his file to the Ministry for consideration and release, because the camp had only the right to keep, not to release.

Nguyễn Mạnh Côn resolutely refused, asking them to release him immediately because he had already served a full three-year rehabilitation sentence. There was no reason to hold him captive. They felt that bribing with fish and meat (in the prison, there is even no salt, not to dream of fish or meat) was not enough. They had a bloody plan. Pampering, giving in was not working. At first, he was still in the room next to me, still talking and laughing. What I just told you was what he said to me with his own mouth.

A few days later, when we returned from work, we found that he was no longer in the room, so they had moved him to another room. This room was not far from our room, just finished and not yet occupied. They locked him in there alone, the police guarded him day and night, not allowing anyone to come near. Every time we came back from work, we looked in from afar, but we couldn't see anything, so we didn't know what his condition was. Asking the foremen of the camp was also not a way, because they are not allowed to go near. A few days later in the afternoon, when returning from work, we could hear his voice screaming: 'So thirsty, so thirsty.' It turned out that the Communists were brutal, seeing that he was on a hunger strike, they didn't let him drink water. That means—both hungry and thirsty. We can go without food for one or two weeks, as long as we still drink enough water. I used to know people who, for the sake of healing, sometimes had to fast for seven weeks, that is, seven times seven which is 49 days.

He was starved and thirsty, even though he cried day and night until he was exhausted. We could not help him, even if it was not far away. His groans could be heard clearly. But because the police guarded very strictly there was no way to supply him with drinking water."[51]

In the end, the jailer broke his will. He was forced to confess his crime openly. Đặng Hà recalled this humiliating scene:

After a period of about a month, I don't know how the prison Communists had seduced and threatened him. They forced him to submit and humiliated him by forcing him to stand in front of the entire camp and read the confession of guilt. That day, I saw him as a person

[50] Vương Trùng Dương. "Nguyễn Mạnh Côn, nhà văn can đảm chọn cái chết trong tù."
[51] Ibid.

who had lost his soul and had no vitality anymore. At that time, there were many people who thought he was so despicable, unworthy of the title of a scholar, among them was the writer Duyên Anh, a junior of Nguyễn Mạnh Côn. Côn is the one who raised Duyên Anh from an unknown person to become a famous writer, from the first short story 'My Flute,' published in the magazine *Chỉ Đạo* directed by the writer Nguyễn Mạnh Côn as editor ...[52]

After the public humiliation came the punishment. Vương Trùng Dương described, citing Đặng Hà, how the jailers then treated the broken writer:

When they had humiliated him in front of all the prisoners and the prison police, they took him to live in the room of criminals, means living with thugs, robbers, and rapists. They did not let him come back to live with us again. Please remember that in the re-education camp, the rooms are not allowed to communicate with each other, if caught, they will be disciplined, if they are caught in a light case, they will be admonished and visitors cut, in hard cases, hand and feat are tied, and the rations will be reduced to nine kilograms of rice per month, which means you eat only thin rice soup. Therefore, I only knew that Mr. Côn was in that room, but he was completely isolated.[53]

The eyewitness Đặng Hà cited in Vương Trùng Dương's account also reported his knowledge about Nguyễn Mạnh Côn's death. He wrote:

Finally, on the morning of 1 June 1979, we received news of his death. It rained that morning, so we didn't have to go to work. I looked through the bars of the door and saw some criminal prisoners carrying his coffin on a modified vehicle, taking it out to the cemetery at the edge of the forest to bury. Heaven may also mourn for a great talent, a great writer of the country who has passed away forever ...

He did something that all the millions of prisoners at that time did not dare to do, dare to say. The Communists at that time only called us to go 'study' for ten days, one month. But who had the courage to stand in front of the whole camp and make a bold statement like he did? If at that time everyone had stood up to respond to his announcement, the situation might have changed. This is fate, you are a lonely hero among wolves, they are ready to cut your skin and humiliate you. He fired the first shot at the lies and deceptions of the Communists and what they called three years of re-education. But they did not release anyone on time, and no one dared to speak but he. So, you don't deserve to be a hero? Fate gave me the opportunity to know him, in the same room. We were the same couple, in the same room, lying next to each other in Xuyên Mộc re-education camp. Witnessing him with my own eyes, he boldly declared that the Communists had to release him according to the sentence they had read. You're gone, but your spirit will forever remain in my heart ... (Đặng Hà, July 23, 2017)."[54]

---

[52] Ibid.
[53] Ibid.
[54] Ibid.

Conclusions

Without any doubt, Nguyễn Mạnh Côn's death was that of a tragic hero. His death corresponds with Gelfert's fourth type, when a person, in his striving for the realization of a value, gets into a state of delusion from an inherent antinomy of that value, so that his positive striving is reversed. Like Michael Kohlhaas, the writer Nguyễn Mạnh Côn wants to push through an absolute value without compromise: justice, which does not exist under a such a regime. As in the case of Kohlhaas, the tragic conflict results from the dialectical structure of the value which is being defended.

His heroine Tuyết Lan is not necessarily a tragic heroine. She followed the VNQDĐ out of sadness for her lost lover. But in the process of revolutionary work and especially in the time of capture in the VM prison, she has no doubt who her main adversary is: the Communists. She has the optimism, through the love she feels for the VNQDĐ and the nationalist leader of Chinese origin, Xương Linh, that she will overcome any obstacle until the final victory. Love transcends all borders! She is depicted as an optimistic hero without fault and blame, a kind of Vietnamese Jeanne d'Arc.

Xương Linh, however, knows already in late 1945, that their struggle might be in vain, as the enemy is stronger, colder, more resolute and more cunning, a cold-blooded power machine which will trample everything under its feet. Linh indeed, could be called a tragic hero, as his counterpart Trọng, who knows the true character of the Communists, but is unable to leave them. He is weak, and therefore an easy object to seduce, curing his unhappy love with opium, and his opium addiction by joining the Communist revolution.

Of course, the author Nguyễn Mạnh Côn has only concentrated on one aspect: why the Vietnamese Communists have won the power struggle against their Vietnamese rivals. Economic questions, like land reform or rural poverty, are totally out of his sight. Characters representing the common people, like the printers in the third or the cab driver in the fourth chapter, remain faint and indistinct.

Naturally, the lower classes respect people "who have learned" as their superiors. The dialogue between Trọng and the cab driver is typical of this attitude, which seems perhaps a little haughty:

> Trọng kept saying: 'Hey, driver, I'm afraid that if you pull any more, you'll faint. Now I'll talk to you to sit there, I'll help you for a bit more, then we'll be at the entrance of Thư Trì district, the road is much higher, it won't be flooded.' The driver was startled and denied 'I don't dare. I don't dare.' Trọng said no matter what, the driver still didn't dare. He said, severely annoyed: 'What you don't dare. The revolution has succeeded, or not?' The driver replied immediately, without thinking: 'Where is there a revolution where we are not the underlings? We never dare to mess with you guys.'[55]

In a natural way, the young intellectuals of petty bourgeois background thought themselves to be the guides and leaders of Vietnam's state and society after independence. They did not even consider winning over the un-educated masses, as Tuyết Lan's thoughts bear witness:

---

[55] Nguyễn Mạnh Côn, 1945, 51. Ist das "Nguyễn Mạnh Côn. *Lạc đường vào lịch sử 1945*".

It means, there were three traitors among the employees of Ido, which were seven altogether. Tuyết Lan thought about these elements in her party, and naturally felt ashamed before the leader of the Hồng Việt unit. The first heated exchanges with Lâm Trọng Ngà were reasonable. To carry out a revolution as they had done, was in reality only satisfying their personal vanity, if it was not mere amateurish work. The revolution is not about calculation, except for the calculation of the kind of Trọng Sơn and Tế! And people like Cuồng Tảo and Xuân, they were nothing else than elements deeply influenced by the spirit of the poor masses, always passive, which meant they had only feelings, but no thoughts, and were always dependent on the intellectuals in their thinking and decision-making. In the printing house Ido, only Quang was an intellectual, but he also was not worthy of being called a true intellectual, so he could not lead other people.[56]

Lenin had raised the principle that even a woman cook must be able to lead the state. All Communist revolutions—in Soviet Russia, Red China, Vietnam, Cuba, North Korea or even, in their own particularly bloody way, in Democratic Kampuchea—had a common point in their programme: the disempowerment of the old and the creation of new, revolutionary elites made up of representatives of the lowest classes.

Exactly, this seems to be the tragedy of these anti-Communist political forces, to whom Côn proudly belonged, that even in 1966, when the book appeared, this basic contradiction had not yet been fully understood. The educated military and civilian elites of the Republic of Vietnam competed for power, rank and privileges in the big cities like Saigon, Đà Nẵng or Huế. More than eighty percent of the population, however, lived in the countryside, a majority of them were poor peasants, not really enthusiastic about the Communists, who caused them hard times, but also with little sympathy for the representatives of the RVN who were seen as the authorities of the rich peasants.[57]

On the one side, there were the "old" elites, refined, for a large part quite sophisticated, French-educated and even to a certain degree cosmopolitan Western intellectuals, for whom Nguyễn Mạnh Côn could serve almost as an exemplary case. They enjoyed a nearly encyclopaedic knowledge of the world, harvested from Western books and journals. From these sources, especially from those depicting the cruel experiences of the USSR, Red China and Northern Vietnam, they apprehended what

---

[56] Nguyễn Mạnh Côn, Lạc đường vào lịch sử 1945, 68.

[57] According to US Army statistics, 17.1 million South Vietnamese lived in the countryside, 3.5 million in the cities (1968). Around 3.3 million people lived in areas fully controlled by the Việt Cộng insurgents (so-called Liberated Areas), where life usually was harsh (high taxes and forced labour for the VC). From three to five million people lived in contested areas, where often the authorities exercised control only during the day-time, and the VC insurgents at nights. According to an American sociological survey conducted in Long An province in the Northern Mekong Delta in 1964, only 40% of the peasants of that province felt positive towards the government, mostly wealthier peasants. The sons of these peasants often served in the RVN army or in the local militias (Bảo An). Around 50% were considered 'fence-sitters,' because they gave no clear opinion. For a large part, they were poorer peasants. Five percent expressed open sympathies for the VC, mostly coming from families who had relatives who had departed in 1954 with the Communists to the North. These and other similar investigations set alarm bells ringing in Washington: the war had to be won in the countryside, or everything was lost! For more information see Engelbert, "Vom Chaos zum Inferno," 178–80.

unnecessary hardships, failures and detours a Communist regime would bring, if it succeeded in South Vietnam. Despite all this knowledge, they did not communicate with and fully understand their own people except for their restricted circle of like-minded companions. They especially lacked understanding of the grievances of those many who lived in life circumstances far less fortunate.

On the other side, there were these power-hungry newcomers from below. These could be modest middle-school teachers who rose, almost without any formal military training, to become supreme commanders (Võ Nguyên Giáp), or petty traders, promoted from guerilla fighters to army generals (Trần Văn Trà) or even landless peasants who could work first as underground party cadres and later climb the ladder to become highest government leaders (Võ Văn Kiệt).

The real tragedy of the RVN's inglorious end lies, for a large part, in this misunderstanding and miscommunication. According to Nguyễn Mạnh Côn's book title, Vietnam went a "wrong way into history" (Lạc đường vào lịch sử). Perhaps, his own tragic life and the book presented above bear witness to that.

Nguyễn Mạnh Côn's tragic failure is a vivid illustration for Schelling's definition of the tragic: to fight against doom, and to be terribly punished for a crime that was fatal. The cause is the struggle between human freedom and the power of the objective world, in which the mortal must necessarily succumb. The tragic hero's terrible punishment, however, is at the same time the recognition of human freedom and of the honour that freedom deserves. For Schelling, it is a great and wonderful idea to willingly accept the penalty for an unavoidable crime, and to prove the existence of freedom by losing one's own freedom. Human downfall occurs with a declaration of free will.[58]

Bibliography

Brecht B (1985) Leben des Galilei. Reclam, Leipzig
Côn NM (1965) Lạc đường vào lịch sử: 1945. NXB Giao Điểm, Sài-gòn
Côn NM (1965). Mối tình màu hoà đào. Lý thuyết kể bằng đối thoại. Giao Điểm xết bản, Sài Gòn
Côn NM (1968) Đem tâm tình viết lịch sử. Nguyễn Đình Vương xuất bản, Saigon. www.vietmesse
    nger.com
Doan VT (1980) *Der vietnamesische Gulag*. Kiepenheuer & Witsch, Cologne.
Dương VT (2018) Nguyễn Mạnh Côn, nhà văn can đảm chọn cái chết trong tù. In: Người Việt
    Boston, 15 Tháng Mười Một. www.nguoivietboston.com
Dương VT (2018) Nguyễn Mạnh Côn, nhà văn can đảm chọn cái chết trong tù. In: Văn Việt, 18
    Tháng Mười Một. www.vanviet.info
Dương VT (2019) Văn học miền Nam 54–75 (560): Nguyễn Mạnh Côn (kỳ 11). In: Văn Việt, 9
    Tháng Năm. www.vanviet.info
Engelbert T (2014) *Vom Chaos zum Inferno. Die Übergangszeit von der Ersten zur Zweiten Republik
    Vietnam (1963–1967)*. In: Hamburger Südostasienstudien, vol 9. Südostasien-Abteilung der
    Universität Hamburg
Gelfert, H-D (1995) *Die Tragödie. Theorie und Geschichte*. Vandenhoeck Kleine Reihe, Göttingen

---

[58] Cit. after Szondi, *Versuch über das Tragische*, 13.

Gouvernement Général de l'Indochine (1931) *Annuaire Administratif de l'Indochine*. Imprimerie d'Extrême Orient, Hanoi

Hà Đ (2019) Tưởng nhớ Nguyễn Mạnh Côn. In: *Văn Việt*, 5 tháng Năm. www.vanviet.info

Hòe VĐ (1997). Hồi ký Thanh Nghị. Quyển I, II. NXB Văn học, Hà Nội.

Hòe VĐ (2012) Thuở lập thân. NXB Trẻ, TP HCM

Khanh NV (2018) Văn học miền Nam 1954–1975. Quyển Thượng, Hạ. Nguyễn Publishings, Toronto

Koestler, A (2018)*Ein spanisches Testament*. Neuausgabe auf der Grundlage der im Jahre 1938 von Arthur Koestler und dem Europa-Verlag Zürich herausgegeben Ausgabe. EuropaPocket, München.

Masters R (2018) Arthur Koestler (1905–1983). In: Wallhead CM (ed) More writers on the Spanish Civil War: experience put to use, Chapter Six. Peter Lang, Bern/Berlin, pp 233–284

Nietzsche F (2005) Gesammelte Werke. Gondrom-Verlag, Bindlach

Schiller F (1792) Über den Grund des Vergnügens an tragischen Gegenständen. In: Neue Thalia, vol 1, pp 92–125.

Szondi P (1961) Versuch über das Tragische. Insel, Frankfurt am Main

Thomas Engelbert received his PhD in Vietnamese Studies and a second doctorate (Habilitation) in Southeast Asian history from Humboldt University, Berlin. Since 2002, he has worked as a Professor of Vietnamese Language and Culture in the Department of Southeast Asian Languages and Cultures at the Asia-Africa Institute, University of Hamburg. His research focuses on Vietnamese and Southeast Asian history, especially Việt folklore, literature, and relations between ethnic minority and majority groups.

Notes on Nationalism in South Vietnam: Vulnerable Indian Migrants

Chi P. Pham

In mainstream Vietnamese history, written by communist intellectuals, the Republic of Vietnam (South Vietnam) occurs as an alien, marginal political entity because its nation-building ideologies were allegedly not derived from what is called "Vietnamese nationalism." Politics of nation-building by South Vietnam are negatively reduced to pure anticommunism and imperialism (or to existing as a puppet of American imperialism).[1] Meanwhile, Vietnamese nationalism—united political and intellectual attempts to establish Vietnam as a culturally and materially homogenous and hegemonic nation—is seen as the attribute, adequate, and exclusive, of nation-building by the communism-oriented Democratic Republic of Vietnam (North Vietnam).[2] By way of attaching nationalism to the communist Party-led government, the official Vietnamese history tends to include only North Vietnam's nation-building as having a legitimate, glorious role while it excludes South Vietnam, which is perceived as a historically illegitimate episode. The politics of exclusion as such is explicit, given that official Vietnamese history conflates Vietnamese communism with Vietnamese nationalism, which has been conflated with traditional, native patriotism, an emotional loyalty to one's homeland and a determination to defend it from foreign domination.[3] Accordingly, South Vietnam, with its alleged nonexistence or weakness of Vietnamese nationalism, is officially seen as national betrayal,[4]

---

[1] Trần Trọng Đăng Đàn. *Văn hóa, văn nghệ,* 28–118; Trần Thục Nga *Lịch sử,* 89–90; Nguyễn Lập Duy. *Unimagined Community,* 175–213.

[2] Moise, "Nationalism," 6–22; Tran Anh Nu, *Contested Identities,* 1–22.

[3] Kim Khánh Huỳnh, *Vietnamese Communism,* 27; Moise, "Nationalism," 6–22.

[4] Ban chỉ đạo soạn sử Việt Nam. *Lịch sử,* 430–432.

C. P. Pham (✉)
Institute of Literature, Vietnam Academy of Social Sciences, Hanoi, Vietnam
e-mail: chiphamvvh@gmail.com

© The Author(s), under exclusive license to Springer Nature Singapore Pte Ltd. 2023
T. Engelbert and C. P. Pham (eds.), *Global Vietnam: Across Time,*
Space and Community, Reading South Vietnam's Writers,
https://doi.org/10.1007/978-981-99-1043-4_11

leading to its deserved ultimate collapse in 1975.[5] This essay examines the vulnerability of the Indian migrants in the context of dynamic nationalist projects in South
Vietnam. It aims at arguing that nationalism, largely in the form of constructing ethnic
and economical homogeneity and hegemony of the Vietnamese nation, did exist,
vitally and relentlessly, in South Vietnam. By way of critically reading of administrative documents, largely stored at the Vietnamese National Archive 2 and the
Archive Center of Ho Chi Minh City's People Committee, this paper will show how
Republic policy-makers implemented bureaucratic reforms to diminish the ethnic
and economic dominance of the Indian migrants, ultimately firmly establishing Vietnamese ethnicity in the Vietnamese national landscape. In other words, the ousting of
the Indian migrants and the gradual disappearance of the Indians as an ethnic group
reveals the existence of the nationalist culture, vital, and ceaseless, in South Vietnam.
So doing, the paper suggests the legitimate status of South Vietnam's nation-building
in the official national history of Vietnam.

The Indians are those who migrated from the Indian subcontinent to Vietnam
in the early nineteenth century. V. M. Reddi (1982) identifies two main groups of
Indians in Indochina—then Cambodia, Laos, and Vietnam. The first group comprised
Indians who gained French citizenship by renouncing their personal native citizenship, through various laws, or through French Indian paternity. The French of Indian
origin largely worked in the French colonial administration, in French firms and
the French military, as tenders, running commercial enterprises, tax collectors, and
teachers.[6] In 1880, French migrants of Indian origin, under the Ministry of Colonies,
obtained the approval to receive benefits similar to French bureaucrats in the colony.
This approval also defined the Indian French as different from the local population in particular and Asians in general.[7] The second group mainly included British
Indians and French subjects of India who refused to become French citizens by way
of renouncing their native laws; this population mostly ran their own businesses
in Indochina. They were largely involved in financial and trading activities, either
private or French-associated, which, as commonly written in official Vietnamese
historiography, shared a common objective of exploiting the colonial population.[8]
Nowadays, descendants of the Indians who migrated to Vietnam during the colonial period form a small and marginalized group in Vietnam; many members of this
group have been in Vietnam for generations and have participated in the economic
and political revolutions of Vietnam.[9]

Most existing scholarship about the Indian migrants in Vietnam has agreed that
the disappearance of this population from the host country was the consequence of
Communist Party-led Vietnamese nationalism, which is national- and class-struggle

---

[5] Tran Anh Nu, *Contested Identities*, 1–22.

[6] Brocheux, *The Mekong,* 103–104; Pairaudeau, *Indians*, 85–127; Ha, *French Women*, 103–104.

[7] Peters, *Appetites*, 201.

[8] Phạm Cao Dương, *Thực trạng*, 169–170; Pairaudeau, *Indians*, 14–18; Chanda, "Indians in," 31–32).

[9] Read Pham Chi P, *Literature and Nation Building.*

oriented. Accordingly, the Indians migrants once played a distinctive, often controversial role in Vietnamese society, particularly in the economic and cultural life from the French colonial period. Many Indian migrants had to give up their lives in Vietnam when the Vietnamese government, under the Party leadership, constructed the socialist image of nation in the north during 1954–1975,[10] and implemented the people's national democratic revolution in the south in 1975 after the Fall of the Republic of Vietnam government.[11] In this people's national democratic revolution, the Indians living in South Vietnam became the target, given their supposed economic status as businessmen and well-off Indians in general.[12] Most Indian bankers and traders, categorized as comprador bourgeoisie, had to "hand over" their property and left Vietnam.[13] However, an examination of South Vietnam's nationalism will reveal the earlier forced disappearance of this population from Vietnam.

Minimizing the Indians' Economic Influences Over Southern Vietnam

Since the early time of its establishment, South Vietnam's government had issued policies and constructed discourse attacking the Indians' economic domination over the country. The Republic of Vietnam issued laws and implemented social regulations and cultural controls to prevent the Indian population from their main ways of earning a living, that of money-lending. In the years of 1955–1956, several ministries of South Vietnam together worked on policies to respond to the so-called money-lending pandemic. On 26 May 1956, the Ministry of Public Administration and Traffic (PAT) issued the document 372-CC/M proposing methods to deal with the bankruptcy of many railway employees, supposedly due to debt owed to the "gangs of Indians" (bọn chà). On 27 May 1956, the South Vietnam government set up an inter-ministry committee (Ủy ban liên bộ), discussing methods of limiting the spread of the "pandemic." Efforts of the South Vietnam ministries apparently aimed to get rid of the Indian money-lenders. One of the proposed methods was to request all officers and workers not to take a loan from Indians and bet with their salaries.[14] The other method was to invalidate mortgaged salary documents, which would make it impossible for the Indians to withdraw the borrowers' wages to cover the debts they could not pay.[15] South Vietnam officials announced their strategies of unearthing loopholes in the provisions of the law and of interpreting the laws differently, all

---

[10] Pham Chi P, *Literature and Nation Building*, 80–101.

[11] Chanda, "Indians," 31–45.

[12] Võ. *Vietnam*, 64-72; Devare, "Rising India," 290.

[13] Archived document: Ủy ban nhân dân thành phố Hồ Chí Minh (1978). Quyết định cho phép ông [A] mang đồ thờ cúng về Ấn Độ (Quyết định 4056/QĐ-UB on 26 December 1978). Ho Chi Minh City: Ho Chi Minh City People's Committee (name of the person was omitted for security reasons).

[14] The document 373-CC/M issued by the Ministry of Public Administrative and Traffic (PAT).

[15] BCC-GT/2813.

aimed to find legal grounds for decriminalization of mortgaged payroll documents.[16] Another method was to form state sponsored-financial organizations such as banks, credit funds, and local pawn shops to replace the private ones that were mostly owned by the Indians by that time.[17] These methods demonstrate South Vietnam officials' attempts to "take the position of the Indians" in money-lending businesses in the south. All the methods were meant to eliminate the main means of livelihood of the Indian community in Saigon.

In addition to crafting legal rationales, South Vietnam policy-makers also constructed the identity of the Indians as foreigners who had harmed the nation economically and socially. In administrative documents published in the period of 1955–1956, the Indians occur as exploiters of local Vietnamese people and as a destructive force of national economy and culture. In that sense, the practice of money-lending was named as a "trap" that many workers, officers, and high officials in the south fell into. They borrowed money from the Indians, mortgaging their salary papers. As reported by the Ministry of Public Administration and Traffic (PAT), the number of railway department's employees in particular and of other economic sectors in general who became the debtors of Indians increased considerably: 450 and 3000 people, respectively. The monthly interest was, $400,000 and $1,200,000, respectively.[18] This situation was critical, given that per capita GNP of South Vietnam in 1969 was $240 and in 1972 $200. Many debtors were unable to repay the loan, so the Indian money-lenders brought the mortgaged paybook to the debtors' offices to collect their salaries, leaving them with no monthly income. As a result, many civil servants and workers of Saigon fell into bankruptcy. It is this difficult economic condition that, as interpreted by southern officials, had degraded humanity in Southern employees.[19] Representative of PAT, as indicated in the documented numbered 967-CC/M, dated on 21 September 1955, agreed that the existing Indian money-lending system was the main cause of the so-called rising social impurity which means the economic decline and moral decay of civil servants and workers in the South. Such a way of highlighting social and moral degeneration as the consequence of the Indians' practice of money-lending aimed to outlaw the Indians' source of wealth, eliminating their essential role in Southerners' economic and social lives.

In order to further marginalize the Indians from Southern society, the language of administrative documents constructed the image of Indians as exploiters of the local people. A document, without number, marked confidential, proposes that the fact that the Indians kept filing the mortgaged salaries of the debtors "indirectly helped the Indian foreigners to exploit our employees."[20] The term "exploiter" was constantly

---

[16] These documents are handwritten on letterheads of the Ministries of Domestic Affairs and of the Judiciary. Dates and numbers are left blank.

[17] Archived document, as written, was issued by the Ministry of Judicial on November [?], 1955.

[18] Number 120-CC/M, dated 20 February 1956.

[19] Number 120-CC/M, dated 20 February 1956.

[20] The document, addressed to Director of the Official of the Ministry of Judicial, dated 19 September 1955, was written by the Director of the Office of PAT.

used to address the Indians' relationship with the local population.[21] The governmental offices agreed to treat the Indian people as exploiters of the local people; all money-related businesses by this foreign population were portrayed as solely aimed to fleecing the native people.[22] Thus, local populations were asked to keep themselves away from these so-called symbols of cunningness and exploitation.[23] The letter BCC-GT/2813 by PAT addressed to the President opens with the accusation that the Indians exploited "our" governmental employees by conspiring to lend them money. This letter ends with a call to boycott "the contagious usury from *time immemorial*." Another letter by the Ministry of the Judiciary and the Ministry of Domestic Affairs highlights that *"for many generations*, there have been a gang of foreigners operating heavy money-lending on this land." "The letter calls to stop the pandemic of heavy moneylending that has existed *for generations.*"[24] The presence of adverbs of time, italicized, in these administrative documents indicates the tendency among South Vietnam officials to generalize the Indians as being traditionally unwelcome migrants, and aimed at marginalizing this population in Southern society.

Discernibly, such marginalization of the Indians aimed not to simply solve the debt problem of the local population, but rather to highlight southern officials' will for national homogeneity and hegemony. Southern officials' attempts to end the existence of the Indians in the South were explicitly tied to the question of national survival. The way of addressing the Indians as some force that polluted Southern society and harmed national culture and economy in general pervades many administrative writings. In the letters, quoted in the previous paragraph, Southern officials highlight the position of the Indians as foreign migrants that had been threatening the individual and the nation's prosperity for centuries. In another document by PAT, the Indians are depicted as "the insult" and "the sins" of "our nation" that needed to be "washed out... to build a purer nation." The long presence of the Indians in the Vietnamese region was considered to have made it corrupted and sinful. Thus, wiping out such presence ensured national purity.[25] The repeated expressions of "national purity" were apparently associated with South Vietnam's attempt at an early establishment of nationalism. Ethnic homogeneity and hegemony historically formed the central point in the national projects of the republic's leaders. Ngô Đình Diệm continuously issued policies to construct a national figure that was entirely Vietnamese:

---

[21] As indicated in a number of documents such as the documents numbered 23 XH/PC/M by the Ministry of Society and Health on 4 April 1956, the document numbered 2979-BTP/NCPL by the Ministry of Judicial on 3 April 1956, and the one numbered 914/BTC/TN by the Ministry of Finance on 9 April 1956. All these documents were to respond to the letters, marked "confidential," numbered 222-CC/M by PAT on 30 March 1956 and numbered 120-CC/M, asking for solutions to help officials and workers who were subjected to excessive interest rates by Indian loan sharks.

[22] Document No. 120-CC/M, dated 20 February 1956.

[23] Document No. 120-CC/M, dated 20 February 1956.

[24] These ideas are quoted in the minute of the inter-governmental meeting on 27 April 1956.

[25] The letter addressed to the Ministry of the Judiciary by director of the Office of PAT, highlights the need of amending article 1690 in the Civil Law in order to make unauthenticated mortgaged salary papers so that Indian money lenders cannot take the mortgaged salaries of the local debtors.

the citizen should be spiritually, culturally, and morally Asiatic and humanist. His government issued policies to limit the dominance of foreigners, particularly Indians and Chinese, in the essential economic activities of South Vietnam.[26] In a number of his public speeches in Vietnam and abroad, Diệm constantly called for constructing a national figure that was culturally homogenous and advanced. Interchangeable terms such as "Asian civilizations," "Asian culture," "reconstruction of Asia by Asians," and "authentic sources of Asian thought" appear constantly in Ngô Đình Diệm's public speeches.[27] That Ngô Đình Diệm's government persistently strived for the economic, political, and cultural sovereignty and unity of Vietnam indicate that nationalism was the attribute of not only the communist Party-led Vietnamese regime. South Vietnam's attempts to marginalize the Indians were historically part of South Vietnam's struggle for legitimacy by promoting the historical narrative of Vietnam's long resistance to outside invaders and of traditional loyalty and sacrifice for the homeland—a narrative that Vietnamese communists of the North used to win over the masses.[28] It is this nationalist narrative with which the Ngô Đình Diệm government could generate support from disparate political and social groups and "win the hearts" of the population.[29] That is to say, regardless of their politically different ideologies, South Vietnam and North Vietnam shared the language of nationalism.

Continuing to Drive the Indians Out of Vietnamese Land

The Second Republic continued the idealized national homogeneity and hegemony partly in a way of further marginalizing the Indians and removing them from prominent positions in the economic and social life of the South. In 1966, South Vietnam's policy-makers revised Decree 53, attempting to exclude the Indians from main livelihoods to a greater extent. Decree 53, initiated by the Ngô Đình Diệm government in 1956, banned foreigners from businesses that dealt with goods essential for the Vietnamese people. These were fish and meat, "chạp phô" (daily miscellany), coal and wood, oil, pawnshops, textiles, metal and bronze, rice, transportation, and rice gridding businesses. This ban obviously targeted especially the Chinese migrants in Saigon, given that this population occupied most of the banned businesses. The Decree was apparently part of Ngô Đình Diệm's nationalist narrative—with its account of Vietnam's long tradition of heroically opposing foreign invasion and Chinese control[30]; it aimed to legitimize the early South Vietnamese government. The revision of Decree 53 in 1966 by the second Republic explicitly attacked the

---

[26] Pham, *Literature and Nationalism*, 20–40.

[27] *President Ngo Dinh Diem on Asia*; Thien Phuc, *President Ngo*; Bouscaren, *The Last of the Manderins*, 77–86.

[28] Masur, "Exhibiting Signs," 293–294.

[29] Masur, "Exhibiting Signs," 295.

[30] Masur, "Exhibiting Signs," 294.

Indian population, given that this Decree outlawed the Indians' money-lending business. This population was even addressed in the Decree as the dominant operator of that business. Other administrative documents continued highlighting the social and economic dangers of the Indians' money-lending business, repeatedly calling for the replacement with Vietnamese for running the essential trades of the country. The letter dated 27 October 1966 by the Economy Department of Saigon highlights that the business of money-lending run by the Indians only aimed at exploiting poor people. On 7 November 1966, this Department encouraged the discontinuation of pawnshops run by Indians, asking for the replacement with Vietnamese people in this business. It rationalized that the "City has enough budget to open pawn shops to fulfill the needs of borrowing money among mass people."[31] This effort of replacing the Indians with the Vietnamese in important businesses is a continuation of similar efforts by the First Republic. In 1957, the Ministry of Economy was open about the goal of Decree 53 being to prohibit foreigners from controlling goods and services that were essential for the masses and to encourage Vietnamese businessmen to take responsibility for distributing those goods and services to their compatriots.[32] As a consequence, to maintain their lives in Vietnam, the foreigners had to either acquire Vietnamese citizenship, transfer their ownership to their Vietnamese wives or sons, or contribute capital with Vietnamese entrepreneurs at the rate prescribed by the government.[33] These attempts definitely aimed for diminishing the foreigners' influence, increasing the power of the local population and what Olga Dror calls "Vietnameseness" over the economic activities of the South.[34] That is to say, both the Republics had advocated for national homogeneity and hegemony.[35]

South Vietnam's constant projects of eliminating foreigners' economic and social influence made Indians increasingly vulnerable, economically and socially. Cases of Indians struggling for survival in the face of South Vietnam's opposition to foreign influence demonstrate the vitality and vibrancy of nationalist advocacies. Take the case of Indians who constantly changed their nationality and wavered between leaving or staying in Vietnam during the Second Republic period as an example. By law, all Vietnamese male citizens, when turning 18 years old, had to "go to the battle" (đi lính).[36] Many Indians with Vietnamese nationality, resulting from Decree 53, applied to renounce their citizenship in order to avoid military service; they then tried to regain the Vietnamese nationality in order not to be forced to leave Vietnam. The Indians' constant change of nationality was considered by the Vietnamese officials as disloyalty to the Vietnamese nation. Most decisions by South Vietnamese officials in respect to Indians' application for nationality change were

---

[31] Document 1483/SKT/ [?].

[32] Document 6966/BKT/NC on 25 July 1957.

[33] Numbers 502/BKT/BC/M2 and [?]BKT/BC/N on 27 July 1957.

[34] Dror, "Foundational Myths," 124–159.

[35] For attempts of the second republic for "the entire people… [and] the great Vietnamese family" in terms of culture and religion, read Dror, Foundational Myths, 131–134.

[36] Documents 1135-BTP/HOV on 1 February 1967; 5057-BTP/HOV on 31 May 1968.

made with scrutiny as to the matter of the age of the applicants, carefully evaluating their loyalty to the nation.[37] Nguyễn Hiệp Hòa (Indian name: Abdul Wahid), a Vietnamese of Indian origin, several times applied to change his nationality. He was born in 1918 at Rajaguiry (India). He moved to Vietnam with his parents, residing at "60/3/14, Ngô Tùng Châu, Saigon." In 1960, Abdul Wahid applied for Vietnamese citizenship successfully in response to Decree 53. In 1967, Abdul Wahid attempted to return to his Indian citizenship. In his application, he explained that only with Indian citizenship could he inherit property that his parents left in India. He went through many interviews with Vietnamese authorities expressing their doubts; in the end, he was allowed to change back to his original nationality. However, Vietnamese officials started keeping negative notes about this man, emphasizing his supposed sole self-interest. The report by the Ministry of the Judiciary to the President on 10 June 1968 includes the police department's account of the supposed true motivation behind Abdul Wahid's change of nationality. As narrated, this man expected that his three sons—by that time having Vietnamese citizenship—could follow him, adopting the Indian citizenship to avoid military service. In 1971, the Ministry of the Judiciary continued its negative notes on Abdul Wahid when he applied to return to Vietnamese citizenship. This application was in response to South Vietnam's increasing policies of pushing the Indians out of the country (more details in the later part of this paper). The notes highlight his supposed ingratitude to and ignorance of the Vietnamese nation which allowed him to earn his living there for generations. As written, this man "is politically reluctant and dishonest"; "he solely aimed at making convenience for himself and his own family"; the Indians "just want to live and work in Vietnam but do not want to take duties assigned along with the Vietnamese citizenship."[38] Ultimately, the South Vietnamese government expelled this man and his family from the country. This account of the Indian's vulnerable life in Vietnam shows the constant efforts of the South Vietnamese officials for the hegemony and homogeneity of Vietnameseness and the Vietnamese nation.

The will to expel Indians out of Southern Vietnam was more fervent in the early 1970s when the alliance between North Vietnam and the Indian government became apparent. In 1970, the Indian government invited Nguyễn Thị Bình, minister of the Ministry of Foreign Affairs of the North Vietnam-led Provisional Revolutionary Government (PRG) and other representatives of PRG to visit India. The PRG government, observed by the Republic of Vietnam, includes "more than 80% of communists." In 1972, the Indian government decided to promote the Indian Consulate to the rank of Embassy in North Vietnam. The Ministry of Labor in a document dated 13 May 1972, openly talked about the association of South Vietnam's current policies of diminishing the Indian migrants with increasing commitments between the Indian government and the North Vietnam government. As written, "in the face of the pro-communist attitude of the Indian government, which has been creating anger

---

[37] For example, documents 74565-BTP/HOV on 30 December 1966; 877-bTP/HOV, 31 January 1973; 3825-BTP/HOV on 14 May 1970; 3826-BTP/HOV on 24 [May?] 1970; 5895-BTP/HOV on 20 July 1970; 6060/BTP/HOV on 27 July 1970.

[38] Document BTP/HOV; April, 1971.

among Vietnamese officials and the masses," the Ministry of Labor, permitted by the President, "will implement methods of denying Indians to immigrate for work in Vietnam and of rejecting all of their applications for work extension."[39]

In the years of 1972–1973, Southern policy-makers agreed to work harder to drive the Indians out of Vietnam. They decided that at first, governmental ministries must work to "decrease the number of Indians who have jobs in Vietnam" in order to "protect rights of Vietnamese laborers;"[40] and such limitations would be later implemented to effect the entire population of Indian migrants. The letter by the Ministry of Domestic Affairs (MDA), addressed to the President's Cabinet on 10 April 1972, exposes the cooperation of different ministries in issuing laws to mini-mize the involvement of Indians in the labor landscape of Vietnam. MDA agreed with the Ministry of Labor on "not extending work permits for temporary Indian residents in Vietnam." The Ministry of Labor further determined that the law of not allowing more Indians to come to work in Vietnam and not extending the existing Indians' work permit was applicable to foreigners working for companies. The law problemat-ically left the Indians who were owners, freelancers, or even jobless unsolved.[41] This "hole," analyzed by MDA, created the condition for the Indians who were not workers to keep staying in Vietnam, "running their own shops or being self-employed." This "hole" would also allow the Indian workers who were rejected in their application for work extension, to change to running their own shops to qualify for staying longer in Vietnam.[42] MDA called for the necessity of the implementation of more methods for putting an end to the Indians' stay in Vietnam. The aim of diminishing number of Indians in Vietnam occurs more explicitly in the following exchanges among South Vietnam's ministries. A letter by the President's Cabinet sent to the Ministry of Economy and Finance on 22 May 1972 was entitled "About Methods to Limit the Indian Residency in Vietnam."[43] On 12 June 1972, the Ministry of Finance wrote a three-page letter, addressed the Ministry of Labor and the Cabinet, introducing strategies to put the residence of all Indians in Vietnam in a vulnerable position. It interpreted Decree 53 in a way that provided MDA with legitimate power to diminish all types of businesses run by Indians.[44] In response, DA issued a decision, marked "confidential," closing all doors toward Indians' further migration to and longer stays in Vietnam:

1. Stop the Indians who want to migrate to Vietnam as company owners or the Indians who want to move to Vietnam by identifying themselves as relatives of the Indian owners in Vietnam. The Ministry of Labor forbids these people to work in Vietnam,

---

[39] Number 07220/BLD/NNC. The document numbered 051/BNV/XNDT/20-M, dated on 10 April 1972 by DA also stated openly about the reason for changes in policies related to the Indians.

[40] Number 051/BNV/XNDT/20-M, dated on 10 April 1972 by MDA.

[41] Number 0771a/BLD/NNC, dated 13 May 1972.

[42] The letter by MDA addressed to the President Cabinet on 10 April 1972.

[43] Number 606-PTh.T/PC1/1-M.

[44] Number 6864/BTC/TV/M1.

2. Only consider extending residency for the Indians who are permanent residents or were born [in Vietnam], given that these people have not violated national rules and public security.[45]

At this point, attempts to decreasing the Indian population from Vietnamese land was disclosed officially and was carried out with consensus among different governmental ministries. And as explicitly noted in point 2, quoted above, such elimination was oriented toward making the Vietnamese identity prominent in the ethnic landscape of Vietnam.

Not only the governmental office but also mass organizations in South Vietnam attacked the Indians' resident status in the name of national pride and integrity. In 1972–1973, in Saigon, students and youth censured the Indians' convenient conditions in Vietnam with the aim of criticizing the pro-North Vietnam attitude—a political betrayal—of the Indian government. Vietnamese undergraduate and high school students, according to a police report dated 12 January 1972, broke into and set on fire financial organizations and trading centers belonging to Indians. According to another report dated the same day, the General Association of Vietnamese Wounded Veterans made a petition to the government, asking to remove the Indians from Vietnam, threatening to "eliminate" (thanh toán) any Indians who walked separately on roads and to destroy private houses of these foreigners. The letter dated 27 July 1972 by the President of Vũng Tàu reported that one hundred Vietnamese veterans and thirty children hung up six slogans demanding the Republic government to realize six points. Out of six points, five points addressed the Indians, including:

1. Highlighting the national pride of the Republic of Vietnam,
2. Requesting the government to confiscate Indian property,
3. Disproving the pro-communist diplomatic policy of the Indian government,
4. Calling for the Vietnamese compatriots to not to pay mortgaged land and money to the Indian money-lenders,
5. Boycotting all businesses run by Indians.

The order of the slogans indicates that nationalist inspiration was the driving force of the urgent calls for the disappearance of Indians from Vietnamese land. It appears that local Vietnamese took advantage of the political tensions between South Vietnam and the Indian government to promote their long-lasting concerns about the Indians' influence on Southern lives.

Not only raising nationalist fervor, protests against Indians in South Vietnam in the early 1970s promoted the idea of class-struggle. Driving the Indians off of Vietnamese land was meant to bring material benefits to the poor, the low-class, "the exploited." In January 1972, the Committee of the Association of Victims of Indian Diasporas was formed with its office located at 14 Lê Văn Duyệt street, Saigon. The committee included deputies, congressmen, professors, and labor union officials who were members of the Party of Workers and Farmers of Vietnam. In an appeal sent to the Cabinet Director dated on 21 January 1972, the committee repeatedly accused the Indians of not sacrificing for Vietnam and not respecting the

---

[45] Number 074/BNV/XNDT/20/M dated on 6 June 1972.

Vietnamese national pride: they were "arrogant, looking down at the national pride of the Republic of Vietnam"; they delve more deeply into political imbalances, and rudely trample on the pride of the Vietnamese people of a nation-state, who are in favor of freedom and democracy"; the Indian "disgraces bone and blood of many Vietnamese people who sacrificed their lives for the freedom and the nation." The committee then called for that the "Vietnamese nation should no longer be more tolerant to the Indians"; instead, it should uncover all foxy and evil conspiracies of the Indians in Vietnam." The appeal is filled with nationalist sentiments. More noticeably, the appeal is explicitly class-struggle oriented.[46] Out of the three missions that the committee identified for themselves, two concern the grass-roots class. As claimed, the committee would "fight to recover the rights and pride of the Vietnamese people, those who were and are being 'suppressed and exploited' by the Indians" and "promote the movement": "Vietnamese land belongs to Vietnamese people and the Vietnamization of property of the cunning and rude Indians." Here, the way of addressing the issues of Indians' presence in Vietnam became similar to the ways of addressing feudal landlords, capitalists, and foreign invaders by national and class revolutionaries.[47] In other words, the Indians were presented as the enemy of the class and national struggles of Southerners.[48] Such a way of associating the Indians with the class and national enemy is more critical in the committee's analyses of the Indians' economic influence in the region of Vietnam. The committee argued that the Indians imitated the French colonizing regime in the way they "directly obtained property, land and houses of the Vietnamese people" and the way they "use a cunning scheme of heavy money-lending in order to take property of Vietnamese people." The appeal potentially provoked more resentments against the Indians by way of depicting the Indians solely as blood-suckers, who "live prosperous lives" and create prosperity out of the "blood and bone and wretched miseries of our compatriots." So, not only being seen as national invaders, the Indians were denounced as the exploiters of laborers. Such a way of depicting the Indians was part of ongoing nationalism, which occurred in forms of anticolonialism and anti-feudalism in South Vietnam.[49]

The Indians' residence in South Vietnam was more critical, given that they were neglected by the Indian government. The letter by the Indian consul addressing the Ministry of Foreign Affairs on 12 January 1972, relegated the Indians to Vietnamese culture, politics, and society, denying to take any responsibility to take care of this population. It said that the Indian community in South Vietnam was not alien to Vietnam in the strict sense of the term. Most Indians living in South Vietnam had been there for generations. "Many were born in Vietnam, they are inter-married with Vietnamese nationals and are, therefore, fully integrated in Vietnamese life and

---

[46] For discussions about complex resistance to the idea of class-struggle in South Vietnam, read Tuan Hoang, Ideology in Urban South Vietnam, 99–167.

[47] For discussions about class equality and national independence in South Vietnam's nationalism, read Lương Thu Hiền, Vietnamese Existential Philosophy, 147–153.

[48] For more details about this idea, read Pham, *Literature and Nation-building*.

[49] Tran Anh Nu emphasizes the presence of these forms in the early First Republic. Read Tran Anh Nu, *Contested Identities*, 52–90.

society." The letter particularly emphasizes cultural ties of the Indians to Vietnam instead of India: "many of them do not even speak Indian languages, they only communicate in Vietnamese."[50] The ignorance of the Indian authority toward their overseas compatriots was all the more pointed in that the movements for "spitting on and kicking all the Indians out of Vietnam" were rising in the South. That means the Indians were denied by both sides, their host country and their original country.

Consequently, in the early 1970, Indians' lives in South Vietnam became even more vulnerable. The administrative documents, stored at the National Archive Center 2, show that Indians desperately struggled to stay in Vietnam. Take the case of thirty-nine Indians, who were denied by MDA to extend their residency in Vietnam, as one example. They had immigrated to Vietnam in 1965 and worked as domestics in families of the Indian businessmen. They were responsible for "services that need confidentiality." They earned great credibility from their Indian bosses.[51] As the rejection by MDA went into effect, these Indian people became illegal residents. The Association of Indians in South Vietnam made an appeal to the South Vietnam government, asking to extend residency for those Indians. Along with the appeal, the community donated 500.000 piaster to the Foundation of Soldier Seasonal Trees (Cây mùa chiến sĩ).[52] Leaders of this association highlighted their loyalty and attachment to South Vietnam in order to convince the RVN government to approve their aim of staying in Vietnam. On 24 January 1973, five Indian people, represented by many associations of Indians in South Vietnam, had a meeting with South Vietnamese authorities. The letter they brought to the meeting affirmed their positive sentiments toward Vietnam, their trust, and their hopes for the "reasonability" and "humanity" of the South Vietnam government. The prominent point is the fact that they had been living very long in Vietnam: "We, a small group of Indian people had been living and working in Vietnam for more than one century." They were mostly businessmen and staff working in Indian trading centers. The Indians expressed their gratitude for South Vietnam government's special treatments and acknowledged its political advantages:

> We are fortunate to enjoy South Vietnam, we experience the freedom as much as Vietnamese citizens in the aspects of trading, religions, etc. We live peacefully with the Vietnamese nation. We highly appreciate the caring treatments of the Vietnam government to us. We are always willing to take part in works to serve Vietnamese society.

The repeated use of the word "Vietnam" in the short paragraph apparently aimed to impress the listeners—South Vietnamese authority—about the loyalty of the Indian population. In a stronger attempt to convince the Vietnamese authority of their heart

---

[50] Letter No.SAI/102(2)/72.

[51] Letter by the Vice-President to the President on 24 January 1973. The letter was numbered 21/VP/Ph.Th.T/TT.

[52] The document numbered 67/TCCTCT/UB,CMX dated on 1 February 1973 by the Ministry of Military confirmed the reception of 500.000 piasters from the Association of Indian Diasporas in Vietnam. The document numbered 578-PThT/PC1/1, dated on 13 February 1973 by the Cabinet, recorded the cash issuance to the French-Asian bank check of 500.000 piaster.

and mind attachment to the Vietnamese nation, representatives of the Indian community invoked the Tết occasion, asking the President for an exceptional approval as he normally did.[53]

However, all the attempts of the Indians were in vain. On 15 March 1973, just one month after meeting, the President's Cabinet issued the final decision, rejecting the application for work permits of the 39 Indian immigrants. The administrative documents, stored at the National Archive Center 2, record one case of an Indian who resisted the decision, desperately struggling to stay in Vietnam. The archival resource includes an application for residence extension of this man dated more than one year after the rejection. That means he had stayed in Vietnam for one year, constantly trying to find ways to remain in Vietnam. In his application in 1974, he asked for an extension with the reason that he had a job as a clothes-seller in Cần Thơ. His application was denied. Then, he applied the second time with the recommendation of another Indian who was the director of a company named Bombay Catinat (6 Lê Lợi, Saigon) that he would work as an employee in that company. However, he was denied again. His third application was denied more quickly with an accusation that he had been illegally residing in Vietnam since 1972, thus, his application was not eligible for consideration.[54] Negotiation and resistance did not work to save the Indians from having to leave Vietnam. Administrative documents by South Vietnam include notes about the Indians' repatriation. An employee working for Bombay Catinat left Vietnam, as noted in a document by the Ministry of Labor, "on his own," without getting permission from authorities ("tự ý").[55] The letter addressed to the President by the Indian Community includes details about the departure of the Indians in early 1973. It has a complaint that the current law exclusively considered Indian bosses' petitions, while most Indians were employees; concurrently "some Indian employees left Vietnam and never returned."[56]

It is apparent that the Indians gradually disappeared from South Vietnam as a result of its ongoing nationalism. The vulnerable existence of the Indians, or the constant struggle for survival of this migrant population is indicative of the vital existence of nationalism in South Vietnam. In other words, constructing an ethnically homogenous and economically and politically sovereign face of the Vietnamese nation did not cease to be part of Southern nation-builders' work. Persistent will and the constant efforts of Southern intellectuals in resisting foreign imposition and occupation, establishing the hegemony and homogeneity of the Vietnamese identity, and realizing class warfare—these narratives of South Vietnam's nation-building potentially became part of the mainstream idea of Vietnamese nationalism.

---

[53] The letter was signed by S.G Mahtani, dated on 4 January 1973.

[54] Document numbered 1124/HCPC1/2 by the General Secretary of the Cabinet, 4 January 1974; Document 146-P.Th.T/HCPC1/2 on 17 January 1975; Document P.Th.T/HCPC1/2; Document 1457/BLD/TNND/ND3 on 18 November 1974; Document 10338/BNV/XNDT/1 on 4 October 1974.

[55] Document 1124/HCPC1/2.

[56] The document numbered [24]-PC1/1 by the General Secretary of the Cabinet, dated 1 January 1974.

Bibliography

Ban chỉ đạo soạn sử Việt Nam (2005) Lịch sử Chính phủ Việt Nam: 1955–1976. NXB Chính trị quốc gia, Hà Nội

Bouscaren AT (1965) The last of the Mandarins: diem of Vietnam. Duquesne University Press, Pittsburgh

Brocheux P (1995) The Mekong Delta: ecology, economy and revolution, 1860–1960. University of Wisconsin Press, Madison

Chanda N (1993) Indians in Indochina. In: Sandhu, KS, Mani A (eds) Indian communities in Southeast Asia. Institute of Southeast Asian Studies, Singapore, pp 31–45

Devare S (2008) Rising India and Indians in Cambodia, Laos and Vietnam. In: Kesavapany K, Mani A, Ramasamy P (eds) Rising India and Indian Communities in East Asia. Institute of Southeast Asian Studies, Singapore, pp 287–300.

Dror O (2017) Foundational myths in the Republic of Vietnam (1955–1975): "harnessing" the Hùng Kings against Ngô Đình Diệm Communists, Cowboys, and Hippies for unity, peace, and Vietnameseness. J Soc Hist 51(1):124–159

Ha M-P (2014) French women and the empire: the case of Indochina. Oxford University Press, Oxford

Kim KH (1982) Vietnamese Communism, 1925–1945. Cornell University Press, Ithaca

Lương HT (2009) Vietnamese existential philosophy: a critical reappraisal. Dissertation. Temple University.

Masur M (2009) Exhibiting signs of resistance: South Vietnam's struggle for legitimacy, 1954–1960. Dipl Hist 33(2):293–313. http://www.jstor.org/stable/44214039

Moise EE (1988) Nationalism and Communism in Vietnam. J Third World Stud 5:6–22.

Nguyen AT (2009) American coming to terms. Xlibris, Philadelphia

Nguyen LD (2020) The unimagined community: imperialism and culture in South Vietnam. Manchester University Press, Manchester

Pairaudeau N (2009) Indians as French citizens in colonial Indochina, 1858–1940. PhD diss, University of London

Peters EJ (2012) Appetites and aspirations in Vietnam: food and drink in the long nineteenth. AltaMira Press, Lanham, MD

Pham CP (2021) Literature and nation-building in Vietnam: The invisibilization of the Indians. Routedlge, New York

Phạm CD (1966) Thực trạng của giới nông dân Việt Nam dưới thời Pháp thuộc [Realities of Vietnamese farmers under the French colonialism]. Khai-Trí, Saigon

President Ngo Dinh Diem on Asia (Extracts from speeches by President Ngo Dinh Diem (1957) Presidency of the Republic of Vietnam, Press Office, Saigon

Reddi VM (1982) Indians in the Indochina states and their problems. In: Bahadur Singh IJ (ed) Indians in Southeast Asia. Sterling, New Delhi, pp 150–160

Thien Phuc (1956) President Ngo Dinh Diem's political philosophy. Review Horizons, Saigon

Tran AN (2013) Contested identities: nationalism in the Republic of Vietnam (1954–1963). PhD diss, University of California, Berkeley

Trần TN (1987) Lịch sử Việt Nam, 1945–1975. Giáo dục, Hà Nội

Trần TĐĐ (1992) Văn hóa, văn nghệ Nam Việt Nam, 1954–1975. Thông tin, Hà Nội

Tuan H (2013) Ideology in Urban South Vietnam (1950–1975). Dissertation, Pepperdine University

Vo NT (1990) Vietnam's economic policy after 1975? Ashgate Pub Co, Farnham

Chi P. Pham is a tenured researcher at the Institute of Literature, Vietnam Academy of Social Sciences. She received her first PhD degree in Literary Theory in Vietnam and her second PhD degree in Comparative Literature in the United States. She was an Alexander von Humboldt Post-doctoral Fellow at the Institute of Asian and African Studies, University of Hamburg, Germany.

She has published articles in Vietnamese and English on post-colonial literature and nation-building. Her most recent monograph is *Literature and Nation-building in Vietnam: The Invisibilization of the Indians*. New York: Routledge, 2021.